The World's Religions

Our Great Wisdom Traditions

HUSTON SMITH

HarperSanFrancisco

A Division of HarperCollins*Publishers*

THE WORLD'S RELIGIONS: *Our Great Wisdom Traditions*. Copyright © 1991 by Huston Smith. Original copyright © 1958 by Huston Smith; copyright renewed in 1986 by Huston Smith. All rights reserved. Printed in the United States of America. No part of this book may be used or reproduced in any manner whatsoever without written permission except in the case of brief quotations embodied in critical articles and reviews. For information address HarperCollins Publishers, 10 East 53rd Street, New York, NY 10022.

HarperCollins books may be purchased for educational, business, or sales promotional use. For information please write: Special Markets Department, Harper-Collins Publishers, 10 East 53rd Street, New York, NY 10022.

HarperCollins Web Site: http://www.harpercollins.com
HarperCollins®, 📖®, and HarperSanFrancisco™ are trademarks of HarperCollins Publishers Inc.

Library of Congress Cataloging-in-Publication Data
Smith, Huston.
    The world's religions / Huston Smith.
      p. cm.
    Rev. and updated ed. of : The religions of man. 1958.
    Includes bibliographical references and index.
    ISBN 0–06–250799–0 (cloth)
    ISBN 0–06–250811–3 (pbk.)
    1. Religions. I. Smith, Huston. Religions of man. II. Title.
BL80.2.S645   1991
291—dc20   90–56449

  99 00 01 02 RRDH 32 31 30 29 28 27 26 25

When I behold the sacred liao wo* my thoughts return
To those who begot me, raised me, and now are tired.
I would repay the bounty they have given me,
But it is as the sky: it can never be approached.

*A species of grass symbolizing parenthood.

. . . the life of religion as a whole is mankind's most important function. —William James

The essence of education is that it be religious.
—Alfred North Whitehead

We need the courage as well as the inclination to consult, and profit from, the "wisdom traditions of mankind."
—E. F. Schumacher

In 1970 I wrote of a "post-traditional world." Today I believe that only living traditions make it possible to have a world at all.
—Robert N. Bellah

Contents

Foreword

The reissue of this book has the feel of a fortieth-anniversary edition, and it puts me in a distinct mood. If I were at a Pentecostal testimonial meeting—several of which I witnessed as a boy in Missouri and Arkansas—I would rise to my feet and testify. We are familiar with the typical format of such testimonials. It has three parts. Part One: "No one was as deep in the gutter as I was." Part Two: "But look at me now," said with wreaths of smiles and an erect carriage that exudes confidence and self-esteem. Then comes the punch line: "Not of my doing! It all came from Above." The "Above" part I shall keep to myself, but I welcome this opportunity to document the "not of my doing" part.

Had the St. Louis station of what evolved into the Public Broadcasting System not asked me in its second year to mount a television series on the world's religions, I am not sure that I would ever have written a book on the subject. I was teaching those religions but had other writing priorities. The response of the viewing public to that series changed my priorities. Click! Not my initiative.

Even if eventually I had written a book on the subject, it would not have been this book. It would have been in the standard textbook mode with the normal audience and life span of that particular genre. As it was, the first "draft" of my book was delivered to a television audience, and the director of the series never let me forget that audience. This is not a classroom where you have a captive audience, he kept reminding me. If you lose their attention for thirty seconds they will switch stations and you won't get them back. So, make your points if you must—you're a professor so you have to make points. *But illustrate them immediately,* with an example, an anecdote, a fragment of poetry, something that will connect your point to things your audience can relate to. That advice—at the time it felt more like a command—has made all the difference. There are many books on world religions that in their own ways are better than mine. But if they haven't received the audience that mine has, it is because they didn't grow out of television series with directors as severely wise as Mayo Simon. It's a miracle that we have remained close friends after all these years, seeing as how I still cannot get his scathing verdicts on the dry runs of my programs out of my ears. "Doesn't sound too red-hot to me," he would say, meaning back to the drawing boards. Click. Not of my doing.

If the feminist movement—not of my doing, despite pointed prods from my wife—had not come along, *The Religions of Man* (as the book was originally titled) would never have been rewritten in inclusive gender with the explicative "man" deleted from its title. The rewriting had the important corollary of providing the opportunity for me to add to the text things that I had learned from thirty years of additional teaching. I am especially glad that I will not go to my grave having let stand a book on religions that omitted its primal, oral, tribal members.

If the directors of Labyrinth Publishing in London and Harper San Francisco had not decided that the time was ripe for a book on the world's great religious art and asked me to abridge *The World's Religions* to provide its accompanying text, *The Illustrated World's Religions* would not have come into existence. Once more, not of my doing.

Finally, without the careful shepherding that the book has received from HarperCollins at every step of its odyssey, it is difficult for me to imagine that there could have been this happy occasion of a fortieth-anniversary printing. Recently, in going through old papers, I came upon a letter that its original editor, Virginia Hilu, wrote to me in 1958 when the book was first published, and the best way I can think of to document the solicitous shepherding I refer to is to quote its closing paragraph:

> *I have re-read your book several times over the summer. When you are an old man, I am certain you will look back on its author with a great deal of affection, admiration, and respect.*

I do, provided that the "not of my doing" part is solidly in place.

Huston Smith
Berkeley, California
December 1998

Preface to the Second Edition

In the years that have elapsed since this book first appeared, people have grown more sensitive to the gender biases in language; so I have changed the book's original title, *The Religions of Man*, to *The World's Religions*. No book can include all of the world's religions. Here the major ones—as determined by their longevity, historical impact, and number of current adherents—are dealt with individually, and smaller, tribal ones considered as a class.

In addition to switching to gender-inclusive language, I have added a short note on Sikhism and sections on Tibetan Buddhism and Sufism, the mystical dimension of Islam. A section on "The Confucian Project" has been inserted, Taoist materials have been considerably reworked, the chapter on Judaism now includes a section on Messianism, and the historical Jesus is treated in greater detail.

I have also added a short concluding chapter on the oral traditions. This is partly to acknowledge that the historical religions the book covers are latecomers; for the bulk of human history, religion was lived in tribal and virtually timeless mode. A strong supporting reason, however, is to allow us to affirm our human past. Recent decades have witnessed a revival of concern for the feminine and the earth, concerns that the historical religions (with the exception of Taoism) tended to lose sight of, but which tribal religions have retained.

The somewhat informal—though not unserious—tone of the book derives from the fact that it evolved from a television series on what is now the Public Broadcasting System. Mention of that allows me to acknowledge again my indebtedness to Mayo Simon, my producer, for what success in communication the book achieves. The book's aim remains the same as the one we set for that series: to carry intelligent laypeople into the heart of the world's great enduring faiths to the point where they might see, and even feel, why and how they guide and motivate the lives of those who live by them.

Huston Smith
Berkeley, California
December 1998

Acknowledgments

If this book achieves something in the way of substance as well as range, it will be due in good part to my having had such good and helpful friends.

Students at the Massachusetts Institute of Technology, Syracuse University, Hamline University, San Diego State University, and the University of California at Berkeley have joined those at Washington University in Saint Louis (who were involved with the book's first edition) in providing stimulating contexts in which concepts took form.

The chapter that remains closest to its version in the first edition is the one on Hinduism which retains the authoritative stamp of Swami Satprakashananda who was then the spiritual director of the Vedanta Society of Saint Louis. Professors K. R. Sundararajan and Frank Podgorski have checked the slightly modified draft for this second edition. Dr. Gurudharm Singh Khalsa checked the appendix on Sikhism.

The other substantive chapters have been improved by suggestions from the following consultants:

Buddhism: Professor Masao Abe and Dr. Edwin Bernbaum.

Confucianism: Professor Tu Wei-ming.

Taoism: Professors Ray Jordan and Whalen Lai, and Steven Tainer.

Islam: Professors Seyyed Hossein Nasr and Daniel Peterson, and Alan Godlas and Barbara Von Schlegell.

Judaism: Professors Irving Gefter and Rabbi Aryeh Wineman.

Christianity: Professors Marcus Borg and Robert Scharlemann, Fathers Owen Carroll and Leonidas Contas, and Brother David Steindl-Rast.

The Primal Religions: Chief Oren Lyons of the Onondaga Nation, and Professors Robert Bellah, Joseph Brown, Sam Gill, Charles Long, and Jill Raitt.

Stephen Mitchell cast his poet's eye over the entire book and improved its style appreciably. Scott Whittaker was invaluable in checking bibliographical references. John Loudon has been a model editor.

I am immensely grateful to all of the above, while exonerating them from responsibility for the uses to which I have put their suggestions.

In an altogether separate category, what I said about the chief support for the book's first edition holds even more for this second. When authors acknowledge a wife's help, the picture usually conjured up is that of a patient spouse respectfully tiptoeing through the household tasks, exuding, perhaps, an ineffable aura of admiration and support. While these virtues are not absent in the present case, something must be added to the image; a partner happily involved in every sentence, pruning with zeal, revising with skill and imagination, and (in the case of this second edition) contributing substantively to the section on Theravada Buddhism. It is because of these virtues that "her husband is known in the gates, when he sits among the elders of the land."

I. Point of Departure

Although the individuals that I name are now only memories for me, I begin this second edition of this book with the four paragraphs that launched its first edition.

I write these opening lines on a day widely celebrated throughout Christendom as World-Wide Communion Sunday. The sermon in the service I attended this morning dwelt on Christianity as a world phenomenon. From mud huts in Africa to the Canadian tundra, Christians are kneeling today to receive the elements of the Holy Eucharist. It is an impressive picture.

Still, as I listened with half my mind, the other half wandered to the wider company of God-seekers. I thought of the Yemenite Jews I watched six months ago in their synagogue in Jerusalem: dark-skinned men sitting shoeless and cross-legged on the floor, wrapped in the prayer shawls their ancestors wore in the desert. They are there today, at least a quorum of ten, morning and evening, swaying backwards and forwards like camel riders as they recite their Torah, following a form they inherit unconsciously from the centuries when their fathers were forbidden to ride the desert horse and developed this pretense in compensation. Yalcin, the Muslim architect who guided me through the Blue Mosque in Istanbul, has completed his month's Ramadan fast, which was beginning while we were together; but he too is praying today, five times as he prostrates himself toward Mecca. Swami Ramakrishna, in his tiny house by the Ganges at the foot of the Himalayas, will not speak today. He will continue the devotional silence that, with the exception of three days each year, he has kept for five years. By this hour U Nu is probably facing the delegations, crises, and cabinet meetings that are the lot of a prime minister, but from four to six this morning, before the world broke over him, he too was alone with the eternal in the privacy of the Buddhist shrine that adjoins his home in Rangoon. Dai Jo and Lai San, Zen monks in Kyoto, were ahead of him by an hour. They have been up since three this morning, and until eleven tonight will spend most of the day sitting immovable in the lotus position as they seek with intense absorption to plumb the Buddha-nature that lies at the center of their being.

What a strange fellowship this is, the God-seekers in every land, lifting their voices in the most disparate ways imaginable to the God of all life. How does it sound from above? Like bedlam, or do the strains blend in strange, ethereal harmony? Does one faith carry the lead, or do the parts share in counterpoint and antiphony where not in full-throated chorus?

We cannot know. All we can do is try to listen carefully and with full attention to each voice in turn as it addresses the divine.

Such listening defines the purpose of this book. It may be wondered if the purpose is not too broad. The religions we propose to consider belt the world. Their histories stretch back thousands of years, and they are motivating more people today than ever before. Is it possible to listen seriously to them within the compass of a single book?

The answer is that it is, because we shall be listening for well-defined themes. These must be listed at the outset or the pictures that emerge from these pages will be distorted.

1. This is not a textbook in the history of religions. This explains the scarcity of names, dates, and social influences in what follows. There are useful books that focus on such material.[1] This one too could have been swollen with their facts and figures, but it is not its intent to do their job in addition to its own. Historical facts are limited here to the minimum that is needed to locate in space and time the *ideas* the book focuses on. Every attempt has been made to keep scholarship out of sight—in foundations that must be sturdy, but not as scaffolding that would obscure the structures being examined.

2. Even in the realm of meanings the book does not attempt to give a rounded view of the religions considered, for each hosts differences that are too numerous to be delineated in a single chapter. One need only think of Christendom. Eastern Orthodox Christians worship in ornate cathedrals, while Quakers consider even steeples

desecrations. There are Christian mystics and Christians who reject mysticism. There are Christian Jehovah's Witnesses and Christian Unitarians. How is it possible to say in a manageable chapter what Christianity means to all Christians?

The answer, of course, is that it is not possible—selection is unavoidable. The question facing an author is not whether to select among points of view; the questions are *how many* to present, and *which ones*. In this book the first question is answered economically; I try to do reasonable justice to several perspectives instead of attempting to catalogue them all. In the case of Islam, this has meant ignoring Sunni/Shi'ite and traditional/modernist divisions, while noting different attitudes toward Sufism. In Buddhism I distinguish its Hinayana, Mahayana, and Vajrayana traditions, but the major schools within Mahayana are bypassed. The subdivisions never exceed three lest trees obscure the woods. Put the matter this way: If you were trying to describe Christianity to an intelligent and interested but busy Thailander, how many denominations would you include? It would be difficult to ignore the differences between Roman Catholic, Greek Orthodox, and Protestant, but you would probably not get into what separates Baptists from Presbyterians.

When we turn to *which* views to present, the guideline has been relevance to the interests of the intended reader. Three considerations have figured in determining this relevance. First, there is the simple matter of numbers. There are some faiths that every citizen should be acquainted with, simply because hundreds of millions of people live by them. The second consideration has been relevance to the modern mind. Because the ultimate benefit that may accrue from a book such as this is help in the ordering of the reader's own life, I have given priority to what (with caution yet a certain confidence) we may regard as these religions' contemporary expressions. The third consideration is universality. Every religion mixes universal principles with local peculiarities. The former, when lifted out and made clear, speak to what is generically human in us all. The latter, rich compounds of rites and legends, are not easy for outsiders to comprehend. It is one of the illusions of rationalism that the universal principles of religion are more important than the rites and rituals that feed them; to make that claim is like contending that the branches and leaves of a tree are more important than the roots from which they grow. But for this book, principles are more important than contexts, if for no other reason than that they are what the author has spent his years working with.

I have read books that have brought contexts themselves to life: Heather Wood's *Third Class Ticket* for India, Lin Yu-tang's *My Country and My People* for China, and Shalom Rabinowitz's *The Old Country* for Eastern European Jews. Perhaps someday someone will write a book about the great religions that roots them to their social settings. This, though, is a book I shall read, not write. I know my limitations and attend to areas from which ideas can be extracted.

3. This book is not a balanced account of its subject. The warning is important. I wince to think of the shock if the reader were to close the chapter on Hinduism and step directly into the Hinduism described by Nehru as "a religion that enslaves you": its Kali Temple in Calcutta, the curse of her caste system, her two million cows revered to the point of nuisance, her *fakirs* offering their bodies as sacrifice to bedbugs. Or what if the reader were transported to Bali, with its theaters named the Vishnu-Hollywood and its bookstores that do brisk business in *Klasik Comics*, in which Hindu gods and goddesses mow down hosts of unsightly demons with cosmic ray guns? I know the contrast. I sense it sharply between what I have written of Taoism and the Taoism that surrounded me as a boy in China: its almost complete submergence in augury, necromancy, and superstition. It is like the contrast between the Silent Christ and the Grand Inquisitor, or between the stillness of Bethlehem and department stores blaring "Silent Night" to promote Christmas shopping. The full story of religion is not rose-colored; often it is crude. Wisdom and charity are intermittent, and the net result is profoundly ambiguous. A balanced view of religion would include human sacrifice and scapegoating, fanaticism and persecution, the Christian Crusades and the holy wars of Islam. It would include witch hunts in Massachusetts, monkey trials in Tennessee, and snake worship in the Ozarks. The list would have no end.

Why then are these things not included in the pages that follow? My answer is so simple that it may sound ingenuous. This is a book about values. Probably as much bad music as good has been composed in the course of human history, but we do not expect courses in music appreciation to give it equal attention. Time being at a premium, we assume that they will attend to the best. I have adopted a similar strategy with respect to religion. A recent book on legal science carries the author's confession that he has written lovingly of the law. If something as impersonal as the law can enamor one author, it should come as no surprise that religion—again at its best—has enamored another. Others will be interested in trying to determine if religion in its entirety has been a blessing or a curse. That has not been my concern.

Having said what my concern is—the world's religions at their best—let me say what I take that best to be, beginning with what it is not. Lincoln Steffens has a fable of a man who climbed to the top of a mountain and, standing on tiptoe, seized hold of the Truth. Satan, suspecting mischief from this upstart, had directed one of his underlings to tail him; but when the demon reported with alarm the man's success—that he had seized hold of the Truth—Satan was unperturbed. "Don't worry," he yawned. "I'll tempt him to institutionalize it."

That story helps to separate the best from the ambiguous in religion. The empowering theological and metaphysical truths of the world's religions are, this book is prepared to argue, inspired. Institutions—religious institutions emphatically included—are another story. Constituted as they are of people with their inbuilt frailties, institutions are built of vices as well as virtues. When the vices— in-group versus out-group loyalties, for example—get compounded by numbers, the results can be horrifying to the point of suggesting (as some wag has) that the biggest mistake religion ever made was to get mixed up with people. Actually, this is not true, however, for to hold aloof from people would have resulted in leaving no mark on history. Given the choice—to remain aloof as disembodied insights or to establish traction in history by institutionalizing those insights— religion chose the wiser course.

This book honors that choice without following its story—I have already said that it is not a book about religious history. It adopts what in ways is the easier course of skimming off the cream of that history: the truths that religious institutions preserve, and which in turn empower those institutions. When religions are sifted for those truths, a different, cleaner side appears. They become the world's wisdom traditions. ("Where is the knowledge that is lost in information? Where is the wisdom that is lost in knowledge?"—T. S. Eliot.) They begin to look like data banks that house the winnowed wisdom of the human race. As this book concentrates on those wisdom deposits, it could have been titled alternatively "The World's Great Wisdom Traditions."

4. Finally, this is not a book on comparative religions in the sense of seeking to compare their worth. Comparisons always tend to be

odious, those among religions the most odious of all. So there is no assumption here that one religion is, or for that matter is not, superior to others. "There is no one alive today," Arnold Toynbee observed, "who knows enough to say with confidence whether one religion has been greater than all others." I have tried to let the best in each faith shine through by presenting it in the way I have found its most impressive adherents envisioning it. Readers may press on with comparisons if they wish to do so.

In saying what this book is not, I have already started to say what it is, but let me be explicit.

1. It is a book that seeks to embrace the world. In one sense, of course, that wish must fail. Even when stretched to the maximum, a single pair of arms falls short, and feet must be planted somewhere. To begin with the obvious, the book is written in English, which to some extent anchors it from the start. Next come cross-references, introduced to ease entry onto foreign turf. There are proverbs from China, tales from India, paradoxes from Japan, but most of the illustrations are Western: a line from Shakespeare, a verse from the Bible, a suggestion from psychoanalysis—Eliot and Toynbee have already been quoted. Beyond idiom, however, the book is incorrigibly Western in being targeted for the contemporary Western mind. That being the author's mind, he had no choice in the matter; but it must be accepted with the recognition that the book would have been different had it been written by a Zen Buddhist, a Muslim Sufi, or a Polish Jew.

This book, then, has a home—a home whose doors swing freely in and out, a base from which to journey forth and return, only to hit the road again in study and imaginings when not in actual travel. If it is possible to be homesick for the world, even places one has never been and suspects one will never go, this book is born of such homesickness.

We live in a fantastic century. I brush aside the incredible discoveries of science, and the razor's edge between doom and fulfillment onto which they have pushed us, to speak of the new situation among peoples. Lands across the planet have become our neighbors, China across the street, the Middle East at our back door. Young people with backpacks are everywhere, and those who remain at home are treated to an endless parade of books, documentaries, and visitors from abroad. We hear that East and West are meeting, but it is an understatement. They are being flung at one another, hurled with the force of atoms, the speed of jets, the restlessness of minds impatient to learn the ways of others. When historians look back on our century, they may remember it most, not for space travel or the release of nuclear energy, but as the time when the peoples of the world first came to take one another seriously.

The change that this new situation requires of us all—we who have been suddenly catapulted from town and country onto a world stage—is staggering. Twenty-five hundred years ago it took an exceptional man like Diogenes to exclaim, "I am not an Athenian or a Greek but a citizen of the world." Today we must all be struggling to make those words our own. We have come to the point in history when anyone who is only Japanese or American, only Oriental or Occidental, is only half human. The other half that beats with the pulse of all humanity has yet to be born.

To borrow an image from Nietzsche, we have all been summoned to become Cosmic Dancers who do not rest heavily on a single spot but lightly turn and leap from one position to another. As World Citizen, the Cosmic Dancer will be an authentic child of its parent culture, while closely related to all. The dancer's roots in family and community will be deep, but in those depths they will strike the water table of a common humanity. For is the dancer not also human? If only she might see what has interested others, might it not interest her as well? It is an exciting prospect. The softening of divisions will induce borrowings that sometimes produce hybrids, but for the most part simply enrich species and sustain their vigor.

The motives that impel us toward world understanding are varied. I was once taxied by bomber to an air force base to lecture to officers on other peoples' faiths. Why? Obviously, because those officers might some day have to deal with those peoples as allies or antagonists. This is one reason for coming to know them. It may be a necessary reason, but one hopes that there are others. Even the goal of avoiding military engagement through diplomacy is provisional because instrumental. The final reason for understanding another is intrinsic—to enjoy the wider angle the vision affords.

I am, of course, speaking metaphorically of vision and view, but an analogue from ocular sight fits perfectly. Without two eyes— binocular vision—there is no awareness of space's third dimension. Until sight converges from more than one angle, the world looks as flat as a postcard. The rewards of having two eyes are practical; they keep us from bumping into chairs and enable us to judge the speed of approaching cars. But the final reward is the deepened view of the world itself—the panoramas that unroll before us, the vistas that extend from our feet. It is the same with "the eye of the soul," as Plato called it. "What do they know of England, who only England know?"

I have acknowledged that the practical gains that come from being able to look at the world through others' eyes are major. They enable corporations to do business with China, and diplomats to stumble less often. But the greatest gains need no tally. To glimpse what belonging means to the Japanese; to sense with a Burmese grandmother what passes in life and what endures; to understand how Hindus can regard their personalities as masks that overlay the Infinite within; to crack the paradox of a Zen monk who assures you that everything is holy but scrupulously refrains from certain acts— to swing such things into view is to add dimensions to the glance of spirit. It is to have another world to live in. The only thing that is good without qualification is not (as Kant argued) the good will, for a will can mean well in cramped quarters. The only thing that is unquali-fiedly good is extended vision, the enlargement of one's understand-ing of the ultimate nature of things.

These thoughts about world understanding lead directly to the world's religions, for the surest way to the heart of a people is through its faith, if that faith has not fossilized. Which distinction—between religion alive and dead—brings us to the second constructive intent of this book.

2. It is a book that takes religion seriously. It is not a tourist guide. There will be no pandering to curiosity seekers, no riffling through peoples' faiths to light on what has shock value; no ascetics on beds of nails, no crucifixions among Penitentes in Mexico, no Parsi Towers of Silence that expose the dead for vultures' consumption, no erotic sculpture or excursions into Tantric sex. The great religions house such material, but to focus on it is the crudest kind of vulgarization.

There are subtler ways to belittle religion. One of these is to acknowledge its importance, but for other people—people of the past, people of other cultures, people whose ego strength needs bol-stering. This, too, will not be our approach. Our parts of speech will be in the third person. We shall be talking about Hindus, Buddhists, Confucianists, Muslims—it will be "they" and "them" all the way. But behind these fronts our deepest concern is for ourselves. The chief reason I find myself returning to the world's great wisdom traditions is for help on issues I have not myself been able to circumvent. Given the essential similarity in human nature—we are all more human than otherwise—I assume that the issues engage the readers of this book as well.

Even the subtlest way to patronize religion will be avoided, the way that honors it not for itself but for its yields—its contributions to art, or to peace of mind, or to group cohesion. This is a book about religion that exists, in William James's contrast, not as a dull habit but as an acute fever. It is about religion alive. And when religion jumps to life it displays a startling quality. It takes over. All else, while not silenced, becomes subdued and thrown into a supporting role.

Religion alive confronts the individual with the most momentous option life can present. It calls the soul to the highest adventure it can undertake, a proposed journey across the jungles, peaks, and deserts of the human spirit. The call is to confront reality, to master the self. Those who dare to hear and follow that secret call soon learn the dangers and difficulties of its lonely journey.

A sharpened edge of a razor, hard to traverse,
A difficult path is this—the poets declare![2]

Science makes major contributions to minor needs, Justice Holmes was fond of saying, adding that religion, however small its successes, is at least at work on the things that matter most. When, then, a lone spirit succeeds in breaking through to major conquests here, it becomes more than a king or queen. It becomes a world redeemer. Its impact stretches for millennia, blessing the tangled course of history for centuries. "Who are . . . the greatest benefactors of the living generation of mankind?" Toynbee asked. "I should say: 'Confucius and Laotze, the Buddha, the Prophets of Israel and Judah, Zoroaster, Jesus, Mohammed and Socrates.'"[3]

His answer should not surprise, for authentic religion is the clearest opening through which the inexhaustible energies of the cosmos enter human life. What then can rival its power to inspire life's deepest creative centers? Moving outward from there through myth and rite, it provides the symbols that carry history forward, until at length its power is spent and life awaits a new redemption. This recurrent pattern leads even the impish, like George Bernard

Shaw, to conclude that religion is the only real motive force in the world. (Alfred North Whitehead added science, which raises the number to two.)[4] It is religion as empowering that will be our object in the chapters ahead.

3. Finally, this book makes a real effort to communicate. I think of it as a work of translation, one that tries not only to penetrate the worlds of the Hindus, Buddhists, and Muslims, but to throw bridges from those worlds to the reader's world. The study of religion can be as technical and academic as any, but I have tried not to lose sight of the relevance this material has for the problems that human beings face today. "If you cannot—in the long run—tell everyone what you have been doing," wrote a great scientist who was also a superb communicator, "your doing has been worthless."[5]

This interest in communication leads back to the book's stance toward historical scholarship that was touched on earlier.

As far as I am aware there is nothing in these pages contrary to the facts of historical evidence, but beyond the avoidance of outright inaccuracy, the issue is less simple. I have deleted enormously, simplifying where historical details seemed to be slowing the pace and obscuring the essential. Occasionally, I have supplied corollaries that seemed to be implied, and I have introduced examples that appear to be in keeping with the theme but are not in the texts themselves. These liberties may lead some to feel that the book "sits loose to the facts," but historical accuracy is not the basic issue. Religion is not primarily a matter of facts; it is a matter of meanings. An analogy from biochemistry is helpful here. "Despite a knowledge of the structure of protein molecules down to the very placement of their atoms in exact three-dimensional space, we do not have the faintest idea of what the rules are for folding them up into their natural form."[6] The religious analogue to the biochemist's atoms are the facts that history, sociology, anthropology, and textual studies marshall about religion. These could be as complete as the biochemists' knowledge of the atomic structure of protein molecules; by themselves they are as lifeless. Implicitly, not explicitly, I have tried in these chapters to apply the "rules" that "fold" religious facts "into their natural form." I have tried to make them live religiously.

We are about to begin a voyage in space and time and eternity. The places will often be distant, the times remote, the themes beyond space and time altogether. We shall have to use words that are foreign — Sanskrit, Chinese, and Arabic. We shall try to describe states of consciousness that words can only hint at. We shall use logic to try to corner insights that laugh at our attempt. And ultimately, we shall fail; being ourselves of a different cast of mind, we shall never quite understand the religions that are not our own. But if we take those religions seriously, we need not fail miserably. And to take them seriously we need do only two things. First, we need to see their adherents as men and women who faced problems much like our own. And second, we must rid our minds of all preconceptions that could dull our sensitivity or alertness to fresh insights. If we lay aside our preconceptions about these religions, seeing each as forged by people who were struggling to see something that would give help and meaning to their lives; and if we then try without prejudice to see ourselves what they saw — if we do these things, the veil that separates us from them can turn to gauze.

A great anatomist used to close his opening lecture to beginning medical students with words that apply equally to our own undertaking. "In this course," he would say, "we shall be dealing with flesh and bones and cells and sinews, and there are going to be times when it's all going to seem terribly cold-blooded. But never forget. It's alive!"

Notes

1. A standard one is John B. Noss, *Man's Religions* (New York: Macmillan, 1984).
2. *Katha Upanishad* I.iii.14.
3. Arnold Toynbee, *Civilization on Trial* (New York: Oxford University Press, 1948), 156.
4. A. N. Whitehead, *Science and the Modern World* (New York: Free Press, 1967), 181.
5. Erwin Schrodinger, *Science and Humanism* (Cambridge: Cambridge University Press, 1952), 9.
6. R. C. Lewontin, in *The New York Review of Books* (April 27, 1989): 18.

II. Hinduism

If I were asked under what sky the human mind . . . has most deeply pondered over the greatest problems of life, and has found solutions to some of them which well deserve the attention even of those who have studied Plato and Kant—I should point to India. And if I were to ask myself from what literature we who have been nurtured almost exclusively on the thoughts of Greeks and Romans, and of one Semitic race, the Jewish, may draw the corrective which is most wanted in order to make our inner life more perfect, more comprehensive, more universal, in fact more truly human a life . . . again I should point to India.

—Max Müller

On July 16, 1945, in the deep privacy of a New Mexico desert, an event occurred that may prove to be the most important single happening of the twentieth century. A chain reaction of scientific discoveries that began at the University of Chicago and centered at "Site Y" at Los Alamos was culminated. The first atomic bomb was, as we say, a success.

No one had been more instrumental in this achievement than Robert Oppenheimer, director of the Los Alamos project. An observer who was watching him closely that morning has given us the following account: "He grew tenser as the last seconds ticked off. He scarcely breathed. He held on to a post to steady himself. . . . When the announcer shouted 'Now!' and there came this tremendous burst of light, followed . . . by the deep-growling roar of the explosion, his face relaxed in an expression of tremendous relief." This much from the outside. But what flashed through Oppenheimer's own mind during those moments, he recalled later, were two lines from the *Bhagavad-Gita* in which the speaker is God:

> *I am become death, the shatterer of worlds;*
> *Waiting that hour that ripens to their doom.*

This incident provides a profound symbol for this chapter's opening, and Mahatma Gandhi's life can join it in setting the stage for the faith we are about to explore. In an age in which violence and peace faced each other more fatefully than ever before, Gandhi's name became, in the middle of our century, the counterpoise to those of Stalin and Hitler. The achievement for which the world credited this man (who weighed less than a hundred pounds and whose worldly possessions when he died were worth less than two dollars) was the British withdrawal from India in peace, but what is less known is that among his own people he lowered a barrier more formidable than that of race in America. He renamed India's untouchables *harijan*, "God's people," and raised them to human stature. And in doing so he provided the nonviolent strategy as well as the inspiration for Martin Luther King, Jr.'s comparable civil rights movement in the United States.

Gandhi's own inspiration and strategy carries us directly into this chapter's subject, for he wrote in his *Autobiography:* "Such power as I possess for working in the political field has derived from my experiments in the spiritual field." In that spiritual field, he went on to say, "truth is the sovereign principle, and the *Bhagavad-Gita* is the book *par excellence* for the knowledge of Truth."

What People Want

If we were to take Hinduism as a whole — its vast literature, its complicated rituals, its sprawling folkways, its opulent art — and compress it into a single affirmation, we would find it saying: You can have what you want.

This sounds promising, but it throws the problem back in our laps. For what *do* we want? It is easy to give a simple answer — not easy to give a good one. India has lived with this question for ages and has her answer waiting. People, she says, want four things.

They begin by wanting pleasure. This is natural. We are all born with built-in pleasure-pain reactors. If we ignored these, leaving our hands on hot stoves or stepping out of second-story windows, we would soon die. What could be more obvious, then, than to follow the promptings of pleasure and entrust our lives to it?

Having heard—for it is commonly alleged—that India is ascetic, other-worldly, and life-denying, we might expect her attitude toward hedonists to be scolding, but it is not. To be sure, India has not made pleasure her highest good, but this is different from condemning enjoyment. To the person who wants pleasure, India says in effect: Go after it—there is nothing wrong with it; it is one of the four legitimate ends of life. The world is awash with beauty and heavy with sensual delights. Moreover, there are worlds above this one where pleasures increase by powers of a million at each rung, and these worlds, too, we shall experience in due course. Like everything else, hedonism requires good sense. Not every impulse can be followed with impunity. Small immediate goals must be sacrificed for long-range gains, and impulses that would injure others must be curbed to avoid antagonisms and remorse. Only the stupid will lie, steal, or cheat for immediate profit, or succumb to addictions. But as long as the basic rules of morality are obeyed, you are free to seek all the pleasure you want. Far from condemning pleasure, Hindu texts house pointers on how to enlarge its scope. To simple people who seek pleasure almost exclusively, Hinduism presents itself as little more than a regimen for ensuring health and prosperity; while at the other end of the spectrum, for sophisticates, it elaborates a sensual aesthetic that shocks in its explicitness. If pleasure is what you want, do not suppress the desire. Seek it intelligently.

This India says, and waits. It waits for the time—it will come to everyone, though not to everyone in one's present life—when one realizes that pleasure is not all that one wants. The reason everyone eventually comes to this discovery is not because pleasure is wicked, but because it is too trivial to satisfy one's total nature. Pleasure is essentially private, and the self is too small an object for perpetual enthusiasm. Søren Kierkegaard tried for a while what he called the aesthetic life, which made enjoyment its guiding principle, only to experience its radical failure, which he described in *Sickness Unto Death*. "In the bottomless ocean of pleasure," he wrote in his *Journal*, "I have sounded in vain for a spot to cast anchor. I have felt the almost irresistible power with which one pleasure drags another after it, the kind of adulterated enthusiasm which it is capable of producing, the boredom, the torment which follow." Even playboys—a type seldom credited with profundity—have been known to conclude, as one did recently, that "The glamour of yesterday I have come to see as tinsel." Sooner or later everyone wants to experience more than a kaleidoscope of momentary pleasures, however delectable.

When this time comes the individual's interests usually shift to the second major goal of life, which is worldly success[1] with its three prongs of wealth, fame, and power. This too is a worthy goal, to be neither scorned nor condemned. Moreover, its satisfactions last longer, for (unlike pleasure) success is a social achievement, and as such it involves the lives of others. For this reason it commands a scope and importance that pleasure cannot boast.

This point does not have to be argued for a contemporary Western audience. The Anglo-American temperament is not voluptuous. Visitors from abroad do not find English-speaking peoples enjoying life a great deal, or much bent on doing so—they are too busy. Being enamored not of sensualism but of success, what takes arguing in the West is not that achievement's rewards exceed those of the senses but that success too has its limitations—that "What is he worth?" does not come down to "How much has he got?"

India acknowledges that drives for power, position, and possessions run deep. Nor should they be disparaged per se. A modicum of worldly success is indispensable for supporting a household and discharging civic duties responsibly. Beyond this minimum, worldly achievements confer dignity and self-respect. In the end, however, these rewards too have their term. For they all harbor limitations that we can detail:

1. Wealth, fame, and power are exclusive, hence competitive, hence precarious. Unlike mental and spiritual values, they do not multiply when shared; they cannot be distributed without diminishing one's own portion. If I own a dollar, that dollar is not yours; while I am sitting on a chair, you cannot occupy it. Similarly with fame and power. The idea of a nation in which everyone is famous is a contradiction in terms; and if power were distributed equally, no one would be powerful in the sense in which we customarily use the word. From the competitiveness of these goods to their precariousness is a short step. As other people want them too, who knows when success will change hands?

2. The drive for success is insatiable. A qualification is needed here, for people do get enough money, fame, and power. It is when they make these things their chief ambition that their lusts cannot be satisfied. For these are not the things people really want, and people can never get enough of what they do not really want. In Hindu idiom, "To try to extinguish the drive for riches with money is like trying to quench a fire by pouring butter over it."

The West, too, knows this point. "Poverty consists, not in the decrease of one's possessions, but in the increase of one's greed," wrote Plato, and Gregory Nazianzen, a theologian, concurs: "Could you from all the world all wealth procure, more would remain, whose lack would leave you poor." "Success is a goal without a satiation point," a psychologist has recently written, and sociologists who studied a midwestern town found "both business men and working men running for dear life in the business of making the money they earn keep pace with the even more rapid growth of their subjective wants." It was from India that the West appropriated the parable of the donkey driver who kept his beast moving by dangling before it a carrot attached to a stick that was fixed to its own harness.

3. The third problem with worldly success is identical with that of hedonism. It too centers meaning in the self, which proves to be too small for perpetual enthusiasm. Neither fortune nor station can obscure the realization that one lacks so much else. In the end everyone wants more from life than a country home, a sports car, and posh vacations.

4. The final reason why worldly success cannot satisfy us completely is that its achievements are ephemeral. Wealth, fame, and power do not survive bodily death —"You can't take it with you," as we routinely say. And since we cannot, this keeps these things from satisfying us wholly, for we are creatures who can envision eternity and must instinctively rue by contrast the brief purchase on time that worldly success commands.

Before proceeding to the other two things that Hinduism sees people wanting, it will be well to summarize the ones considered thus far. Hindus locate pleasure and success on the Path of Desire. They use this phrase because the personal desires of the individual have thus far been foremost in charting life's course. Other goals lie ahead, but this does not mean that we should berate these preliminaries. Nothing is gained by repressing desires wholesale or pretending that we do not have them. As long as pleasure and success is what we think we want, we should seek them, remembering only the provisos of prudence and fair play.

The guiding principle is not to turn from desire until desire turns from you, for Hinduism regards the objects of the Path of Desire as if they were toys. If we ask ourselves whether there is anything wrong with toys, our answer must be: On the contrary, the thought of children without them is sad. Even sadder, however, is the prospect of adults who fail to develop interests more significant than dolls and trains. By the same token, individuals whose development is not arrested will move through delighting in success and the senses to the point where their attractions have been largely outgrown.

But what greater attractions does life afford? Two, say the Hindus. In contrast with the Path of Desire, they constitute the Path of Renunciation.

The word renunciation has a negative ring, and India's frequent use of it has been one of the factors in earning for it the reputation of being a life-denying spoilsport. But renunciation has two faces. It can stem from disillusionment and despair, the feeling that it's not worthwhile to extend oneself; but equally it can signal the suspicion that life holds more than one is now experiencing. Here we find the back-to-nature people—who renounce affluence to gain freedom from social rounds and the glut of things—but this is only the beginning. If renunciation always entails the sacrifice of a trivial now for a more promising yet-to-be, religious renunciation is like that of athletes who resist indulgences that could deflect them from their all-consuming goal. Exact opposite of disillusionment, renunciation in this second mode is evidence that the life force is strongly at work.

We must never forget that Hinduism's Path of Renunciation comes after the Path of Desire. If people could be satisfied by following their impulses, the thought of renunciation would never arise. Nor does it occur only to those who have failed on the former path—the disappointed lover who enters a monastery or nunnery to compensate. We can agree with the disparagers that for such people renunciation is a salvaging act—the attempt to make the best of personal defeat. What forces us to listen attentively to Hinduism's hypothesis is the testimony of those who stride the Path of Desire famously and still find themselves wishing for more than it offers. These people—not the ones who renounce but the ones who see nothing to renounce for — are the world's real pessimists. For to live, people must believe in that for the sake of which they live. As long as they sense no futility in pleasure and success, they can believe that those are worth living for. But if, as Tolstoy points out in his *Confessions*, they can no longer believe in the finite, they will believe in the infinite or they will die.

Let us be clear. Hinduism does not say that everyone in his or her present life will find the Path of Desire wanting. For against a vast time scale, Hinduism draws a distinction the West too is familiar with — that between chronological and psychological age. Two people, both forty-six, are the same age chronologically, but psychologically one may be still a child and the other an adult. The Hindus extend this distinction to cover multiple life spans, a point we shall take up explicitly when we come to the idea of reincarnation. As a consequence we shall find men and women who play the game of desire with all the zest of nine-year-old cops and robbers; though they know little else, they will die with the sense of having lived to the full and enter their verdict that life is good. But equally, there will be others who play this game as ably, yet find its laurels paltry. Why the difference? The enthusiasts, say the Hindus, are caught in the flush of novelty, whereas the others, having played the game over and over again, seek other worlds to conquer.

We can describe the typical experience of this second type. The world's visible rewards still attract them strongly. They throw themselves into enjoyment, enlarging their holdings and advancing their status. But neither the pursuit nor the attainment brings true happiness. Some of the things they want they fail to get, and this makes them miserable. Some they get and hold onto for a while, only to have them suddenly snatched away, and again they are miserable. Some they both get and keep, only to find that (like the Christmases of many adolescents) they do not bring the joy that was expected. Many experiences that thrilled on first encounter pall on the hundredth. Throughout, each attainment seems to fan the flames of new desire; none satisfies fully; and all, it becomes evident, perish with time. Eventually, there comes over them the suspicion that they are caught on a treadmill, having to run faster and faster for rewards that mean less and less.

When that suspicion dawns and they find themselves crying, "Vanity, vanity, all is vanity!" it may occur to them that the problem stems from the smallness of the self they have been scrambling to serve.

What if the focus of their concern were shifted? Might not becoming a part of a larger, more significant whole relieve life of its triviality?

That question announces the birth of religion. For though in some watered-down sense there may be a religion of self-worship, true religion begins with the quest for meaning and value beyond self-centeredness. It renounces the ego's claims to finality.

But what is this renunciation for? The question brings us to the two signposts on the Path of Renunciation. The first of these reads "the community," as the obvious candidate for something greater than ourselves. In supporting at once our own life and the lives of others, the community has an importance no single life can command. Let us, then, transfer our allegiance to it, giving its claims priority over our own.

This transfer marks the first great step in religion. It produces the religion of duty, after pleasure and success the third great aim of life in the Hindu outlook. Its power over the mature is tremendous. Myriads have transformed the will-to-get into the will-to-give, the will-to-win into the will-to-serve. Not to triumph but to do their best—to acquit themselves responsibly, whatever the task at hand—has become their prime objective.

Hinduism abounds in directives to people who would put their shoulders to the social wheel. It details duties appropriate to age, temperament, and social status. These will be examined in subsequent sections. Here we need only repeat what was said in connection with pleasure and success: Duty, too, yields notable rewards, only to leave the human spirit unfilled. Its rewards require maturity to be appreciated, but given maturity, they are substantial. Faithful performance of duty brings respect and gratitude from one's peers. More important, however, is the self-respect that comes from doing one's part. But in the end even these rewards prove insufficient. For even when time turns community into history, history, standing alone, is finite and hence ultimately tragic. It is tragic not only because it must end—eventually history, too, will die—but in its refusal to be perfected. Hope and history are always light-years apart. The final human good must lie elsewhere.

What People Really Want

"There comes a time," Aldous Huxley wrote, "when one asks even of Shakespeare, even of Beethoven, is this all?"

It is difficult to think of a sentence that identifies Hinduism's attitude toward the world more precisely. The world's offerings are not bad. By and large they are good. Some of them are good enough to command our enthusiasm for many lifetimes. Eventually, however, every human being comes to realize with Simone Weil that "there is no true good here below, that everything that appears to be good in this world is finite, limited, wears out, and once worn out, leaves necessity exposed in all its nakedness."² When this point is reached, one finds oneself asking even of the best this world can offer, "Is this all?"

This is the moment Hinduism has been waiting for. As long as people are content with the prospect of pleasure, success, or service, the Hindu sage will not be likely to disturb them beyond offering some suggestions as to how to proceed more effectively. The critical point in life comes when these things lose their original charm and one finds oneself wishing that life had something more to offer. Whether life does or does not hold more is probably the question that divides people more sharply than any other.

The Hindu answer to the question is unequivocal. Life holds other possibilities. To see what these are we must return to the question of what people want. Thus far, Hinduism would say, we have been answering this question too superficially. Pleasure, success, and duty are never humanity's ultimate goals. At best they are means that we assume will take us in the direction of what we really want. What we really want are things that lie at a deeper level.

First, we want being. Everyone wants to be rather than not be; normally, no one wants to die. A World War II correspondent once described the atmosphere of a room containing thirty-five men who had been assigned to a bombing mission from which, on average, only one-fourth returned. What he felt in those men, the correspondent noted, was not so much fear as "a profound reluctance to give up the future." Their sentiment holds for us all, the Hindus would say. None of us take happily to the thought of a future in which we shall have no part.

Second, we want to know. Whether it be scientists probing the secrets of nature, a typical family watching the nightly news, or neighbors catching up on local gossip, we are insatiably curious. Experiments have shown that even monkeys will work longer and harder to discover what is on the other side of a trapdoor than they will for either food or sex.

The third thing people seek is joy, a feeling tone that is the opposite of frustration, futility, and boredom.

These are what people really want. To which we should add, if we are to complete the Hindu answer, that they want these things infinitely. A distinctive feature of human nature is its capacity to think of something that has no limits: the infinite. This capacity affects all human life, as de Chirico's painting "Nostalgia of the Infinite" poignantly suggests. Mention any good, and we can imagine more of it—and, so imagining, want that more. Medical science has doubled life expectancy, but has living twice as long made people readier to die? To state the full truth, then, we must say that what people would really like to have is infinite being, infinite knowledge, and infinite bliss. They might have to settle for less, but this is what they really want. To gather the wants into a single word, what people really want is liberation *(moksha)*—release from the finitude that restricts us from the limitless being, consciousness, and bliss our hearts desire.

Pleasure, success, responsible discharge of duty, and liberation—we have completed the circuit of what people think they want and what they want in actuality. This takes us back to the staggering conclusion with which our survey of Hinduism began. What people most want, that they can have. Infinite being, infinite awareness, and infinite bliss are within their reach. Even so, the most startling statement yet awaits. Not only are these goods within peoples' reach, says Hinduism. People already possess them.

For what is a human being? A body? Certainly, but anything else? A personality that includes mind, memories, and propensities that have derived from a unique trajectory of life-experiences? This, too, but anything more? Some say no, but Hinduism disagrees. Underlying the human self and animating it is a reservoir of being that never dies, is never exhausted, and is unrestricted in consciousness and bliss. This infinite center of every life, this hidden self or *Atman,* is no less than *Brahman,* the Godhead. Body, personality, and *Atman-Brahman*—a human self is not completely accounted for until all three are noted.

But if this is true and we really are infinite in our being, why is this not apparent? Why do we not act accordingly? "I don't feel particularly unlimited today," one may be prompted to observe. "And my neighbor—I haven't noticed his behavior to be exactly Godlike." How can the Hindu hypothesis withstand the evidence of the morning newspaper?

The answer, say the Hindus, lies in the depth at which the Eternal is buried under the almost impenetrable mass of distractions, false assumptions, and self-regarding instincts that comprise our surface selves. A lamp can be covered with dust and dirt to the point of obscuring its light completely. The problem life poses for the human self is to cleanse the dross of its being to the point where its infinite center can shine forth in full display.

The Beyond Within

"The aim of life," Justice Holmes used to say, "is to get as far as possible from imperfection." Hinduism says its purpose is to pass beyond imperfection altogether.

If we were to set out to compile a catalogue of the specific imperfections that hedge our lives, it would have no end. We lack strength and imagination to effect our dreams; we grow tired, fall ill, and are foolish. We fail and become discouraged; we grow old and die. Lists of this sort could be extended indefinitely, but there is no need, for all specific limitations reduce to three basic variants. We are limited in joy, knowledge, and being, the three things people really want.

Is it possible to pass beyond the strictures that separate us from these things? Is it feasible to seek to rise to a quality of life that, because less circumscribed, would be life indeed?

To begin with the strictures on our joy, these fall into three subgroups: physical pain, frustration that arises from the thwarting of desire, and boredom with life in general.

Physical pain is the least troublesome of the three. As pain's intensity is partly due to the fear that accompanies it, the conquest of fear can reduce pain concomitantly. Pain can also be accepted when it has a purpose, as a patient welcomes the return of life and feeling, even painful feeling, to a frozen arm. Again, pain can be overridden by an urgent purpose, as in a football game. In extreme cases of useless pain, it may be possible to anesthetize it through drugs or control of the senses. Ramakrishna, the greatest Hindu saint of the nineteenth century, died of cancer of the throat. A doctor who was examining him in the last stages of the disease probed his degenerating tissue and Ramakrishna flinched in pain. "Wait a minute," he said;

then, "Go ahead," after which the doctor could probe without resistance. The patient had focused his attention to the point where nerve impulses could barely gain access. One way or another it seems possible to rise to a point where physical pain ceases to be a major problem.

More serious is the psychological pain that arises from the thwarting of specific desires. We want to win a tournament, but we lose. We want to profit, but the deal falls through. A promotion goes to our competitor. We would like to have been invited, but are snubbed. Life is so filled with disappointments that we are likely to assume that they are built into the human condition. On examination, however, there proves to be something disappointments share in common. Each thwarts an expectation of the individual ego. If the ego were to have no expectations, there would be nothing to disappoint.

If this sounds like ending an ailment by killing the patient, the same point can be stated positively. What if the interests of the self were expanded to the point of approximating a God's-eye view of humanity? Seeing all things under the aspect of eternity would make one objective toward oneself, accepting failure as on a par with success in the stupendous human drama of yes and no, positive and negative, push and pull. Personal failure would be as small a cause for concern as playing the role of loser in a summer theater performance. How could one feel disappointed at one's own defeat if one experienced the victor's joy as also one's own; how could being passed over for a promotion touch one if one's competitor's success were enjoyed vicariously? Instead of crying "impossible," we should perhaps content ourselves with noting how different this would feel from life as it is usually lived, for reports of the greatest spiritual geniuses suggest that they rose to something like this perspective. "Inasmuch as you have done it unto the least of these, you have done it unto me"—are we to suppose that Jesus was posturing when he uttered those words? We are told that Sri Ramakrishna once

howled with pain when he saw two boatmen quarrelling angrily. He came to identify himself with the sorrows of the whole world, however impure and murderous they might be, until his heart was scored with scars. But he knew that he must love God in all sorts and conditions of men, however antagonistic and hostile, and in all forms of thought controlling their existence and often setting them at variance to one another.[3]

Detachment from the finite self or attachment to the whole of things—we can state the phenomenon either positively or negatively. When it occurs, life is lifted above the possibility of frustration and above ennui—the third threat to joy—as well, for the cosmic drama is too spectacular to permit boredom in the face of such vivid identification.

The second great limitation of human life is ignorance. The Hindus claim that this, too, is removable. The Upanishads speak of a "knowing of That the knowledge of which brings knowledge of everything." It is not likely that "everything" here implies literal omniscience. More probably, it refers to an insight that lays bare the point of everything. Given that summarizing insight, to ask for details would be as irrelevant as asking the number of atoms in a great painting. When the point is grasped, who cares about details?

But is transcendent knowledge even in this more restricted sense possible? Clearly, mystics think that it is. Academic psychology has not followed them all the way, but it is convinced that there is far more to the mind than appears on its surface. Psychologists liken the mind to an iceberg, most of which is invisible. What does the mind's vast, submerged ballast contain? Some think it contains every memory and experience that has come its way, nothing being forgotten by the deep mind that never sleeps. Others, like Carl Jung, think it includes racial memories that summarize the experience of the entire human species. Psychoanalysis aims a few pinpoints of light at this mental darkness. Who is to say how far the darkness can be dispelled?

As for life's third limitation, its restricted being, to profitably consider this we have first to ask how the boundary of the self is to be defined. Not, certainly, by the amount of physical space our bodies occupy, the amount of water we displace in the bathtub. It makes more sense to gauge our being by the size of our spirits, the range of reality with which they identify. A man who identifies with his family, finding his joys in theirs, would have that much reality; a woman who could identify with humankind would be that much greater. By this criterion people who could identify with being as a whole would be unlimited. Yet this seems hardly right, for they would still die. The object of their concerns would continue, but they themselves would be gone.

We need, therefore, to approach this question of being not only spatially, so to speak, but also in terms of time. Our everyday experience provides a wedge for doing so. Strictly speaking, every moment of our lives is a dying; the I of that moment dies, never to be reborn. Yet despite the fact that in this sense my life consists of nothing but funerals, I do not conceive of myself as dying each moment, for I do not equate myself with my individual moments. I endure through them — experiencing them, without being identical with any of them in its singularity. Hinduism carries this notion a step further. It posits an extensive self that lives successive lives in the way a single life lives successive moments.

A child's heart is broken by misfortunes we consider trivial. It identifies completely with each incident, being unable to see it against the backdrop of a whole, variable lifetime. A lot of living is required before the child can withdraw its self-identification from the individual moment and approach, thereby, adulthood. Compared with children we are mature, but compared with saints we are children. No more capable of seeing our total selves in perspective than a three-year-old who has dropped its ice cream cone, our attention is fixated on our present life span. If we could mature completely we would see that lifespan in a larger setting, one that is, actually, unending.

This is the basic point in the Hindu estimate of the human condition. We have seen that psychology has accustomed us to the fact that there is more to ourselves than we suspect. Like the eighteenth century European view of the earth, our minds have their own darkest Africas, their unmapped Borneos, their Amazonian basins. Their bulk continues to await exploration. Hinduism sees the mind's hidden continents as stretching to infinity. Infinite in being, infinite in awareness, there is nothing beyond them that remains unknown. Infinite in joy, too, for there is nothing alien to them to mar their beatitude.

Hindu literature is studded with metaphors and parables that are designed to awaken us to the realms of gold that are hidden in the depths of our being. We are like kings who, falling victim to amnesia, wander our kingdoms in tatters not knowing who we really are. Or like a lion cub who, having become separated from its mother, is raised by sheep and takes to grazing and bleating on the assumption that it is a sheep as well. We are like a lover who, in his dream, searches the wide world in despair for his beloved, oblivious of the fact that she is lying at his side throughout.

What the realization of our total being is like can no more be described than can a sunset to one born blind; it must be experienced. The biographies of those who have made the discovery provide us with clues, however. These people are wiser; they have more strength and joy. They seem freer, not in the sense that they go around breaking the laws of nature (though the power to do exceptional things is often ascribed to them) but in the sense that they seem not to find the natural order confining. They seem serene, even radiant. Natural peacemakers, their love flows outward, alike to all. Contact with them strengthens and purifies.

Four Paths to the Goal

All of us dwell on the brink of the infinite ocean of life's creative power. We carry it within us: supreme strength, the fullness of wisdom, unquenchable joy. It is never thwarted and cannot be destroyed. But it is hidden deep, which is what makes life a problem. The infinite is down in the darkest, profoundest vault of our being, in the forgotten well-house, the deep cistern. What if we could bring it to light and draw from it unceasingly?

This question became India's obsession. Her people sought religious truth not simply to increase their store of general information; they sought it as a chart to guide them to higher states of being. Religious people were ones who were seeking to transform their natures, reshape them to a superhuman pattern through which the infinite could shine with fewer obstructions. One feels the urgency of the quest in a metaphor the Hindu texts present in many guises. Just as a man carrying on his head a load of wood that has caught fire would go rushing to a pond to quench the flames, even so will the seeker of truth, scorched by the fires of life—birth, death, self-deluding futility—go rushing to a teacher wise to the ways of the things that matter most.

Hinduism's specific directions for actualizing the human potential come under the heading of *yoga*. The word once conjured images of shaggy men in loincloths, twisting their bodies into human pretzels while brandishing occult powers. Now that the West has appropriated the term, however, we are more likely to think of lithe women exercising to retain their trim suppleness. Neither image is totally divorced from the real article, but they relate only to its bodily aspects. The word *yoga* derives from the same root as does the English word yoke, and yoke carries a double connotation: to unite (yoke together), and to place under disciplined training (to bring under the yoke, or "take my yoke upon you"). Both connotations are present in the Sanskrit word. Defined generally, then, *yoga* is a method of training designed to lead to integration or union. But integration of what?

Some people are chiefly interested in their bodies. Needless to say, they have their Indian counterparts—people who make their bodies the prime objects of their concern and endeavor. For such people India, through centuries of experimentation, has devised the most fantastic school of physical culture the world has ever seen.[4] Not that she has been more interested in the body than the West; her interest has simply taken a different turn. Whereas the West has sought strength and beauty, India has been interested in precision and control, ideally complete control over the body's every function. How many of her incredible claims in this area can be scientifically corroborated remains to be seen.[5] It is enough here to note that her extensive instructions on the subject comprise an authentic *yoga*, *hatha yoga*. Originally it was practiced as preliminary to spiritual *yoga*, but it has largely lost this connection so it need not concern us here. The judgment of the Hindu sages on this matter can be ours as well. Incredible things can be done with the body if you are willing to give your life to the project, but these things have little to do with enlightenment. If their cultivation stems from a desire to show off, they can actually impede spiritual growth.

The *yogas* that do concern us are those designed to unite the human spirit with the God who lies concealed in its deepest recesses. "Since all the Indian spiritual [as distinct from bodily] exercises are devoted seriously to this practical aim—not to a merely fanciful contemplation or discussion of lofty and profound ideas—they may well be regarded as representing one of the most realistic, matter-of-fact, practical-minded systems of thought and training ever set up by the human mind. How to come to Brahman [God in Sanskrit] and remain in touch with Brahman; how to become identified with Brahman, living out of it; how to become divine while still on earth — transformed, reborn adamantine while on the earthly plane; that is the quest that has inspired and deified the human spirit in India throughout the ages."[6]

The spiritual trails that Hindus have blazed toward this goal are four. At first this may seem surprising. If there is one goal, should there not be one path to it? This might be the case if we were all starting from the same point, though even then different modes of transport — walking, driving, flying — might counsel alternate routes. As it is, people approach the goal from different directions, so there must be multiple trails to the common destination.

Where one starts from depends on the kind of person one is. The point has not been lost on Western spiritual directors. One of the most noted of these, Father Surin, for example, criticized "directors who get a plan into their heads which they apply to all the souls who come to them, trying to bring them into line with it like one who should wish all to wear the same clothes." St. John of the Cross called attention to the same danger when he wrote in *The Living Flame* that the aim of spiritual directors should "not be to guide souls by a way suitable to themselves, but to ascertain the way by which God Himself is pointing them." What is distinctive in Hinduism is the amount of attention it has devoted to identifying basic spiritual personality types and the disciplines that are most likely to work for each. The result is a recognition, pervading the entire religion, that there are multiple paths to God, each calling for its distinctive mode of travel.

The number of the basic spiritual personality types, by Hindu count, is four. (Carl Jung built his typology on the Indian model, while modifying it in certain respects.) Some people are primarily reflective. Others are basically emotional. Still others are essentially active. Finally, some are experimentally inclined. For each of these personality types Hinduism prescribes a distinct *yoga* that is designed to capitalize on the type's distinctive strength. The types are not sealed in watertight compartments, for every human being possesses all four talents to some degree, just as most hands of cards contain all four suits. But it makes sense to lead with the suit that is strongest.

All four paths begin with moral preliminaries. As the aim of the *yoga*s is to render the surface self transparent to its underlying divinity, it must first be cleansed of its gross impurities. Religion is always more than morality, but if it lacks a moral base it will not stand. Selfish acts coagulate the finite self instead of dissolving it; ill-will perturbs the flow of consciousness. The first step of every *yoga*, therefore, involves the cultivation of such habits as non-injury, truth-fulness, non-stealing, self-control, cleanliness, contentment, self-discipline, and a compelling desire to reach the goal.

Keeping these common preliminaries in mind, we are ready for the *yogas'* distinctive instructions.

The Way to God through Knowledge

Jnana yoga, intended for spiritual aspirants who have a strong reflective bent, is the path to oneness with the Godhead through knowledge. Such knowledge—the Greeks' *gnosis* and *sophia*—has nothing to do with factual information; it is not encyclopedic. It is, rather, an intuitive discernment that transforms, turning the knower eventually into that which she knows. ("She" is appropriate here because in the principal Western source-languages—Hebrew, Latin, and Greek—the words for knowledge in this mode are usually feminine in gender.) Thinking is important for such people. They live in their heads a lot because ideas have for them an almost palpable vitality; they dance and sing for them. And if such thinkers are parodied as philosophers who walk around with their heads in the clouds, it is because they sense Plato's Sun shining above those clouds. Thoughts have consequences for such people; their minds animate their lives. Not many people are convinced by Socrates' claim that "to know the good is to do it," but in his own case he may have been reporting a straightforward fact.

For people thus given to knowing, Hinduism proposes a series of demonstrations that are designed to convince the thinker that she possesses more than her finite self. The rationale is straightforward. Once the *jnana yogi* grasps this point, her sense of self will shift to a deeper level.

The key to the project is discrimination, the power to distinguish between the surface self that crowds the foreground of attention and the larger self that is out of sight. Cultivating this power proceeds through three stages, the first of which is learning. Through listening to sages and scriptures and treatises on the order of Thomas Aquinas's *Summa Theologica*, the aspirant is introduced to the prospect that her essential being is Being itself.

The second step is thinking. By prolonged, intensive reflection, that which the first step introduced as a hypothesis must assume life. The *Atman* (God within) must change from concept to realization. A number of lines of reflection are proposed for this project. For example, the disciple may be advised to examine our everyday language and ponder its implications. The word "my" always implies a distinction between the possessor and what is possessed; when I speak of my book or my jacket, I do not suppose that I am those things. But I also speak of my body, my mind, or my personality, giving evidence thereby that in some sense I consider myself as distinct from them as well. What is this "I" that possesses my body and mind, but is not their equivalent?

Again, science tells me that there is nothing in my body that was there seven years ago, and my mind and my personality have undergone comparable changes. Yet, throughout their manifold revisions, I have remained in some way the same person, the person who believed now this, now that; who once was young and is now old. What is this something in my makeup, more constant than body or mind, that has endured the changes? Seriously pondered, this question can disentangle one's Self from one's lesser identifications.

Our word "personality" comes from the Latin *persona*, which originally referred to the mask an actor donned as he stepped onto the stage to play his role, the mask through *(per)* which he sounded *(sonare)* his part. The mask registered the role, while behind it the actor remained hidden and anonymous, aloof from the emotions he enacted. This, say the Hindus, is perfect; for roles are precisely what our personalities are, the ones into which we have been cast for the moment in this greatest of all tragi-comedies, the drama of life itself in which we are simultaneously coauthors and actors. As a good actress gives her best to her part, we too should play ours to the hilt. Where we go wrong is in mistaking our presently assigned part for what we truly are. We fall under the spell of our lines, unable to remember previous roles we have played and blind to the prospect of future ones. The task of the *yogi* is to correct this false identification. Turning her awareness inward, she must pierce the innumerable layers of her personality until, having cut through them all, she reaches the anonymous, joyfully unconcerned actress who stands beneath.

The distinction between self and Self can be assisted by another image. A man is playing chess. The board represents his world. There are pieces to be moved, bishops to be won and lost, an objective to be gained. The game can be won or lost, but not the player himself. If he has worked hard, he has improved his game and indeed his faculties; this happens in defeat fully as much as in victory. As the contestant is related to his total person, so is the finite self of any particular life-time related to its underlying *Atman*.

Metaphors continue. One of the most beautiful is found in the Upanishads, as also (by interesting coincidence) in Plato. There is a rider who sits serene and motionless in his chariot. Having delegated responsibility for the journey to his charioteer, he is free to sit back and give full attention to the passing landscape. In this image resides a metaphor for life. The body is the chariot. The road over which it travels are the sense objects. The horses that pull the chariot over the road are the senses themselves. The mind that controls the senses when they are disciplined is represented by the reins. The decisional faculty of the mind is the driver, and the master of the chariot, who is in full authority but need never lift a finger, is the Omniscient Self.

If the *yogi* is able and diligent, such reflections will eventually induce a lively sense of the infinite Self that underlies one's transient, finite self. The two will become increasingly distinct in one's mind, separating like water and oil where formerly they mixed like water and milk. One is then ready for the third step on the path of knowl-edge, which consists in shifting her self-identification to her abiding part. The direct way for her to do this is to think of herself as Spirit, not only during periods of meditation that are reserved for this pur-pose, but also as much as possible while performing her daily tasks. This latter exercise, though, is not easy. She needs to drive a wedge between her skin-encapsulated ego and her *Atman,* and an aid in doing so is to think of the former in the third person. Instead of "I am walking down the street," she thinks, "There goes Sybil walking down Fifth Avenue," and tries to reinforce the assertion by visualizing her-self from a distance. Neither agent nor patient, her approach to what happens is, "I am the Witness." She watches her unsubstantial history with as much detachment as she lets her hair blow in the wind. Just as a lamp that lights a room is unconcerned with what goes on within it, even so the *yogi* watches what transpires in his house of pro-toplasm, the texts tell us. "Even the sun, with all its warmth, is mar-velously detached" was found scribbled somewhere on a prison wall. Life's events are simply allowed to proceed. Seated in the dentist's chair, Sybil notes, "Poor Sybil. It will soon be over." But she must play fair and adopt the same posture when fortune visits her and she would like nothing better than bask in the praise she is receiving.

Thinking of oneself in the third person does two things simultaneously. It drives a wedge between one's self-identification and one's surface self, and at the same time forces this self-identification to a deeper level until at last, through a knowledge identical with being, one becomes in full what one always was at heart. "That thou art, other than Whom there is no other seer, hearer, thinker, or agent."[7]

The Way to God through Love

The *yoga* of knowledge is said to be the shortest path to divine realization. It is also the steepest. Requiring as it does a rare combination of rationality and spirituality, it is for a select few.

By and large, life is powered less by reason than by emotion; and of the many emotions that crowd the human heart, the strongest is love. Even hate can be interpreted as a rebound from the thwarting of this impulse. Moreover, people tend to become like that which they love, with its name written on their brows. The aim of *bhakti yoga* is to direct toward God the love that lies at the base of every heart. "As the waters of the Ganges flow incessantly toward the ocean," says God in the *Bhagavata Purana*, "so do the minds of the *bhakta* move constantly toward Me, the Supreme Person residing in every heart, immediately they hear about My qualities."

In contrast to the way of knowledge, *bhakti yoga* has countless followers, being, indeed, the most popular of the four. Though it originated in antiquity, one of its best-known proponents was a sixteenth-century mystical poet named Tulsidas. During his early married life he was inordinately fond of his wife, to the point that he could not abide her absence even for a day. One day she went to visit her parents. Before the day was half over, Tulsidas turned up at her side, whereupon his wife exclaimed, "How passionately attached to me you are! If only you could shift your attachment to God, you would reach him in no time." "So I would," thought Tulsidas. He tried it, and it worked.

All the basic principles of *bhakti yoga* are richly exemplified in Christianity. Indeed, from the Hindu point of view, Christianity is one great brilliantly lit *bhakti* highway toward God, other paths being not neglected, but less clearly marked. On this path God is conceived differently than in *jnana*. In *jnana yoga* the guiding image was of an infinite sea of being underlying the waves of our finite selves. This sea typified the all-pervading Self, which is as much within us as without, and with which we should seek to identify. Thus envisioned, God is impersonal, or rather transpersonal, for personality, being something definite, seems to be finite whereas the *jnanic* Godhead is infinite. To the *bhakti*, for whom feelings are more real than thoughts, God appears different on each of these counts.

First, as healthy love is out-going, the *bhakta* will reject all suggestions that the God one loves is oneself, even one's deepest Self, and insist on God's otherness. As a Hindu devotional classic puts the point, "I want to taste sugar; I don't want to be sugar."

> *Can water quaff itself?*
> *Can trees taste of the fruit they bear?*
> *He who worships God must stand distinct from Him,*
> *So only shall he know the joyful love of God;*
> *For if he say that God and he are one,*
> *That joy, that love, shall vanish instantly away.*
>
> *Pray no more for utter oneness with God:*
> *Where were the beauty if jewel and setting were one?*
> *The heat and the shade are two,*
> *If not, where were the comfort of shade?*
> *Mother and child are two,*
> *If not, where were the love?*
> *When after being sundered, they meet,*
> *What joy do they feel, the mother and child!*
> *Where were joy, if the two were one?*
> *Pray, then, no more for utter oneness with God.* [8]

Second, being persuaded of God's otherness, the *bhakta's* goal, too, will differ from the *jnani's*. The *bhakta* will strive not to identify with God, but to adore God with every element of his or her being. The words of Bede Frost, though written in another tradition, are directly applicable to this side of Hinduism: "The union is no Pantheist absorption of the man in the one, but is essentially personal in character. More, since it is preeminently a union of love, the kind of knowledge which is required is that of friendship in the very highest sense of the word."[9] Finally, in such a context God's personality, far from being a limitation, is indispensable. Philosophers may be able to love pure being, infinite beyond all attributes, but they are exceptions. The normal object of human love is a person who possesses attributes.

All we have to do in this *yoga* is to love God dearly—not just claim such love, but love God in fact; love God only (other things being loved in relation to God); and love God for no ulterior reason (not even from the desire for liberation, or to be loved in return) but for love's sake alone. Insofar as we succeed in this we know joy, for no experience can compare with that of being fully and authentically in love. Moreover, every strengthening of our affections toward God will weaken the world's grip. Saints may, indeed will, love the world more than do the profane; but they will love it in a very different way, seeing in it the reflected glory of the God they adore.

How is such love to be engendered? Obviously, the task will not be easy. The things of this world clamor for our affection so incessantly that it may be marveled that a Being who can neither be seen nor heard can ever become their rival.

Enter Hinduism's myths, her magnificent symbols, her several hundred images of God, her rituals that keep turning night and day like never-ending prayer wheels. Valued as ends in themselves these could, of course, usurp God's place, but this is not their intent. They are matchmakers whose vocation is to introduce the human heart to what they represent but themselves are not. It is obtuse to confuse Hinduism's images with idolatry, and their multiplicity with polytheism. They are runways from which the sense-laden human spirit can rise for its "flight of the alone to the Alone." Even village priests will frequently open their temple ceremonies with the following beloved invocation:

> *O Lord, forgive three sins that are due to my human limitations:*
> *Thou art everywhere, but I worship you here;*
> *Thou art without form, but I worship you in these forms;*
> *Thou needest no praise, yet I offer you these prayers and*
>   *salutations.*
> *Lord, forgive three sins that are due to my human limitations.*

A symbol such as a multi-armed image, graphically portraying God's astounding versatility and superhuman might, can epitomize an entire theology. Myths plumb depths that the intellect can see only obliquely. Parables and legends present ideals in ways that make hearers long to embody them—vivid support for Irwin Edman's contention that "it is a myth, not a mandate, a fable, not a logic by which people are moved." The value of these things lies in their power to recall our minds from the world's distractions to the thought of God and God's love. In singing God's praises, in praying to God with wholehearted devotion, in meditating on God's majesty and glory, in reading about God in the scriptures, in regarding the entire universe as God's handiwork, we move our affections steadily in God's direction. "Those who meditate on Me and worship Me without any attachment to anything else," says Lord Krishna in the *Bhagavad-Gita,* "those I soon lift from the ocean of death."

Three features of the *bhakta*'s approach deserve mention: *japam,* ringing the changes on love, and the worship of one's chosen ideal.

Japam is the practice of repeating God's name. It finds a Christian parallel in one of the classics of Russian spirituality, *The Way of a Pilgrim.* This is the story of an unnamed peasant whose first concern is to fulfill the biblical injunction to "pray without ceasing." Seeking for someone who can explain how it is possible to do this, he wanders through Russia and Siberia with a knapsack of dried bread for food and the charity of locals for shelter, consulting many authorities, only to be disappointed until at last he meets an old man who teaches him "a constant, uninterrupted calling upon the divine Name of Jesus with the lips, in the spirit, in the heart, during every occupation, at all times, in all places, even during sleep." The pilgrim's teacher trains him until he can repeat the name of Jesus more than 12,000 times a day without strain. This frequent service of the lips imperceptibly becomes a genuine appeal of the heart. The prayer becomes a constant, warming presence within him that brings a bubbling joy. "Keep the name of the Lord spinning in the midst of all your activities" is a Hindu statement of the same point. Washing or weaving, planting or shopping, imperceptibly but indelibly these verbal droplets of aspiration soak down into the subconscious, loading it with the divine.

Ringing the changes on love puts to religious use the fact that love assumes different nuances according to the relationship involved. The love of the parent for the child carries overtones of protectiveness, whereas a child's love includes dependence. The love of friends is different from the conjugal love of woman and man. Different still is

the love of a devoted servant for its master. Hinduism holds that all of
these modes have their place in strengthening the love of God and
encourages *bhaktas* to make use of them all. In practice Christianity
does the same. Most frequently it envisions God as benevolent protec-
tor, symbolized as lord or parent, but other modes are not absent.
"What a Friend we have in Jesus" is a familiar Christian hymn, and "my
Master and my Friend" figures prominently in another Christian favorite. God figures as spouse in the Song of Songs and in Christian mystical
writings where the marriage of the soul to Christ is a standing metaphor. The attitude of regarding God as one's child sounds somewhat
foreign to Western ears, yet much of the magic of Christmas derives
from this being the one time in the year when God enters the heart
as a child, eliciting thereby the tenderness of the parental instinct.

We come finally to the worship of God in the form of one's chosen ideal. The Hindus have represented God in innumerable forms.
This, they say, is appropriate. Each is but a symbol that points to
something beyond; and as none exhausts God's actual nature, the
entire array is needed to complete the picture of God's aspects and
manifestations. But though the representations point equally to God,
it is advisable for each devotee to form a lifelong attachment to one of
them. Only so can its meaning deepen and its full power become
accessible. The representation selected will be one's *ishta,* or
adopted form of the divine. The *bhakta* need not shun other forms,
but this one will never be displaced and will always enjoy a special
place in its disciple's heart. The ideal form for most people will be
one of God's incarnations, for God can be loved most readily in
human form because our hearts are already attuned to loving people.
Many Hindus acknowledge Christ as a God-man, while believing
that there have been others, such as Rama, Krishna, and the Buddha.
Whenever the stability of the world is seriously threatened, God
descends to redress the imbalance.

> *When goodness grows weak,*
> *When evil increases,*
> *I make myself a body.*
>
> *In every age I come back*
> *To deliver the holy,*
> *To destroy the sin of the sinner,*
> *To establish the righteous.*   (Bhagavad-Gita, IV:7–8)

The Way to God through Work

The third path toward God, intended for persons of active bent, is *karma yoga*, the path to God through work.

An examination of the anatomy and physiology of human bodies discloses an interesting fact. All organs of digestion and respiration serve to feed the blood with nutritive materials. The circulatory apparatus delivers this nourishing blood throughout the body, maintaining bones, joints, and muscles. Bones provide a framework without which the muscles could not operate, while joints supply the flexibility needed for movement. The brain envisions the movements that are to be made, and the spinal nervous system executes them. The vegetative nervous system, helped by the endocrine system, maintains the harmony of the viscera on which the motor muscles depend. In short, the entire body, except for the reproductive apparatus, converges on action. "The human machine," a physician writes, "seems indeed to be made for action."[10]

Work is the staple of human life. The point is not simply that all but a few people must work to survive. Ultimately, the drive to work is psychological rather than economic. Forced to be idle, most people become irritable; forced to retire, they decline. Included here are compulsive housekeepers as well as great scientists, such as Mme. Curie. To such people Hinduism says, You don't have to retire to a cloister to realize God. You can find God in the world of everyday affairs as readily as anywhere.[11] Throw yourself into your work with everything you have; only do so wisely, in a way that will bring the highest rewards, not just trivia. Learn the secret of work by which every movement can carry you Godward even while other things are being accomplished, like a wristwatch that winds itself as other duties are performed.

How this is to be done depends on the other components in the worker's nature. By choosing the path of work, the *karma yogi* has already shown an inclination toward activity, but there remains the question of whether the supporting disposition is predominantly affective or reflective. The answer to that question determines whether the *yogi* approaches work intellectually or in the spirit of love. In the language of the four *yogas*, *karma yoga* can be practiced in either mode: *jnana* (knowledge), or *bhakti* (devoted service).

As we have seen, the point of life is to transcend the smallness of the finite self. This can be done either by identifying oneself with the transpersonal Absolute that resides at the core of one's being, or by shifting one's interest and affection to a personal God who is experienced as distinct from oneself. The first is the way of *jnana*, the second of *bhakti*. Work can be a vehicle for self-transcendence in either approach, for according to Hindu doctrine every action performed upon the external world reacts on the doer. If I chop down a tree that blocks my view, each stroke of the ax unsettles the tree; but it leaves its mark on me as well, driving deeper into my being my determination to have my way in the world. Everything I do for my private wellbeing adds another layer to my ego, and in thickening it insulates me more from God. Conversely, every act done without thought for myself diminishes my self-centeredness until finally no barrier remains to separate me from the Divine.

The best way for the emotionally inclined to render work selfless is to bring their ardent and affectionate natures into play and work for God's sake instead of their own. "He who performs actions without attachment, resigning them to God, is untainted by their effects as the lotus leaf by water."[12] Such a one is as active as before, but works for a different reason, out of dedication. Acts are no longer undertaken for their personal rewards. Not only are they now performed as service to God; they are regarded as prompted by God's will and enacted by God's energy as channeled through the devotee. "Thou art the Doer, I the instrument." Performed in this spirit, actions lighten the ego instead of encumbering it. Each task becomes a sacred ritual, lovingly fulfilled as a living sacrifice to God's glory. "Whatsoever you do, whatever you eat, whatever you offer in sacrifice, whatever you give, whatever austerity you practice, O Son of Kunti, do this as an offering to Me. Thus shall you be free from the bondages of actions that bear good and evil results," says the *Bhagavad-Gita*. "They have no desire for the fruits of their actions," echoes the *Bhagavata Purana*. "These persons would not accept even the state of union with Me; they would always prefer My service."

A young woman, newly married and in love, works not for herself alone. As she works the thought of her beloved is in the back of her mind, giving meaning and purpose to her labors. So too with a devoted servant. He claims nothing for himself. Regardless of personal cost he does his duty for his master's satisfaction. Just so is

God's will the joy and satisfaction of the devotee. Surrendering to the Lord of all, he remains untouched by life's vicissitudes. Such people are not broken by discouragements, for winning is not what motivates them; they want only to be on the right side. They know that if history changes it will not be human beings that change it but its Author—when human hearts are ready. Historical figures lose their center when they become anxious over the outcome of their actions. "Do without attachment the work you have to do. Surrendering all action to Me, freeing yourself from longing and selfishness, fight—unperturbed by grief" (*Bhagavad-Gita*).

Once all claims on work have been renounced, including whether it will succeed in its intent, the *karma yogi's* actions no longer swell the ego. They leave on the mind no mark that could vector its subsequent responses. In this way the *yogi* works out the accumulated impressions of previous deeds without acquiring new ones. Whatever one thinks of this *karmic* way of putting the matter, the psychological truth involved is readily apparent. A person who is completely at the disposal of others barely exists. The Spanish ask wryly: "Would you like to become invisible? Have no thought of yourself for two years and no one will notice you."

Work as a path toward God takes a different turn for people whose dispositions are more reflective than emotional. For these too the key is work done unselfishly, but they approach the project differently. Philosophers tend to find the idea of Infinite Being at the center of one's self more meaningful than the thought of a divine Creator who watches over the world with love. It follows, therefore, that their approach to work should be adapted to the way they see things.

The way that leads to enlightenment is work performed in detachment from the empirical self. Specifically, it consists in drawing a line between the finite self that acts, on the one hand, and on the other the eternal Self that observes the action. People usually approach work in terms of its consequences for their empirical selves—the pay or acclaim it will bring. This inflates the ego. It thickens its insulation and thereby its isolation.

The alternative is work performed detachedly, almost in dissociation from the empirical self. Identifying with the Eternal, the worker works; but as the deeds are being performed by the empirical self, the True Self has nothing to do with them. "The knower of Truth, being centered in the Self should think, 'I do nothing at all.' While seeing, breathing, speaking, letting go, holding, opening and closing the eyes, he observes only senses moving among sense objects."[13]

As the *yogi's* identification shifts from her finite to her infinite Self, she will become increasingly indifferent to the consequences that flow from her finite actions. More and more she will recognize the truth of the *Gita's* dictum: "To work you have the right, but not to the fruits thereof." Duty for duty's sake becomes her watchword.

> *He who does the task*
> *Dictated by duty,*
> *Caring nothing*
> *For the fruit of the action,*
> *He is a yogi.* (*Bhagavad-Gita*, VI:1)

Hence the story of the *yogi* who, as he sat meditating on the banks of the Ganges, saw a scorpion fall into the water. He scooped it out, only to have it bite him. Presently, the scorpion fell into the river again. Once more the *yogi* rescued it, only again to be bitten. The sequence repeated itself twice more, whereupon a bystander asked the *yogi,* "Why do you keep rescuing that scorpion when its only gratitude is to bite you?" The *yogi* replied: "It is the nature of scorpions to bite. It is the nature of *yogis* to help others when they can."

Karma yogis will try to do each thing as it comes as if it were the only thing to be done and, having done it, turn to the next duty in similar spirit. Concentrating fully and calmly on each duty as it presents itself, they will resist impatience, excitement, and the vain attempt to do or think of half a dozen things at once. Into the various tasks that fall their lot they will put all the strokes they can, for to do otherwise would be to yield to laziness, which is another form of selfishness. Once they have done this, however, they will dissociate themselves from the act and let the chips fall where they may.

> *One to me is loss or gain,*
> *One to me is fame or shame,*
> *One to me is pleasure, pain.* (*Bhagavad-Gita,* XII)

Mature individuals do not resent correction, for they identify more with their long-range selves that profit from correction than with the momentary self that is being advised. Similarly, the *yogi* accepts loss, pain, and shame with equanimity, knowing that these too are teachers. To the degree that *yogis* repose in the Eternal, they experience calm in the midst of intense activity. Like the center of a rapidly spinning wheel, they seem still — emotionally still — even when they are intensely busy. It is like the stillness of absolute motion.

Though the conceptual frameworks within which philosophical and affectionate natures practice *karma yoga* are different, it is not difficult to perceive their common pursuit. Both are engaged in a radical reducing diet, designed to starve the finite ego by depriving it of the consequences of action on which it feeds. Neither gives the slightest purchase to that native egoism that the world considers healthy self-regard. The *bhakta* seeks "self-naughting" by giving heart and will to the Eternal Companion and finding them enriched a thousandfold thereby. The *jnani* is equally intent on shrinking the ego, being convinced that to the degree that the venture succeeds there will come into view a nucleus of selfhood that differs radically from its surface mask, "a sublime inhabitant and onlooker, transcending the spheres of the former conscious-unconscious system, aloofly unconcerned with the tendencies that formerly supported the individual biography. This anonymous 'diamond being' is not at all what we were cherishing as our character and cultivating as our faculties, inclinations, virtues, and ideals; for it transcends every horizon of unclarified consciousness. It was enwrapped within the sheaths of the body and personality; yet the dark, turbid, thick [layers of the surface self] could not disclose its image. Only the translucent essence of [a self in which all private wants have been dispersed] permits it to become visible — as through a glass, or in a quiet pond. And then, the moment it is recognized, its manifestation bestows an immediate knowledge that this is our true identity. The life-monad is remembered and greeted, even though it is distinct from everything in this phenomenal composite of body and psyche, which, under the delusion caused by our usual ignorance and undiscriminating consciousness we had crudely mistaken for the real and lasting essence of our being."[14]

The Way to God through Psychophysical Exercises

Because of the dazzling heights to which it leads, *raja yoga* has been known in India as "the royal *(raj)* road to reintegration." Designed for people who are of scientific bent, it is the way to God through psychophysical experiments.

The West has honored empiricism in the laboratory but has often distrusted it in spiritual matters, on grounds that it deifies personal experience by making it the final test of truth. India has not had such misgivings. Arguing that affairs of the spirit can be approached as empirically as can outer nature, she encourages people who possess the requisite inclination and willpower to seek God in laboratory fashion. The approach calls for a strong suspicion that our true selves are more than we now realize and a passion to plumb their full extent. For those who possess these qualifications, *raja yoga* outlines a series of steps that are to be followed as rigorously as the steps in a physics experiment. If these do not produce the expected consequences, the hypothesis has been disproved, at least for this experimenter. The claim, however, is that the experiences that unfold will confirm the hypothesis in question.

Unlike most experiments in the natural sciences, those of *raja yoga* are on one's self, not external nature. Even where science does turn to self-experiment—as in medicine, where ethics prescribes that dangerous experiments may be performed only on oneself—the Indic emphasis is different. The *yogi* experiments not on his body (though we shall find the body definitely involved) but on his mind. The experiments take the form of practicing prescribed mental exercises and observing their subjective effects.

No dogmas need be accepted, but experiments require hypotheses they are designed to confirm or negate. The hypothesis that underlies *raja yoga* is the Hindu doctrine of the human self; and though it has been described several times already, it needs to be restated as the background against which the steps of *raja yoga* proceed.

The theory postulates that the human self is a layered entity. We need not go into the detailed Hindu analyses of these layers; the accounts are technical, and future science may show them to be more metaphorical than literally accurate. For our purposes it is enough to summarize the hypothesis by reducing the principal layers to four. First and most obviously, we have bodies. Next comes the conscious layer of our minds. Underlying these two is a third region, the realm of the individual subconscious. This has been built up through our individual histories. Most of our past experiences have been lost to our conscious memory, but those experiences continue to shape our lives in ways that contemporary psychoanalysis tries to understand. With these three parts of the self, the West is in full agreement. What is distinctive in the Hindu hypothesis is its postulation of a fourth component. Underlying the other three, less perceived by the conscious mind than even its private subconscious (though related to it fully as much), stands Being Itself, infinite, unthwarted, eternal. "I am smaller than the minutest atom, likewise greater than the greatest. I am the whole, the diversified-multicolored-lovely-strange universe. I am the Ancient One. I am Man, the Lord. I am the Being-of-Gold. I am the very state of divine beatitude." [15]

Hinduism agrees with psychoanalysis that if only we could dredge up portions of our individual unconscious — the third layer of our being — we would experience a remarkable expansion of our powers, a vivid freshening of life. But if we could uncover something forgotten not only by ourselves but by humanity as a whole, something that provides clues not simply to our individual personalities and quirks but to all life and all existence, what then? Would this not be momentous?

The call, clearly, is to retreat from the world's inconsequential panorama to the deep-lying causal zones of the psyche where the real problems and answers lie. Beyond this, however, *raja yoga*'s response cannot be described, quite, as an answer to any articulated call. Rather, it is a determined refusal to allow the pitter-patter of daily existence to distract from the unknown demands of some waiting urgency within: a kind of total strike against the terms of routine, prosaic existence. The successful *yogi* succeeds in carrying life's problem to this plane of new magnitude and there resolving it. The insights of such people will pertain not so much to passing personal and social predicaments as to the unquenchable source by which all peoples and societies are renewed, for their inspiration will be drawn from direct contact with this primary spring. In body they will remain individuals. In spirit each will have become unspecific, universal, perfected.

The purpose of *raja yoga* is to demonstrate the validity of this fourfold estimate of the human self by leading the inquirer to direct personal experience of "the beyond that is within." Its method is willed introversion, one of the classic implements of creative genius in any line of endeavor, here carried to its logical term. Its intent is to drive the psychic energy of the self to its deepest part to activate the lost continent of the true self. Risks are of course involved; if the venture is bungled, at best considerable time will have been lost, and at worst consciousness can disintegrate into psychosis. Rightly done, however, under a director who knows the terrain, the *yogi* will be able to integrate the insights and experiences that come into view and will emerge with heightened self-knowledge and greater self-control.

With the hypothesis *raja yoga* proposes to test before us, we are prepared to indicate the eight steps of the experiment itself.

1 and 2. The first two concern the moral preliminaries with which all four *yogas* begin. Anyone who sits down to this task of self-discovery discovers that distractions lie in wait. Two of the most obvious are bodily cravings and mental inquietude. Just as concentration is about to begin in earnest, the *yogi* may experience an urge for a cigarette or drink of water. Or resentments, envies, and pangs of conscience obtrude. The first two steps of *raja yoga* seek to clear the field of such static and to lock the door against further intrusions. The first involves the practice of five abstentions: from injury, lying, stealing, sensuality, and greed. The second involves the practice of five observances: cleanliness, contentment, self-control, studiousness, and contemplation of the divine. Together they constitute the five finger exercises of the human spirit in anticipation of more intricate studies to come. Chinese and Japanese officers who used to practice variations of *raja yoga* in Buddhist monasteries with no religious interest whatsoever—simply to increase their mental clarity and vitality— discovered that even in their case a certain amount of moral comportment was a necessary condition for success.

3. *Raja yoga* works with the body even while being ultimately concerned with the mind. More precisely, it works through the body to the mind. Beyond general health, its chief object here is to keep the body from distracting the mind while it concentrates. This is no small object, for an untrained body cannot go for long without itching or fidgeting. Each sensation is a bid for attention that distracts from the project at hand. The object of this third step is to exclude such distractions—to get Brother Ass, as Saint Francis called his body, properly tethered and out of the way. What is attempted is a bodily state midway between discomfort, which rouses and disturbs, and at the opposite pole a relaxation so complete that it sinks into drowsiness. The Hindu discoveries for achieving this balance are called *asanas*, a word usually translated "postures" but which carries

connotations of balance and ease. The physical and psychological benefits of at least some of these postures are now widely recognized. That the Hindu texts describe eighty-four postures indicates extensive experimentation in the area, but only about five are considered important for meditation.

Of these, the one that has proved most important is the world-renowned lotus position in which the *yogi* sits — ideally on a tiger skin, symbolizing energy, overlaid with a deerskin, symbolizing calm — with legs crossed in such a way that each foot rests sole up on its opposing thigh. The spine, with allowance for its natural curvature, is erect. Hands are placed, palms up, in the lap, one atop the other with thumbs touching lightly. The eyes may be closed or allowed to gaze unfocused on the ground or floor. People who undertake this position after their bodies have reached maturity find it painful, for it imposes strains on the tendons which require months of conditioning to be accommodated. When the position has been mastered, however, it is surprisingly comfortable and seems to place the mind in a state that conduces to meditation. Given that standing induces fatigue, chairs invite slumping, and reclining encourages sleep, there may be no other position in which the body can remain for as long a stretch both still and alert.

4. *Yogic* postures protect the meditator from disruptions from the body in its static aspects, but there remain bodily activities, such as breathing. The *yogi* must breathe, but untrained breathing can shatter the mind's repose. Newcomers to meditation are surprised by the extent to which unbridled breathing can intrude upon the task. Bronchial irritations and congestions trigger coughs and clearings of the throat. Each time the breath sinks too low, a deep sigh erupts to shatter the spell. Nor are such obvious irregularities the sole offenders; through concentrated silence, a "normal" breath can rip like a crosscut, sending the hush shivering, flying. The purpose of *raja yoga*'s fourth step is to prevent such disruptions through the mastery of respiration. The exercises prescribed toward this end are numerous and varied. Some, like learning to breathe in through one nostril and out through the other, sound bizarre, but studies suggest that they may help to balance the brain's two hemispheres. On the whole the exercises work toward slowing the breath, evening it, and reducing the amount of air required. A typical exercise calls for breathing so gently across goose down touching the nostrils that an

observer cannot tell if air is moving in or out. Breath suspension is particularly important, for the body is most still when it is not breathing. When, for example, the *yogi* is doing a cycle of sixteen counts inhaling, sixty-four holding, and thirty-two exhaling, there is a stretch during which animation is reduced to the point that the mind seems disembodied. These are cherished moments for the task at hand. "The light of a lamp," says the *Bhagavad-Gita*, "does not flicker in a windless place."

5. Composed, body at ease, its breathing regular, the *yogi* sits absorbed in contemplation. Suddenly, a door creaks, a sliver of moonlight shimmers on the ground ahead, a mosquito whines, and he is back in the world.

> *Restless the mind is,*
> *So strongly shaken*
> *In the grip of the senses.*
> *Truly I think*
> *The wind is no wilder.*   (*Bhagavad-Gita*, VI:34)

The senses turn outward. As bridges to the physical world they are invaluable, but the *yogi* is seeking something else. On the track of more interesting prey—the interior universe in which (according to reports) is to be found the final secret of life's mystery—the *yogi* wants no sense bombardments. Fascinating in its own way, the outer world has nothing to contribute to the present task. For the *yogi* is tracking the underpinning of life's facade. Behind its physical front, where we experience the play of life and death, the *yogi* seeks a deeper life that knows no death. Is there, beneath our surface accounting of objects and things, a dimension of awareness that is different not just in degree but in kind? The *yogi* is testing a hypothesis: that the deepest truth is opened only to those who turn their attention inward, and in this experiment the physical senses can be nothing but busybodies. "The senses turn outward," observe the Upanishads. "People, therefore, look toward what is outside and see not the inward being. Rare are the wise who shut their eyes to outward things and behold the glory of the Atman within." Five hundred years later the *Bhagavad-Gita* repeats that refrain:

> *Only that yogi*
> *Whose joy is inward,*

Inward his peace,
And his vision inward
Shall come to Brahman
And know Nirvana.

It is against the background of three millennia of this postulate that Mahatma Gandhi proposed to our extroverted century: "Turn the spotlight inward."

The final, transitional step in the process of effecting this turn from the external to the internal world is to close the doors of perception, for only so can the clatter of the world's boiler factory be effectively shut out. That this can be done, and without bodily mutilation, is a common experience. A man calls his wife to remind her that they should leave for a social engagement. Five minutes later she insists that she did not hear him; he insists that she must have heard him, for he was in the adjoining room and spoke distinctly. Who is right? It is a matter of definition. If hearing means that sound waves of sufficient amplitude beat on healthy eardrums, she heard; if it means that they were noticed, she did not. There is nothing esoteric about such occurrences; their explanation is simply concentration — the woman was at her computer and deeply engrossed. Similarly, there is no catch in this fifth step in *raja yoga*. It seeks to carry the *yogi* beyond the point the wife had reached, first, by turning concentration from a chance occurrence into a power that is controlled; and second, by raising the talent to a point where drumbeats in the same room can escape notice. The technique, though, is identical. Concentration on one thing excludes other things.

6. At last the *yogi* is alone with his mind. The five steps enumerated thus far all point to this eventuality; one by one the intrusions of cravings, a troubled conscience, body, breath, and the senses have been stopped. But the battle is not yet won; at close quarters it is just beginning. For the mind's fiercest antagonist is itself. Alone with itself it still shows not the slightest inclination to settle down or obey. Memories, anticipations, daydreams, chains of reverie held together by the flimsiest, most unexpected links imaginable close in from all sides, causing the mind to ripple like a lake beneath a breeze, alive with ever-changing, self-shattering reflections. Left to itself the mind never stays still, smooth as a mirror, crystal clear, reflecting the Sun of all life in perfect replica. For such a condition to prevail, it is not

enough that entering rivulets be dammed; this the five preceding steps effectively accomplished. There remain lake-bottom springs to be stopped and fantasies to be curbed. Obviously, much remains to be done.

Or switch the metaphor to one less serene. The motions of the average mind, say the Hindus, are about as orderly as those of a crazed monkey cavorting about its cage. Nay, more; like the prancings of a drunk, crazed monkey. Even so we have not conveyed its restlessness; the mind is like a drunken, crazed monkey that has St. Vitus' Dance. To do justice to our theme, however, we must go a final step. The mind is like a drunken crazed monkey with St. Vitus' Dance who has just been stung by a wasp.

Few who have seriously tried to meditate will find this metaphor extreme. The trouble with the advice to "leave your mind alone" is the unimpressive spectacle that remains. I tell my hand to rise and it obeys. I tell my mind to be still and it mocks my command. How long can the average mind think about one thing—one thing only, without slipping first into thinking about *thinking* about that thing and taking off from there on a senseless chain of irrelevancies? About three and a half seconds, psychologists tell us. Like a ping-pong ball, the mind will alight where its owner directs it, but only to take off immediately on a jittery flight of staccato bounces that are completely out of hand.

What if the mind could be turned from a ping-pong ball into a lump of dough, which when thrown sticks to a wall until deliberately removed? Would not its power increase if it could be thus held in focus? Would not its strength be compounded, like the strength of a light bulb when ringed by reflectors? A normal mind can be held to a reasonable extent by the world's objects. A psychotic mind cannot; it slips at once into uncontrollable fantasy. What if a third condition of mind could be developed, as much above the normal mind as the psychotic mind is below it, a condition in which the mind could be induced to focus protractedly on an object to fathom it deeply? This is the aim of concentration, the sixth step of *raja yoga*. An elephant's trunk that sways to and fro as the elephant walks and reaches out for objects on either side will settle down if it is given an iron ball to hold. The purpose of concentration is comparable: to teach the restless mind to hold unswervingly to the object it is directed to. "When all the senses are stilled, when the mind is at rest, when the intellect wavers not—that, say the wise, is the highest state."[16]

The method proposed for reaching this state is not exotic, only arduous. One begins by relaxing the mind to allow thoughts that need release to exorcize themselves from the subconscious. Then one selects something to concentrate on—the glowing tip of a joss stick, the tip of one's nose, an imaged sea of infinite light, the object does not much matter—and practices keeping the mind on the object until success increases.

7. The last two steps are stages in which this process of concentration progressively deepens. In the preceding step the mind was brought to the point where it would flow steadily toward its object, but it did not lose consciousness of itself as an object distinct from the one it was focusing on. In this seventh step, in which concentration deepens into meditation, the union between the two is tightened to the point where separateness vanishes: "The subject and the object are completely merged so that the self-consciousness of the individual subject has disappeared altogether."[17] In this moment the duality of knower and known is resolved into a perfect unity. In the words of Schelling, "the perceiving self merges in the self-perceived. At that moment we annihilate time and the duration of time; we are no longer in time, but time, or rather eternity itself, is in us."

8. There remains the final, climactic state for which the Sanskrit word *samadhi* should be retained. Etymologically *sam* parallels the Greek prefix *syn*, as in synthesis, synopsis, and syndrome. It means "together with." *Adhi* in Sanskrit is usually translated Lord, paralleling the Hebrew word for Lord in the Old Testament, *Adon* or *Adonai*. *Samadhi*, then, names the state in which the human mind is completely absorbed in God. In the seventh step—that of meditation—concentration had deepened to the point where the self dropped out of sight entirely, all attention being riveted on the object being known. The distinctive feature of *samadhi* is that all of the object's forms fall away. For forms are limiting boundaries; to be one form others must be excluded, and what is to be known in *raja yoga*'s final stage is without limits. The mind continues to think—if that is the right word—but of no thing. This does not mean that it is thinking of nothing, that it is a total blank. It has perfected the paradox of seeing the invisible. It is filled with that which is "separated from all qualities, neither this nor that, without form, without a name."[18]

We have come a long way from Lord Kelvin's assertion that he could not imagine anything of which he could not construct a mechanical model. By that mode in which the knower is united with what is known, the knower has been brought to the knowledge of total being and, for a spell, been dissolved into it.[19] That which the experiment was designed to test has been determined. The *yogi* has attained to the insight "That, verily, That thou art."

We have presented the four *yoga*s as alternatives but, to conclude with a point that was made at the start, Hinduism does not consider them as exclusive of one another. No individual is solely reflective, emotional, active, or experimental, and different life situations call for different resources to be brought into play. Most people will, on the whole, find travel on one road more satisfactory than on others and will consequently tend to keep close to it; but Hinduism encourages people to test all four and combine them as best suits their needs. The major division is between *jnana* and *bhakti*, the reflective and the emotional types. We have seen that work can be adapted to either of these modes, and some meditation is valuable in any case. The normal pattern, therefore, will be for individuals to cast their religion in either a philosophical or a devotional mold, adapt their work to the one that is chosen, and meditate to whatever extent is practicable. We read in the *Bhagavad-Gita* that some "realize the *Atman* through contemplation. Some realize the *Atman* philosophically. Others realize it by following the yoga of right action. Others worship God as their teachers have taught them. If these faithfully practice what they have learned, they will pass beyond death's power."

The Stages of Life

People are different. Few observations could be more banal, yet serious attention to it is one of Hinduism's distinctive features. The preceding sections traced its insistence that differences in human nature call for a variety of paths toward life's fulfillment. We have now to note the same insistence pressed from another quarter. Not only do individuals differ from one another; each individual moves through different stages, each of which calls for its own appropriate conduct. As each day passes from morning through noon and afternoon into evening, so every life likewise passes through four phases, each possessing distinct aptitudes that dictate distinct modes of response. If we ask, therefore, how should we live? Hinduism answers, that depends not only on what kind of person you are but also on the stage of life you are in.

The first stage India marked off as that of the student. Traditionally, this stage began after the rite of initiation, between the ages of eight and twelve. It lasted for twelve years, during which the student typically lived in the home of the teacher, rendering service for instruction received. Life's prime responsibility at this stage was to learn, to offer a receptive mind to all that the teacher, standing, as it were, on the pinnacle of the past, could transmit. Soon enough responsibilities would announce themselves copiously; for this gloriously suspended moment the student's only obligation was to store up against the time when much would be demanded. What was to be learned included factual information, but more; for India — dreamy, impractical India — has had little interest in knowledge for knowledge's sake. The successful student was not to emerge a walking encyclopedia, a reference library wired for sound. Habits were to be cultivated, character acquired. The entire training was more like an apprenticeship in which information became incarnated in skill. The liberally educated student was to emerge as equipped to turn out a good and effective life as a potter's apprentice to turn out a well-wrought urn.

The second stage, beginning with marriage, was that of the householder. Here during life's noonday, with physical powers at their zenith, interests and energies naturally turn outward. There are three fronts on which they can play with satisfaction: family, vocation, and the community to which one belongs. Normally, attention will be divided between the three. This is the time for satisfying the first three human wants: pleasure, through marriage and family primarily; success, through vocation; and duty, through civic participation.

Hinduism smiles on the happy fulfillment of these wants but does not try to prime them when they begin to ebb. That attachment to them should eventually decline is altogether appropriate, for it would be unnatural for life to end while action and desire are at their zenith. It is not ordained that it do so. If we follow the seasons as they come, we shall notice a time when sex and the delights of the senses (pleasure) as well as achievement in the game of life (success) no longer yield novel and surprising turns; when even the responsible discharge of a human vocation (duty) begins to pall, having grown repetitious and stale. When this season arrives it is time for the individual to move on to the third stage in life's sequence.

Some never do. Their spectacle is not a pretty one, for pursuits appropriate in their day become grotesque when unduly prolonged. A playboy of twenty-five may have considerable appeal, but spare us the playboys of fifty. How hard they work at their pose, how little they receive in return. It is similar with people who cannot bring themselves to relinquish key positions when a younger generation with more energy and new ideas should be stepping into them.

Still, such people cannot be censured; for seeing no other frontier to life, they have no option but to hang on to what they know. The question they pose is, bluntly, "Is old age worthwhile?" With medical science increasing life expectancy dramatically, more and more people are having to face that question. Poets have always given their nod to autumn leaves and the sunset years, but their phrases sound suspect. If we rest our case with poetry, "Grow old along with me, the best is yet to be" carries not half the conviction of "Gather ye rosebuds while ye may. . . . Tomorrow we'll be dying."

Whether life has a future beyond middle age depends in the end not on poetry but on fact, on what the values of life really are. If they are supremely those of body and sense, we may as well resign ourselves to the fact that life after youth must be downhill. If worldly achievement and the exercise of power is best, middle age, the stage of the householder, will be life's apex. But if vision and self-understanding carry rewards equal to or surpassing these others, old age has its own opportunities, and we can come to happiness at the time when the rivers of our lives flow gently.

Whether or not the later years do hold such rewards depends on the scene that is disclosed when the curtain of ignorance lifts. If reality is a monotonous and depressing wasteland and self no more than subtle cybernetics, the rewards of vision and self-knowledge cannot possibly rival the ecstasies of sense or the satisfactions of social achievement. We have seen, however, that in Hinduism they are held to be more. "Leave all and follow Him! Enjoy his inexpressible riches," say the Upanishads. No joy can approximate the beatific vision, and the Self to be discovered is great beyond all report. It follows that succeeding the stages of student and householder, Hinduism will mark with confidence a third stage into which life should move.

This is the stage of retirement. Any time after the arrival of a first grandchild, the individual may take advantage of the license of age

and withdraw from the social obligations that were thus far shoul-
dered with a will. For twenty to thirty years society has exacted its
dues; now relief is in order, lest life conclude before it has been
understood. Thus far society has required the individual to special-
ize; there has been little time to read, to think, to ponder life's meaning without interruption. This is not resented; the game has carried
its own satisfactions. But must the human spirit be indentured to
society forever? The time has come to begin one's true adult education, to discover who one is and what life is about. What is the secret
of the "I" with which one has been on such intimate terms all these
years, yet which remains a stranger, full of inexplicable quirks,
baffling surds, and irrational impulses? Why are we born to work and
struggle, each with a portion of happiness and sorrow, only to die too
soon? Generation after generation swells briefly like a wave, then
breaks on the shore, subsiding into the anonymous fellowship of
death. To find meaning in the mystery of existence is life's final and
fascinating challenge.

Traditionally, those who responded fully to this lure of spiritual
adventure were known as forest dwellers, for—husband and wife
together if she wished to go, husband alone if she did not—they
would take their leave of family, the comforts and constraints of
home, and plunge into the forest solitudes to launch their program of
self-discovery. At last their responsibilities were to themselves alone.
"Business, family, secular life, like the beauties and hopes of youth
and the successes of maturity, have now been left behind; eternity
alone remains. And so it is to that—not to the tasks and worries of this
life, already gone, which came and passed like a dream—that the
mind is turned."[20] Retirement looks beyond the stars, not to the village streets. It is the time for working out a philosophy, and then
working that philosophy into a way of life; a time for transcending the
senses to find, and dwell with, the reality that underlies this natural
world.

Beyond retirement, the final stage wherein the goal is actually
reached is the state of the *sannyasin*, defined by the *Bhagavad-Gita*
as "one who neither hates nor loves anything."

The pilgrim is now free to return to the world for, the intent of
the forest discipline achieved, time and place have lost their hold.
Where in all the world can one be totally free if not everywhere? The
Hindus liken the *sannyasin* to a wild goose or swan, "which has no

fixed home but wanders, migrating with the rain-clouds north to the Himalayas and back south again, at home on every lake or sheet of water, as also in the infinite, unbounded reaches of the sky." The marketplace has now become as hospitable as the forests. But though the *sannyasin* is back, he is back as a different person. Having discovered that complete release from every limitation is synonymous with absolute anonymity, the *sannyasin* has learned the art of keeping the finite self dispersed lest it eclipse the infinite.

Far from wanting to "be somebody," the *sannyasin's* wish is the opposite: to remain a complete nonentity on the surface in order to be joined to all at root. How could one possibly wish to make oneself up again as an individual, restore the posturings and costumes of a limiting self-identity, the persona that conceals the purity and radiance of the intrinsic self? The outward life that fits this total freedom best is that of a homeless mendicant. Others will seek to be economically independent in their old age; the *sannyasin* proposes to cut free of economics altogether. With no fixed place on earth, no obligations, no goal, no belongings, the expectations of body are nothing. Social pretensions likewise have no soil from which to sprout and interfere. No pride remains in someone who, begging bowl in hand, finds himself at the back door of someone who was once his servant and would not have it otherwise.

The *sannyasin* saints of Jainism, an offshoot of Hinduism, went about "clothed in space," stark naked. Buddhism, another offshoot, dressed its counterparts in ochre, the color worn by criminals ejected from society and condemned to death. Good to have all status whisked away at a stroke, for all social identities prevent identification with the imperishable totality of existence. "Taking no thought of the future and looking with indifference upon the present," read the Hindu texts, the *sannyasin* "lives identified with the eternal Self and beholds nothing else." "He no more cares whether his body falls or remains, than does a cow what becomes of the garland that someone has hung around her neck; for the faculties of his mind are now at rest in the Holy Power, the essence of bliss."[21]

The unwise life is one long struggle with death the intruder — an uneven contest in which age is obsessively delayed through artifice and the denial of time's erosions. When the fever of desire slackens, the unwise seek to refuel it with more potent aphrodisiacs. When they are forced to let go, it is grudgingly and with self-pity, for they cannot see the inevitable as natural, and good as well. They have no comprehension of Tagore's insight that truth comes as conqueror only to those who have lost the art of receiving it as friend.

The Stations of Life

People are different—we are back a third time to this cardinal Hindu tenet. We have traced its import for the different paths people should follow toward God, and the different patterns of life appropriate at various stages in the human career. We come now to its implications for the station the individual should occupy in the social order.

This brings us to the Hindu concept of caste. On no other score is Hinduism better known or more roundly denounced by the outside world. Caste contains both point and perversion. Everything in the discussion of this subject depends on our ability to distinguish between the two.

How caste arose is one of the confused topics of history. Central, certainly, was the fact that during the second millennium B.C. a host of Aryans possessing a different language, culture, and physiognomy (tall, fair-skinned, blue-eyed, straight-haired) migrated into India. The clash of differences that followed burgeoned the caste system, if it did not actually create it. The extent to which ethnic differences, color, trade guilds harboring professional secrets, sanitation restrictions between groups with different immunity systems, and magico-religious taboos concerning pollution and purification contributed to the pattern that emerged may never be fully unraveled. In any event the outcome was a society that was divided into four groups: seers, administrators, producers, and followers.

Let us record at once the perversions that entered in time, however they originated. To begin with, a fifth group—of outcastes or untouchables—appeared. Even in speaking of this category there are mitigating points to be remembered. In dealing with her lowest social group, India did not sink to slavery as have most civilizations; outcastes who in their fourth stage of life renounced the world for God were regarded as outside social classifications and were revered, even by the highest caste, the *brahmins*;[22] from Buddha through Dayananda to Gandhi, many religious reformers sought to remove untouchability from the caste system; and contemporary India's constitution outlaws the institution. Still, the outcaste's lot through

India's history has been a wretched one and must be regarded as the basic perversion the caste system succumbed to. A second deterioration lay in the proliferation of castes into subcastes, of which there are today over three thousand. Third, proscriptions against intermarriage and interdining came to complicate social intercourse enormously. Fourth, privileges entered the system, with higher castes benefiting at the expense of the lower. Finally, caste became hereditary. One remained in the caste into which one was born.

With these heavy counts against it, it may come as a surprise to find that there are contemporary Indians, thoroughly familiar with Western alternatives, who defend caste—not, to be sure, in its entirety, especially what it has become, but in its basic format.[23] What lasting values could such a system possibly contain?

What is called for here is recognition that with respect to the ways they can best contribute to society and develop their own potentialities, people fall into four groups. (1) The first group India called *brahmins* or seers. Reflective, with a passion to understand and a keen intuitive grasp of the values that matter most in human life, these are civilization's intellectual and spiritual leaders. Into their province fall the functions our more specialized society has distributed among philosophers, artists, religious leaders, and teachers; things of the mind and spirit are their raw materials. (2) The second group, the *kshatriyas*, are born administrators,[24] with a genius for orchestrating people and projects in ways that makes the most of available human talents. (3) Others find their vocation as producers; they are artisans and farmers, skillful in creating the material things on which life depends. These are the *vaishyas*. (4) Finally, *shudras*, can be characterized as followers or servants. Unskilled laborers would be another name for them. These are people who, if they had to carve out a career for themselves, commit themselves to long periods of training, or go into business for themselves, would founder. Their attention spans are relatively short, which makes them unwilling to sacrifice a great deal in the way of present gains for the sake of future rewards. Under supervision, however, they are capable of hard work and devoted service. Such people are better off, and actually happier, working for others than being on their own. We, with our democratic and egalitarian sentiments, do not like to admit that there are such people, to which the orthodox Hindu replies: What you would *like* is not the point. The question is what people actually are.

Few contemporary Hindus defend the lengths to which India eventually went in keeping the castes distinct. Her proscriptions regulating intermarriage, interdining, and other forms of social contact made her, in her first prime minister's wry assessment, "the least tolerant nation in social forms while the most tolerant in the realm of ideas." Yet even here a certain point lies behind the accursed proliferations. That proscriptions against different castes drinking from the same source were especially firm suggests that differences in immunity to diseases may have played a part. The presiding reasons, however, were broader than this. Unless unequals are separated in some fashion, the weak must compete against the strong across the board and will stand no chance of winning anywhere. Between castes there was no equality, but within each caste the individual's rights were safer than if he or she had been forced to fend alone in the world at large. Each caste was self-governing, and in trouble one could be sure of being tried by one's peers. Within each caste there was equality, opportunity, and social insurance.

Inequalities between the castes themselves aimed for due compensation for services rendered. The well-being of society requires that some people assume, at the cost of considerable self-sacrifice, responsibilities far beyond average. While most young people will plunge early into marriage and employment, some must postpone those satisfactions for as much as a decade to prepare themselves for demanding vocations. The wage earner who checks out at five o'clock is through for the day; the employer must take home the ever-present insecurities of the entrepreneur, and often homework as well. The question is partly whether employers would be willing to shoulder their responsibilities without added compensation, but also whether it would be just to ask them to do so. India never confused democracy with egalitarianism. Justice was defined as a state in which privileges were proportionate to responsibilities. In salary and social power, therefore, the second caste, the administrators, rightly stood supreme; in honor and psychological power, the *brahmins*. But only (according to the ideal) because their responsibilities were proportionately greater. In precise reverse of the European doctrine that the king could do no wrong, the orthodox Hindu view came very near to holding that the shudras, the lowest caste, could do no wrong, its members being regarded as children from whom not much should be expected. Classical legal doctrine stipulated that for the same offense "the punishment of the Vaishya [producer] should be twice as heavy as that of the shudra, that of the *kshatriya* [administrator] twice as heavy again, and that of the *brahmin* twice or even four times as heavy again."[25] In India the lowest caste was exempt from many of the forms of probity and self-denial that the upper castes were held to. Its widows might remarry, and proscription against meat and alcohol were less exacting.

Stated in modern idiom, the ideal of caste emerges something like this: At the bottom of the social scale is a class of routineers—domestics, factory workers, and hired hands—who can put up with an unvaried round of duties but who, their self-discipline being marginal, must punch time clocks if they are to get in a day's work, and who are little inclined to forego present gratification for the sake of long-term gains. Above them is a class of technicians. Artisans in preindustrial societies, in an industrial age they are the people who understand machines, repair them, and keep them running. Next comes the managerial class. In its political wing it includes party officials and elected representatives; in its military branch, officers and chiefs-of-staff; in its industrial arm, entrepreneurs, managers, board members, and chief executive officers.

If, however, society is to be not only complex but good, if it is to be wise and inspired as well as efficient, there must be above the administrators—in esteem but not in pay, for one of the defining marks of this class must lie in its indifference to wealth and power—a fourth class, which in our specialized society would include religious leaders, teachers, writers, and artists. Such people are rightly called seers in the literal sense of this word, for they are the eyes of the community. As the head (administrators) rests on the body (laborers and technicians), so the eyes are placed at the top of the head. Members of this class must possess enough willpower to counter the egoism and seductions that distort perception. They command respect because others recognize both their own incapacity for such restraint and the truth of what the seer tells them. It is as if the seer sees clearly what other types only suspect. But such vision is fragile; it yields sound discernments only when carefully protected. Needing leisure for unhurried reflection, the seer must be protected from overinvolvement in the day-to-day exigencies that clutter and cloud the mind, as a navigator must be free from serving in the galley or stoking in the hold in order to track the stars to keep the ship on course. Above all, this final caste must be protected from temporal power. India considered Plato's dream of the philosopher king unrealistic, and it is true that when *brahmins* assumed social power, they became corrupt. For temporal power subjects its wielder to pressures and temptations that to some extent refract judgment and distort it. The role of the seer is not to crack down but to counsel, not to drive but to guide. Like a compass needle, guarded that it may point, the *brahmin* is to ascertain, then indicate, the true north of life's meaning and purpose, charting the way to civilization's advance.

Caste, when it has decayed, is as offensive as any other corrupting corpse. Whatever its character at the start, it came in time to neglect Plato's insight that "a golden parent may have a silver son, or a silver parent a golden son, and then there must be a change of rank; the son of the rich must descend, and the child of the artisan rise, in the social scale; for an oracle says 'that the state will come to an end if governed by a man of brass or iron.' " As one of the most thoughtful recent advocates of the basic idea of caste has written, "we may expect that the coming development will differ chiefly in permitting intermarriage and choice or change of occupation under certain conditions, though still recognizing the general desirability of marriage within the group and of following one's parents' calling."[26] Insofar as caste has come to mean rigidity, exclusiveness, and undeserved privilege, Hindus today are working to clear the corruption from their polity. But there remain many who believe that to the problem no country has yet solved, the problem of how society ought to be ordered to insure the maximum of fair play and creativity, the basic theses of caste continue to warrant attention.

Up to this point we have approached Hinduism in terms of its practical import. Beginning with its analysis of what people want, we have traced its suggestions concerning the ways these wants might be met and the responses appropriate to various stages and stations of human life. The remaining sections of this chapter shift the focus from practice to theory, indicating the principal philosophical concepts that rib the Hindu religion.

"Thou Before Whom All Words Recoil"

The first principle of Japanese *ikebana* flower arrangement is to learn what to leave out. This is also the first principle to be learned in speaking of God, the Hindus insist. People are forever trying to lay hold of Reality with words, only in the end to find mystery rebuking their speech and their syllables swallowed by silence. The problem is not that our minds are not bright enough. The problem lies deeper. Minds, taken in their ordinary, surface sense, are the wrong kind of instrument for the undertaking. The effect, as a result, is like trying to ladle the ocean with a net, or lasso the wind with a rope. The awe-inspiring prayer of Shankara, the Thomas Aquinas of Hinduism, begins with the invocation, "Oh Thou, before whom all words recoil."

The human mind has evolved to facilitate survival in the natural world. It is adapted to deal with finite objects. God, on the contrary, is infinite and of a completely different order of being from what our minds can grasp. To expect our minds to corner the infinite is like asking a dog to understand Einstein's equation with its nose. This analogy becomes misleading if, pressed in a different direction, it suggests that we can never know the Abysmal God. The *yogas*, we have seen, are roads to precisely such realization. But the knowledge to which they lead transcends the knowledge of the rational mind; it rises to the deep yet dazzling darkness of the mystical consciousness.[27] The only literally accurate description of the Unsearchable of which the ordinary mind is capable is *neti . . . neti*, not this . . . not this. If you traverse the length and breadth of the universe saying of everything you can see and conceive, "not this . . . not this," what remains will be God.[28]

And yet words and concepts cannot be avoided. Being the only equipment at our mind's disposal, any conscious progress toward God must be made with their aid. Though concepts can never carry the mind to its destination, they can point in the right direction.

We may begin simply with a name to hang our thoughts on. The name the Hindus give to the supreme reality is *Brahman*, which has a dual etymology, deriving as it does from both *br*, to breathe, and *brih*, to be great. The chief attributes to be linked with the name are *sat, chit*, and *ananda;* God is being, awareness, and bliss. Utter reality, utter consciousness, and utterly beyond all possibility of frustration —this is the basic Hindu view of God. Even these words cannot claim to describe God literally, however, for the meanings they carry for us are radically unlike the senses in which they apply to God. What pure being would be like, being infinite with absolutely nothing excluded, of this we have scarcely an inkling. Similarly with awareness and joy. In Spinoza's formulation God's nature resembles our words about as much as the dog star resembles a dog. The most that can be said for these words is that they are pointers; our minds do better to move in their direction than in the opposite. God lies on the further side of being as we understand it, not nothingness; beyond minds as we know them, not mindless clay; beyond ecstasy, not agony.

This is as far as some minds need go in their vision of God: infinite being, infinite consciousness, infinite bliss — all else is at best commentary, at worst retraction. There are sages who can live in this austere, conceptually thin atmosphere of the spirit and find it invigorating; they can understand with Shankara that "the sun shines even without objects to shine upon." Most people, however, cannot be gripped by such high-order abstractions. That C. S. Lewis is among their number is proof that their minds are not inferior, only different. Professor Lewis tells us that while he was a child his parents kept admonishing him not to think of God in terms of any form, for these could only limit his infinity. He tried his best to heed their instructions, but the closest he could come to the idea of a formless God was an infinite sea of grey tapioca.

This anecdote, the Hindus would say, points up perfectly the circumstance of the man or woman whose mind must bite into something concrete and representational if it is to find life-sustaining meaning. Most people find it impossible to conceive, much less be motivated by, anything that is removed very far from direct experience. Hinduism advises such people not to try to think of God as the supreme instance of abstractions like being or consciousness, and instead to think of God as the archetype of the noblest reality they encounter in the natural world. This means thinking of God as the supreme person (*Ishvara* or *Bhagavan*), for people are nature's noblest crown. Our discussion of *bhakti yoga*, the path to God through love and devotion, has already introduced us to God conceived in this way. This, in Pascal's Western idiom, is the God of Abraham, Isaac, and Jacob, not the God of the philosophers. It is God as parent, lovingly merciful, omniscient, almighty, our eternal contemporary, the companion who understands.

God so conceived is called *Saguna Brahman*, or God-with-attributes as distinct from the philosophers' more abstract *Nirguna Brahman*, or God-without-attributes. *Nirguna Brahman* is the ocean without a ripple; *Saguna Brahman* the same ocean alive with swells and waves. In the language of theology, the distinction is between personal and transpersonal conceptions of God. Hinduism has included superb champions of each view, notably Shankara for the transpersonal and Ramanuja for the personal; but the conclusion that does most justice to Hinduism as a whole and has its own explicit champions like Sri Ramakrishna is that both are equally correct. At first blush this may look like a glaring violation of the law of the excluded middle. God may be either personal or not, we are likely to insist, but not both. But is this so? What the disjunction forgets, India argues, is the distance our rational minds are from God in the first place. Intrinsically, God may not be capable of being two contradictory things—we say may not because logic itself may melt in the full blaze of the divine incandescence. But concepts of God contain so much alloy to begin with that two contradictory ones may be true, each from a different angle, as both wave and particles may be equally accurate heuristic devices for describing the nature of light.[29] On the whole India has been content to encourage the devotee to conceive of *Brahman* as either personal or transpersonal, depending on which carries the most exalted meaning for the mind in question.

God's relation to the world likewise varies according to the symbolism that is embraced. Conceived in personal terms, God will stand in relation to the world as an artist to his or her handiwork. God will be Creator (Brahma), Preserver (Vishnu), and Destroyer (Shiva), who in the end resolves all finite forms back into the primordial nature from which they sprang. On the other hand, conceived transpersonally, God stands above the struggle, aloof from the finite in every respect. "As the sun does not tremble, although its image trembles when you shake the cup filled with water in which the sun's light is reflected; thus the Lord also is not affected by pain, although pain be felt by that part of him which is called the individual soul."[30] The world will still be God-dependent. It will have emerged in some unfathomable way from the divine plenitude and be sustained by its power. "He shining, the sun, the moon and the stars shine after Him; by His light all is lighted. He is the Ear of the ear, the Mind of the mind, the Speech of the speech, the Life of life, the Eye of the eye."[31] But God will not have intentionally willed the world, nor be affected by its inherent ambiguity, imperfections, and finitude.

The personalist will see little religious availability in this idea of a God who is so far removed from our predicaments as to be unaware of our very existence. Is it not religion's death to despoil the human heart of its final treasure, the diamond of God's love? The answer is that God serves an entirely different function for the transpersonalist, one that is equally religious, but different all the same. If one is struggling against a current it is comforting to have a master swimmer by one's side. It is equally important that there be a shore, solid and serene, that lies beyond the struggle as the terminus of all one's splashings. The transpersonalist has become so possessed by the goal as to forget all else, even the encouragement of supporting companions.

Coming of Age in the Universe

With God in pivotal position in the Hindu scheme, we can return to human beings to draw together systematically the Hindu concept of their nature and destiny.

Individual souls, or *jivas*, enter the world mysteriously; by God's power we may be sure, but how or for what reason we are unable fully to explain. Like bubbles that form on the bottom of a boiling teakettle, they make their way through the water (universe) until they break free into the limitless atmosphere of illumination (liberation). They begin as the souls of the simplest forms of life, but they do not vanish with the death of their original bodies. In the Hindu view spirit no more depends on the body it inhabits than body depends on the clothes it wears or the house it lives in. When we outgrow a suit or find our house too cramped, we exchange these for roomier ones that offer our bodies freer play. Souls do the same.

> *Worn-out garments*
> *Are shed by the body:*
> *Worn-out bodies*
> *Are shed by the dweller.*   (*Bhagavad-Gita*, II:22)

This process by which an individual *jiva* passes through a sequence of bodies is known as reincarnation or transmigration of the soul—in Sanskrit *samsara*, a word that signifies endless passage through cycles of life, death, and rebirth. On the subhuman level the passage is through a series of increasingly complex bodies until at last a human one is attained. Up to this point the soul's growth is virtually automatic. It is as if the soul were growing as steadily and normally as a plant and receiving at each successive embodiment a body that, being more complex, provides the needed largess for its new capabilities.

With the soul's graduation into a human body, this automatic, escalator-like mode of ascent comes to an end. Its entry into this exalted habitation is evidence that the soul has reached self-consciousness, and with this estate come freedom, responsibility, and effort.

The mechanism that ties these new acquisitions together is the law of *karma*. The literal meaning of *karma* (as we encountered it in *karma yoga*) is work, but as a doctrine it means, roughly, the moral law of cause and effect. Science has alerted the West to the importance of causal relationships in the physical world. Every physical event, we are inclined to believe, has its cause, and every cause will have its determinate effects. India extends this concept of causation to include moral and spiritual life as well. To some extent the West has as well. "As a man sows, so shall he reap"; or again, "Sow a thought and reap an act, sow an act and reap a habit, sow a habit and reap a character; sow a character and reap a destiny"—these are ways the West has put the point. The difference is that India tightens up and extends its concept of moral law to see it as absolute; it brooks no exceptions. The present condition of each interior life—how happy it is, how confused or serene, how much it sees—is an exact product of what it has wanted and done in the past. Equally, its present thoughts and decisions are determining its future experiences. Each act that is directed upon the world has its equal and opposite reaction on oneself. Each thought and deed delivers an unseen chisel blow that sculpts one's destiny.

This idea of *karma* and the completely moral universe it implies carries two important psychological corollaries. First, it commits the Hindu who understands it to complete personal responsibility. Each individual is wholly responsible for his or her present condition and will have exactly the future he or she is now creating. Most people are not willing to admit this. They prefer, as the psychologists say, to project—to locate the source of their difficulties outside themselves. They want excuses, someone to blame so that they may be exonerated. This, say the Hindus, is immature. Everybody gets exactly what is deserved—we have made our beds and must lie in them. Conversely, the idea of a moral universe closes the door on chance or accident. Most people have little idea how much they secretly bank on luck—hard luck to justify past failures, good luck to bring future successes. How many people drift through life simply waiting for the breaks, for that moment when a lucky lottery number brings riches and a dizzying spell of fame. If you approach life this way, says Hinduism, you misjudge your position pathetically. Breaks have nothing to do with protracted levels of happiness, nor do they happen by chance. We live in a world in which there is no chance or accident. Those words are simply covers for ignorance.

Because *karma* implies a lawful world, it has often been interpreted as fatalism. However often Hindus may have succumbed to this interpretation, it is untrue to the doctrine itself. *Karma* decrees that every decision must have its determinate consequences, but the decisions themselves are, in the last analysis, freely arrived at. To approach the matter from the other direction, the consequences of one's past decisions condition one's present lot, as a card player finds himself dealt a particular hand while remaining free to play that hand in a variety of ways. This means that the career of a soul as it threads its course through innumerable human bodies is guided by its choices, which are controlled by what the soul wants and wills at each stage of the journey.

What its wants are, and the order in which they appear, can be summarized quickly here, for previous sections have considered them at length. When it first enters a human body, a *jiva* (soul) wants nothing more than to taste widely of the sense delights its new physical equipment makes possible. With repetition, however, even the most ecstatic of these falls prey to habituation and grows monotonous, whereupon the *jiva* turns to social conquests to escape boredom. These conquests—the various modes of wealth, fame, and power—can hold the individual's interest for a considerable time. The stakes are high and their attainment richly gratifying. Eventually, however, this entire program of personal ambition is seen for what it is: a game—a fabulous, exciting, history-making game, but a game all the same.

As long as it holds one's interest, it satisfies. But when novelty wears off, when a winner has acknowledged with the same bow and pretty little speech the accolades that have come so many times before, he or she begins to yearn for something new and more deeply satisfying. Duty, the total dedication of one's life to one's community, can fill the need for a while, but the ironies and anomalies of history make this object too a revolving door. Lean on it and it gives, but in time one discovers that it is going round and round. After social dedication the only good that can satisfy is one that is infinite and eternal, whose realization can turn all experience, even the experience of time and apparent defeat, into splendor, as storm clouds drifting through a valley look different viewed from a peak that is bathed in sunshine. The bubble is approaching the water's surface and is demanding final release.

The soul's progress through these ascending strata of human wants does not take the form of a straight line with an acute upward angle. It fumbles and zigzags its way toward what it really needs. In the long run, however, the trend of attachments will be upward— everyone finally gets the point. By "upward" here is meant a gradual relaxation of attachment to physical objects and stimuli, accompanied by a progressive release from self-interest. We can almost visualize the action of *karma* as it delivers the consequences of what the soul reaches out for. It is as if each desire that aims at the ego's gratification adds a grain of concrete to the wall that surrounds the individual self and insulates it from the infinite sea of being that surrounds it; while, conversely, each compassionate or disinterested act dislodges a grain from the confining dike. Detachment cannot be overtly assessed, however; it has no public index. The fact that someone withdraws to a monastery is no proof of triumph over self and craving, for these may continue to abound in the imaginations of the heart. Conversely, an executive may be heavily involved in worldly responsibilities; but if he or she manages them detachedly—living in the world as a mudfish lives in the mud, without the mud's sticking to it—the world becomes a ladder to ascend.

Never during its pilgrimage is the human spirit completely adrift and alone. From start to finish its nucleus is the *Atman,* the God within, exerting pressure to "out" like a jack-in-the-box. Underlying its whirlpool of transient feelings, emotions, and delusions is the self-luminous, abiding point of the transpersonal God. Though it is buried too deep in the soul to be normally noticed, it is the sole ground of human existence and awareness. As the sun lights the world even when cloud-covered, "the Immutable is never seen but is the Witness; It is never heard but is the Hearer; it is never thought, but is the Thinker; is never known, but is the Knower. There is no other witness but This, no other knower but This."[32] But God is not only the empowering agent in the soul's every action. In the end it is God's radiating warmth that melts the soul's icecap, turning it into a pure capacity for God.

What happens then? Some say the individual soul passes into complete identification with God and loses every trace of its former separateness. Others, wishing to taste sugar, not be sugar, cherish the hope that some slight differentiation between the soul and God will still remain—a thin line upon the ocean that provides nevertheless a remnant of personal identity that some consider indispensable for the beatific vision.

Christopher Isherwood has written a story based on an Indian fable that summarizes the soul's coming of age in the universe. An old man seated on a lawn with a group of children around him tells them of the magic Kalpataru tree that fulfills all wishes. "If you speak to it and tell it a wish; or if you lie down under it and think, or even dream, a wish, then that wish will be granted." The old man proceeds to tell them that he once obtained such a tree and planted it in his garden. "In fact," he tells them, "that is a Kalpataru over there."

With that the children rush to the tree and begin to shower it with requests. Most of these turn out to be unwise, ending in either indigestion or tears. But the Kalpataru grants them indiscriminately. It has no interest in giving advice.

Years pass, and the Kalpataru is forgotten. The children have now grown into men and women and are trying to fulfill new wishes that they have found. At first they want their wishes to be fulfilled instantly, but later they search for wishes that can be fulfilled only with ever-increasing difficulty.

The point of the story is that the universe is one gigantic Wishing Tree, with branches that reach into every heart. The cosmic process decrees that sometime or other, in this life or another, each of these wishes will be granted—together, of course, with consequences. There was one child from the original group, however, so the story concludes, who did not spend his years skipping from desire to desire, from one gratification to another. For from the first he had understood the real nature of the Wishing Tree. "For him, the Kalpataru was not the pretty magic tree of his uncle's story—it did not exist to grant the foolish wishes of children—it was unspeakably terrible and grand. It was his father and his mother. Its roots held the world together, and its branches reached beyond the stars. Before the beginning it had been — and would be, always."[33]

The World—Welcome and Farewell

A ground plan of the world as conceived by Hinduism would look something like this: There would be innumerable galaxies comparable to our own, each centering in an earth from which people wend their ways to God. Ringing each earth would be a number of finer worlds above and coarser ones below, to which souls repair between incarnations according to their just desserts.

"Just as the spider pours forth its thread from itself and takes it back again, even so the universe grows from the Imperishable."[34] Periodically the thread is withdrawn; the cosmos collapses into a Night of Brahma, and all phenomenal being is returned to a state of pure potentiality. Thus, like a gigantic accordion, the world swells out and is drawn back in. This oscillation is built into the scheme of things; the universe had no beginning and will have no end. The time frame of Indian cosmology boggles the imagination and may have something to do with the proverbial oriental indifference to haste. The Himalayas, it is said, are made of solid granite. Once every thousand years a bird flies over them with a silk scarf in its beak, brushing their peaks with its scarf. When by this process the Himalayas have been worn away, one day of a cosmic cycle will have elapsed.

When we turn from our world's position in space and time to its moral character, the first point has already been established in the preceding section. It is a just world in which everyone gets what is deserved and creates his or her own future.

The second thing to be said is that it is a middle world. This is so, not only in the sense that it hangs midway between heavens above and hells below. It is also middle in the sense of being middling, a world in which good and evil, pleasure and pain, knowledge and ignorance, interweave in about equal proportions. And this is the way things will remain. All talk of social progress, of cleaning up the world, of creating the kingdom of heaven on earth — in short, all dreams of utopia — are not just doomed to disappointment; they misjudge the world's purpose, which is not to rival paradise but to provide a training ground for the human spirit. The world is the soul's gymnasium, its school and training field. What we do is important; but ultimately, it is important for the discipline it offers our individual character. We delude ourselves if we expect it to change the world fundamentally. Our work in the world is like bowling in an uphill alley; it can build muscles, but we should not think that our rolls will permanently deposit the balls at the alley's other end. They all roll back eventually, to confront our children if we ourselves have passed on. The world can develop character and prepare people to look beyond it—for these it is admirably suited. But it cannot be perfected. "Said Jesus, blessed be his name, this world is a bridge: pass over, but build no house upon it." It is true to Indian thought that this apocryphal saying, attributed to the poet Kabir, should have originated on her soil.

If we ask about the world's metaphysical status, we shall have to continue the distinction we have watched divide Hinduism on every major issue thus far; namely, the one between the dual and the non-dual points of view. On the conduct of life this distinction divides *jnana yoga* from *bhakti yoga;* on the doctrine of God it divides the personal from the transpersonal view; on the issue of salvation it divides those who anticipate merging with God from those who aspire to God's company in the beatific vision. In cosmology an extension of the same line divides those who regard the world as being from the highest perspective unreal from those who believe it to be real in every sense.

All Hindu religious thought denies that the world of nature is self-existent. It is grounded in God, and if this divine base were removed it would instantly collapse into nothingness. For the dualist the natural world is as real as God is, while of course being infinitely less exalted. God, individual souls, and nature are distinct kinds of beings, none of which can be reduced to the others. Non-dualists, on the other hand, distinguish three modes of consciousness under which the world can appear. The first is hallucination, as when we see pink elephants, or when a straight stick appears bent under water. Such appearances are corrected by further perceptions, including those of other people. Second, there is the world as it normally appears to the human senses. Finally, there is the world as it appears to *yogis* who have risen to a state of superconsciousness. Strictly speaking, this is no world at all, for here every trait that characterizes the world as normally perceived—its multiplicity and materiality—vanishes. There is but one reality, like a brimming ocean, boundless as the sky, indivisible, absolute. It is like a vast sheet of water, shoreless and calm.

The non-dualist claims that this third perspective is the most accurate of the three. By comparison, the world that normally appears to us is *maya*. The word is often translated "illusion," but this is misleading. For one thing it suggests that the world need not be taken seriously. This the Hindus deny, pointing out that as long as it appears real and demanding to us we must accept it as such. Moreover, *maya* does have a qualified, provisional reality.

Were we asked if dreams are real, our answer would have to be qualified. They are real in the sense that we have them, but they are not real inasmuch as what they depict need not exist objectively. Strictly speaking, a dream is a psychological construct, a mental fabrication. The Hindus have something like this in mind when they speak of *maya*. The world appears as the mind in its normal condition perceives it; but we are not justified in thinking that reality as it is in itself is as it is thus seen. A young child seeing its first movie will mistake the moving pictures for actual objects, unaware that the lion growling from the screen is projected from a booth at the rear of the theater. It is the same with us; the world we see is conditioned, and in that sense projected, by our perceptual mechanisms. To change the metaphor, our sense receptors register only a narrow band of electromagnetic frequencies. With the help of microscopes and other amplifiers, we can detect some additional wavelengths, but superconsciousness must be cultivated to know reality itself. In that state our receptors would cease to refract, like a prism, the pure light of being into a spectrum of multiplicity. Reality would be known as it actually is: one, infinite, unalloyed.

Maya comes from the same root as magic. In saying the world is *maya*, non-dual Hinduism is saying that there is something tricky about it. The trick lies in the way the world's materiality and multiplicity pass themselves off as being independently real—real apart from the stance from which we see them—whereas in fact reality is undifferentiated *Brahman* throughout, even as a rope lying in the dust remains a rope while being mistaken for a snake. *Maya* is also seductive in the attractiveness in which it presents the world, trapping us within it and leaving us with no desire to journey on.

But again we must ask, if the world is only provisionally real, will it be taken seriously? Will not responsibility flag? Hinduism thinks not. In a sketch of the ideal society comparable to Plato's *Republic,* the *Tripura Rahasya* portrays a prince who achieves this outlook on the world and is freed thereby from "the knots of the heart" and "the identification of the flesh with the Self." The consequences depicted are far from asocial. Thus liberated, the prince performs his royal duties efficiently but dispassionately, "like an actor on the stage." Following his teachings and example, his subjects attain a comparable freedom and are no longer motivated by their passions, though they still possess them. Worldly affairs continue, but the citizens are relieved of old resentments and are less buffeted by fears and desires. "In their everyday life, laughing, rejoicing, wearied or angered, they behaved like men intoxicated and indifferent to their own affairs." Wherefore the sages that visited there called it "the City of Resplendent Wisdom."

If we ask why Reality, which is in fact one and perfect, is seen by us as many and marred; why the soul, which is really united with God throughout, sees itself for a while as sundered; why the rope appears to be a snake—if we ask these questions we are up against the question that has no answer, any more than the comparable Christian question of why God created the world has an answer. The best we can say is that the world is *lila,* God's play. Children playing hide and seek assume various roles that have no validity outside the game. They place themselves in jeopardy and in conditions from which they must escape. Why do they do so when in a twinkling they could free themselves by simply stepping out of the game? The only answer is that the game is its own point and reward. It is fun in itself, a spontaneous overflow of creative, imaginative energy. So too in some mysterious way must it be with the world. Like a child playing alone, God is the Cosmic Dancer, whose routine is all creatures and all worlds. From the tireless stream of God's energy the cosmos flows in endless, graceful reenactment.

Those who have seen images of the goddess Kali dancing on a prostrate body while holding in her hands a sword and a severed head; those who have heard that there are more Hindu temples dedicated to Shiva (whose haunt is the crematorium and is God in his aspect of destroyer) than there are temples to God in the form of creator and preserver combined—those who know these things will not jump quickly to the conclusion that the Hindu worldview is gentle. What they overlook is that what Kali and Shiva destroy is the finite in order to make way for the infinite.

> *Because Thou lovest the Burning-ground,*
> *I have made a Burning-ground of my heart—*
> *That Thou, Dark One, hunter of the Burning-ground,*
> *Mayest dance Thy eternal dance.*   (Bengali hymn)

Seen in perspective, the world is ultimately benign. It has no permanent hell and threatens no eternal damnation. It may be loved without fear; its winds, its ever-changing skies, its plains and woodlands, even the poisonous splendor of the lascivious orchid—all may be loved provided that they are not dallied over indefinitely. For all is *maya, lila,* the spell-binding dance of the cosmic magician, beyond which lies the boundless good, which all will achieve in the end. It is no accident that the only art form India failed to produce was tragedy.

In sum: To the question, "What kind of world do we have?" Hinduism answers:

1. A multiple world that includes innumerable galaxies horizontally, innumerable tiers vertically, and innumerable cycles temporally.

2. A moral world in which the law of *karma* is never suspended.

3. A middling world that will never replace paradise as the spirit's destination.

4. A world that is *maya,* deceptively tricky in passing off its multiplicity, materiality, and dualities as ultimate when they are actually provisional.

5. A training ground on which people can develop their highest capacities.

6. A world that is *lila,* the play of the Divine in its Cosmic Dance—untiring, unending, resistless, yet ultimately beneficent, with a grace born of infinite vitality.

Many Paths to the Same Summit

That Hinduism has shared her land for centuries with Jains, Buddhists, Parsees, Muslims, Sikhs, and Christians may help explain a final idea that comes out more clearly through her than through the other great religions; namely, her conviction that the various major religions are alternate paths to the same goal. To claim salvation as the monopoly of any one religion is like claiming that God can be found in this room but not the next, in this attire but not another. Normally, people will follow the path that rises from the plains of their own civilization; those who circle the mountain, trying to bring others around to their paths, are not climbing. In practice India's sects have often been fanatically intolerant, but in principle most have been open. Early on, the Vedas announced Hinduism's classic contention that the various religions are but different languages through which God speaks to the human heart. "Truth is one; sages call it by different names."

It is possible to climb life's mountain from any side, but when the top is reached the trails converge. At base, in the foothills of theology, ritual, and organizational structure, the religions are distinct. Differences in culture, history, geography, and collective temperament all make for diverse starting points. Far from being deplorable, this is good; it adds richness to the totality of the human venture. Is life not more interesting for the varied contributions of Confucianists, Taoists, Buddhists, Muslims, Jews, and Christians? "How artistic," writes a contemporary Hindu, "that there should be room for such variety—how rich the texture is, and how much more interesting than if the Almighty had decreed one antiseptically safe, exclusive, orthodox way. Although he is Unity, God finds, it seems, his recreation in variety!"[35] But beyond these differences, the same goal beckons.

For evidence of this, one of Hinduism's nineteenth-century saints sought God successively through the practices of a number of the world's great religions. In turn he sought God through the person of Christ, the imageless, God-directed teachings of the Koran, and a variety of Hindu God-embodiments. In each instance the result was the same: The same God (he reported) was revealed, now incarnate in Christ, now speaking through the Prophet Muhammad, now in the guise of Vishnu the Preserver or Shiva the Completer. Out of these experiences came a set of teachings on the essential unity of the great religions that comprise Hinduism's finest voice on this topic. As tone is as important as idea here, we shall come closer to the Hindu position if we relinquish the remainder of this section to Ramakrishna's words instead of trying the paraphrase them.[36]

God has made different religions to suit different aspirations, times, and countries. All doctrines are only so many paths; but a path is by no means God Himself. Indeed, one can reach God if one follows any of the paths with whole-hearted devotion. One may eat a cake with icing either straight or sidewise. It will taste sweet either way.

As one and the same material, water, is called by different names by different peoples, one calling it water, another eau, *a third* aqua, *and another* pani, *so the one Everlasting-Intelligent-Bliss is invoked by some as God, by some as Allah, by some as Jehovah, and by others as Brahman.*

As one can ascend to the top of a house by means of a ladder or a bamboo or a staircase or a rope, so diverse are the ways and means to approach God, and every religion in the world shows one of these ways.

Bow down and worship where others kneel, for where so many have been paying the tribute of adoration the kind Lord must manifest himself, for he is all mercy.

The Saviour is the messenger of God. He is like the viceroy of a mighty monarch. As when there is some disturbance in a far-off province, the king sends his viceroy to quell it, so wherever there is a decline of religion in any part of the world, God sends his Saviour there. It is one and the same Saviour that, having plunged into the ocean of life, rises up in one place and is known as Krishna, and diving down again rises in another place and is known as Christ.

Everyone should follow one's own religion. A Christian should follow Christianity, a Muslim should follow Islam, and so on. For the Hindus the ancient path, the path of the Aryan sages, is the best.

People partition off their lands by means of boundaries, but no one can partition off the all-embracing sky overhead. The indivisible sky surrounds all and includes all. So people in ignorance say, "My religion is the only one, my religion is the best." But when a heart is illumined by true knowledge, it knows that above all these wars of sects and sectarians presides the one indivisible, eternal, all-knowing bliss.

As a mother, in nursing her sick children, gives rice and curry to one, and sago arrowroot to another, and bread and butter to a third, so the Lord has laid out different paths for different people suitable for their natures.

There was a man who worshipped Shiva but hated all other deities. One day Shiva appeared to him and said, "I shall never be pleased with you so long as you hate the other gods." But the man was inexorable. After a few days Shiva again appeared to him and said, "I shall never be pleased with you so long as you hate." The man kept silent. After a few days Shiva again appeared to him. This time one side of his body was that of Shiva, and the other side that of Vishnu. The man was half pleased and half displeased. He laid his offerings on the side representing Shiva, and did not offer anything to the side representing Vishnu. Then Shiva said, "Your bigotry is unconquerable. I, by assuming this dual aspect, tried to convince you that all gods and goddesses are but various aspects of the one Absolute Brahman.*

Appendix on Sikhism

Hindus are inclined to regard Sikhs (literally disciples) as somewhat wayward members of their own extended family, but Sikhs reject this reading. They see their faith as having issued from an original divine revelation that inaugurated a new religion.

The revelation was imparted to Guru Nanak, *guru* being popularly explained as a dispeller of ignorance or darkness *(gu)* and bringer of enlightenment *(ru)*. Nanak, pious and reflective from his birth in 1469, around the year 1500 mysteriously disappeared while bathing in a river. On reappearing three days later he said: "Since there is neither Hindu nor Muslim, whose path shall I follow? I will follow God's path. God is neither Hindu nor Muslim, and the path I follow is God's." His authority for those assertions, he went on to explain, derived from the fact that in his three-day absence he had been taken to God's court, where he was given a cup of nectar *(amrit,* from which Amritsar, Sikhism's holy city, is named) and was told:

This is the cup of the adoration of God's name. Drink it. I am with you. I bless you and raise you up. Whoever remembers you will enjoy my favor. Go, rejoice in my name and teach others to do so also. Let this be your calling.

That Nanak began by distinguishing his path from both Hinduism and Islam underscores the fact that Sikhism arose in a Hindu culture — Nanak was born into the *kshatriya* caste — that was under Muslim domination. Sikhism's homeland is the Punjab, "the land of the five rivers" in northwest India, where Muslim invaders were in firm control. Nanak valued his Hindu heritage while also recognizing the nobility of Islam. Here were two religions, each in itself inspired, but which in collision were exciting hatred and slaughter.

If the two sides had agreed to negotiate their differences, they could hardly have reached a more reasonable theological compromise than the tenets of Sikhism afford. In keeping with Hinduism's *sanatana dharma* (Eternal Truth), the revelation that was imparted to Nanak affirms the ultimacy of a supreme and formless God who is beyond human conceiving. In keeping with the Islamic revelation, however, it rejects the notion of *avatars* (divine incarnations), caste distinctions, images as aids to worship, and the sanctity of the Vedas. Having departed from Hinduism in these respects, however, the Sikh revelation leans back toward it in endorsing, as against Islam, the doctrine of reincarnation.

This relatively even division between Hindu and Muslim doctrines has led outsiders to suspect that in his deep, intuitive mind, if not consciously, Nanak worked out a faith he hoped might resolve the conflict religion had produced in his region. As for the Sikhs themselves, they acknowledge the conciliatory nature of their faith, but ascribe its origins to God. Only in a secondary sense was Guru Nanak a *guru*. The only True *Guru* is God. Others qualify as *gurus* in proportion as God speaks through them.

The official Sikh *gurus* are ten in number and, beginning with Guru Nanak, the Sikh community took shape through their ministrations. The tenth in this lineage, Guru Gobind Singh, announced that he was the last of this line; following his death the Sacred Text that had taken shape would replace human *gurus* as the head of the Sikh community. Known as the Guru Granth Sahib, or Collection of Sacred Wisdom, this scripture has ever since been revered by the Sikhs as their living *Guru;* it lives in the sense that the will and words of God are alive within it. For the most part it consists of poems and hymns that came to six of the *Gurus* as they meditated on God in the deep stillness of their hearts and emerged to sing joyfully God's praises.

Sikhism has been under heavy assault during much of its history. At a time when the faith was particularly hard pressed, the Tenth *Guru* called for those who were prepared to commit their lives unreservedly to the faith to step forward. To the "beloved five" who responded he gave a special initiation, thereby instituting the *Khalsa*, or Pure Order, which continues to this day. Open to men and women alike who are willing to fulfill its regulations, it requires that those who enter it abstain from alcohol, meat, and tobacco, and that they wear "the five Ks," so-called because in Punjabi all begin with the letter "k." The five are uncut hair, a comb, a sword or dagger, a steel bracelet, and undershorts. Originally, all five of these had protective as well as symbolic sides. Together with the comb, uncut hair (typically gathered in a turban) shielded the skull while tying in with the *yogic* belief that uncut hair conserves vitality and draws it upward; the comb for its part symbolized cleanliness and good order. The steel bracelet provided a small shield, while at the same time "shackling" its wearer to God as a reminder that hands should always be in God's service. Undershorts, which replaced the Indian *dhoti*, meant that one was always dressed for action. The dagger, now largely symbolic, was originally needed for self-defense.

At the same time that he instituted the *Khalsa*, Guru Gobind Singh extended his name Singh (literally lion, and by extension stalwart and lionhearted) to all Sikh men, and to women he gave the name Kaur, or princess. The names remain in force for Sikhs, right down to today.

These matters concern religious forms. Centrally, Sikhs seek salvation through union with God by realizing, through love, the Person of God, who dwells in the depths of their own being. Union with God is the ultimate goal. Apart from God life has no meaning; it is separation from God that causes human suffering. In the words of Nanak, "What terrible separation it is to be separated from God and what blissful union to be united with God!"

World renunciation does not figure in this faith. The Sikhs have no tradition of renunciation, asceticism, celibacy, or mendicancy. They are householders who support their families with their earnings and donate one-tenth of their income to charity.

Today there are some 13 million Sikhs in the world, most of them in India. Their headquarters are in the famed Golden Temple, which is located in Amritsar.

Suggestions for Further Reading

Before turning to books, let me note that my half-hour videotape (with Elda Hartley), titled "India and the Infinite: The Soul of a People," places the ideas of this chapter in their audio-visual context. It can be purchased or rented from Hartley Film Foundation, Cat Rock Road, Cos Cob, CT 06807.

David Kinsley's *Hinduism: A Cultural Perspective* (Englewood Cliffs, NJ: Prentice-Hall, 1982) provides a clear overview of Hinduism. It grounds it in its geographical setting, outlines its historical development, and calls attention to the tremendous variety this religion includes.

Heinrich Zimmer's *The Philosophies of India* (Princeton, NJ: Princeton University Press, 1969) and Swami Prabhavananda's *The Spiritual Heritage of India* (Hollywood, CA: Vedanta Press, 1980) develop at greater length the philosophical and religious dimension of Hinduism that my chapter focuses on.

Diana Eck's *Darshan: Seeing the Divine Image in India* (Chambersburg, PA: Anima Books, 1985) provides a graphic sense of Hindu devotion.

The Hindu scriptures are of enormous scope, but two portions are of universal import. The *Bhagavad-Gita* now belongs to the world, and Barbara Stoler Miller's translation (New York: Bantam Books, 1986) is eminently serviceable. The Upanishads require more interpretation, and Swami Nikhilananda's four-volume translation of the principal ones, with running commentary (New York: Ramakrishna-Vivekananda Center, 1975–79), can be recommended. For a one-volume edition of the Upanishads, without commentary but with a helpful introduction, see the translation by Juan Mascaro (New York: Penguin Books, 1965).

On Sikhism *The Sikhs: Their Religious Beliefs and Practices* by W. Owen Cole and Piara Singh Sambhi (New York: Routledge, Chapman & Hall, 1986), and the chapter on "The Faith of the Sikhs" in John Koller's *The Indian Way* (New York: Macmillan, 1982) are recommended.

Notes

1. The Sanskrit word here is *artha*, which literally means "thing, object, substance," and so is usually translated "wealth" or "material possession." I have translated it "worldly success" because the Hindu texts deal in fact with this larger theme, not just wealth. This wording is appropriate considering the normal connection of prestige and power with material possessions.

2. Simone Weil, *Waiting for God,* 1951. Reprint. (New York: Harper & Row, 1973), 210.

3. D. G. Mukerji, *The Face of Silence,* as paraphrased in Romain Rolland, *The Life of Ramakrishna* (Mayavati, Almora, Himalayas: Advaita Ashrama, 1954), 80.

4. B. K. S. Iyengar's *Light on Yoga* (1965. Reprint. [New York: Schocken Books, 1979]) presents one of the best overviews of this side of *yoga.*

5. As instances of the kinds of claims that need to be sifted, in the September 14, 1954, issue of *The Reporter,* Jean Lyon tells of witnessing a *yogi* being buried and exhumed alive after eight days, when Western physicians calculated that his air supply would suffice for only two. And in the January 21, 1982, issue of *Nature,* Herbert Benson of the Harvard Medical School and five colleagues reported experiments on three Tibetan *yogis* who, through mind control, were able to increase the temperature in their fingers and toes by as much as 14.9 degrees Fahrenheit.

6. Heinrich Zimmer, *The Philosophies of India,* 1951. Reprint. (Princeton, NJ: Princeton University Press: 1969), 80–81.

7. A refrain that, with minor variations, runs throughout the Upanishads.

8. Song by Tukaram. Translated by John S. Hoyland in *An Indian Peasant Mystic,* 1932. Reprint. (Dublin, IN: Prinit Press, 1978).

9. Bede Frost, *The Art of Mental Prayer,* 1950. Reprint. (London: Curzon Press, 1988), 29–30.

10. Hubert Benoit, *The Supreme Doctrine,* 1955. Reprint. (New York: Pantheon Books, 1969), 22.

11. There is something here that parallels Luther's determination to ease the distinction between clergy and the laity by sanctifying the common life. One recalls him crying to magistrate, farmer, artisan, and servant that if they approach their station in the right spirit, none on earth can be higher. Indeed, any of these can be "a status higher than that of a bishop."

12. *Bhagavad-Gita,* V:10.

13. Swami Swarupananda, trans., *Srimad-Bhagavad-Gita* (Mayavati, Himalayas: Advaita Ashrama, 1933), 125.

14. Zimmer, *Philosophies of India,* 303–4.

15. Quoted in Zimmer, *Philosophies of India.*

16. *Katha Upanishad,* II.iii.10.

17. Paul Deussen, *The Philosophy of the Upanishads,* 1908. Reprint. (New York: Dover Publications, 1966).

18. A description that, with minor variations, recurs throughout the Upanishads.

19. For a description of a man who spent six months in this condition, see Romain Rolland, *Life of Ramakrishna,* 1952. Reprint. (Calcutta, India: Advaita Ashrama, 1965) 77–78.

20. Zimmer, *Philosophies of India,* 44.

21. Zimmer, *Philosophies of India,* 157–58. This entire description of the four stages has drawn heavily on Zimmer's account.

22. So little has this fact been recognized in recent discussions of caste that it will be well to document it through three quotations. An ancient and authoritative lawgiver writes: "Learn supreme knowledge and service even from the man of low birth; and even from the *chandala* [outcaste]; learn by serving him the way to salvation." Quoted in *The Complete Works of Swami Vivekananda* (Mayabati, India: Advaita Ashrama, 1932), vol. 3, 381. Swami Tyagisananda's translation of the seventy-second aphorism of Narada's *Bhakti-Sutras* (Madras, India: Sri Ramakrishna Math, 1943) reads, "In [the lovers of God] there is no distinction based on caste or culture." Most forceful of all is Sri Krishna's statement in the *Mahabharata:* "The devotees of the Lord are not shudras [the lowest caste]; Shudras are they who have no faith in the Lord whichever be their caste. A wise man should not slight even an outcaste if he is devoted to the Lord; he who looks down on him will fall into hell."

23. For one of the most thoughtful of such defenses, see "What has India Contributed to Human Welfare?" in Ananda Coomaraswamy, *The Dance of Shiva,* 1957. Reprint. (New York: Dover Publications, 1985). For perhaps the best overview, and judicious assessment of the caste system, see Louis Dumont, *Homo Hierarchicus* (Chicago: University of Chicago Press, 1980).

24. The Sanskrit word *kshatriya* originally connoted warior as well as ruler, because the latter were expected to protect the weak and subdue the wicked.

25. Coomaraswamy, *Dance of Shiva,* 12.

26. Coomaraswamy, *Dance of Shiva,* 125.

27. Compare Thomas à Kempis: "There is a distance incomparable between the things men imagine by natural reason and those which illuminated men hold by contemplation."

28. Western parallels to this *via negativa,* the way to God through radical negation, are to be found in the writings of most of her great mystics and theologians. There is St. Bernard's *"nescio, nescio,"* and Angela of Foligno's "Not this! Nor this! I blaspheme," as she struggles to put her overwhelming experience of God into words. "Then only is there truth in what we know concerning God," says St. Gregory, "when we are made sensible that we

cannot know anything concerning Him." And Meister Eckhart insists that God must be loved "as not-God, not-spirit, no-person, not-image, just be loved as He is, a sheer pure absolute One, sundered from all twoness, and in whom we must eternally sink from nothingness to nothingness."

29. A Western parallel to the Hindu view on this point occurs in Simone Weil's *Waiting for God* (1951. Reprint. [New York: Harper & Row, 1973], 32): "A case of contradictories, both of them true. There is a God. There is no God. Where is the problem? I am quite sure that there is a God in the sense that I am sure my love is no illusion. I am quite sure there is no God, in the sense that I am sure there is nothing which resembles what I can conceive when I say the word."

30. Abbreviated from Shankara's Commentary on *The Brahma Sutra*, II.iii.46.

31. Composite, drawn from *Katha Upanishad*, II.ii.15; *Mundaka Upanishad*, II.ii.10; *Svetasvatara*, V.vi.14.

32. *Brihadaranyaka Upanishad*, III.vii.23.

33. Christopher Isherwood, "The Wishing Tree," in *Vedanta for the Western World* (Hollywood: Vedanta Press, 1945), 448–51.

34. *Mundaka Upanishad*, I.i.7.

35. Prema Chaitanya, "What Vedanta Means to Me," in *Vedanta and the West*, 1948. Reprint. (London: Allen & Unwin, 1961), 33.

36. The balance of this section consists of teachings of Sri Ramakrishna as compiled by Swami Abhedananda in *The Sayings of Sri Ramakrishna* (New York: The Vedanta Society, 1903), with minor editorial changes.

III. Buddhism

The Man Who Woke Up

Buddhism begins with a man. In his later years, when India was afire with his message and kings themselves were bowing before him, people came to him even as they were to come to Jesus asking what he was.[1] How many people have provoked this question — not "Who are you?" with respect to name, origin, or ancestry, but "*What* are you? What order of being do you belong to? What species do you represent?" Not Caesar, certainly. Not Napoleon, or even Socrates. Only two: Jesus and Buddha. When the people carried their puzzlement to the Buddha himself, the answer he gave provided an identity for his entire message.

"Are you a god?" they asked. "No." "An angel?" "No." "A saint?" "No." "Then what are you?"

Buddha answered, "I am awake."

His answer became his title, for this is what Buddha means. The Sanskrit root *budh* denotes both to wake up and to know. Buddha, then, means the "Enlightened One," or the "Awakened One." While the rest of the world was wrapped in the womb of sleep, dreaming a dream known as the waking state of human life, one of their number roused himself. Buddhism begins with a man who shook off the daze, the doze, the dream-like vagaries of ordinary awareness. It begins with a man who woke up.

His life has become encased in loving legend. We are told that the worlds were flooded with light at his birth. The blind so longed to see his glory that they received their sight; the deaf and mute conversed in ecstasy of the things that were to come. Crooked became straight; the lame walked. Prisoners were freed from their chains and the fires of hell were quenched. Even the cries of the beasts were hushed as peace encircled the earth. Only Mara, the Evil One, did not rejoice.

The historical facts of his life are roughly these: He was born around 563 B.C. in what is now Nepal, near the Indian border. His full name was Siddhartha Gautama of the Sakyas. Siddhartha was his given name, Gautama his surname, and Sakya the name of the clan to which his family belonged. His father was a king, but as there were then many kingdoms in the subcontinent of India, it would be more accurate to think of him as a feudal lord. By the standards of the day his upbringing was luxurious. "I wore garments of silk and my attendants held a white umbrella over me. My unguents were always from Banaras." He appears to have been exceptionally handsome, for there are numerous references to "the perfection of his visible body." At sixteen he married a neighboring princess, Yasodhara, who bore a son whom they called Rahula.

He was, in short, a man who seemed to have everything: family, "the venerable Gautama is well born on both sides, of pure descent"; appearance, "handsome, inspiring trust, gifted with great beauty of complexion, fair in color, fine in presence, stately to behold"; wealth, "he had elephants and silver ornaments for his elephants." He had a model wife, "majestic as a queen of heaven, constant ever, cheerful night and day, full of dignity and exceeding grace," who bore him a beautiful son. In addition, as heir to his father's throne, he was destined for fame and power.

Despite all this there settled over him in his twenties a discontent, which was to lead to a complete break with his worldly estate.

The source of his discontent is impounded in the legend of The Four Passing Sights, one of the most celebrated calls to adventure in all world literature. When Siddhartha was born, so this story runs, his father summoned fortunetellers to find out what the future held for his heir. All agreed that this was no usual child. His career, however, was crossed with one basic ambiguity. If he remained with the world, he would unify India and become her greatest conqueror, a *Chakravartin* or Universal King. If, on the other hand, he forsook the world, he would become not a world conqueror but a world redeemer. Faced with this option, his father determined to steer his son toward the former destiny. No effort was spared to keep the prince attached to the world. Three palaces and 40,000 dancing girls were placed at his disposal; strict orders were given that no ugliness intrude upon the courtly pleasures. Specifically, the prince was to be shielded from contact with sickness, decrepitude, and death; even when he went riding, runners were to clear the roads of these sights. One day, however, an old man was overlooked, or (as some versions have it) miraculously incarnated by the gods to effect the needed lesson: a man decrepit, broken-toothed, gray-haired, crooked and bent of body, leaning on a staff, and trembling. That day Siddhartha learned the fact of old age. Though the king extended his guard, on a second ride Siddhartha encountered a body racked with disease, lying by the roadside; and on a third journey, a corpse. Finally, on a fourth occasion he saw a monk with shaven head, ochre robe, and bowl, and on that day he learned of the life of withdrawal from the world. It is a legend, this story, but like all legends it embodies an important truth. For the teachings of the Buddha show unmistakably that it was the body's inescapable involvement with disease, decrepitude, and death that made him despair of finding fulfillment on the physical plane. "Life is subject to age and death. Where is the realm of life in which there is neither age nor death?"

Once he had perceived the inevitability of bodily pain and passage, fleshly pleasures lost their charm. The singsong of the dancing girls, the lilt of lutes and cymbals, the sumptuous feasts and processions, the elaborate celebration of festivals only mocked his brooding mind. Flowers nodding in the sunshine and snows melting on the Himalayas cried louder of the evanescence of worldly things. He determined to quit the snare of distractions his palace had become and follow the call of a truth-seeker. One night in his twenty-ninth year he made the break, his Great Going Forth. Making his way in the post-midnight hours to where his wife and son were locked in sleep, he bade them both a silent goodbye, and then ordered the gate-keeper to bridle his great white horse. The two mounted and rode off toward the forest. Reaching its edge by daybreak, Gautama changed clothes with the attendant who returned with the horse to break the news, while Gautama shaved his head and, "clothed in ragged raiment," plunged into the forest in search of enlightenment.

Six years followed, during which his full energies were concentrated toward this end. "How hard to live the life of the lonely forest-dweller . . . to rejoice in solitude. Verily, the silent groves bear heavily upon the monk who has not yet won to fixity of mind!" The words bear poignant witness that his search was not easy. It appears to have moved through three phases, without record as to how long each lasted or how sharply the three were divided. His first act was to seek out two of the foremost Hindu masters of the day and pick their minds for the wisdom in their vast tradition. He learned a great deal—about *raja yoga* especially, but about Hindu philosophy as well; so much in fact that Hindus came to claim him as their own, holding that his criticisms of the religion of his day were in the order of reforms and were less important than his agreements. In time, however, he concluded that he had learned all that these *yogis* could teach him.

His next step was to join a band of ascetics and give their way an honest try. Was it his body that was holding him back? He would break its power and crush its interference. A man of enormous will-power, the Buddha-to-be outdid his associates in every austerity they proposed. He ate so little—six grains of rice a day during one of his fasts—that "when I thought I would touch the skin of my stomach I actually took hold of my spine." He would clench his teeth and press his tongue to his palate until "sweat flowed from my armpits." He would hold his breath until it felt "as if a strap were being twisted around my head."[2] In the end he grew so weak that he fell into a faint; and if companions had not been around to feed him some warm rice gruel, he could easily have died.

This experience taught him the futility of asceticism. He had given this experiment all anyone could, and it had not succeeded—it had not brought enlightenment. But negative experiments carry their own lessons, and in this case asceticism's failure provided Gautama with the first constructive plank for his program: the principle of the Middle Way between the extremes of asceticism, on the one hand, and indulgence on the other. It is the concept of the rationed life, in which the body is given what it needs to function optimally, but no more.

Having turned his back on mortification, Gautama devoted the final phase of his quest to a combination of rigorous thought and mystic concentration along the lines of *raja yoga*. One evening near Gaya in northeast India, south of the present city of Patna, he sat down under a peepul tree that has come to be known as the Bo Tree (short for *bodhi* or enlightenment). The place was later named the Immovable Spot, for tradition reports that the Buddha, sensing that a breakthrough was near, seated himself that epoch-making evening vowing not to arise until enlightenment was his.

The records offer as the first event of the night a temptation scene reminiscent of Jesus' on the eve of his ministry. The Evil One, realizing that his antagonist's success was imminent, rushed to the spot to disrupt his concentrations. He attacked first in the form of Kama, the God of Desire, parading three voluptuous women with their tempting retinues. When the Buddha-to-be remained unmoved, the Tempter switched his guise to that of Mara, the Lord of Death. His powerful hosts assailed the aspirant with hurricanes, torrential rains, and showers of flaming rocks, but Gautama had so emptied himself of his finite self that the weapons found no target to strike and turned into flower petals as they entered his field of concentration. When, in final desperation, Mara challenged his right to do what he was doing, Gautama touched the earth with his right fingertip, whereupon the earth responded, thundering, "I bear you witness" with a hundred, a thousand, and a hundred thousand roars. Mara's army fled in rout, and the gods of heaven descended in rapture to tend the victor with garlands and perfumes.

Thereafter, while the Bo Tree rained red blossoms that full-mooned May night, Gautama's meditation deepened through watch after watch until, as the morning star glittered in the transparent sky of the east, his mind pierced at last the bubble of the universe and shattered it to naught, only, wonder of wonders, to find it miraculously restored with the effulgence of true being. The Great Awakening had arrived. Gautama's being was transformed, and he emerged the Buddha. The event was of cosmic import. All created things filled the morning air with their rejoicings and the earth quaked six ways with wonder. Ten thousand galaxies shuddered in awe as lotuses bloomed on every tree, turning the entire universe into "a bouquet of flowers set whirling through the air."[3] The bliss of this vast experience kept the Buddha rooted to the spot for seven entire days. On the eighth he tried to rise, but another wave of bliss broke over him. For a total of forty-nine days he was lost in rapture, after which his "glorious glance" opened onto the world.

Mara was waiting for him with one last temptation. He appealed this time to what had always been Gautama's strong point, his reason.

Mara did not argue the burden of reentering the world with its banal-
ities and obsessions. He posed a deeper challenge. Who could be
expected to understand truth as profound as that which the Buddha
had laid hold of? How could speech-defying revelation be translated
into words, or visions that shatter definitions be caged in language?
In short, how show what can only be found, teach what can only be
learned? Why bother to play the idiot before an uncomprehending
audience? Why not wash one's hands of the whole hot world—be
done with the body and slip at once into *nirvana?* The argument was
so persuasive that it almost carried the day. At length, however, the
Buddha answered, "There will be some who will understand," and
Mara was banished from his life forever.

Nearly half a century followed, during which the Buddha trudged
the dusty paths of India until his hair was white, step infirm, and
body nothing but a burst drum, preaching his ego-shattering, life-
redeeming message. He founded an order of monks, challenged the
deadness of *brahmin* society, and accepted in return the resentment,
queries, and bewilderment his stance provoked. His daily routine
was staggering. In addition to training monks and overseeing the
affairs of his order, he maintained an interminable schedule of public
preaching and private counseling, advising the perplexed, encourag-
ing the faithful, and comforting the distressed. "To him people come
right across the country from distant lands to ask questions, and he
bids all welcome." Underlying his response to these pressures and
enabling him to stand up under them was the pattern of withdrawal
and return that is basic to all creativity. The Buddha withdrew for six
years, then returned for forty-five. But each year was likewise divided: nine months in the world, followed by a three-month retreat
with his monks during the rainy season. His daily cycle, too, was pat-
terned to this mold. His public hours were long, but three times a day
he withdrew, to return his attention (through meditation) to its
sacred source.

After an arduous ministry of forty-five years, at the age of eighty
and around the year 483 B.C., the Buddha died from dysentery after
eating a meal of dried boar's flesh in the home of Cunda the smith.
Even on his deathbed his mind moved toward others. In the midst of
his pain, it occurred to him that Cunda might feel responsible for his
death. His last request, therefore, was that Cunda be informed that of
all the meals he had eaten during his long life, only two stood out as

having blessed him exceptionally. One was the meal whose strength had enabled him to reach enlightenment under the Bo Tree, and the other the one that was opening to him the final gates to *nirvana*. This is but one of the deathbed scenes that *The Book of the Great Decease* has preserved. Together they present a picture of a man who passed into the state in which "ideas and consciousness cease to be" without the slightest resistance. Two sentences from his valedictory have echoed through the ages. "All compounded things decay. Work out your own salvation with diligence."

The Silent Sage

To understand Buddhism it is of utmost importance to gain some sense of the impact of Buddha's life on those who came within its orbit.

It is impossible to read the accounts of that life without emerging with the impression that one has been in touch with one of the greatest personalities of all time. The obvious veneration felt by almost all who knew him is contagious, and the reader is soon caught up with his disciples in the sense of being in the presence of something close to wisdom incarnate.

Perhaps the most striking thing about him was his combination of a cool head and a warm heart, a blend that shielded him from sentimentality on the one hand and indifference on the other. He was undoubtedly one of the greatest rationalists of all times, resembling in this respect no one as much as Socrates. Every problem that came his way was automatically subjected to cool, dispassionate analysis. First, it would be dissected into its component parts, after which these would be reassembled in logical, architectonic order with their meaning and import laid bare. He was a master of dialogue and dialectic, and calmly confident. "That in disputation with anyone whomsoever I could be thrown into confusion or embarrassment— there is no possibility of such a thing."

The remarkable fact, however, was the way this objective, critical component of his character was balanced by a Franciscan tenderness so strong as to have caused his message to be subtitled "a religion of infinite compassion." Whether he actually risked his life to free a goat that was snagged on a precipitous mountainside may be historically uncertain, but the act would certainly have been in character, for his life was one continuous gift to the famished crowds. Indeed, his self-giving so impressed his biographers that they could explain it only in terms of a momentum that had acquired its trajectory in the animal stages of his incarnations. The *Jataka Tales* have him sacrificing himself for his herd when he was a stag, and hurling himself as a hare into a fire to feed a starving *brahmin*. Dismiss these *post facto* accounts as legends if we must; there is no question but that in his life as the Buddha the springs of tenderness gushed abundant. Wanting to draw the arrows of sorrow from everyone he met, he gave to each his sympathy, his enlightenment, and the strange power of soul, which, even when he did not speak a word, gripped the hearts of his visitors and left them transformed.

Socially, the Buddha's royal lineage and upbringing were of great advantage. "Fine in presence," he moved among kings and potentates with ease, for he had been one of them. Yet his poise and sophistication seem not to have distanced him from simple villagers. Surface distinctions of class and caste meant so little to him that he often appears not even to have noticed them. Regardless of how far individuals had fallen or been rejected by society, they received from the Buddha a respect that stemmed from the simple fact that they were fellow human beings. Thus many an outcaste and derelict, encountering for the first time the experience of being understood and accepted, found self-respect emerging and gained status in the community. "The venerable Gautama bids everyone welcome, is congenial, conciliatory, not supercilious, accessible to all."[4]

There was indeed an amazing simplicity about this man before whom kings bowed. Even when his reputation was at its highest he would be seen, begging-bowl in hand, walking through streets and alleys with the patience of one who knows the illusion of time. Like vine and olive, two of the most symbolic plants that grow from the meagerest of soils, his physical needs were minimal. Once at Alavi during the frosts of winter he was found resting in meditation on a few leaves gathered on a cattle path. "Rough is the ground trodden by the hoofs of cattle; thin is the couch; light the monk's yellow robe; sharp the cutting wind of winter," he admitted. "Yet I live happily with sublime uniformity."

It is perhaps inaccurate to speak of Buddha as a modest man. John Hay, who was President Lincoln's secretary, said it was absurd to call Lincoln modest, adding that "no great human being is modest."

Certainly, the Buddha felt that he had risen to a plane of understanding that was far above that of anyone else in his time. In this respect he simply accepted his superiority and lived in the self-confidence this acceptance bequeathed. But this is different from vanity or humorless conceit. At the final assembly of one of his *sangha's* (order's) annual retreats, the Exalted One looked round over the silent company and said, "Well, ye disciples, I summon you to say whether you have any fault to find with me, whether in word or in deed." And when a favorite pupil exclaimed, "Such faith have I, Lord, that methinks there never was nor will be nor is now any other greater or wiser than the Blessed One," the Buddha admonished:

"Of course, Sariputta, you have known all the Buddhas of the past."

"No, Lord."

"Well then, you know those of the future?"

"No, Lord."

"Then at least you know me and have penetrated my mind thoroughly?"

"Not even that, Lord."

"Then why, Sariputta, are your words so grand and bold?"

Notwithstanding his own objectivity toward himself, there was constant pressure during his lifetime to turn him into a god. He rebuffed all these categorically, insisting that he was human in every respect. He made no attempt to conceal his temptations and weaknesses — how difficult it had been to attain enlightenment, how narrow the margin by which he had won through, how fallible he still remained. He confessed that if there had been another drive as powerful as sex he would never have made the grade. He admitted that the months when he was first alone in the forest had brought him to the brink of mortal terror. "As I tarried there, a deer came by, a bird caused a twig to fall, and the wind set all the leaves whispering; and I thought: 'Now it is coming — that fear and terror.'" As Paul Dahlke remarks in his *Buddhist Essays*, "One who thus speaks need not allure with hopes of heavenly joy. One who speaks like this of himself attracts by that power with which the Truth attracts all who enter her domain."

Buddha's leadership was evidenced not only by the size to which his order grew, but equally by the perfection of its discipline. A king visiting one of their assemblies, which was prolonged into a full-moon night, burst out at last, "You are playing me no tricks? How can it be that there should be no sound at all, not a sneeze, nor a cough, in so large an Assembly, among 1,250 of the Brethren?" Watching the Assembly, seated as silent as a clear lake, he added, "Would that my son might have such calm."

Like other spiritual geniuses—one thinks of Jesus spotting Zacchaeus in a tree—the Buddha was gifted with preternatural insight into character. Able to size up, almost at sight, the people who approached him, he seemed never to be taken in by fraud and front but would move at once to what was authentic and genuine. One of the most beautiful instances of this was his encounter with Sunita the flower-scavenger, a man so low in the social scale that the only employment he could find was picking over discarded bouquets to find an occasional blossom that might be bartered to still his hunger. When the Buddha arrived one day at the place where he was sorting through refuse, Sunita's heart was filled with awe and joy. Finding no place to hide—for he was an outcaste—he stood as if stuck to the wall, saluting with clasped hands. The Buddha "marked the conditions of Arahatship [sainthood] in the heart of Sunita, shining like a lamp within a jar," and drew near, saying, "Sunita, what to you is this wretched mode of living? Can you endure to leave the world?" Sunita, "experiencing the rapture of one who has been sprinkled with ambrosia, said, 'If such as I may become a monk of yours, may the Exalted One suffer me to come forth!'" He became a renowned member of the order.[5]

The Buddha's entire life was saturated with the conviction that he had a cosmic mission to perform. Immediately after his enlightenment he saw in his mind's eye "souls whose eyes were scarcely dimmed by dust and souls whose eyes were sorely dimmed by dust"[6]—the whole world of humanity, milling, lost, desperately in need of help and guidance. He had no alternative but to agree with his followers that he had been "born into the world for the good of the many, for the happiness of the many, for the advantage, the good, the happiness of gods and men, out of compassion for the world."[7] His acceptance of this mission without regard for personal cost won India's heart as well as her mind. "The monk Gautama has gone forth into the religious life, giving up the great clan of his relatives, giving up much money and gold, treasure both buried and above ground. Truly while he was still a young man without gray hair on his head, in the beauty of his early manhood he went forth from the household life into the homeless state."[8]

Encomiums to the Buddha crowd the texts, one reason undoubtedly being that no description ever satisfied his disciples completely. After words had done their best, there remained in their master the essence of mystery—unplumbed depths their language could not express because thought could not fathom them. What they could understand they revered and loved, but there was more than they could hope to exhaust. To the end he remained half light, half shadow, defying complete intelligibility. So they called him Sakyamuni, "silent sage *(muni)* of the Sakya clan," symbol of something beyond what could be said and thought. And they called him Tathagata, the "Thus-come," the "Truth-winner," the "Perfectly Enlightened One," for "he alone thoroughly knows and sees, face to face, this universe." "Deep is the Tathagata, unmeasurable, difficult to understand, even like the ocean."[9]

The Rebel Saint

In moving from Buddha the man to Buddhism the religion, it is imperative that the latter be seen against the background of the Hinduism out of which it grew. Unlike Hinduism, which emerged by slow, largely imperceptible spiritual accretion, the religion of the Buddha appeared overnight, fully formed. In large measure it was a religion of reaction against Hindu perversions—an Indian protestantism not only in the original meaning of that word, which emphasized witnessing for *(testis pro)* something, but equally in its latter-day connotations, which emphasize protesting against something. Buddhism drew its lifeblood from Hinduism, but against its prevailing corruptions Buddhism recoiled like a whiplash and hit back—hard.

To understand the teachings of the Buddha, then, we shall need a minimal picture of the existing Hinduism that partly provoked it. And to lead into this, several observations about religion are in order.

Six aspects of religion surface so regularly as to suggest that their seeds are in the human makeup. One of these is authority. Leaving divine authority aside and approaching the matter in human terms only, the point begins with specialization. Religion is not less complicated than government or medicine. It stands to reason, therefore, that talent and sustained attention will lift some people above the average in matters of spirit; their advice will be sought and their counsels generally followed. In addition, religion's institutional, organized side calls for administrative bodies and individuals who occupy positions of authority, whose decisions carry weight.

A second normal feature of religion is ritual, which was actually religion's cradle, for anthropologists tell us that people danced out their religion before they thought it out. Religion arose out of celebration and its opposite, bereavement, both of which cry out for collective expression. When we are crushed by loss or when we are exuberant, we want not only to be with people; we want to interact with them in ways that make the interactions more than the sum of their parts — this relieves our isolation. The move is not limited to the human species. In northern Thailand, as the rising sun first touches the treetops, families of gibbons sing half-tone descending scales in unison as, hand over hand, they swoop across the topmost branches.

Religion may begin in ritual, but explanations are soon called for, so speculation enters as a third religious feature. Whence do we come, whither do we go, why are we here?—people want answers to these questions.

A fourth constant in religion is tradition. In human beings it is tradition rather than instinct that conserves what past generations have learned and bequeath to the present as templates for action.

A fifth typical feature of religion is grace, the belief—often difficult to sustain in the face of facts—that Reality is ultimately on our side. In last resort the universe is friendly; we can feel at home in it. "Religion says that the best things are the more eternal things, the things in the universe that throw the last stone, so to speak, and say the final word." [10]

Finally, religion traffics in mystery. Being finite, the human mind cannot begin to fathom the Infinite it is drawn to.

Each of these six things — authority, ritual, speculation, tradition, grace, and mystery—contributes importantly to religion, but equally each can clog its works. In the Hinduism of the Buddha's day they had done so, all six of them. Authority, warranted at the start, had become hereditary and exploitative as *brahmins* took to hoarding their religious secrets and charging exorbitantly for ministrations. Rituals became mechanichal means for obtaining miraculous results. Speculation had lost its experiential base and devolved into meaningless hair-splitting. Tradition had turned into a dead weight, in one specific by insisting that Sanskrit—no longer understood by the masses—remain the language of religious discourse. God's grace was being misread in ways that undercut human responsibility, if indeed responsibility any longer had meaning where *karma*, likewise misread, was confused with fatalism. Finally, mystery was confused with mystery-mongering and mystification—perverse obsession with miracles, the occult, and the fantastic.

Onto this religious scene—corrupt, degenerate, and irrelevant, matted with superstition and burdened with worn-out rituals—came the Buddha, determined to clear the ground that truth might find new life. The consequence was surprising. For what emerged was (at the start) a religion almost entirely devoid of each of the above-mentioned ingredients without which we would suppose that religion could not take root. This fact is so striking that it warrants being documented.

⁓ 1. Buddha preached a religion devoid of authority. His attack on authority had two prongs. On the one hand he wanted to break the monopolistic grip of the *brahmins* on religious teachings, and a good part of his reform consisted of no more than making generally accessible what had hitherto been the possession of a few. Contrasting his own openness with the guild secrecy of the *brahmins*, he pointed out that "there is no such thing as closed-fistedness in the Buddha." So important did he regard this difference that he returned to it on his deathbed to assure those about him: "I have not kept anything back."[11] But if his first attack on authority was aimed at an institution—the *brahmin* caste—his second was directed toward individuals. In a time when the multitudes were passively relying on *brahmins* to tell them what to do, Buddha challenged each individual to do his own religious seeking. "Do not accept what you hear by report, do not accept tradition, do not accept a statement because it is found in our books, nor because it is in accord with your belief, nor because it is the saying of your teacher. Be lamps unto yourselves. Those who, either now or after I am dead, shall rely upon themselves only and not look for assistance to anyone besides themselves, it is they who shall reach the topmost height."[12]

⁓ 2. Buddha preached a religion devoid of ritual. Repeatedly, he ridiculed the rigmarole of *Brahmanic* rites as superstitious petitions to ineffectual gods. They were trappings—irrelevant to the hard, demanding job of ego-reduction. Indeed, they were worse than irrelevant; he argued that "belief in the efficacy of rites and ceremonies" is one of the Ten Fetters that bind the human spirit. Here, as apparently everywhere, the Buddha was consistent. Discounting Hinduism's forms, he resisted every temptation to institute new ones of his own, a fact that has led some writers to characterize his teachings (unfairly) as a rational moralism rather than a religion.

— 3. Buddha preached a religion that skirted speculation. There is ample evidence that he could have been one of the world's great metaphysicians if he had put his mind to the task. Instead, he skirted "the thicket of theorizing." His silence on that front did not pass unnoticed. "Whether the world is eternal or not eternal, whether the world is finite or not, whether the soul is the same as the body or whether the soul is one thing and the body another, whether a Buddha exists after death or does not exist after death—these things," one of his disciples observed, "the Lord does not explain to me. And that he does not explain them to me does not please me, it does not suit me."[13] There were many it did not suit. Yet despite incessant needling, he maintained his "noble silence." His reason was simple. On questions of this sort, "greed for views . . . tends not to edification."[14] His practical program was exacting, and he was not going to let his disciples be diverted from the hard road of practice into fields of fruitless speculation.

His famous parable of the arrow smeared thickly with poison puts the point with precision.

It is as if a man had been wounded by an arrow thickly smeared with poison, and his friends and kinsmen were to get a surgeon to heal him, and he were to say, I will not have this arrow pulled out until I know by what man I was wounded, whether he is of the warrior caste, or a brahmin, *or of the agricultural or the lowest caste. Or if he were to say, I will not have this arrow pulled out until I know of what name of family the man is; —or whether he is tall, or short, or of middle height; or whether he is black, or dark, or yellowish; or whether he comes from such and such a village, or town, or city; or until I know whether the bow with which I was wounded was a* chapa *or a* kodanda, *or until I know whether the bow-string was of swallow-wort, or bamboo fiber, or sinew, or hemp, or of milk-sap tree, or until I know whether the shaft was*

*from a wild or cultivated plant; or whether it was feathered from
a vulture's wing or a heron's or a hawk's, or a peacock's; or whether
it was wrapped round with the sinew of an ox, or of a buffalo, or
of a ruru-deer, or of a monkey; or until I know whether it was an
ordinary arrow, or a razor-arrow, or an iron arrow, or of a calf-
tooth arrow. Before knowing all this, that man would die.*

*Similarly, it is not on the view that the world is eternal, that
it is finite, that body and soul are distinct, or that the Buddha
exists after death, that a religious life depends. Whether these
views or their opposites are held, there is still rebirth, there is old
age, there is death, and grief, lamentation, suffering, sorrow, and
despair. . . . . I have not spoken to these views because they do not
conduce to absence of passion, or to tranquillity and Nirvana.*

*And what have I explained? Suffering have I explained, the
cause of suffering, the destruction of suffering, and the path that
leads to the destruction of suffering have I explained. For this is
useful.* [15]

4. Buddha preached a religion devoid of tradition. He stood on top
of the past and its peaks extended his vision enormously, but he saw
his contemporaries as largely buried beneath those peaks. He
encouraged his followers, therefore, to slip free from the past's burden.
"Do not go by what is handed down, nor on the authority of your traditional teachings. When you know of yourselves: 'These teachings are
not good: these teachings when followed out and put in practice conduce to loss and suffering'—then reject them." [16] His most important
personal break with archaism lay in his decision—comparable to Martin Luther's decision to translate the Bible from Latin into German—to
quit Sanskrit and teach in the vernacular of the people.

5. Buddha preached a religion of intense self-effort. We have
noted the discouragement and defeat that had settled over the India
of Buddha's day. Many had come to accept the round of birth and
rebirth as unending, which was like resigning oneself to a nightmar-
ish sentence to hard labor for eternity. Those who still clung to the
hope of eventual release had resigned themselves to the *brahmin*-
sponsored notion that the process would take thousands of lifetimes,
during which they would gradually work their way into the *brahmin*
caste as the only one from which release was possible.

Nothing struck the Buddha as more pernicious than this prevailing fatalism. He denies only one assertion, that of the "fools" who say there is no action, no deed, no power. "Here is a path to the end of suffering. Tread it!" Moreover, every individual must tread this path himself or herself, through self-arousal and initiative. "Those who, relying upon themselves only, shall not look for assistance to any one besides themselves, it is they who shall reach the topmost height."[17] No god or gods could be counted on, not even the Buddha himself. When I am gone, he told his followers in effect, do not bother to pray to me; for when I am gone I will be really gone. "Buddhas only point the way. Work out your salvation with diligence."[18] The notion that only *brahmins* could attain enlightenment the Buddha considered ridiculous. Whatever your caste, he told his followers, you can make it in this very lifetime. "Let persons of intelligence come to me, honest, candid, straightforward; I will instruct them, and if they practice as they are taught, they will come to know for themselves and to realize that supreme religion and goal."

—6. Buddha preached a religion devoid of the supernatural. He condemned all forms of divination, soothsaying, and forecasting as low arts, and, though he concluded from his own experience that the human mind was capable of powers now referred to as paranormal, he refused to allow his monks to play around with those powers. "By this you shall know that a man is *not* my disciple—that he tries to work a miracle." For all appeal to the supernatural and reliance on it amounted, he felt, to looking for shortcuts, easy answers, and simple solutions that could only divert attention from the hard, practical task of self-advance. "It is because I perceive danger in the practice of mystic wonders that I strongly discourage it."

Whether the Buddha's religion—without authority, ritual, theology, tradition, grace, and the supernatural—was also a religion without God will be reserved for later consideration. After his death all the accoutrements that the Buddha labored to protect his religion from came tumbling into it, but as long as he lived he kept them at bay. As a consequence original Buddhism presents us with a version of religion that is unique and therefore historically invaluable, for every insight into the forms that religion can take increases our understanding of what in essence religion really is. Original Buddhism can be characterized in the following terms:

1. It was empirical. Never has a religion presented its case with such unequivocal appeal to direct validation. On every question personal experience was the final test of truth. "Do not go by reasoning, nor by inferring, nor by argument."[19] A true disciple must "know for himself."

2. It was scientific. It made the quality of lived experience its final test, and directed its attention to discovering cause-and-effect relationships that affected that experience. "That being present, this becomes; that not being present, this does not become."[20] There is no effect without its cause.

3. It was pragmatic — a transcendental pragmatism if one wishes, to distinguish it from the kind that focuses on practical problems in everyday life, but pragmatic all the same in being concerned with problem solving. Refusing to be sidetracked by speculative questions, Buddha kept his attention riveted on predicaments that demanded solution. Unless his teachings were useful tools, they had no value whatsoever. He likened them to rafts; they help people cross streams, but are of no further value once the further shore is reached.

4. It was therapeutic. Pasteur's words, "I do not ask you either your opinions or your religion; but what is your suffering?" could equally have been his. "One thing I teach," said the Buddha: "suffering and the end of suffering. It is just Ill and the ceasing of Ill that I proclaim."[21]

5. It was psychological. The word is used here in contrast to metaphysical. Instead of beginning with the universe and moving to the place of human beings within it, the Buddha invariably began with the human lot, its problems, and the dynamics of coping with them.

6. It was egalitarian. With a breadth of view unparalleled in his age and infrequent in any, he insisted that women were as capable of enlightenment as men. And he rejected the caste system's assumption that aptitudes were hereditary. Born a *kshatriya* (warrior, ruler) yet finding himself temperamentally a *brahmin,* he broke caste, opening his order to all regardless of social status.

7. It was directed to individuals. Buddha was not blind to the social side of human nature; he not only founded a religious order *(sangha)* — he insisted on its importance in reinforcing individual

resolves. Yet in the end his appeal was to the individual, that each should proceed toward enlightenment through confronting his or her individual situation and predicaments.

> *Therefore, O Ananda, be lamps unto yourselves. Betake yourselves to no external refuge. Hold fast as a refuge to the Truth. Work out your own salvation with diligence.*[22]

The Four Noble Truths

When the Buddha finally managed to break through the spell of rapture that rooted him to the Immovable Spot for the forty-nine days of his enlightenment, he arose and began a walk of over one hundred miles toward India's holy city of Banaras. Six miles short of that city, in a deer park at Sarnath, he stopped to preach his first sermon. The congregation was small — only five ascetics who had shared his severe austerities but had broken with him in anger when he renounced that approach, only to have now become his first disciples. His subject was the Four Noble Truths. His first formal discourse after his awakening, it was a declaration of the key discoveries that had come to him as the climax of his six-year quest.

Asked to list in propositional form their four most considered convictions about life, most people would probably stammer. The Four Noble Truths constitute Buddha's answer to that request. Together they stand as the axioms of his system, the postulates from which the rest of his teachings logically derive.

The First Noble Truth is that life is *dukkha*, usually translated "suffering." Though far from its total meaning, suffering is an important part of that meaning and should be brought to focus before proceeding to other connotations.

Contrary to the view of early Western interpreters, the Buddha's philosophy was not pessimistic. A report of the human scene can be as grim as one pleases; the question of pessimism does not arise until we are told whether it can be improved. Because the Buddha was certain that it could be, his outlook falls within Heinrich Zimmer's observation that "everything in Indian thought supports the basic insight that, fundamentally, all is well. A supreme optimism prevails everywhere." But the Buddha saw clearly that life as typically lived is unfulfilling and filled with insecurity.

He did not doubt that it is possible to have a good time and that having a good time is enjoyable, but two questions obtruded. First, how much of life is thus enjoyable. And second, at what level of our being does such enjoyment proceed. Buddha thought the level was superficial, sufficient perhaps for animals but leaving deep regions of the human psyche empty and wanting. By this understanding even pleasure is gilded pain. "Earth's sweetest joy is but disguised pain," William Drummond wrote, while Shelley speaks of "that unrest which men miscall delight." Beneath the neon dazzle is darkness; at the core—not of reality but of unregenerated human life—is the "quiet desperation" Thoreau saw in most peoples' lives. That is why we seek distractions, for distractions divert us from what lies beneath the surface. Some may be able to distract themselves for long periods, but the darkness is unrelieved.

> *Lo! as the wind is, so is mortal life:*
> *A moan, a sigh, a sob, a storm, a strife.* [23]

That such an estimate of life's usual condition is prompted more by realism than by morbidity is suggested by the extent to which thinkers of every stripe have shared it. Existentialists describe life as a "useless passion," "absurd," "too much *(de trop)*." Bertrand Russell, a scientific humanist, found it difficult to see why people should take unhappily to news that the universe is running down, inasmuch as "I do not see how an unpleasant process can be made less so [by being] indefinitely repeated." Poetry, always a sensitive barometer, speaks of "the pitiful confusion of life" and "time's slow contraction on the most hopeful heart." The Buddha never went further than Robert Penn Warren:

> *Oh, it is real. It is the only real thing.*
> *Pain. So let us name the truth, like men.*
> *We are born to joy that joy may become pain.*
> *We are born to hope that hope may become pain.*
> *We are born to love that love may become pain.*
> *We are born to pain that pain may become more*
> *Pain, and from that inexhaustible superflux*
> *We may give others pain as our prime definition.* [24]

Even Albert Schweitzer, who considered India pessimistic, echoed the Buddha's appraisal almost to idiom when he wrote, "Only at quite rare moments have I felt really glad to be alive. I could not but feel with a sympathy full of regret all the pain that I saw around me, not only that of men, but of the whole creation."

Dukkha, then, names the pain that to some degree colors all finite existence. The word's constructive implications come to light when we discover that it was used in Pali to refer to wheels whose axles were off-center, or bones that had slipped from their sockets. (A modern metaphor might be a shopping cart we try to steer from the wrong end.) The exact meaning of the First Noble Truth is this: Life (in the condition it has got itself into) is dislocated. Something has gone wrong. It is out of joint. As its pivot is not true, friction (interpersonal conflict) is excessive, movement (creativity) is blocked, and it hurts.

Having an analytical mind, the Buddha was not content to leave this First Truth in this generalized form. He went on to pinpoint six moments when life's dislocation becomes glaringly apparent. Rich or poor, average or gifted, all human beings experience:

1. The trauma of birth. Psychoanalysts have in our time made a great deal of this point. Though Freud came to deny that the birth trauma was the source of all later anxiety, to the end he considered it anxiety's prototype. The birth experience "involves just such a concatenation of painful feelings, of discharges and excitation, and of bodily sensations, as have become a prototype for all occasions on which life is endangered, ever after to be reproduced again in us as the dread of 'anxiety' conditions."[25]

2. The pathology of sickness.

3. The morbidity of decrepitude. In the early years sheer physical vitality joins with life's novelty to render life almost automatically good. In later years the fears arrive: fear of financial dependence; fear of being unloved and unwanted; fear of protracted illness and pain; fear of being physically repulsive and dependent on others; fear of seeing one's life as a failure in some important respect.

4. The phobia of death. On the basis of years of clinical practice, Carl Jung reported that he found death to be the deepest terror in every patient he had analyzed who had passed the age of forty. Existentialists join him in calling attention to the extent to which the fear of death mars healthy living.

5. To be tied to what one dislikes. Sometimes it is possible to break away, but not always. An incurable disease, a stubborn character defect—for better or for worse there are martyrdoms to which people are chained for life.

6. To be separated from what one loves.

No one denies that the shoe of life pinches in these six places. The First Noble Truth pulls them together by concluding that the five *skandas* (life components) are painful. As these *skandas* are body, sensations, thoughts, feelings, and consciousness—in short, the sum of what we generally consider life to be—the statement amounts to the assertion that the whole of human life (again, as usually lived) is suffering. Somehow life has become estranged from reality, and this estrangement precludes real happiness until it is overcome.

For the rift to be healed we need to know its cause, and the Second Noble Truth identifies it. The cause of life's dislocation is *tanha*. Again imprecisions of translations—all are to some degree dishonest—make it wise to stay close to the original word. *Tanha* is usually translated as "desire." There is some truth in this—the kind we encounter in *Heartbreak House* when George Bernard Shaw has Ellie exclaim, "I feel now as if there was nothing I could not do, because I want nothing," which assertion moves Captain Shotover to his one enthusiasm in the play: "That's the only real strength. That's genius. That's better than rum." But if we try to make desire *tanha's* equivalent, we run into difficulties. To begin with, the equivalence would make this Second Truth unhelpful, for to shut down desires, all desires, in our present state would be to die, and to die is not to solve life's problem. But beyond being unhelpful, the claim of equivalence would be flatly wrong, for there are some desires the Buddha explicitly advocated—the desire for liberation, for example, or for the happiness of others.

Tanha is a specific kind of desire, the desire for private fulfillment. When we are selfless we are free, but that is precisely the difficulty—to maintain that state. *Tanha* is the force that ruptures it, pulling us back from the freedom of the all to seek fulfillment in our egos, which ooze like secret sores. *Tanha* consists of all "those inclinations which tend to continue or increase separateness, the separate existence of the subject of desire; in fact, all forms of selfishness, the essence of which is desire for self at the expense, if necessary, of all other forms of life. Life being one, all that tends to separate one aspect from another must cause suffering to the unit which even unconsciously works against the Law. Our duty to our fellows is to understand them as extensions, other aspects, of ourselves — fellow facets of the same Reality."[26]

This is some distance from the way people normally understand their neighbors. The customary human outlook lies a good halfway toward Ibsen's description of a lunatic asylum in which "each shuts himself in a cask of self, the cask stopped with a bung of self and seasoned in a well of self." Given a group photograph, whose face does one scan for first? It is a small but telling symptom of the devouring cancer that causes sorrow. Where is the man who is as concerned that no one go hungry as that his own children be fed? Where is the woman who is as concerned that the standard of living for the entire world rise, as that her own salary be raised? Here, said the Buddha, is where the trouble lies; this is why we suffer. Instead of linking our faith and love and destiny to the whole, we persist in strapping these to the puny burros of our separate selves, which are certain to stumble and give out eventually. Coddling our individual identities, we lock ourselves inside "our skin-encapsulated egos" (Alan Watts), and seek fulfillment through their intensification and expanse. Fools to suppose that imprisonment can bring release! Can we not see that "tis the self by which we suffer"? Far from being the door to abundant life, the ego is a strangulated hernia. The more it swells, the tighter it shuts off the free-flowing circulation on which health depends, and the more pain increases.

The Third Noble Truth follows logically from the Second. If the cause of life's dislocation is selfish craving, its cure lies in the overcoming of such craving. If we could be released from the narrow limits of self-interest into the vast expanse of universal life, we would be relieved of our torment. The Fourth Noble Truth prescribes how the cure can be accomplished. The overcoming of *tanha*, the way out of our captivity, is through the Eightfold Path.

The Eightfold Path

The Buddha's approach to the problem of life in the Four Noble Truths was essentially that of a physician. He began by examining carefully the symptoms that provoke concern. If everything were going smoothly, so smoothly that we noticed ourselves as little as we normally notice our digestion, there would be nothing to worry about and we would have to attend no further to our way of life. But this is not the case. There is less creativity, more conflict, and more pain than we feel there should be. These symptoms the Buddha summarized in the First Noble Truth, with the declaration that life is *dukkha,* or out of joint. The next step was diagnosis. Throwing rites and faith to the winds, he asked, practically, what is causing these abnormal symptoms? Where is the seat of the infection? What is always present when suffering is present, and absent when suffering is absent? The answer was given in the Second Noble Truth: the cause of life's dislocation is *tanha,* or the drive for private fulfillment. What, then, of the prognosis? The Third Noble Truth is hopeful: the disease can be cured by overcoming the egoistic drive for separate existence. This brings us to prescription; how is this overcoming to be accomplished? The Fourth Noble Truth provides the answer. The way to the overcoming of self-seeking is through the Eightfold Path.

The Eightfold Path, then, is a course of treatment. But it is not an external treatment, to be accepted passively by the patient as coming from without. It is not treatment by pills, or rituals, or grace. Instead, it is treatment by training. People routinely train for sports and their professions, but with notable exceptions like Benjamin Franklin, they are inclined to assume that one cannot train for life itself. The Buddha disagreed. He distinguished two ways of living. One—a random, unreflective way, in which the subject is pushed and pulled by impulse and circumstance like a twig in a storm drain—he called "wandering about." The second, the way of intentional living, he called the Path. What he proposed was a series of changes designed to release the individual from ignorance, unwitting impulse, and *tanha.* It maps a complete course; steep grades and dangerous curves are posted, and rest spots indicated. By long and patient discipline, the Eightfold Path intends nothing less than to pick one up where one is and set one down as a different human being, one who has been cured of crippling disabilities. "Happiness he who seeks may win," the Buddha said, "if he practice."

What is this practice the Buddha is talking about? He breaks it down into eight steps. They are preceded, however, by a preliminary he does not include in his list, but refers to so often elsewhere that we may assume that he was presupposing it here. This preliminary step is right association. No one has recognized more clearly than the Buddha the extent to which we are social animals, influenced at every turn by the "companioned example" of our associates, whose attitudes and values affect us profoundly. Asked how one attains illumination, the Buddha began: "An arouser of faith appears in the world. One associates oneself with such a person." Other injunctions follow, but right association is so basic that it warrants another paragraph.

When a wild elephant is to be tamed and trained, the best way to begin is by yoking it to one that has already been through the process. By contact, the wild one comes to see that the condition it is being led toward is not wholly incompatible with being an elephant — that what is expected of it does not contradict its nature categorically and heralds a condition that, though startlingly different, is viable. The constant, immediate, and contagious example of its yoke-fellow can teach it as nothing else can. Training for the life of the spirit is not different. The transformation facing the untrained is neither smaller than the elephant's nor less demanding. Without visible evidence that success is possible, without a continuous transfusion of courage, discouragement is bound to set in. If (as scientific studies have now shown) anxieties are absorbed from one's associates, may not persistence be assimilated equally? Robert Ingersoll once remarked that had he been God he would have made health contagious instead of disease; to which an Indian contemporary responded: "When shall we come to recognize that health *is* as contagious as disease, virtue as contagious as vice, cheerfulness as contagious as moroseness?" One of the three things for which we should give thanks every day, according to Shankara, is the company of the holy; for as bees cannot make honey unless together, human beings cannot make progress on the Way unless they are supported by a field of confidence and concern that Truthwinners generate. The Buddha agrees. We should associate with Truthwinners, converse with them, serve them, observe their ways, and imbibe by osmosis their spirit of love and compassion.

With this preliminary step in place we may proceed to the Path's eight steps proper.

1. Right Views.   A way of life always involves more than beliefs, but it can never bypass them completely, for in addition to being social animals, as was just noted, human beings are also rational animals. Not entirely, to be sure — the Buddha would have been quick to acknowledge this. But life needs some blueprint, some map the mind can trust if we are to direct our energies purposively. To return to the elephant for illustration, however great the danger in which it finds itself, it will make no move to escape until it has first assured itself that the track it must tread will bear its weight. Without this conviction it will remain trumpeting in agony in a burning wagon rather than risk a fall. Reason's most vociferous detractors must admit that it plays at least this much of a role in human life. Whether or not it has the power to lure, it clearly holds power of veto. Until reason is satisfied, an individual cannot proceed in any direction wholeheartedly.

Some intellectual orientation, therefore, is needed if one is to set out other than haphazardly. The Four Noble Truths provide this orientation. Suffering abounds, it is occasioned by the drive for private fulfillment, that drive can be tempered, and the way to temper it is by traveling the Eightfold Path.

2. Right Intent. Whereas the first step summoned us to make up our minds as to what life's problem basically is, the second advises us to make up our hearts as to what we really want. Is it really enlightenment, or do our affections swing this way and that, dipping like kites with every current of distraction? If we are to make appreciable headway, persistence is indispensable. People who achieve greatness are almost invariably passionately invested in some one thing. They do a thousand things each day, but behind these stands the one thing they count supreme. When people seek liberation with single-mindedness of this order, they may expect their steps to turn from sliding sandbank scrambles into ground-gripping strides.

3. Right Speech. In the next three steps we take hold of the switches that control our lives, beginning with attention to language. Our first task is to become aware of our speech and what it reveals about our character. Instead of starting with a resolve to speak nothing but the truth — one that is likely to prove ineffective at the outset because it is too advanced — we will do well to start further back, with a resolve to notice how many times during the day we deviate from the truth, and to follow this up by asking why we did so. Similarly with uncharitable speech. Begin not by resolving never to speak an unkind word, but by watching one's speech to become aware of the motives that prompt unkindness.

After this first step has been reasonably mastered, we will be ready to try some changes. The ground will have been prepared, for once we become aware of how we do talk, the need for changes will become evident. In what directions should the changes proceed? First, toward veracity. The Buddha approached truth more ontologically than morally; he considered deceit more foolish than evil. It is foolish because it reduces one's being. For why do we deceive? Behind the rationalizations, the motive is almost always fear of revealing to others or to ourselves what we really are. Each time we give in to this "protective tariff," the walls of our egos thicken to further imprison us. To expect that we can dispense with our defenses at a stroke would be unrealistic, but it is possible to become progressively aware of them and recognize the ways in which they hem us in.

The second direction in which our speech should move is toward charity. False witness, idle chatter, gossip, slander, and abuse are to be avoided, not only in their obvious forms but also in their covert ones. The covert forms—subtle belittling, "accidental" tactlessness, barbed wit—are often more vicious because their animus is veiled.

4. *Right Conduct.*   Here, too, the admonition (as the Buddha detailed it in his later discourses) involves a call to understand one's behavior more objectively before trying to improve it. The trainee is to reflect on actions with an eye to the motives that prompted them. How much generosity was involved, and how much self-seeking? As for the direction in which change should proceed, the counsel is again toward selflessness and charity. These general directives are detailed in the Five Precepts, the Buddhist version of the second or ethical half of the Ten Commandments:

Do not kill. Strict Buddhists extend this proscription to animals and are vegetarians.

Do not steal.

Do not lie.

Do not be unchaste. For monks and the unmarried, this means continence. For the married it means restraint in proportion to one's interests in, and distance along, the Path.

Do not drink intoxicants. It is reported that an early Russian Czar, faced with the decision as to whether to choose Christianity, Islam, or Buddhism for his people, rejected the latter two because both included this fifth proscription.

5. Right Livelihood.   The word "occupation" is well devised, for our work does indeed occupy most of our waking attention. Buddha considered spiritual progress to be impossible if the bulk of one's doings pull against it: "The hand of the dyer is subdued by the dye in which it works." Christianity has agreed. While explicitly including the hangman as a role society regrettably requires, Martin Luther disallowed usurers and speculators.

For those who are intent enough on liberation to give their entire lives to the project, right livelihood requires joining the monastic order and subscribing to its discipline. For the layperson it calls for engaging in occupations that promote life instead of destroying it. Again the Buddha was not content with generalizing. He named names—the professions of his day he considered incompatible with spiritual seriousness. Some of these are obvious: poison peddler, slave trader, prostitute. Others if adopted worldwide would be revolutionary: butcher, brewer, arms maker, tax collector (profiteering was then routine). One of the number continues to be puzzling. Why did the Buddha condemn the occupation of caravan trader?

While the Buddha's explicit teachings about work were aimed at helping his contemporaries decide between occupations that were conducive to spiritual progress and ones that impeded it, there are Buddhists who suggest that if he were teaching today he would be less concerned with specifics than with the danger that people forget that earning a living is life's means, not life's end.

6. Right Effort.   The Buddha laid tremendous stress on the will. Reaching the goal requires immense exertion; there are virtues to be developed, passions to be curbed, and destructive mind states to be expunged so compassion and detachment can have a chance. "'He robbed me, he beat me, he abused me'—in the minds of those who think like this, hatred will never cease." But the only way such crippling sentiments can be dispelled, indeed the only way to shake off fetters of any sort, is by what William James called "the slow dull heave of the will." "Those who follow the Way," said Buddha, "might well follow the example of an ox that marches through the deep mire carrying a heavy load. He is tired, but his steady gaze, looking forward, will never relax until he comes out of the mire, and it is only then he takes a respite. O monks, remember that passion and sin are more than the filthy mire, and that you can escape misery only by earnestly and steadily thinking of the Way."[27] Velleity—a low level of volition, a mere wish not accompanied by effort or action to obtain it—won't do.

In discussing right effort, the Buddha later added some afterthoughts about timing. Inexperienced climbers, out to conquer their first major peak, are often impatient with the seemingly absurd saunter at which their veteran guide sets out, but before the day is over his staying pace is vindicated. The Buddha had more confidence in the steady pull than in the quick spurt. Stretched too taut, a string will snap; a plane that ascends too sharply will crash. In China the author of the *Tao Te Ching* made the point with a different image: "He who takes the longest strides does not walk farthest."

Because the West has found the last two steps in the Eightfold Path of special importance for the understanding of the human mind and its workings—there are several meditation centers in the United States, catering disproportionately to mental health professionals, that are dedicated exclusively to their practice—these will be discussed at greater length.

7. Right Mindfulness.   No teacher has credited the mind with more influence over life than did the Buddha. The best loved of all Buddhist texts, the *Dhammapada*, opens with the words, "All we are is the result of what we have thought." And respecting the future, it assures us that "all things can be mastered by mindfulness."[28]

Among Western philosophers, Spinoza stands closest to the Buddha on the mind's potential. Spinoza's dictum—"to understand something is to be delivered of it"—comes close to summarizing his entire ethic. The Buddha would have agreed. If we could really understand life, if we could really understand ourselves, we would find neither a problem. Humanistic psychology proceeds on the same assumption. When "awareness of experience is fully operating," Carl Rogers writes, "human behavior is to be trusted, for in these moments the human organism becomes aware of its delicacy and tenderness towards others." The Buddha saw ignorance, not sin, as the offender. More precisely, insofar as sin is our fault, it is prompted by a more fundamental ignorance—most specifically, the ignorance of our true nature.

To gradually overcome this ignorance, the Buddha counsels such continuous self-examination as to make us wilt (almost) at the prospect, but he thought it necessary because he believed that freedom—liberation from unconscious, robot-like existence—is achieved by self-awareness. To this end he insisted that we seek to understand ourselves in depth, seeing everything minutely, "as it really is." If we maintain a steady attention to our thoughts and feelings, we perceive that they swim in and out of our awareness, and are in no way permanent parts of us. We should witness all things non-reactively, especially our moods and emotions, neither condemning some nor holding on to others. A miscellany of other practices are recommended, some of which are these: The aspirant is to keep the mind in control of the senses and impulses, rather than being driven by them. Fearful and disgusting sights are to be meditated on until one no longer experiences aversion toward them. The entire world should be pervaded with thoughts of loving-kindness.

Out of the semi-alertness that comprises the consciousness of the average human being, this seventh step summons the seeker to steady awareness of every action that is taken, and every content that turns up in one's stream of consciousness. The adept becomes aware of the moment when sleep takes over, and whether breath was coming in or going out at that moment. Obviously, this takes practice. In addition to working at it continuously to some extent, special times should be allotted for undistracted introspection. Periods of complete withdrawal for the purpose must also be built into one's schedule.

Here is a Western observer's description of monks in Thailand practicing this seventh step:

> One of them spends hours each day slowly walking about the grounds of the wat in absolute concentration upon the minutest fraction of every action connected with each step. The procedure is carried into every single physical act of daily life until, theoretically, the conscious mind can follow every step that goes into the generation of a feeling, perception or thought. A fifty-year-old monk meditates in a small graveyard adjoining his wat, because

*he's undisturbed there. He seats himself, cross-legged and immo-
bile but with his eyes open, for hours on end—through the driving
rain at midnight or the blistering heat of noonday. His usual
length of stay is two or three hours.* [29]

Through this practice one arrives at a number of insights: (1)
Every emotion, thought, or image is accompanied by a body sensation, and vice versa. (2) One discerns obsessive patterns in what
arises in one's mind and how these patterns constitute our misery
(dukkha). For some it is a nursing of old grievances; others find themselves preoccupied with longings and self-pity, and still others simply
feel at sea. With continuing practice the obsessive grip of these patterns loosens. (3) Every mental and physical state is in flux; none is
solid and enduring. Even physical pain is a series of discrete sensations that can suddenly change. (4) The meditator realizes how little
control we have over our minds and our physical sensations, and how
little awareness we normally have of our reactions. (5) Most important, one begins to realize that there is nobody *behind* the men-
tal/physical events, orchestrating them. When the capacity for
microscopic attention is refined, it becomes apparent that consciousness itself is not continuous. Like the light from a light bulb,
the on/off is so rapid that consciousness seems to be steady, whereas
in fact it is not. With these insights, the belief in a separate self-
existent self begins to dissolve.

8. Right Concentration.   This involves substantially the techniques we have already encountered in Hinduism's *raja yoga* and
leads to substantially the same goal.

In his later years the Buddha told his disciples that his first intimations of deliverance came to him before he left home when, still a
boy and sitting one day in the cool shade of an apple tree in deep
thought, he found himself caught up into what he later identified as
the first level of the absorptions. It was his first faint foretaste of deliverance, and he said to himself, "This is the way to enlightenment." It
was nostalgia for the return and deepening of this experience, as
much as his disillusionment with the usual rewards of worldly life,
that led him to his decision to devote his life completely to spiritual
adventure. The result, as we have seen, was not simply a new philosophy of life. It was regeneration: change into a different kind of

creature, who experienced the world in a new way. Unless we see this, we shall be unequipped to fathom the power of Buddhism in human history. Something happened to the Buddha under that Bo Tree, and something has happened to every Buddhist since who has persevered to the final step of the Eightfold Path. Like a camera, the mind had been poorly focused, but the adjustment has now been made. With the "extirpation of delusion, craving, and hostility," the three poisons, we see that things were not as we had supposed. Indeed, suppositions of whatsoever sort have vanished, to be replaced by direct perception. The mind reposes in its true condition.

Basic Buddhist Concepts

The Buddha's total outlook on life is as difficult to be certain of as that of any personage in history. Part of the problem stems from the fact that, like most ancient teachers, he wrote nothing. There is a gap of almost a century and a half between his spoken words and the first written records, and though memory in those times appears to have been incredibly faithful, a gap of that length is certain to raise questions. A second problem arises from the wealth of material in the texts themselves. Buddha taught for forty-five years, and a staggering corpus has come down to us in one form or another. While the net result is doubtless a blessing, the sheer quantity of materials is bewildering; for though his teachings remained remarkably consistent over the years, it was impossible to say things for many minds and in many ways without creating problems of interpretation. These interpretations constitute the third barrier. By the time texts began to appear, partisan schools had sprung up, some intent on minimizing the Buddha's break with Brahmanic Hinduism, others intent on sharpening it. This makes scholars wonder how much in what they are reading is the Buddha's actual thought and how much is partisan interpolation.

Undoubtedly, the most serious obstacle to the recovery of the Buddha's rounded philosophy, however, is his own silence at crucial points. We have seen that his burning concerns were practical and therapeutic, not speculative and theoretical. Instead of debating cosmologies, he wanted to introduce people to a different kind of life. It would be wrong to say that theory did not interest him. His dialogues show that he analyzed certain abstract problems meticulously; that

he possessed, indeed, a brilliant metaphysical mind. It was on principle that he resisted philosophy, as someone with a sense of mission
might shun hobbies as a waste of time.

His decision makes so much sense that it may seem a betrayal to
insert a section like this one, which tries forthrightly to identify—and
to some extent define—certain key notions in the Buddha's outlook.
In the end, however, the task is unavoidable for the simple reason
that metaphysics is unavoidable. Everyone harbors some notions
about ultimate questions, and these notions affect interpretations of
subsidiary issues. The Buddha was no exception. He refused to initiate philosophical discussions, and only occasionally did he let himself be pried from his "noble silence" to engage in them, but certainly
he had views. No one who wishes to understand him can escape the
hazardous task of trying to discover what they were.

We may begin with *nirvana*, the word the Buddha used to name
life's goal as he saw it. Etymologically it means "to blow out," or "to
extinguish," not transitively, but as a fire ceases to draw. Deprived of
fuel, the fire goes out, and this is *nirvana*. From such imagery it has
been widely supposed that the extinction to which Buddhism points
is complete, total annihilation. If this were so there would be grounds
for the accusation that Buddhism is life-denying and pessimistic. As
it is, scholars of the last half-century have exploded this view. *Nirvana*
is the highest destiny of the human spirit and its literal meaning is
extinction, but we must be precise as to what is to be extinguished. It
is the boundaries of the finite self. It does not follow that what is left
will be nothing. Negatively, *nirvana* is the state in which the faggots
of private desire have been completely consumed and everything
that restricts the boundless life has died. Affirmatively, it is that
boundless life itself. Buddha parried every request for a positive
description of the unconditioned, insisting that it was "incomprehensible, indescribable, inconceivable, unutterable"; for after we elimi-
nate every aspect of the only consciousness we have known, how can
we speak of what is left?[30] One of Buddha's heirs, Nagasena, preserves this point in the following dialogue. Asked what *nirvana* is like,
Nagasena countered with a question of his own:

"Is there such a thing as wind?"

"Yes, revered sir."

"Please, sir, show the wind by its color or configuration or as thin
or thick or long or short."

"But it is not possible, revered Nagasena, for the wind to be shown; for the wind cannot be grasped in the hand or touched; yet wind exists."

"If, sir, it is not possible for the wind to be shown, well then, there is no wind."

"I, revered Nagasena, know that there is wind; I am convinced of it, but I am not able to show the wind."

"Even so, sir, nirvana exists; but it is not possible to show nirvana."[31]

Our final ignorance is to imagine that our final destiny is conceivable. All we can know is that it is a condition that is beyond—beyond the limitations of mind, thoughts, feelings, and will, all these (not to mention bodily things) being confinements. The Buddha would venture only one affirmative characterization. "Bliss, yes bliss, my friends, is *nirvana*."

Is *nirvana* God? When answered in the negative, this question has led to opposite conclusions. Some conclude that since Buddhism professes no God, it cannot be a religion; others, that since Buddhism obviously is a religion, religion doesn't require God. The dispute requires that we take a quick look at what the word "God" means.

Its meaning is not single, much less simple. Two meanings must be distinguished for its place in Buddhism to be understood.

One meaning of God is that of a personal being who created the universe by deliberate design. Defined in this sense, *nirvana* is not God. The Buddha did not consider it personal because personality requires definition, which *nirvana* excludes. And while he did not expressly deny creation, he clearly exempted *nirvana* from responsibility for it. If absence of a personal Creator-God is atheism, Buddhism is atheistic.

There is a second meaning of God, however, which (to distinguish it from the first) has been called the Godhead. The idea of personality is not part of this concept, which appears in mystical traditions throughout the world. When the Buddha declared, "There is, O monks, an Unborn, neither become nor created nor formed. . . . Were there not, there would be no deliverance from the formed, the made, the compounded,"[32] he seemed to be speaking in this tradition. Impressed by similarities between *nirvana* and the Godhead, Edward Conze has compiled from Buddhist texts a series of attributes that apply to both. We are told

that Nirvana is permanent, stable, imperishable, immovable, age-
less, deathless, unborn, and unbecome, that it is power, bliss and
happiness, the secure refuge, the shelter, and the place of unassail-
able safety; that it is the real Truth and the supreme Reality; that
it is the Good, the supreme goal and the one and only consumma-
tion of our life, the eternal, hidden and incomprehensible Peace.[33]

We may conclude with Conze that *nirvana* is not God defined as personal creator, but that it stands sufficiently close to the concept of
God as Godhead to warrant the name in that sense.[34]

The most startling thing the Buddha said about the human self is
that it has no soul. This *anatta* (no soul) doctrine has again caused
Buddhism to seem religiously peculiar. But again the word must be
examined. What was the *atta* (Pali for the Sanskrit *Atman* or soul)
that the Buddha denied? At the time it had come to signify (a) a spiritual substance that, in keeping with the dualistic position in Hinduism, (b) retains its separate identity forever.

Buddha denied both these features. His denial of spiritual substance—the soul as homunculus, a ghostly wraith within the body that
animates the body and outlasts it—appears to have been the chief point
that distinguished his concept of transmigration from prevailing Hindu
interpretations. Authentic child of India, the Buddha did not doubt that
reincarnation was in some sense a fact, but he was openly critical of
the way his *Brahmanic* contemporaries interpreted the concept. The
crux of his criticism may be gathered from the clearest description he
gave of his own view on the subject. He used the image of a flame being
passed from candle to candle. As it is difficult to think of the flame on
the final candle as being the original flame, the connection would seem
to be a causal one, in which influence was transmitted by chain reaction but without a perduring substance.

When to this image of the flame we add the Buddha's acceptance
of *karma,* we have the gist of what he said about transmigration. A
summary of his position would run something like this: (1) There is a
chain of causation threading each life to those that have led up to it,
and to those that will follow. Each life is in its present condition
because of the way the lives that led up to it were lived. (2) Throughout this causal sequence the will remains free. The lawfulness of
things makes the present state the product of prior acts, but within
the present the will is influenced but not controlled. People remain

at liberty to shape their destinies. (3) The two preceding points affirm the causal connectedness of life, but they do not entail that a substance of some sort be transmitted. Ideas, impressions, feelings, streams of consciousness, present moments — these are all that we find, no spiritual substrate. Hume and James were right: If there is an enduring self, subject always, never object, it never shows itself.

An analogy can suggest the Buddha's views of *karma* and reincarnation in a supporting way. (1) The desires and dislikes that influence the contents of my mind — what I pay attention to and what I ignore — have not appeared by accident; they have definite lineages. In addition to attitudes that I have taken over from my culture, I have formed mental habits. These include cravings of various sorts, tendencies to compare myself with others in pride or envy, and dispositions toward contentment and its opposite, aversion. (2) Although habitual reactions tend to become fixed, I am not bound by my personal history; I can have new ideas and changes of heart. (3) Neither the continuity nor the freedom these two points affirm requires that thoughts or feelings be considered entities — things, or mental substances that are transported from mind to mind, or from moment to moment. Acquiring a concern for justice from my parents did not mean that a substance, however ethereal and ghostlike, leapt from their heads into mine.

This denial of spiritual substance was only an aspect of Buddha's wider denial of substance of every sort. Substance carries both a general and a specific connotation. Generally, it refers to something relatively permanent that underlies surface changes in the thing in question; specifically, this more basic something is thought to be matter. The psychologist in Buddha rebelled against the latter notion, for to him mind was more basic than matter. The empiricist in him, for its part, challenged the implications of a generalized notion of substance. It is impossible to read much Buddhist literature without catching its sense of the transitoriness *(anicca)* of everything finite, its recognition of the perpetual perishing of every natural object. It is this that gives Buddhist descriptions of the natural world their poignancy. "The waves follow one after another in an eternal pursuit." Or,

Life is a journey.
Death is a return to the earth.

The universe is like an inn.
The passing years are like dust.

The Buddha listed impermanence *(anicca)* as the first of his Three Marks of Existence—characteristics that apply to everything in the natural order—the other two being suffering *(dukkha)* and the absence of permanent identity or a soul *(anatta)*. Nothing in nature is identical with what it was the moment before; in this the Buddha was close to modern science, which has discovered that the relatively stable objects of the macro-world derive from particles that barely exist. To underscore life's fleetingness the Buddha called the components of the human self *skandas*—skeins that hang together as loosely as yarn—and the body a "heap," its elements no more solidly assembled than grains in a sandpile. But why did the Buddha belabor a point that may seem obvious? Because, he believed, we are freed from the pain of clutching for permanence only if the acceptance of continual change is driven into our very marrow. Followers of the Buddha know well his advice:

Regard this phantom world
As a star at dawn, a bubble in a stream,
A flash of lightning in a summer cloud,
A flickering lamp—a phantom—and a dream.[35]

Given this sense of the radical impermanence of all things finite, we might expect the Buddha's answer to the question "Do human beings survive bodily death?" to be a flat no, but actually his answer was equivocal. Ordinary people when they die leave strands of finite desire that can only be realized in other incarnations; in this sense at least these persons live on.[36] But what about the *Arhat*, the holy one who has extinguished all such desires; does such a one continue to exist? When a wandering ascetic put this question, the Buddha said:

"The word reborn does not apply to him."

"Then he is not reborn?"

"The term not-reborn does not apply to him."

"To each and all of my questions, Gotama, you have replied in the negative. I am at a loss and bewildered."

"You ought to be at a loss and bewildered, Vaccha. For this doctrine is profound, recondite, hard to comprehend, rare, excellent, beyond dialectic, subtle, only to be understood by the wise. Let me therefore question you. If there were a fire blazing in front of you, would you know it?"

"Yes, Gotama."

"If the fire went out, would you know it had gone out?"

"Yes."

"If now you were asked in what direction the fire had gone, whether to east, west, north, or south, could you give an answer?"

"The question is not rightly put, Gotama." Whereupon Buddha brought the discussion to a close by pointing out that "in just the same way" the ascetic had not rightly put his question. "Feelings, perceptions, forces, consciousness — everything by which the *Arhat* might be denoted has passed away for him. Profound, measureless, unfathomable, is the *Arhat* even as the mighty ocean; reborn does not apply to him nor not-reborn, nor any combination of such terms."[37]

It contributes to the understanding of this conversation to know that the Indians of that day thought that expiring flames do not really go out but return to the pure, invisible condition of fire they shared before they visibly appeared. But the real force of the dialogue lies elsewhere. In asking where the fire, conceded to have gone out, had gone, the Buddha was calling attention to the fact that some problems are posed so clumsily by our language as to preclude solution by their very formulation. The question of the illumined soul's existence after death is such a case. If the Buddha had said, "Yes, it does live on," his listeners would have assumed the persistence of our present mode of experiencing, which the Buddha did not intend. On the other hand, if he had said, "The enlightened soul ceases to exist," his hearers would have assumed that he was consigning it to total extinction, which too he did not intend. On the basis of this rejection of extremes we cannot say much with certainty, but we can venture something. The ultimate destiny of the human spirit is a condition in which all identification with the historical experience of the finite self will disappear, while experience as such not only remains but is heightened beyond recognition. As an inconsequential dream vanishes completely on awakening, as the stars go out in deference to the morning sun, so individual awareness will be eclipsed in the blazing light of total awareness. Some say, "The dewdrop slips into the shining sea." Others prefer to think of the dewdrop as opening to receive the sea itself.

If we try to form a more detailed picture of the state of *nirvana*, we shall have to proceed without the Buddha's help, not only because he realized almost to despair how far the condition transcends the power of words, but also because he refused to wheedle his hearers with previews of coming attractions. Even so, it is possible to form some notion of the logical goal toward which his Path points. We have seen that the Buddha regarded the world as one of lawful order in which events are governed by the pervading law of cause and effect. The life of the *Arhat*, however, is one of increasing independence from the causal order of nature. It does not violate that order, but the *Arhat's* spirit grows in autonomy as the world's hold decreases. In this sense the *Arhat* is increasingly free not only from the passions and worries of the world but also from its happenings in general. With every growth of inwardness, peace and freedom replace the turbulent bondage of those whose lives are prey to circumstance. As long as spirit remains tied to body, its freedom from the particular, the temporal, and the changing cannot be complete. But sever this connection with the *Arhat's* final death, and freedom from the finite will be complete. We cannot imagine what the state would be like, but the trajectory toward it is discernible.

Spiritual freedom brings largeness of life. The Buddha's disciples sensed that he embodied immeasurably more of reality—and in that sense was more real—than anyone else they knew; and they testified from their own experience that advance along his path enlarged their lives as well. Their worlds seemed to expand, and with each step they felt themselves more alive than they had been before. As long as they were limited by their bodies, there were limits beyond which they could not go; but if all ties were loosed, might not they be completely free? Once more, we cannot concretely imagine such a state, but the logic of the progression seems clear. If increased freedom brings increased being, total freedom should be being itself.

> *A thousand questions remain, but the Buddha is silent.*
> *Others abide our questions. Thou are free.*
> *We ask and ask; thou smilest and art still.*[38]

Big Raft and Little

Thus far we have been looking at Buddhism as it appears from its earliest records. We turn now to Buddhist history and the record it provides of the variations that can enter a tradition as it seeks to minister to the needs of masses of people and multiple personality types.

When we approach Buddhist history with this interest, what strikes us immediately is that it splits. Religions invariably split. In the West the twelve Hebrew tribes split into Israel and Judah. Christendom split into the Eastern and Western churches, the Western church split into Roman Catholicism and Protestantism, and Protestantism splinters. The same happens in Buddhism. The Buddha dies, and before the century is out the seeds of schism have been sown. One approach to the question of why Buddhism split would be through analyzing the events, personalities, and environments the religion became implicated with in its early centuries. We can cut through all that, however, by saying, simply, that Buddhism divided over the questions that have always divided people.

How many such questions are there? How many questions will divide almost every assemblage of people whether in India, New York, or Madrid? Three come to mind.

First, there is the question of whether people are independent or interdependent. Some people are most aware of their individuality; for them, their freedom and initiative is more important than their bondings. The obvious corollary is that they see people as making their own ways through life; what each achieves will be largely of his or her own doing. "I was born in the slums, my father was an alcoholic, all of my siblings went to the dogs—don't talk to me about heredity or environment. I got to where I am by myself!" This is one attitude. On the other side of the fence are those for whom life's interconnectedness prevails. To them the separateness of people seems tenuous; they see themselves as supported and vectored by social fields that are as strong as those of physics. Human bodies are of course separate, but on a deeper level we are joined like icebergs in a common floe. "Send not to ask for whom the bell tolls, it tolls for thee."

A second question concerns the relation in which human beings stand, not this time to their fellows, but to the universe. Is the universe friendly—helpful on the whole toward creatures? Or is it indifferent, if not hostile? Opinions differ. On bookstore shelves we find volumes with titles like *Man Stands Alone,* and next to them *Man Does not Stand Alone* and *Man Is Not Alone.* Some people see history as a thoroughly human project in which humanity raises itself by its own bootstraps or progress doesn't happen. For others it is powered by "a higher power that makes for good."

A third dividing question is: What is the best part of the human self, its head or its heart? A popular parlor game used to revolve around the question, "If you had to choose, would you rather be loved or respected?" It is the same point with a different twist. Classicists rank thoughts above feelings; romantics do the opposite. The first seek wisdom; the second, if they had to choose, prefer compassion. The distinction probably also relates to William James's contrast between the tough-minded and the tender-minded.

Here are three questions that have probably divided people as long as they have been human and continue to divide them today. They divided the early Buddhists. One group took as its motto the Buddha's valedictory, "Be lamps unto yourselves; work out your salvation with diligence." Whatever progress those in this group make will be the fruit of wisdom—insight into the cause of suffering as gained through meditation. The other group held that compassion is the more important feature of enlightenment, arguing that to seek enlightenment by oneself and for oneself is a contradiction in terms. For them, human beings are more social than individual, and love is the greatest thing in the world.

Other differences gathered around these fundamental ones. The first group insisted that Buddhism was a full-time job; those who made *nirvana* their central object would have to give up the world and become monks. The second group, perhaps because it did not rest all its hopes on self-effort, was less demanding. It held that its outlook was as relevant for the layperson as for the professional; that in its own way it was as applicable in the world as in the monastery. This difference left its imprint on the names of the two outlooks. Both called themselves *yanas*, rafts or ferries, for both claimed to carry people across life's sea to the shores of enlightenment. The second group, however, pointing to its doctrine of cosmic help (grace) and its ampler regard for laypeople, claimed to be "Buddhism for the people" and thereby the larger of the two vehicles. Accordingly it preempted the name *Mahayana*, the Big Raft, *maha* meaning "great," as in *Mahatma* (the Great Souled) Gandhi. As this name caught on, the other group came to be known, by default, as *Hinayana*, or the Little Raft.

Not exactly pleased with this invidious designation, the Hinayanists have preferred to call their Buddhism *Theravada*, the Way of the Elders. In doing so they regained the initiative by claiming to represent original Buddhism, the Buddhism taught by Gautama himself. The claim is justified if we confine ourselves to the explicit teachings of the Buddha as they are recorded in the earliest texts, the Pali Canon, for on the whole those texts do support the Theravada position. But this fact has not discouraged the Mahayanists from their counterclaim that it is they who represent the true line of succession. For, they argue, the Buddha taught more eloquently and profoundly by his life and example than by the words the Pali Canon records. The decisive fact about his life is that he did not remain in *nirvana* after his enlightenment but returned to devote his life to others. Because he did not belabor this fact, Theravadins (attending too narrowly to his initial spoken words, the Mahayanists contend) overlook the importance of his "great renunciation," and this causes them to read his mission too narrowly.[39]

We can leave to the two schools their dispute over apostolic succession; our concern is not to judge but to understand the positions they embody. The differences that have come out thus far may be summarized by the following pairs of contrasts, if we keep in mind that they are not absolute but denote differences in emphasis.

1. For Theravada Buddhism progress is up to the individual; it depends on his or her understanding and resolute application of the will. For Mahayanists the fate of the individual is linked to that of all life, and they are ultimately undivided. Two lines from John Whittier's "The Meeting" summarize the latter outlook:

He findeth not who seeks his own
The soul is lost that's saved alone.

2. Theravada holds that humanity is on its own in the universe. No gods exist to help us over the humps, so self-reliance is our only recourse.

By ourselves is evil done,
By ourselves we pain endure,
By ourselves we cease from wrong,
By ourselves become we pure.
No one saves us but ourselves,
No one can and no one may;

> *We ourselves must tread the Path:*
> *Buddhas only show the way.*

For Mahayana, in contrast, grace is a fact. We can be at peace because a boundless power draws—or if you prefer, propels—everything to its appointed goal. In the words of a famous Mahayana text, "There is a Buddha in every grain of sand."

3. In Theravada Buddhism the prime attribute of enlightenment is wisdom (*bodhi*), meaning profound insight into the nature of reality, the causes of anxiety and suffering, and the absence of a separate core of selfhood. From these realizations flow automatically the Four Noble Virtues: loving-kindness, compassion, equanimity, and joy in the happiness and wellbeing of others. From the Mahayana perspective *karuna* (compassion) cannot be counted on to be an automatic fruit. From the beginning compassion must be given priority over wisdom. Meditation yields a personal power that can be destructive if a person has not deliberately cultivated compassionate concern for others as the motive for arduous discipline. "A guard I would be to them who have no protection," runs a typical Mahayana invocation; "a guide to the voyager, a ship, a well, a spring, a bridge for the seeker of the other shore." The theme has been beautifully elaborated by Shantideva, a poet-saint who has been called the Thomas à Kempis of Buddhism:

> *May I be a balm to the sick, their healer and servitor until*
> *sickness come never again;*
> *May I quench with rains of food and drink the anguish of*
> *hunger and thirst;*
> *May I be in the famine of the age's end their drink and meat;*
> *May I become an unfailing store for the poor, and serve them*
> *with manifold things for their need.*
> *My own being and my pleasures, all my righteousness in the*
> *past, present and future, I surrender indifferently,*
> *That all creatures may win through to their end.*[40]

4. The *sangha* (Buddhist monastic order) is at the heart of Theravada Buddhism. Monasteries (and to a lesser extent nunneries) are the spiritual dynamos in lands where it predominates, reminding everyone of a higher truth behind visible reality. Monks and nuns—only partially isolated from society because they are dependent on

local people to put into their begging bowls their one daily meal—
are accorded great respect. This veneration is extended to people
who assume monastic vows for limited periods (a not uncommon
practice) in order to practice mindfulness meditation intensively. In
Burma "taking the robe" for a three-month monastic retreat has virtually marked the passage into male adulthood. Mahayana Buddhism, on the contrary, is primarily a religion for laypeople. Even its
priests usually marry, and they are expected to make service to the
laity their primary concern.

   5. It follows from these differences that the ideal type as projected
by the two schools will differ appreciably. For the Theravadins the ideal
was the *Arhat*, the perfected disciple who, wandering like the lone rhi-
noceros, strikes out alone for *nirvana* and, with prodigious concentration, proceeds unswervingly toward that goal. The Mahayana ideal, on
the contrary, was the *boddhisattva*, "one whose essence (*sattva*) is perfected wisdom (*bodhi*)"—a being who, having reached the brink of *nirvana*, voluntarily renounces that prize and returns to the world to make
nirvana available to others. The *boddhisattva* deliberately sentences
himself—or herself: the best loved of all *boddhisattvas* is the Goddess
of Mercy, Kwan Yin, in China—to age-long servitude in order that
others, drawing vicariously on the merit thus accumulated, may enter *nirvana* first.

   The difference between the two types is illustrated in the story of
four men who, journeying across an immense desert, come upon a
compound surrounded with high walls. One of the four determines
to find out what is inside. He scales the wall, and on reaching the top
gives a whoop of delight and jumps over. The second and third do
likewise. When the fourth man gets to the top of the wall, he sees
below him an enchanted garden with sparkling streams, pleasant
groves, and luscious fruit. Though longing to jump over, he resists the
temptation. Remembering other wayfarers who are trudging the
burning deserts, he climbs back down and devotes himself to directing them to the oasis. The first three men were *Arhats*; the last was a
boddhisattva, one who vows not to desert this world "until the grass
itself be enlightened."

   6. This difference in ideal naturally floods back to color the two
schools' estimates of the Buddha himself. For one he was essentially

a saint, for the other a savior. Theravadins revere him as a supreme
sage, who through his own efforts awakened to the truth and became
an incomparable teacher who laid out a path for them to follow. A
man among men, his very humanness is the basis for the Theravadins'
faith that they, too, have the potential for enlightenment. But the
Buddha's direct personal influence ceased with his *paranirvana*
(entrance into *nirvana* at death). He knows nothing more of this
world of becoming and is at perfect peace. The reverence felt by
the Mahayanists could not be satisfied with this humanness — extraordinary, to be sure, but human nonetheless. For them the Buddha
was a world savior who continues to draw all creatures toward him
"by the rays of his jewel hands." The bound, the shackled, the suffering on every plane of existence, galaxy beyond galaxy, worlds beyond
worlds, all are drawn toward liberation by the glorious "gift rays" of
the Lord.

These differences are the central ones, but several others may be
mentioned to piece out the picture. Whereas the Theravadins followed their founder in considering speculation a useless diversion,
Mahayana spawned elaborate cosmologies replete with many-leveled
heavens and hells. The only kind of prayer the Theravadins countenanced was meditation and invocations to deepen faith and loving-
kindness, whereas the Mahayanists added supplication, petition, and
calling on the name of the Buddha for spiritual strength. Finally,
whereas Theravada remained conservative to the point of an almost
fundamentalistic adherence to the early Pali texts, Mahayana was
liberal in almost every respect. It accepted later texts as equally
authoritative, was less strict in interpreting disciplinary rules, and
had a higher opinion of the spiritual possibilities of women and the
laity in general.

Thus, in the end, the wheel comes full circle. The religion that
began as a revolt against rites, speculation, grace, and the supernatural, ends with all of them back in full force and its founder (who was
an atheist as far as a personal God was concerned) transformed into
such a God himself. We can schematize the differences that divide
the two great branches of Buddhism as follows, if we bear in mind
that the differences are not absolute:

THERAVADA	MAHAYANA
Human beings are emancipated by self-effort, without supernatural aid.	Human aspirations are supported by divine powers and the grace they bestow.
Key virtue: wisdom.	Key virtue: compassion.[41]
Attainment requires constant commitment, and is primarily for monks and nuns.	Religious practice is relevant to life in the world, and therefore to laypeople.
Ideal: the *Arhat* who remains in *nirvana* after death	Ideal: the *boddhisattva*.
Buddha a saint, supreme teacher, and inspirer.	Buddha a savior.
Minimizes metaphysics.	Elaborates metaphysics.
Minimizes ritual.	Emphasizes ritual.
Practice centers on meditation.	Includes petitionary prayer.

Which one wins? Inwardly, there is no measure (or better, no such thing as winning); but outwardly (in terms of numbers), the answer is Mahayana. Part of the reason may lie in the fact that it converted one of the greatest kings the world has known. In the history of ancient royalty the figure of Asoka (c. 272–232 B.C.) stands out like a Himalayan peak, clear and resplendent against a sunlit sky. If we are not all Buddhists—Mahayana Buddhists—today it was not Asoka's fault. Not content to board the Big Raft himself and commend it to his subjects—his Buddhist wheel of the law waves on India's flag today—he strove to extend it over three continents. Finding Buddhism an Indian sect, he left it a world religion.

It would be going too far, however, to suppose that a single historical personage made Buddhism cosmopolitan, and the different ways Asia heard the Buddha's message and took it to heart provides a final touchstone for distinguishing Theravada from Mahayana. The differences that have occupied us thus far have been doctrinal, but there is an important socio-political difference between them as well.[42]

Theravada sought to incarnate a feature of the Buddha's teachings that has not thus far been mentioned: his vision of an entire society—a civilization if you will—that was founded like a tripod on monarchy, the monastic community (*sangha*), and the laity, each with responsibilities to the other two and meriting services from them in return. South Asian countries that remain to this day Theravadin—Sri Lanka, Burma, Thailand, and Cambodia—took this political side of the Buddha's message seriously, and remnants of his model are discernible in those lands right down to today. China's interest in Buddhism (which she transmitted to the other lands that were to become Mahayanist: Korea, Japan, and Tibet) bypassed its social dimensions, which included education as well as politics. In East Asian lands Buddhism appears as something of a graft. Buddhist missionaries persuaded the Chinese that they possessed psychological and metaphysical profundities the Chinese sages had not sounded, but Confucius had thought a lot about the social order, and the Chinese were not about to be lectured to on that subject by aliens. So China discounted the political proposals of the Buddha and took from his corpus its psycho-spiritual components with their cosmic overtones. The world still awaits a history of Buddhism that tells the story of the Theravada/Mahayana divide in terms of the way in which (for geographical and historical reasons) Theravada remained faithful to its founder's vision of a Buddhist civilization, whereas Mahayana becomes Buddhism trimmed to its religious core: a module that could be grafted onto civilizations whose social foundations were securely in place.

The doctrinal differences between Theravada and Mahayana appear to have softened as the centuries have gone by. Following World War II two young Germans who were disillusioned with Europe went to Sri Lanka to dedicate their lives to the Buddha's peaceable way. Both became Theravada monks. One, his name changed to Nyanaponika Thera, continued on that path; but the other, while on a sightseeing trip to north India, met some Tibetans and switched to their tradition, becoming known in the West as Lama Govinda. Toward the close of Nyanaponika's life a visitor asked him about the different Buddhisms the two friends had espoused. With great serenity and sweetness the aging Theravadin replied: "My friend cited the Bodhisattva Vow as the reason for his switch to Mahayana, but I could not see the force of his argument. For if one were to transcend self-centeredness completely, as the *Arhat* seeks to do, what would be left but compassion?"

The Secret of the Flower [43]

After Buddhism split into Theravada and Mahayana, Theravada continued as a fairly unified tradition, whereas Mahayana divided into a number of denominations or schools. The most popular of these, the Pure Land Sect, resembles the Pauline strand in Christianity in relying on faith—in its case faith in the "other power" of one of the Buddhas—to carry devotees to the Pure Land of the Western Paradise. In its popular reading this paradise bears many resemblances to the Christian heaven, though both admit of subtler interpretations in which paradise is regarded as an experiential state rather than a geographical place. Another important Mahayana school (*Ti'en Tai* in Chinese; *Tendai* in Japanese) introduced into Buddhism the Confucian predilections for learning and social harmony. It sought to find a place for all the Buddhist schools in a culminating treatise, *The Lotus Sutra*. We shall not go into these and smaller sects of Mahayana Buddhism; we shall reserve our space for, first, the Buddhism that Taoism profoundly influenced, namely *Ch'an* (*Zen* in Japanese), and second, the Buddhism that evolved in Tibet. The selection is partly determined by the fact that these are the branches of Buddhism that have attracted the most attention in the West, but there is the added advantage that they will take us to two quite different lands in which Buddhism has flourished.

Because the Communist takeover of China disrupted its religious life, we shall pursue the Ch'an/Zen sect in its Japanese guise. Like other Mahayanist sects, this one claims to trace its perspective back to Gautama himself. His teachings that found their way into the Pali Canon, it holds, were those the masses seized upon. His more perceptive followers heard in his message a higher, subtler teaching. The classic instance of this is reported in the Buddha's Flower Sermon. Standing on a mountain with his disciples around him, the Buddha did not on this occasion resort to words. He simply held aloft a golden lotus. No one understood the meaning of this eloquent gesture save Mahakasyapa, whose quiet smile, indicating that he had gotten the point, caused the Buddha to designate him as his successor. The insight that prompted the smile was transmitted in India through twenty-eight patriarchs and carried to China in A.D. 520 by Bodhidharma. Spreading from there to Japan in the twelfth century, it contains the secret of Zen.

Entering Zen is like stepping through Alice's looking glass. One finds oneself in a topsy-turvy wonderland where everything seems quite mad—charmingly mad for the most part, but mad all the same. It is a world of bewildering dialogues, obscure conundrums, stunning paradoxes, flagrant contradictions, and abrupt non sequiturs, all carried off in the most urbane, cheerful, and innocent style imaginable. Here are some examples:

A master, Gutei, whenever he was asked the meaning of Zen, lifted his index finger. That was all. Another kicked a ball. Still another slapped the inquirer.

A novice who makes a respectful allusion to the Buddha is ordered to rinse his mouth out and never utter that dirty word again.

Someone claiming to understand Buddhism writes the following stanza:

The body is the Bodhi-Tree;
The mind is like the mirror bright.
Take heed to keep it always clean,
And let no dust collect upon it.

He is at once corrected by an opposite quatrain, which becomes accepted as the true Zen position:

Bodhi (True Wisdom) is not a tree;
The mind is not a mirror shining.
As there is nothing from the first,
Why talk of wiping off the dust?

A monk approaches a master saying, "I have just come to this monastery. Would you kindly give me some instruction?" The master asks, "Have you eaten your breakfast yet?" "I have." "Then go wash your bowls." The inquirer acquired the understanding he was seeking through this exchange.

A group of Zen masters, gathered for conversation, have a great time declaring that there is no such thing as Buddhism, or Enlightenment, or anything even remotely resembling *nirvana*. They set traps for one another, trying to trick someone into an assertion that might imply the contrary. Practiced as they are, they always artfully elude traps and pitfalls, whereupon the entire company bursts into glorious, room-shaking laughter.

What goes on here? Is it possible to make any sense out of what at first blush looks like Olympian horseplay, if not a direct put-on? Can they possibly be serious in this kind of spiritual doubletalk, or are they simply pulling our legs?

The answer is that they are completely serious, though it is true that they are rarely solemn. And though we cannot hope to convey their perspective completely, it being of Zen's essence that it cannot be impounded in words, we can give some hint as to what they are up to.

Let us admit at the outset that even this is going to be difficult, for we shall have to use words to talk about a position that is acutely aware of their limitations. Words occupy an ambiguous place in life. They are indispensable to our humanity, for without them we would be but howling yahoos. But they can also deceive, or at least mislead, fabricating a virtual reality that fronts for the one that actually exists. A parent can be fooled into thinking it loves its child because it addresses the child in endearing terms. A nation can assume that the phrase "under God" in its Pledge of Allegiance shows that its citizens believe in God when all it really shows is that they believe in *believing* in God. With all their admitted uses, words have three limitations. At worst they construct an artificial world wherein our actual feelings are camouflaged and people are reduced to stereotypes. Second, even when their descriptions are reasonably accurate, descriptions are not the things described—menus are not the meal. Finally, as mystics emphasize, our highest experiences elude words almost entirely.

Every religion that has developed even a modicum of semantic sophistication recognizes to some extent the way words and reason fall short of reality when they do not actually distort it. However much the rationalist may begrudge the fact, paradox and the trans-rational are religion's life blood, and that of art as well. Mystics in every faith report contacts with a world that startles and transforms them with its dazzling darkness. Zen stands squarely in this camp, its only uniqueness being that it makes breaking the language barrier its central concern.

Only if we keep this fact in mind have we a chance of understanding this outlook, which in ways is the strangest expression of mature religion. It was the Buddha himself, according to Zen tradition, who first made the point by refusing (in the Flower Sermon we have already alluded to) to equate his experiential discovery with any verbal expression. Bodhidharma continued in this tradition by defining the treasure he was bringing to China as "a special transmission outside the scriptures." This seems so out of keeping with religion as usually understood as to sound heretical. Think of Hinduism with its Vedas, Confucianism with its Classics, Judaism with its Torah, Christianity with its Bible, Islam with its Koran. All would happily define themselves as special transmissions *through* their scriptures. Zen, too, has its texts; they are intoned in its monasteries morning and evening. In addition to the Sutras, which it shares with other branches of Buddhism, it has its own texts: the *Hekigan Roku*, the *Mumonkan*, and others. But one glance at these distinctive texts will reveal how unlike other scriptures they are. Almost entirely they are given to pressing home the fact that Zen cannot be equated with any verbal formula whatsoever. Account after account will depict disciples interrogating their masters about Zen, only to receive a roared "Ho!" for answer. For the master sees that through such questions, seekers are trying to fill the lack in their lives with words and concepts instead of realizations. Indeed, students will be lucky if they get off with verbal rebuffs. Often a rain of blows will be the retort as the master, utterly uninterested in the disciples' physical comfort, resorts to the most forceful way he can think of to pry the questioner out of his mental rut.

As we might expect, this unique stance toward scripture is duplicated in Zen's attitude toward creeds. In contrast to most religions, which pivot around a creed of some sort, Zen refuses to lock itself into a verbal casing; it is "not founded on written words, and [is] *outside* the established teachings," to return to Bodhidharma's putting of the point. Signposts are not the destination, maps are not the terrain. Life is too rich and textured to be fitted into pigeonholes, let alone equated with them. No affirmation is more than a finger pointing to the moon. And, lest attention turn to the finger, Zen will point, only to withdraw its finger at once. Other faiths regard blasphemy and disrespect for God's word as sins, but Zen masters may order their disciples to rip their scriptures to shreds and avoid words like Buddha or *nirvana* as if they were smut. They intend no disrespect.[44] What they are doing is straining by every means they can think of to blast their novices out of solutions that are only verbal. "Not everyone who says to me, 'Lord, Lord,' will enter the kingdom of heaven"(Matthew

7:21). Zen is not interested in theories about enlightenment; it wants the real thing. So it shouts, and buffets, and reprimands, without ill-will entering in the slightest. All it wants to do is force the student to crash the word-barrier. Minds must be sprung from their verbal bonds into a new mode of apprehending.

Every point can be overstated, so we should not infer from what has been said that Zen forgoes reason and words entirely.[45]

To be sure, it is no more impressed with the mind's attempts to mirror ultimate reality than was Kierkegaard with Hegel's metaphysics; no amount of polishing can enable a brick to reflect the sun. But it does not follow that reason is worthless. Obviously, it helps us make our way in the everyday world, a fact that leads Zennists in the main to be staunch advocates of education. But more. Working in special ways, reason can actually help awareness toward its goal. If the way that it is employed to do this seems at times like using a thorn to remove a thorn, we should add that reason can also play an interpretive role, serving as a bridge to join a newly discovered world to the world of common sense. For there is not a Zen problem whose answer, once discovered, does not make good sense within its own frame of reference; there is no experience that the masters are unwilling to try to describe or explain, given the proper circumstance. The point regarding Zen's relation to reason is simply a double one. First, Zen logic and description make sense only from an experiential perspective radically different from the ordinary. Second, Zen masters are determined that their students attain the experience itself, not allow talk to take its place.

Nowhere is Zen's determination on this latter point more evident than in the method it adopted for its own perpetuation. Whereas on the tricky matter of succession other religions turned to institutionalized mandates, papal succession, or creedal dicta, Zen trusted its future to a specific state of consciousness that was to be transmitted directly from one mind to another, like flame passed from candle to candle, or water poured from cup to cup. It is this "transmission of Buddha-mind to Buddha-mind" that constitutes the "special transmission" Bodhidharma cited as Zen's essence. For a number of centuries this inward transmission was symbolized by the handing down of the Buddha's robe and bowl from patriarch to patriarch, but in the Eighth Century the Sixth Patriarch in China concluded that even this simple gesture was a step toward confounding form with essence and ordered it discontinued. So here is a tradition that centers in a succession of teachers, each of whom has in principle inherited from his master a mind-state analogous to the one Gautama awakened in Mahakasyapa. Practice falls short of this principle, but the following figures suggest the steps that are taken to keep it in place. The master of the teacher under whom the author of this book studied estimated that he had given personal instruction to some nine hundred probationers. Of these, thirteen completed their Zen training, and four were given the *inka*—which is to say, they were confirmed as *roshis* (Zen masters) and authorized to teach.

And what is the training by which aspirants are brought toward the Buddha-mind that has been thus preserved? We can approach it by way of three key terms: *zazen, koan,* and *sanzen.*

Zazen literally means "seated meditation." The bulk of Zen training takes place in a large meditation hall. Visitors to these are struck by the seemingly endless hours the monks devote to sitting silently on two long, raised platforms that extend the length of the hall on either side, their faces toward the center (or to the walls, depending on which of the two main lineages of Zen the monastery is attached to).[46] Their position is the lotus posture, adopted from India. Their eyes are half closed as their gaze falls unfocused on the tawny straw mats they are sitting on.

Thus they sit, hour after hour, day after day, year after year,[47] seeking to waken the Buddha-mind so they may later relate it to their daily lives. The most intriguing feature of the process is the use they make of one of the strangest devices for spiritual training anywhere to be encountered—the *koan.*

In a general way *koan* means problem, but the problems Zen devises are fantastic. At first glance they look like nothing so much as a cross between a riddle and a shaggy dog story. For example:

> A *master, Wu Tsu, says, "Let me take an illustration from a fable. A cow passes by a window. Its head, horns, and the four legs all pass by. Why did not the tail pass by?"*

> Or again: *What was the appearance of your face before your ancestors were born?*

Another: *We are all familiar with the sound of two hands clapping. What is the sound of one hand clapping?* (If you protest that one hand can't clap, you go to the foot of the class.)

One more: *Li-ku, a high-ranking officer in the T'ang dynasty, asked a famous Ch'an master: "A long time ago a man kept a goose in a bottle. It grew larger and larger until it could not get out of the bottle any more. He did not want to break the bottle, nor did he wish to harm the goose. How would you get it out?*

The master was silent for a few moments, then shouted, "O Officer!"

"Yes."

"It's out!"

Our impulse is to dismiss these puzzles as absurd, but the Zen practitioner is not permitted to do this. He or she is ordered to direct the full force of the mind upon them, sometimes locking logic with them, sometimes dropping them into the mind's deep interior to wait till an acceptable answer erupts, a project that on a single *koan* may take as long as a doctoral dissertation.

During this time the mind is intently at work, but it is working in a very special way. We in the West rely on reason so fully that we must remind ourselves that in Zen we are dealing with a perspective that is convinced that reason is limited and must be supplemented by another mode of knowing.

For Zen, if reason is not a ball and chain, anchoring mind to earth, it is at least a ladder too short to reach to truth's full heights. It must, therefore, be surpassed, and it is just this surpassing that *koans* are designed to assist. If they look scandalous to reason, we must remember that Zen is not trying to placate the mundane mind. It intends the opposite: to upset the mind — unbalance it and eventually provoke revolt against the canons that imprison it. But this puts the matter too mildly. By forcing reason to wrestle with what from its normal point of view is flat absurdity; by compelling it to conjoin things that are ordinarily incompatible, Zen tries to drive the mind to a state of agitation wherein it hurls itself against its logical cage with the desperation of a cornered rat. By paradox and non sequitur Zen provokes, excites, exasperates, and eventually exhausts the mind until it sees that thinking is never more than thinking *about*, or feeling more than feeling *for*. Then, having gotten the rational mind where it wants it—reduced to an impasse—it counts on a flash of sudden insight to bridge the gap between secondhand and firsthand life.

> *Light breaks on secret lots. . . .*
> *Where logics die*
> *The secret grows through the eye.*[48]

Before we dismiss this strange method as completely foreign, it is well to remember that Kierkegaard regarded meditation on the paradox of the Incarnation—the logical absurdity of the Infinite becoming finite, God becoming man—as the most rewarding of all Christian exercises. The *koan* appears illogical because reason proceeds within structured perimeters. Outside those perimeters the *koan* is not inconsistent; it has its own logic, a "Riemannian" logic we might say. Once the mental barrier has been broken, it becomes intelligible. Like an alarm clock, it is set to awaken the mind from its dream of rationality. A higher lucidity is at hand.

Struggling with his *koan*, the Zen monk is not alone. Books will not avail, and *koans* that are being worked on are not discussed with fellow monks, for this could only produce secondhand answers. Twice a day, though, on average, the monk confronts the master in private "consultation concerning meditation"—*sanzen* in Rinzai and *dokusan* in the Soto sect. These meetings are invariably brief. The trainee states the *koan* in question and follows it with his or her answer to date. The role of the master is then threefold. In the happy event that the answer is correct, he validates it, but this is his least important role, for a right answer usually comes with a force that is self-validating. A greater service is rendered in rejecting inadequate answers, for nothing so helps the student to put these permanently to one side as the master's categorical rejection of them. This aspect of *sanzen* is fittingly described in the ninth-century *Rules of Hyakujo* as affording "the opportunity for the teacher to make a close personal examination of the student, to arouse him from his immaturity, to beat down his false conceptions and to rid him of his prejudices, just as the smelter removes the lead and quicksilver from the gold in the smelting-pot, and as the jade-cutter, in polishing the jade, discards every possible flaw."[49] The master's other service is, like that of any exacting examiner, to keep the student energized and determined during the long years the training requires.

And to what does this *zazen, koan* training, and *sanzen* lead? The first important breakthrough is an intuitive experience called *kensho* or *satori*. Though its preparation may take years, the experience itself comes in a flash, exploding like a silent rocket deep within the subject and throwing everything into a new perspective. Fearful of being seduced by words, Zennists waste little breath in describing *satoris,* but occasionally accounts appear.

> *Ztt! I entered. I lost the boundary of my physical body. I had my skin, of course, but I felt I was standing in the center of the cosmos. I saw people coming toward me, but all were the same man. All were myself. I had never known this world before. I had believed that I was created, but now I must change my opinion: I was never created; I was the cosmos. No individual existed.*[50]

From this and similar descriptions we can infer that *satori* is Zen's version of the mystical experience, which, wherever it appears, brings joy, at-one-ment, and a sense of reality that defies ordinary language. But whereas the tendency is to relate such experiences to the zenith of the religious quest, Zen places them close to the point of departure. In a very real sense Zen training begins with *satori*. For one thing, there must be further *satoris* as the trainee learns to move with greater freedom in this realm.[51] But the important point is that Zen, drawing half its inspiration from the practical, common-sense, this-worldly orientation of the Chinese to balance the mystical otherworldly half it derived from India, refuses to permit the human spirit to withdraw—shall we say retreat?—into the mystical state completely. Once we achieve *satori*, we must

> *get out of the sticky morass in which we have been floundering, and return to the unfettered freedom of the open fields. Some people may say: "If I have [achieved satori] that is enough. Why should I go further?" The old masters lashed out at such persons, calling them "earthworms living in the slime of self-accredited enlightenment."*[52]

The genius of Zen lies in the fact that it neither leaves the world in the less-than-ideal state in which it finds it, nor withdraws from the world in aloofness or indifference. Zen's object is to infuse the temporal *with* the eternal—to widen the doors of perception so that the wonder of the *satori* experience can flood the everyday world.

"What," asks the student, "is the meaning of Bodhidharma's coming from the West?" The master answers, "The cypress tree standing in the garden." Being's amazingness must be directly realized, and *satori* is its first discernment. But until—through recognizing the interpenetration and convertibility of all phenomena—its wonder spreads to objects as common as the tree in your backyard and you can perform your daily duties with the understanding that each is equally a manifestation of the infinite, Zen's business has not been completed.

With the possible exception of the Buddha himself, in no one is that business ever completely finished. Yet by extrapolating hints in the Zen corpus we can form some idea of what the condition of "the man who has nothing further to do" would be like.

First, it is a condition in which life seems distinctly good. Asked what Zen training leads to, a Western student who had been practicing for seven years in Kyoto answered, "No paranormal experiences that I can detect. But you wake up in the morning and the world seems so beautiful you can hardly stand it."

Along with this sense of life's goodness there comes, secondly, an objective outlook on one's relation to others; their welfare impresses one as being as important as one's own. Looking at a dollar bill, one's gaze may be possessive; looking at a sunset, it cannot be. Zen attainment is like looking at the sunset. Requiring (as it does) awareness to the full, issues like "whose awareness?" or "awareness of what?" do not arise. Dualisms dissolve. As they do there comes over one a feeling of gratitude to the past and responsibility to things present and future.

Third, the life of Zen (as we have sought to emphasize) does not draw one away from the world; it returns one to the world—the world robed in new light. We are not called to worldly indifference, as if life's object were to spring soul from body as piston from syringe. The call is to discover the satisfaction of full awareness even in its bodily setting. "What is the most miraculous of all miracles?" "That I sit quietly by myself." Simply to see things as they are, as they truly are in themselves, is life enough. It is true that Zen values unity, but it is a unity that is simultaneously empty (because it erases lines that divide) and full (because it replaces those lines with ones that connect). Stated in the form of a Zen algorithm, "All is one, one is none, none is all." Zen wears the air of divine ordinariness: "Have you eaten? Then wash your bowls." If you cannot find the meaning of life in an act as simple as that of doing the dishes, you will not find it anywhere.

> *My daily activities are not different,*
> *Only I am naturally in harmony with them.*
> *Taking nothing, renouncing nothing,*
> *In every circumstance no hindrance, no conflict . . .*
> *Drawing water, carrying firewood,*
> *This is supernatural power, this the marvelous activity.*[53]

With this perception of the infinite in the finite there comes, finally, an attitude of generalized agreeableness. "Yesterday was fair, today it is raining"; the experiencer has passed beyond the opposites of preference and rejection. As both pulls are needed to keep the relative world turning, each is welcomed in its proper turn.

There is a poem by Seng Ts'an on "Trust in the Heart," that stands as the purest expression of this ideal of total acceptance.

> *The perfect way knows no difficulties*
> *Except that it refuses to make preferences;*
> *Only when freed from hate and love*
> *Does it reveal itself fully and without disguise;*
> *A tenth of an inch's difference,*
> *And heaven and earth are set apart.*
> *If you wish to see it before your own eyes*
> *Have no fixed thoughts either for or against it.*
>
> *To set up what you like against what you dislike —*
> *That is the disease of the mind.*
> *The Way is perfect like unto vast space,*
> *With nothing wanting, nothing superfluous.*
> *It is due to making choices*
> *That its Suchness is lost sight of.*
>
> *The One is none other than the All, the All none other than the*
>   *One.*
> *Take your stand on this, and the rest will follow of its own*
>   *accord;*
> *I have spoken, but in vain, for what can words tell*
> *Of things that have no yesterday, tomorrow, or today?*[54]

Even truth and falsity look different. "Do not seek after truth. Merely cease to hold opinions."

Fifth, as the dichotomies between self and other, finite and infinite, acceptance and rejection are transcended, even the dichotomy between life and death disappears.

> *When this realization is completely achieved, never again can one feel that one's individual death brings an end to life. One has lived from an endless past and will live into an endless future. At this very moment one partakes of Eternal Life—blissful, luminous, pure.*[55]

As we leave Zen to its future we may note that its influence on the cultural life of Japan has been enormous. Though its greatest influence has been on pervasive life attitudes, four ingredients of Japanese culture carry its imprint indelibly. In *sumie* or black ink landscape painting, Zen monks, living their simple lives close to the earth, have rivaled the skill and depth of feeling of their Chinese masters. In landscape gardening Zen temples surpassed their Chinese counterparts and raised the art to unrivaled perfection. Flower arrangement began in floral offerings to the Buddha, but developed into an art that until recently was a part of the training of every refined Japanese girl. Finally, there is the celebrated tea ceremony, in which an austere but beautiful setting, a few fine pieces of old pottery, a slow, graceful ritual, and a spirit of utter tranquility combine to epitomize the harmony, respect, clarity, and calm that characterize Zen at its best.

The Diamond Thunderbolt

We have spoken of two *yanas* or paths in Buddhism, but we must now add a third. If Hinayana literally means the Little Way and Mahayana the Great Way, Vajrayana is the Diamond Way.

Vajra was originally the thunderbolt of Indra, the Indian Thunder God who is often mentioned in the early, Pali Buddhist texts; but when Mahayana turned the Buddha into a cosmic figure, Indra's thunderbolt was transformed into the Buddha's diamond scepter. We see here a telling instance of Buddhism's capacity to accommodate itself to local ideas while revaluing them by changing the spiritual center of gravity; for the diamond transforms the thunderbolt, symbol of nature's power, into an emblem of spiritual supremacy, while retaining the connotations of power that the thunderbolt possessed. The diamond is the hardest stone—one hundred times harder than its closest rival—and at the same time the most transparent stone. This makes the Vajrayana the way of strength and lucidity—strength to realize the Buddha's vision of luminous compassion.[56]

We just noted that the roots of the Vajrayana can be traced back to India, and it continues to survive in Japan as Shingon Buddhism; but it was the Tibetans who perfected this third Buddhist path. For Tibetan Buddhism is not just Buddhism with Tibet's pre-Buddhist Bon deities incorporated. Nor is it enough to characterize it as Indian Buddhism in its eighth- and ninth-century heyday, moved northward to be preserved against its collapse in India. To catch its distinctiveness we must see it as the third major Buddhist *yana*, while adding immediately that the essence of the Vajrayana is Tantra. Tibetan Buddhism, the Buddhism here under review, is at heart Tantric Buddhism.

Buddhists have no monopoly on Tantra, which first showed itself in medieval Hinduism where the word had two Sanskrit roots. One of these is "extension." In this meaning Tantra denotes texts, many of them esoteric and secret in nature, that were added to the Hindu corpus to extend its range. This gives us only the formal meaning of the word, however. For the content of those extended texts we should look to the second etymological meaning of Tantra, which derives from the weaving craft and denotes interpenetration. In weaving, the threads of warp and woof intertwine repeatedly. The Tantras are texts that focus on the interrelatedness of things. Hinduism pioneered such texts, but it was Buddhism, particularly Tibetan Buddhism, that gave them pride of place.

The Tibetans say that their religion is nowise distinctive in its goal. What distinguishes their practice is that it enables one to reach *nirvana* in a single lifetime.[57] This is a major claim. How do the Tibetans defend it?

They say that the speed-up is effected by utilizing all of the energies latent in the human make-up, those of the body emphatically included, and impressing them *all* into the service of the spiritual quest.

The energy that interests the West most is sex, so it is not surprising that Tantra's reputation abroad has been built on its sacramental use of this drive. H. G. Wells once said that God and sex were the only two things that really interested him. If we can have both—not be forced to choose between them as in monasticism and celibacy—this is music to modern ears, so much so that in the popular Western mind Tantra and sex are almost equated. This is unfortunate. Not only does it obscure the larger world of Tantra; it distorts its sexual teachings by removing them from that world.

Within that world Tantra's teachings about sex are neither titillating nor bizarre: they are universal. Sex is so important—after all, it keeps life going—that it must be linked quite directly with God. It is the divine Eros of Hesiod, celebrated in Plato's *Phaedrus* and in some way by every people. Even this, though, is too mild. Sex *is* the divine in its most available epiphany. But with this proviso: It is such when joined to love. When two people who are passionately, even madly— Plato's divine madness—in love; when each wants most to receive what the other most wants to give;—at the moment of their mutual climax it is impossible to say whether the experience is more physical or spiritual, or whether they sense themselves as two or as one. The moment is ecstatic because at that moment they stand outside—*ex*, out; *stasis*, standing—themselves in the melded oneness of the Absolute.

Nothing thus far is uniquely Tantric; from the Hebrew *Song of Songs* to the explicit sexual symbolism in mystical marriages to Christ, the principles just mentioned turn up in all traditions. What distinguishes Tantra is the way it wholeheartedly espouses sex as a spiritual ally, working with it explicitly and intentionally. Beyond squeamishness and titillation, both, the Tantrics keep the physical and spiritual components of the love-sex splice in strict conjunction —through their art (which shows couples in coital embrace), in their fantasies (the ability to visualize should be actively cultivated), and in overt sexual engagement, for only one of the four Tibetan priestly orders is celibate. Beyond these generalizations it is not easy to go, so we shall leave the matter with a covering observation. Tantric sexual practice is pursued, not as a law-breaking revel, but under the cautious supervision of a *guru*, in the controlled context of a non-dualist outlook, and as the culminating festival of a long sequence of spiritual disciplines practiced through many lives. The spiritual emotion that is worked for is ecstatic, egoless, beatific bliss in the realization of transcendent identity. But it is not self-contained, for the ultimate goal of the practice is to descend from the non-dual experience better equipped to experience the multiplicity of the world without estrangement.

With Tantra's sexual side thus addressed, we can move on to more general features of its practice. We have already seen that these are distinctive in the extent to which they are body-based, and the physical energies the Tantrics work with most regularly are the ones that are involved with speech, vision, and gestures.

To appreciate the difference in a religious practice that engages these faculties actively, it is useful to think back to the *raja yoga* of Hinduism and Zen in Buddhism. Both of these meditation programs set out to immobilize the body so that for practical purposes the mind might rise above it. A snapshot could capture the body in those practices, whereas with the Tibetans a motion picture camera would be needed, and one that is wired for sound. For, ritualistically engaged, the Tibetans' bodies are always moving. The *lamas* prostrate themselves, weave stylized hand gestures, pronounce sacred syllables, and intone deep-throated chants. Audially and visually, something is always going on.

The rationale they invoke for engaging their bodies in their spiritual pursuits is straightforward. Sounds, sights, and motion *can* distract, they admit, but it does not follow that they *must* do so. It was the genius of the great pioneers of Tantra to discover *upayas* (skillful means) for channeling physical energies into currents that carry the spirit forward instead of derailing it. The most prominent of these currents relate to the sound, sight, and movement we have referred to, and the names for them all begin with the letter "m." *Mantras* convert noise into sound and distracting chatter into holy formulas. *Mudras* choreograph hand gestures, turning them into pantomime and sacred dance. *Mandalas* treat the eyes to icons whose holy beauty draws the beholder in their direction.

If we try to experience our way into the liturgy by which the Tibetans put these Tantric devices into practice, the scene that emerges is something like this. Seated in long, parallel rows; wearing headgear that ranges from crowns to wild shamanic hats; garbed in maroon robes, which they periodically smother in sumptuous vestments of silver, scarlet, and gold, gleaming metaphors for inner states of consciousness, the monks begin to chant. They begin in a deep, guttural, metric monotone, but as the mood deepens those monotones splay out into harmonics that sound like full-throated chords, though actually the monks are not singing in parts; harmony (a Western discovery) is unknown to them. By a vocal device found nowhere else in the world, they reshape their vocal cavities in ways that amplify overtones to the point where they can be heard as discrete tones in their own right.[58] Meanwhile, their hands perform stylized gestures that kinesthetically augment the states of consciousness that are being accessed.

A final, decisive feature of this practice would be lost on observers because it is totally internal. Throughout the exercise the monks visualize the deities they are invoking—visualize them with such intensity (years of practice are required to master the technique) that, initially with closed eyes but eventually with eyes wide open, they are able to see the deities as if they were physically present. This goes a long way toward making them real, but in the meditation's climax, the monks go further. They seek experientially to merge with the gods they have conjured, the better to appropriate their powers and their virtues. An extraordinary assemblage of artistic forms are orchestrated here, but not for art's sake. They constitute a technology, designed to modulate the human spirit to the wavelengths of the tutelary deities that are invoked.

To complete this profile of Tibetan Buddhism's distinctiveness, we must add to this summary of its Tantric practice a unique institution. When in 1989 the Nobel Peace Prize was awarded to His Holiness the Dalai Lama, that institution jumped to worldwide attention.

The Dalai Lama is not accurately likened to the pope, for it is not his prerogative to define doctrine. Even more misleading is the designation God-King, for though temporal and spiritual authority do converge in him, neither of these powers define his essential function. That function is to incarnate on earth the celestial principle of which compassion or mercy is the defining feature. The Dalai Lama is the *bodhisattva* who in India was known as Avalokiteshvara, in China as the Goddess of Mercy Kwan Yin, and in Japan as Kannon. As Chenrezig (his Tibetan name) he has for the last several centuries incarnated himself for the empowerment and regeneration of the Tibetan tradition. Through his person—a single person who has thus far assumed fourteen successive incarnations—there flows an uninterrupted current of spiritual influence, characteristically compassionate in its flavor. Thus in relation to the world generally, and to

Tibet in particular, the office of the Dalai Lama is chiefly neither one of administration nor of teaching but an "activity of presence" that is operative independently of anything he may, as an individual, choose to do or not do. The Dalai Lama is a receiving station toward which the compassion-principle of Buddhism in all its cosmic amplitude is continuously channeled, to radiate thence to the Tibetan people most directly, but by extension to all sentient beings.

Whether the Dalai Lama will reincarnate himself again after his present body is spent is uncertain, for at present the Chinese invaders are determined that there will be no distinct people for him to serve. If there are not, something important will have withdrawn from history. For as rain forests are to the earth's atmosphere, someone has said, so are the Tibetan people to the human spirit in this time of its planetary ordeal.

The Image of the Crossing

We have looked at three modes of transport in Buddhism: the Little Raft; the Big Raft, with special attention to Zen; and, though it sounds odd in the context of a flotilla, the Diamond Raft. These vehicles are so different that we must ask in closing whether, on any grounds other than historical lineage, they deserve to be considered aspects of a single religion.

There are two respects in which they should be so regarded. They all revere a single founder from whom they claim their teachings derive. And all three can be subsumed under a single metaphor. This is the image of the crossing, the simple everyday experience of crossing a river on a ferryboat.

To appreciate the force of this image we must remember the role the ferry played in traditional Asian life. In lands laced by rivers and canals, almost every considerable journey required a ferry. This routine fact underlies and inspires every school of Buddhism, as the use of the word *yana* by all of them attests. Buddhism is a voyage across life's river, a transport from the common-sense shore of ignorance, grasping, and death, to the further bank of wisdom and enlightenment. Compared with this settled fact, the differences within Buddhism are no more than variations in the kind of vehicle one boards, or the stage one has reached on the journey.

What are these stages?

While we are on the first bank it is in effect the world for us. Its earth underfoot is solid and reassuring. The rewards and disappointments of its social life are vivid and compelling. The opposite shore is barely visible and has no impact on our dealings.

If, however, something prompts us to see what the other side is like, we may decide to attempt a crossing. If we are of independent bent, we may decide to make it on our own. In this case we are Theravadins; we follow the Buddha's design for a sturdy craft, but we build ours ourself. Most of us, however, have neither the time nor the talent for a project of such proportions. We are Mahayanists and move down the bank to where a ready-made ferryboat is expected. As the group of explorers clamber aboard at the landing there is an air of excitement. Attention is focused on the distant bank, still indistinct, but the voyagers are still very much like citizens of this side of the river.

The ferry pushes off and moves across the water. The bank we are leaving behind is losing its substance. The shops and streets and ant-like figures are blending together and releasing their hold on us. Meanwhile, the shore toward which we are headed is not in focus either; it seems almost as far away as it ever was. There is an interval in the crossing when the only tangible realities are the water, with its treacherous currents, and the boat, which is stoutly but precariously contending with them. This is the moment for Buddhism's Three Vows: I take refuge in the *Buddha*, the fact that there was an explorer who made this trip and proved to us that it can succeed. I take refuge in the *dharma*, the vehicle of transport, this boat to which we have committed our lives in the conviction that it is seaworthy. I take refuge in the *sangha*, the order, the crew that is navigating this ship, in whom we have confidence. The shoreline of the world has been left behind. Until we set foot on the further bank, these are the only things in which we can trust.

The further shore draws near, becomes real. The craft jolts onto the sand and we step onto solid ground. The land, which had been misty and unsubstantial as a dream, is now fact. And the shore that we left behind, which was so palpable and real, is now only a slender horizontal line, a visual patch, a memory without substance.

Impatient to explore our new surroundings, we nevertheless remember our gratitude for the splendid ship and crew who have brought us safely to what promises to be a rewarding land. It will not be gratitude, however, to insist on packing the boat with us as we plunge into the woods. "Would he be a clever man," the Buddha asked, "if out of gratitude for the raft that has carried him across the stream to safety he, having reached the other shore, should cling to it, take it on his back, and walk about with the weight of it? Would not the clever man be the one who left the raft, no longer of use to him, to the current of the stream and walked ahead without turning back to look at it? Is it not simply a tool to be cast away and forsaken once it has served the purpose for which it was made? In the same way the vehicle of the doctrine is to be cast away and forsaken once the other shore of Enlightenment has been attained."[59]

Here we come to the *Prajnaparamita* or *Perfection of Wisdom* sutras, which are widely considered to be the culminating texts of Buddhism. The Five Precepts and the Eightfold Path; the technical terminology of *dukkha, karma, nirvana,* and their like; the committed order and the person of the Buddha himself—all these are vitally important to the individual in the act of making the crossing. They lose their relevance for those who have arrived. Indeed, to the traveler who has not only reached the promised shore but who keeps moving into its interior, there comes a time when not only the raft but the river itself drops from view. When such a one turns around to look for the land that has been left behind, what appears? What of that land *can* appear to one who has crossed a horizon beyond which the river dividing this shore from that shore has vanished? One looks, and there is no other shore. There is no separating river. There is no raft, no ferryman. These things are not a part of the new world.

Before the river was crossed the two shores, human and divine, had to appear distinct from each other, different as life and death, as day and night. But once the crossing has been made, no dichotomy remains. The realm of the gods is not a distinct place. It is where the traveler stands; and if that stance happens to be in this world, the world itself is transmuted. It is in this sense that we are to read the avowals in *The Perfection of Wisdom* that "this our worldly life is an activity of Nirvana itself; not the slightest distinction exists between them."[60] Introspection having led to a condition described positively as *nirvana* and negatively as Emptiness because it transcends all forms, the "stream-winner" now finds in the world itself this same Emptiness that he discovered within. "Form is emptiness, emptiness is form. Emptiness is not different from form, form is not different from emptiness." The noisy disjunction between acceptance and rejection having been stilled, every moment is affirmed for what it actually is. It is Indra's cosmic net, laced with jewels at every juncture. Each jewel reflects the others, together with all the reflections *in* the others. In such a vision the categories of good and evil disappear. "That which is sin is also Wisdom" we read; and once again, "the realm of Becoming is *Nirvana.*"

> *This earth on which we stand*
> *is the promised Lotus Land,*
> *And this very body*
> *is the body of the Buddha.*[61]

This new-found shore throws light on the *bodhisattva*'s vow not to enter *nirvana* "until the grass itself be enlightened." As grass keeps coming, does this mean that the *bodhisattva* will never be enlightened? Not exactly. It means, rather, that he (or she) has risen to the point where the distinction between time and eternity has lost its force. That distinction, drawn by the rational mind, is dissolved in the lightning-and-thunder insight that annihilates opposites. Time and eternity are now two aspects of the same experiential whole, two sides of the same coin. "The jewel of eternity is in the lotus of birth and death."

From the standpoint of normal, worldly consciousness there must always remain an inconsistency between this climactic insight and worldly prudence. This, though, should not surprise us, for it would be flatly contradictory if the world looked exactly the same to those who have crossed the river of ignorance. Only they can dissolve the world's distinctions—or, perhaps we should say, take them in their stride, for the distinctions persist, but now without difference. Where to eagle vision the river can still be seen, it is seen as connecting the two banks rather than dividing them.

The Confluence of Buddhism and Hinduism in India

Among the surface paradoxes of Buddhism—this religion that began by rejecting ritual, speculation, grace, mystery, and a personal God and ended by bringing them all back into the picture—there is a final one. Today Buddhists abound in every Asian land except India; only recently, after a thousand-year absence, are they beginning in small numbers to reappear. Buddhism triumphs in the world at large, only (it would seem) to forfeit the land of its birth.

This surface appearance is deceptive. The deeper fact is that in India Buddhism was not so much defeated by Hinduism as accommodated within it. Up to around the year 1000, Buddhism persisted in India as a distinct religion. To say that the Muslim invaders then wiped it out will not do, for Hinduism survived. The fact is that in the course of its 1,500 years in India, Buddhism's differences with Hinduism softened. Hindus admitted the legitimacy of many of the Buddha's reforms, and in imitation of the Buddhist *sangha* orders of Hindu *sadhus* (wandering ascetics) came into existence. From the other side, Buddhist teachings came to sound increasingly like Hindu ones as Buddhism opened into the Mahayana, until in the end Buddhism sank back into the source from which it had sprung.

Only if one assumes that Buddhist principles left no mark on subsequent Hinduism can the merger be considered a Buddhist defeat. Actually, almost all of Buddhism's affirmative doctrines found their place or parallel. Its contributions, accepted by Hindus in principle if not always practice, included its renewed emphasis on kindness to all living things, on non-killing of animals, on the elimination of caste barriers in matters religious and their reduction in matters social, and its strong ethical emphasis generally. The *bodhisattva* ideal seems to have left its mark in prayers like the following by Santi Deva in the great Hindu devotional classic, the *Bhagavatam:*

> *I desire not of the Lord the greatness which comes by the attainment of the eightfold powers, nor do I pray him that I may not be born again; my one prayer to him is that I may feel the pain of others, as if I were residing within their bodies, and that I may have the power of relieving their pain and making them happy.*

All in all, the Buddha was reclaimed as "a rebel child of Hinduism"; he was even raised to the status of a divine incarnation. The goal of Theravada Buddhism was acknowledged to be substantially that of non-dual Hinduism, and even the *Prajnaparamita's* contention that eternity is not other than the present moment found its Hindu counterpart:

> *This very world is a mansion of mirth;*
> *Here I can eat, here drink and make merry. (Ramakrishna)*

Especially in Hindu Tantric schools, disciples were brought to the point where they could see meat, wine, and sex—things that had formerly appeared as the most formidable barriers to the divine—as but varying forms of God. "The Mother is present in every house. Need I break the news as one breaks an earthen pot on the floor."[62]

Suggestions for Further Reading

Although written in the 1920s, J. B. Pratt's *The Pilgrimage of Buddhism and a Buddhist Pilgrimage* (New York: AMS Press, 1928) remains a comprehensive, readable account of this religion. More recent and accessible is Richard Robinson and Willard Johnson's *The Buddhist Religion* (Belmont, CA: Wadsworth Publishing Co., 1982).

Edward Conze's *Buddhist Scriptures* (Baltimore: Penguin Books, 1959) selects wisely from original texts.

Vipassana, the insight meditation practice of Theravada Buddhism, is nicely introduced to Westerners through Joseph Goldstein's *The Experience of Insight* (Boston, MA: Shambala, 1987).

Two very different books on Zen that complement each other beautifully are Philip Kapleau's *The Three Pillars of Zen* (New York: Anchor Books, 1989) and Shunryu Suzuki's *Zen Mind, Beginner's Mind* (New York: John Weatherhill, 1970).

Lama Anagarika Govinda's *Foundations of Tibetan Mysticism* (York Beach, ME: Samuel Weiser, 1969) presents the theory of Tibetan Buddhism, while Marco Pallis's *Peaks and Lamas* (London: The Woburn Press, 1974) is one of the finest spiritual travelogues ever written.

My half-hour videotape on Tibetan Buddhism, "Requiem for a Faith," makes available the audiovisual dimensions of the Vajrayana as described in "The Diamond Thunderbolt" section of this chapter. It can be secured from The Hartley Film Foundation, Cat Rock Road, Cos Cob, CT 06807.

Notes

1. The word in the case of Jesus was different, but the direction of the question was the same.
2. Cf. Clarence H. Hamilton, *Buddhism: A Religion of Infinite Compassion,* 1952. Reprint. (New York: The Liberal Arts Press, 1954), 14–15.

3. Cf. Hamilton, *Buddhism*, 3–4.

4. Quoted from *Digha Nikaya* in J. B. Pratt, *The Pilgrimage of Buddhism and a Buddhist Pilgrimage* (New York: AMS Press, 1928), 10.

5. Related in Pratt, *The Pilgrimage*, 12.

6. Quoted in Pratt, *The Pilgrimage*, 8.

7. Quoted in Pratt, *The Pilgrimage*, 9.

8. Quoted in Pratt, *The Pilgrimage*, 10.

9. *Majjhima* LXXII. Quoted in Pratt, *The Pilgrimage*, 13.

10. William James, *The Varieties of Religious Experience* (New York: Macmillan, 1961).

11. Quoted in B. L. Suzuki, *Mahayana Buddhism*, 1948. Rev. ed. (London: Allen & Unwin, 1981), 2.

12. E. A Burtt, *The Teachings of the Compassionate Buddha* (New York: Mentor Books, 1955), 49–50.

13. Burtt, *Teachings*, 18.

14. See, for example, Burtt, *Teachings*, 32.

15. I have paraphrased slightly the discourse as it appears in *Majjhima Nikaya*, Sutta 63, as translated by E. J. Thomas in *Early Buddhist Scriptures* (New York: AMS Press, 1935), 64–67.

16. Quoted in F. L. Woodward, *Some Sayings of the Buddha* (London: Gordon Press, 1939), 283.

17. Quoted in Burtt, *Teachings*, 50.

18. Quoted in Christmas Humphreys, *Buddhism* (Harmondsworth, England: Pelican Books, 1951), 120.

19. Quoted in Woodward, *Some Sayings*, 283.

20. Quoted in A. Coomaraswamy, *Hinduism and Buddhism* (New York: The Philosophical Library, 1943), 62.

21. Woodward, *Some Sayings*, 294.

22. Burtt, *Teachings*, 49.

23. Sir Edwin Arnold, *The Light of Asia*, 1879. Reprint. (Los Angeles: Theosophy Co., 1977).

24. Robert Penn Warren, *Brother to Dragons* (New York: Random House, 1979).

25. Sigmund Freud, *General Introduction to Psychoanalysis* (New York: Liverwright, 1935), 344.

26. Humphreys, *Buddhism*, 91.

27. Quoted in Pratt, *The Pilgrimage*, 40.

28. *Anguttara Nikaya*, 8:83.

29. Lew Ayres, *Altars of the East* (Garden City, NY: Doubleday, 1956), 90–91. Slightly adapted.

30. Precisely this indescribable character of *nirvana* caused later Buddhists to speak of it as *shunyata* or emptiness. It is void, but not in the absolute sense. Rather, it is *de*void of finite, specifiable features, in something of the way the suprasonic is lacking in sounds our ears can register.

31. Quoted in Burtt, *Teachings*, 115.

32. *Iti-vuttaka*, 43; *Udana* VIII, 3. Cf. Pratt, *The Pilgrimage*, 88–89, and Burtt, *Teachings*, 113.

33. Edward Conze, *Buddhism: Its Essence and Development*, 1951. Reprint. (New York: Harper & Row).

34. Compare, for example, its relation to Paul Tillich's "God above God" in *The Courage to Be* (New Haven, CT: The Yale University Press, 1952), 186–190.

35. *Vairacchedika*, 32.

36. This, in passing, was one of the ways in which the Buddha's understanding of reincarnation differed from that of most Hindus of his day. The standard Hindu doctrine attributed rebirth to *karma*, the consequences of actions set in motion during previous lives. As these actions were innumerable, innumerable lives were assumed to be needed to work off these consequences. Characteristically, the Buddha took a more psychological view. Rebirth, he maintained, was due not to *karma* but to *tanha*. As long as the wish to be a separate self persisted, that wish would be granted. It follows that since desire is the key, it is possible to step permanently out of the cycle of rebirth whenever one wishes wholeheartedly to do so.

37. Quoted in Pratt, *The Pilgrimage*, 86.

38. Quoted in Pratt, *The Pilgrimage*, 91.

39. The Tibetan version holds that the Buddha explicitly preached the Mahayana doctrines but in his "glorified body" *(sambogakaya)*, which only the most advanced disciples could perceive.

40. From the *Bodhichayavatara* of Shantideva.

41. Though Mahayana honors wisdom as conducing to compassion.

42. If it seems like mixing politics and religion to say this, we should realize a point that this book, focusing as it does on metaphysics, psychology, and ethics, does not go into; namely, that the great religions entered history, not so much as religions in the narrow meaning of that word, but rather as civilizations. Each staked out for its adherents an entire way of life—a lifeworld that encompassed not only things that we now consider distinctively religious, but also regions of life that the modern world divides into economics, politics, ethics, law, art, philosophy, and education.

43. This section, begun under the influence of Dr. D. T. Suzuki's writings and person, received its final shape from six weeks of Zen training in Kyoto during the summer of 1957—weeks that included daily *sanzen* (consultation concerning meditation) with the eminent Zen master Goto Roshi; celebration of *Gematsu O-Sesshin* (eight days of looking into mind and heart) with monks in the monastery of Myoshinji (Temple of the Marvelous Mind); access to the manuscripts of the Kyoto branch of the First Zen Institute of America; and a number of important conversations with its then director, Ruth Fuller Sasaki.

44. A Western professor, wishing to show that he had grasped Zen's determination to transcend forms, expressed surprise when the abbot of the temple he was visiting bowed reverently to images of the Buddha as they passed

them. "I thought you were beyond such things," he said, adding, "I am; why I would just as soon spit on these images." "Very well," said the abbot in his not quite perfect English. "You spits. I bow."

45. Because of the extent to which reason was interfering with this author's Zen practice, his teacher, Goto Roshi, diagnosed him with having contracted "the philosopher's disease." Immediately, though, he retracted, acknowledging that there was nothing wrong with philosophy as such; he himself had a master's degree in philosophy from one of the better Japanese universities. "However," he continued, "reason can only work with the experience that is available to it. You obviously know how to reason. What you lack is the experience to reason wisely from. For these weeks put reason aside and work for experience."

46. The two are *Soto*, stemming from Dogen, who imported the *Ts'ao-tung* school of Ch'an from China; and *Rinzai*, the Japanese version of the *Lin-chi* school, which Eisai introduced to Japan. The former considers enlightenment a gradual process, whereas the latter contends that it is sudden.

47. I was told that the shortest time on record in which a *koan* (see the next sentence of the text) was solved was overnight, and the longest time was twelve years.

48. Dylan Thomas, "Light Breaks Where No Sun Shines."
    *Koan*s are actually of different types, geared to the stages in the students' progress. As the mind must work differently according to the kind of *koan* it is assigned, a phenomenonological description of the entire sweep of *koan* study would be complex. What I have said here applies to early *koan*s. Miura Roshi and Ruth Fuller Sasaki's *Zen Dust* (New York: Harcourt, Brace & World, 1967) presents a comprehensive account of *koan* training.

49. Quoted in *Cat's Yawn* (New York: The First Zen Institute of America, 1947), 32.

50. Quoted in *Zen Notes* (New York: The First Zen Institute of America [vol. 1, no. 5]), 1.

51. A great master, Dai Osho, reported, "I have experienced Great *Satori* eighteen times, and lost count of the number of small *satoris* I have had."

52. Sasaki, *Zen Dust*.

53. From *The Sayings of the Lay Disciple Ho*. Not published in English.

54. Abridged from D. T. Suzuki's translation in Edward Conze, ed., *Buddhist Scriptures* (Baltimore: Penguin Books, 1973), 171–75.

55. From "Zen—A Religion," an unpublished essay by Ruth Fuller Sasaki.

56. The word the Tibetans used to translate the Sanskrit word *vajra* was *dorje*, which literally meant chief stone *(dorj*, stone; *je*, chief).

57. For a discussion of this point, see Jeffrey Hopkins, *The Tantric Distinction: An Introduction to Tibetan Buddhism* (London: Wisdom Books, 1984), 148–49.

58. I am describing the rituals of Gyume and Gyutö, the two highest Tantric colleges in Tibet, now in exile in India. For particulars relating to their

exceptional chanting, see Huston Smith, "Can One Voice Sing a Chord?" *The Boston Globe* (January 26, 1969); with Kenneth Stevens, "Unique Vocal Ability of Certain Tibetan Lamas," *American Anthropologist* 69 (April 1967): 2; and with K. Stevens and R. Tomlinson, "On an Unusual Mode of Chanting by Certain Tibetan Lamas," *Journal of the Accoustical Society of America* 41 (May 1967): 5.

59. *Majjhima-Nikaya*, 3.2.22.135.
60. Cf. Edward Conze, *Buddhism: Its Essence and Development*, n.d. Reprint. (New York: Harper & Row, 1959), 136.
61. These lines, from Hakuin's "Song in Praise of Zazen," do not come directly from the *Prajnaparamita Sutra* but clearly echo its theme.
62. Ramprasad. Quoted in H. Zimmer, *The Philosophies of India*, 1951. Reprint. (Princeton, NJ: Princeton University Press, 1969), 602.

IV. Confucianism

The First Teacher

If there is one name with which Chinese culture has been associated it is Confucius'— Kung Fu-tzu or Kung the Master. Chinese reverently speak of him as the First Teacher—not that there were no teachers before him, but because he stands first in rank. No one claims that he crafted Chinese culture singlehandedly, and he himself played down his originality by claiming to be no more than "a lover of the ancients."[1] This designation, however, gives him less than his due; it stands as an example of the modesty and reticence he advocated. For though Confucius did not author Chinese culture, he was its supreme editor. Winnowing the past, underscoring here, playing down or discarding there, reordering and annotating throughout, he brought his culture to a focus that has remained remarkably distinct for twenty-five centuries.

The reader who supposes that such an achievement could come only from a dramatic life will be disappointed. Confucius was born around 551 B.C. in the principality of Lu in what is now Shantung province. We know nothing for certain about his ancestors, but it is clear that his early home life was modest. "When young, I was without rank and in humble circumstances." His father died before Confucius was three, leaving his upbringing to a loving but impoverished mother. Financially, therefore, he was forced to make his own way, at first through menial tasks. The hardship and poverty of these early years gave him a tie with the common people, which was to be reflected in the democratic tenor of his entire philosophy.

Though reminiscences of his boyhood contain nostalgic references to hunting, fishing, and archery, thereby suggesting that he was anything but a bookworm, he took early to his studies and did well in them. "On reaching the age of fifteen, I bent my mind to learning." In his early twenties, having held several insignificant government posts and contracted a not too successful marriage, he established himself as a tutor. This was obviously his vocation. The reputation of his personal qualities and practical wisdom spread rapidly, attracting a circle of ardent disciples.

Despite these disciples' conviction that "since the beginning of the human race there has never been a man like our Master," Confucius' career was, in terms of his own ambitions, a failure. His goal was public office, for he believed — how wrongly we shall see — that his theories would not take hold unless he showed that they worked. He had supreme confidence in his ability to reorder society if given a chance. Being told of the growth of population in the state of Wei and asked what should be done, he answered, "Enrich them." And after that? "Educate them," was his famous reply, adding with a sigh, "Were a prince to employ me, in a year something could be done, and in three years the work could be completed!" Doting biographers, unable to conceive that a man so gifted could remain permanently blocked in his life's ambition, credit him with five years of brilliant administration in his early fifties, years in which he is pictured as advancing rapidly from Minister of Public Works through Minister of Justice to Prime Minister, during which Lu became a model state. Dissoluteness and dishonesty hid their heads, the romanticized account continues. "A thing dropped in the streets was not picked up," and loyalty and good faith became the order of the day. The truth is that contemporary rulers were much too afraid of Confucius' candor and integrity to appoint him to any position involving power. When his reputation rose to the point where the ruler of his own state, who had gained his power through usurpation, felt obliged to ask him perfunctorily for advice on how to rule, Confucius replied, tartly, that he had better learn to govern himself before trying to govern others. The ruler did not have him cut into pieces, as he might have done save for Confucius' reputation, but neither did he appoint him prime minister. Instead he tossed him an honorific post with an exalted title but no authority, hoping thus to keep him quiet. Needless to say, once Confucius discovered the ploy he resigned in disgust.

Prompted as if by call —"At fifty I perceived the divine mission"—
he gave his next thirteen years, with many a backward look and resisting footstep, to "the long trek," in which he wandered from state to
state proffering unsolicited advice to rulers on how to improve their
governing and seeking a real opportunity to put his ideas into practice. The opportunity never came; a bystander's prediction as he set
out that "Heaven is going to use the Master as a bell to rouse the people" turned to mockery as the years slipped by. Once he was offered
an official position in the state of Chen, but finding that the official
who issued the invitation was in rebellion against his chief, he
refused to become a party to the intrigue. The dignity and saving
humor with which he carried himself during these difficult years
does great credit to his person. Taunted once by a bystander: "Great
indeed is Confucius! He knows about everything and has made no
name in anything," Confucius responded to his disciples in mock dis-
may: "Now what shall I take up? Charioteering? Archery?" As state
after state disregarded his counsels of peace and concern for the people, recluses and hermits sneered at his efforts to reform society and
advised him to join their quest for a self-mastery sufficient to offset
the ills of a society beyond redemption. Even peasants criticized him
as "a man who knows he cannot succeed but keeps on trying." Only
a small band of faithful disciples stood by him through rebuff, discouragement, and near starvation. Once the records give us a picture
of them together, Confucius' heart swelling with happiness and pride
as he looked at them — Ming Tzu so calm in reserved strength, Tzu Lu
so full of energy, Jan Ch'iu and Tzu Kung so frank and fearless.

In time, with a change of administration in his own state, he was
invited to return. There, recognizing that he was now too old for
office anyway, he spent his last five years quietly teaching and editing
the classics of China's past. In 479 B.C., at the age of seventy-two,
he died.

A failure as a politician, Confucius was undoubtedly one of the
world's greatest teachers. Prepared to instruct in history, poetry, government, propriety, mathematics, music, divination, and sports, he
was, in the manner of Socrates, a one-man university. His method of
teaching was likewise Socratic. Always informal, he seems not to have
lectured but instead to have conversed on problems his students
posed, citing readings and asking questions. He was particularly
skilled at the latter: "The Master's way of asking — how different it is

from that of others!" The openness with which he interacted with his students was likewise striking. Not for a moment assuming that he was a sage himself, sagehood being for him not a stock of knowledge but quality in comportment, he presented himself to his students as their fellow traveler, committed to the task of becoming fully human but modest in how far he had gotten with that task.

> There are four things in the Way of the profound person, none of which I have been able to do. To serve my father as I would expect my son to serve me. To serve my ruler as I would expect my ministers to serve me. To serve my elder brother as I would expect my younger brothers to serve me. To be the first to treat friends as I would expect them to treat me. These I have not been able to do.[2]

At the same time, on the importance of the task on which he was embarked, he was uncompromising. This led him to expect much from his students, for he saw the cause in which he was enrolling them as nothing less than the redressing of the entire social order. This conviction made him a zealot, but humor and a sense of proportion preserved him from being a fanatic. When the skeptic Tsai Wo proposed derisively, "If someone said there is a man in the well, the altruist, I suppose, would go after him," Confucius remarked that "even an altruist would first make certain there really was a man down the well!" When someone was recommended to him as "thinking thrice before he took action," Confucius replied dryly, "Twice is sufficient." Confident as he was, he was always ready to admit that he might be wrong, and, when it was the case, that he had been mistaken.

There was nothing other-worldly about him. He loved to be with people, to dine out, to join in the chorus of a good song, and to drink, though not in excess. His disciples reported that "When at leisure the Master's manner was informal and cheerful. He was affable, yet firm; dignified yet pleasant." His democratic attitudes have already been remarked upon. Not only was he always ready to champion the cause of common people against the oppressive nobility of his day; in his personal relations he cut "scandalously" across class lines and never slighted his poorer students even when they could pay him nothing. He was kind, though capable of sarcasm when he thought it deserved. Of one who had taken to criticizing his companions, Confucius observed, "Obviously Tzu Kung must have become quite perfect himself to have time for this sort of thing. I do not have this much leisure."

It was true, for he remained to the end more exacting of himself than he was of others. "How dare I allow myself to be taken as sage and humane!" he said. "It may rather be said of me that I strive to become such without satiety."[3] He remained faithful to the quest. Power and wealth could have been his for the asking if he had been willing to compromise with those in authority. He preferred, instead, his integrity. He never regretted the choice. "With coarse food to eat, water to drink, and my bended arm for a pillow, I still have joy in the midst of these things. Riches and honors acquired by unrighteousness mean no more to me than the floating clouds."

With his death began his glorification. Among his disciples the move was immediate. Said Tzu Kung, "He is the sun, the moon, which there is no way of climbing over. The impossibility of equalling our Master is like the impossibility of reaching the sky by scaling a ladder." Others came to agree. Within a few generations he was regarded throughout China as "the mentor and model of ten thousand generations." What would have pleased him more was the attention given to his ideas. Until this century, every Chinese school child for two thousand years raised his clasped hands each morning toward a table in the schoolroom that bore a plaque bearing Confucius' name. Virtually every Chinese student has pored over his sayings for hours, with the result that they have become a part of the Chinese mind and trickled down to the illiterate in spoken proverbs. Chinese government, too, has been influenced by him, more deeply than by any other figure. Since the start of the Christian era a large number of governmental offices, including some of the highest, have required of their occupants a knowledge of the Confucian classics. There have been a number of attempts, some of them quasi-official, to elevate him to the stature of divinity.

What produced this influence? — so great that until the Communist takeover observers were still regarding Confucianism as "the greatest single intellectual force" among one-quarter of the world's population. It could hardly have been his personality. Exemplary as this was, it was too undramatic to explain his historical impact. If we turn instead to his teachings, our puzzle only deepens. As edifying anecdotes and moral maxims, they are thoroughly commendable. But how a collection of sayings so patently didactic, so pedestrian that they often appear commonplace, could have molded a civilization, appears at first glance to be one of history's enigmas. Here are some samples:

> Is not he a true philosopher who, though he be unrecognized, cherishes no resentment?
>
> What you do not wish done to yourself, do not do to others.
>
> I will not grieve that others do not know me. I will grieve that I do not know others.
>
> Do not wish for quick results, nor look for small advantages. If you seek quick results, you will not attain the ultimate goal. If you are led astray by small advantages, you will never accomplish great things.
>
> Nobler persons first practice what they preach and afterwards preach according to their practice. If, when you look into your own heart, you find nothing wrong there, what is there to worry about. What is there to fear?
>
> When you know a thing, to recognize that you know it; and when you do not, to know that you do not know—that is knowledge.
>
> To go too far is as bad as to fall short.
>
> When you see someone of worth, think of how you may emulate. When you see someone unworthy, examine your own character.
>
> Wealth and rank are what people desire, but unless they be obtained in the right way they may not be possessed.
>
> Feel kindly toward everyone, but be intimate only with the virtuous. [4]

There is certainly nothing to take exception to in such observations. But where is their power?

The Problem Confucius Faced

For the clue to Confucius' power and influence, we must see both his life and his teaching against the background of the problem he faced. This was the problem of social anarchy.

Early China had been neither more nor less turbulent than other lands. The eighth to the third centuries B.C., however, witnessed a collapse of the Chou Dynasty's ordering power. Rival baronies were left to their own devices, creating a precise parallel to conditions in Palestine in the period of the Judges: "In those days there was no king in Israel; every man did what was right in his own eyes."

The almost continuous warfare of the age began in the pattern of chivalry. The chariot was its weapon, courtesy its code, and acts of generosity were accorded high honor. Confronted with invasion, a baron would send in bravado a convoy of provisions to the invading army. Or to prove that his men were beyond fear and intimidation, he would send, as messengers to his invader, soldiers who would slit their throats in his presence. As in the Homeric age, warriors of opposing armies, recognizing each other, would exchange haughty compliments from their chariots, drink together, and even trade weapons before doing battle.

By Confucius' time, however, the interminable warfare had degenerated from chivalry toward the unrestrained horror of the Period of the Warring States. The horror reached its height in the century following Confucius' death. Contests between charioteers gave way to cavalry, with its surprise attacks and sudden raids. Instead of nobly holding their prisoners for ransom, conquerors put them to death in mass executions. Whole populations unlucky enough to be captured were beheaded, including women, children, and the aged. We read of mass slaughters of 60,000, 80,000, and even 400,000. There are accounts of the conquered being thrown into boiling cauldrons and their relatives forced to drink the human soup.

In such an age the question that eclipsed all others was: How can we keep from destroying ourselves? Answers differed, but the question was always the same. With the invention and proliferation of weapons of ever-increasing destructiveness, it is a question that in the twentieth century has come to haunt the entire world.

As the clue to the power of Confucianism lies in its answer to this problem of social cohesion, we need to see that problem in historical perspective. Confucius lived at a time when social cohesion had deteriorated to a critical point. The glue was no longer holding. What had held society together up to then?

Before life reached the human level, the answer was obvious. The glue that holds the pack, the herd, the hive together is instinct. The cooperation it produces among ants and bees is legendary, but throughout the subhuman world generally it can be counted on to ensure reasonable cooperation. There is plenty of violence in nature, but on the whole it is between species, not within them. Within the species an inbuilt gregariousness, the "herd instinct," keeps life stable.

With the emergence of the human species, this automatic source of social cohesion disappears. Man being "the animal without instincts," no inbuilt mechanism can be counted on to keep life intact. What is now to hold anarchy in check? In the infancy of the species the answer was spontaneous tradition, or as the anthropologists sometimes say, "the cake of custom." Through generations of trial and error, certain ways of behaving prove to contribute to the tribe's well-being. Councils do not sit down to decide what the tribe wants and what behavior patterns will secure those wants; patterns simply take shape over centuries, during which generations fumble their way toward satisfying mores and away from destructive ones. Once the patterns becomes established — societies that fail to evolve viable ones presumably read themselves out of existence, for none have remained for anthropologists to study — they are transmitted from generation to generation unthinkingly. As the Romans would say, they are passed on to the young *cum lacte*, "with the mother's milk."

Modern life has moved so far from the tradition-bound life of tribal societies as to make it difficult for us to realize how completely it is possible for mores to be in control. There are not many areas in which custom continues to reach into our lives to dictate our behavior, but dress and attire remains one of them. Guidelines are weakening even here, but it is still pretty much the case that if a corporation executive were to forget his necktie, he would have trouble getting through the day. Indecent exposure would not be the problem; he would simply have transgressed convention — his profession's assumed (but for the most part not explicitly stated) dress code. This would immediately target him as an outsider; he would be suspected of aberrant, if not subversive, proclivities. His associates would regard him out of the corners of their eyes as — well, different. And this is not a comfortable way to be seen, which is what gives custom its power. Someone has ventured that in a woman's certitude that she is wearing precisely the right thing for the occasion, there is a peace that religion can neither give nor take away.

If we generalize to all areas of life this power of tradition, which we now seldom feel outside matters of attire, we shall have a picture of the tradition-oriented life of tribal societies. Two things about this life are of particular interest here. The first is its phenomenal capacity to keep asocial acts in check. There are tribes among the Eskimos and the Australian aborigines that do not even have words for disobedience. The second impressive thing is the spontaneous, unthinking way socialization by this means proceeds. No laws are formulated with penalties attached; no plans for the moral education of children intentionally devised. Group expectations are so strong and uncompromising that the young internalize them without question or deliberation. The Greenlanders have no conscious program of education, nevertheless anthropologists report that their children are impressively obedient, good-natured, and ready to help. American Indians are still living who remember a time when in their regions' social controls were entirely internal. "There were no laws then. Everybody did what was right."[5]

In early China, custom and tradition probably likewise provided sufficient cohesion to keep the community intact. Vivid evidence of its power has come down to us. There is, for example, the recorded case of a noble lady who was burned to death in a palace fire because she refused to violate convention and leave the house without a chaperon. The historian—a contemporary of Confucius—who reported the incident glosses it in a way that shows that convention had lost some of its force in his thinking but was still very much intact. He suggests that if the lady had been unmarried, her conduct would have been beyond question. But as she was not only a married woman but an elderly one at that, it might not have been "altogether unfitting under the circumstances" for her to have left the burning mansion unaccompanied.[6]

The historian's sensitivity to the past is stronger than most; not everyone in Confucius' day gave even as much ear to tradition as did the reporter just cited. China had reached a new point in its social evolution, a point marked by the emergence of large numbers of individuals in the full sense of that word. Self-conscious rather than group-conscious, these individuals had ceased to think of themselves primarily in the first person plural and were thinking in the first person singular. Reason was replacing social conventions, and self-interest outdistancing the expectations of the group. The fact that others were behaving in a given way or that their ancestors had done so from time immemorial could no longer be relied on as sufficient reason for individuals to follow suit. Proposals for action had now to face peoples' question, "What's in it for me?"

The old mortar that had held society together was chipping and flaking. In working their way out of the "cake of custom," individuals had cracked that cake beyond repair. The rupture did not occur overnight; in history nothing begins or ends on time's knife-edge, least of all cultural change. The first individualists were probably wild mutants, lonely eccentrics who raised strange questions and resisted group identification not out of caprice but from the simple inability to feel themselves completely one with the gang. But individualism and self-consciousness are contagious. Once they appear, they spread like epidemic and wildfire. Unreflective solidarity is a thing of the past.

Rival Answers

When tradition is no longer adequate to hold society together, human life faces the gravest crisis it has encountered. It is a crisis the modern world should have no difficulty in understanding, for in recent years it has returned to haunt humanity in an acute form. The United States provides the clearest example. A genius for absorbing peoples of varying national and ethnic backgrounds has earned for her the reputation of being a melting pot; but in weakening the traditions that immigrant groups brought with them, the United States has not provided them with a compelling replacement. This leaves the nation perhaps the most traditionless society history has known. As the alternative to tradition, the United States has proposed reason. Educate citizens and inform them, and they can be counted on to behave sensibly—this is the Jeffersonian-Enlightenment faith on which the United States was founded. It has not been fulfilled. Until recently the world's leader in education, the United States leads likewise in crime, delinquency, and divorce.

With the Enlightenment's answer to the problem of human coherence having still to vindicate itself, it is of more than antiquarian interest to look at the options that ancient China proposed. One of these was put forward by the Realists.[7] What do you do when people don't behave? Hit them. It is a classic answer to a classic question. What people understand best is force. Once individuals emerge from the chrysalis of tradition and start to steer their lives by reason, the pull of passion and self-interest is so strong that only the threat of heavy reprisal will keep them in line. Prate as you please of reason and morality, in the last analysis it is brute force that carries the day. The only way to avoid universal violence in a society composed of self-seeking individuals is to maintain an effective militia that stands ready to bat people back in line when they transgress. There must be laws that state clearly what is and is not permitted, and penalties for violation must be such that no one will dare to incur them. In short, the Realists' answer to the problem of social order was: laws with teeth in them. It was essentially the answer Hobbes was to propose in the West. Left to the devices of individuals, with no absolute hand to restrain their self-seeking, life is "nasty, brutish, and above all, short."

The application of the Realists' philosophy of social order proceeded by way of an elaborate mechanism of "penalties and rewards." Those who did what the state commanded were to be rewarded; those who did not were to be punished. Given this approach, the list of laws obviously had to be long and detailed — pious generalities, which could be bent out of shape by self-seeking interpretations, would not do. "If a law is too concise," said Han Fei Tzu, the leading spokesman for the Realists, "the common people dispute its intentions. An enlightened ruler, when he makes his laws, sees to it that every contingency is provided for in detail.[8] Not only must the requirements of law be spelled out; penalties for infractions should likewise be clearly specified. And they should be heavy. "Idealists," Han Fei Tzu continues, "are always telling us that punishments should be light. This is the way to bring about confusion and ruin. The object of rewards is to encourage; that of punishments, to prevent. If rewards are high, then what the ruler wants will be quickly effected; if punishments are heavy, what he does not want will be swiftly prevented."

The estimate of human nature from which this political philosophy proceeded was obviously low. It was low in two ways. First, it assumed that base impulses predominate over noble ones. People are naturally lustful, greedy, and jealous. Goodness, if it is to emerge, must be built into them as wood is straightened in a press. "Ordinary people are lazy; it is natural to them to shirk hard work and to delight in idleness."[9] Many will feign moral attitudes when they think these will enable them to get ahead; indeed, a country may reek with sham morality and faked altruism. But when push comes to shove, self-interest will out.

The second way the Realists' view of human nature was low was in judging people to be short-sighted. Rulers must envision the long-term good, but subjects are not capable of this. Consequently, they will not voluntarily accept present sacrifices as necessary for future gains. Suppose a baby has a scalp disease. "If the baby's head is not shaved, there is a return of its malady; if a boil is not lanced, it will go on growing. But while such things are being done to it, though someone holds it close and soothes it and its own mother lovingly performs these operations, the child will nevertheless scream and howl the whole while, not understanding at all that the small pain to which it is being subjected will result in a great gain."[10] Similarly, the masses "want security, but hate the means that produce security." If they are allowed to follow the promptings of immediate pleasure, they will soon be victims of the pains they most dread; whereas if they are made to accept some things they currently dislike, they will be brought in the end to the pleasures they want.

This low estimate of human nature in general did not lead the Realists to deny that nobler sentiments exist. They simply doubted that these were in sufficient supply to keep the state in order. Occasional geniuses appear who are able to draw perfect circles freehand, but can wheel-making wait on these? One person in a thousand may be scrupulously honest, but of what use are these few when millions are involved? For the millions, audits are indispensable. One ruler in a thousand might be able to inspire a people to live cooperatively without sanctions; but to tell the Chinese people, caught as they were in the Period of the Warring States, to wait for another model ruler of the order of the legendary heroes of the past, is like telling a man who is drowning in Middle China to hope that a skilled swimmer from the border provinces will materialize to save him.

Life is hard. We may wish that it were not, but wishing does not change realities.

> *No lake so still but that it has its wave;*
> *No circle so perfect but that it has its blur.*
> *I would change things for you if I could;*
> *As I can't, you must take them as they are.*

The harsh facts of existence call for unwavering realism, for compromises annul action by trying to move two ways at once. "Ice and embers cannot lie in the same bowl."

Actually, a social philosophy as different from the Realists' as fire from ice did exist alongside it in Confucius' China. Known as Mohism after its principal spokesman, Mo Tzu or Mo Ti, it proposed as the solution to China's social problem not force but love—universal love (*chien ai*).[11] One should "feel toward all people under heaven exactly as one feels toward one's own people, and regard other states exactly as one regards one's own state."

> *Mutual attacks among states, mutual usurpation among houses, mutual injuries among individuals, these are [among] the major calamities in the world.*
>
> *But whence do these calamities arise?*
>
> *They arise out of want of mutual love. At present, feudal lords have learned only to love their own state and not those of others. Therefore they do not scruple about attacking other states. The heads of houses have learned only to love their own houses and not those of others. Therefore they do not scruple about usurping other houses. And individuals have learned only to love themselves and not others. Therefore they do not scruple about injuring others. Therefore all the calamities, strifes, complaints, and hatred in the world have arisen out of want of mutual love. . . .*
>
> *How can we have the condition altered?*
>
> *It is to be altered by the way of universal love and mutual aid.*
>
> *But what is the way of universal love and mutual aid?*
>
> *It is to regard the state of others as one's own, the houses of others as one's own, the persons of others as one's self. When all the people in the world love one another, then the strong will not overpower the weak, the many will not oppress the few, the wealthy will not mock the poor, the honored will not disdain the humble, and the cunning will not deceive the simple. And it is all due to mutual love that calamities, strifes, complaints, and hatred are prevented from arising.*[12]

Mo Tzu simply disagreed with charges that his emphasis on love was sentimental and impractical. "If it were not useful, even I would disapprove of it. But how can there be anything that is good but not useful?" It may have been the radicalness of Mo Tzu's position that led him to believe that it was backed by Shang Ti, the Sovereign on High, a personal god who "loves people dearly; ordered the sun, the moon, and the stars; sent down snow, frost, rain, and dew; established the hills and rivers, ravines and valleys; appointed dukes and lords to reward the virtuous and punish the wicked. Heaven loves the whole world universally. Everything is prepared for the good of human beings." [13]

As love is obviously good, and the God who orders the world is good as well, it is inconceivable that we have a world in which love does not pay. For "whoever loves others is loved by others; whoever benefits others is benefited by others; whoever injures others is injured by others." [14]

Confucius' Answer

Neither of these rival answers to the problem of social cohesion impressed Confucius. [15] He rejected the Realists' answer of force because it was clumsy and external. Force regulated by law can set limits to peoples' dealings, but it is too crude to inspire their day-to-day, face-to-face exchanges. With regard to the family, for example, it can stipulate conditions of marriage and divorce, but it cannot generate love and companionship. This holds generally. Governments need what they cannot themselves provide: meaning and motivation.

As for the Mohists' reliance on love, Confucius agreed with the Realists in dismissing it as utopian. A. C. Graham testifies to the decisiveness of Confucius' victory on this point when he observes that in retrospect "Mohism has the appearance of being foreign, not merely to Confucian thinking, but to the whole of Chinese civilization. No one else finds it tolerable to insist that you should be as concerned for the other man's family as for your own." [16] That love has an important place in life, we shall be hearing Confucius insist; but it must be supported by social structures and a collective ethos. To harp exclusively on love is to preach ends without means. Putting it this way helps us to appreciate Confucius' conviction that the Realists and Mohists were equally mistaken, but in opposite ways. The Realists thought that governments could establish peace and harmony through the laws and force that are their domain. Mohists went to the opposite extreme; they assumed that personal commitment could do the job. This overlooks the fact that different circumstances and relationships prompt different sentiments and legitimize different responses. When asked, "Should one love one's enemy, those who do us harm?" Confucius replied, "By no means. Answer hatred with justice, and love with benevolence. Otherwise you would waste your benevolence." Confucius' foremost disciple, Mencius, used this same logic to reject Mo Tzu's call "to love all equally." In ignoring the special affection members of one's own family inspire, Mo Tzu showed himself to be unrealistic.

The West's current approach to the social problem—through the cultivation of reason—probably did not occur to Confucius. If it had he would have dismissed it as not thought through. Those who hold an evolutionary view of intelligence, seeing it as increasing over the centuries, may argue that this was because he was dealing with society in its immaturity—when, like an adolescent, it was too old to spank but too young to reason with. It is more probable that insofar as this issue entered his consciousness at all, Confucius assumed that the mind operates in a context of attitudes and emotions that are conditioned by the individual's group relationships. Unless experiences in this latter area dispose one to cooperate, upgraded reason is likely to do nothing but aid self-interest. Confucius was no child of the Enlightenment. He was closer to philosophers and psychologists who recognize that altruism is not much engendered by exhortation.

Taking this for granted, Confucius was all but obsessed with tradition, for he saw it as the chief shaper of inclinations and attitudes. He loved tradition because he saw it as a potential conduit—one that could funnel into the present behavior patterns that had been perfected during a golden age in China's past, the Age of the Grand Harmony. Because mores were then compelling, people conformed to them; because they were finely wrought, the conformation brought peace and happiness. Confucius may have idealized, even romanticized, this period when China was passing from the second millennium into the first and the Chou Dynasty was at its zenith. Unquestionably, he envied it and wished to replicate it as faithfully as he could. Tradition appeared to him to be the device for appropriating from this glorious past prescriptions that could serve his own troubled times.

Current social theorists would commend his line of thought: Socialization, they tell us, *has to be transmitted from the old to the young, and the habits and the ideas must be maintained as a seamless web of memory among the bearers of the tradition, generation after generation. . . . When the continuity of the traditions of civility is ruptured, the community is threatened. Unless the rupture is repaired, the community will break down into factional . . . wars. For when the continuity is interrupted, the cultural heritage is not being transmitted. The new generation is faced with the task of rediscovering and reinventing and relearning by trial and error most of what [it] needs to know. . . . No one generation can do this.*[17]

Confucius spoke a different language, but he was working on this exact theme.

His regard, even reverence, for the past did not make him an antiquarian. He knew that changes had occurred that precluded the possibility of returning literally to the past. The year 500 B.C. was separated from the year 1000 (to use round numbers) by the Chinese having become individuals. They were now self-conscious and reflective. This being the case, spontaneous tradition — tradition that had emerged without conscious intent and had ruled villages without dissent — could no longer be counted on. Its alternative was deliberate tradition. When tradition is no longer spontaneous and unquestioned, it must be shored up and reinforced through conscious attention.

The solution, simple to the ear but in substance profound, embodied the appositeness of social genius. In times of transition an effective proposal must meet two conditions. It must be continuous with the past, for only by tying in with what people have known and are accustomed to can it be generally accepted—"think not that I came to destroy; I came not to destroy but to fulfill" (Matthew 5:17). At the same time the answer must take clear-eyed account of developments that render the old answer unworkable. Confucius' proposal met both requirements brilliantly. Continuity was preserved by keeping tradition stage center. Don't rush, he seemed to be saying; let's see how it was done in the past—we have heard his claim to being "simply a lover of the ancients." With the perspicacity of a politician taking his stand on the Constitution, he appealed to the Classics as establishing the guidelines for his platform. Yet all the while he was interpreting, modifying, reformulating. Unknown to his people, we can feel confident, he was effecting a momentous reorientation by shifting tradition from an unconscious to a conscious foundation.

Unknown to his people, and for the most part unknown to himself, we should add, for it would be a mistake to suppose that Confucius was fully aware of what he was doing. But genius does not depend upon full, self-conscious understanding of its creations. A poet may have less than a critic's knowledge of why certain words were chosen; the lack in no way precludes the words from being right. Probably all exceptional creativity proceeds more by intuitive feel than by explicit discernment. Clearly, this was so with Confucius. He would not, he could not, have justified or even described his answer in the terms we have used. He merely conceived the answer in the first place, leaving to posterity the secondary task of trying to understand what he had done and why it proved to be effective.

The shift from spontaneous to deliberate tradition requires that the powers of critical intelligence be turned both to keeping the force of tradition intact, and to determining which ends tradition shall henceforth serve. A people must first decide what values are important to their collective well-being; this is why "among the Confucians the study of the correct attitudes was a matter of prime importance."[18] Then every device of education—formal and informal, womb to tomb—should be turned to seeing that these values are universally internalized. As one Chinese has described the process: "Moral ideas were driven into the people by every possible means—temples, theaters, homes, toys, proverbs, schools, history, and stories—until they became habits in daily life. . . . Even festivals and parades were [in this sense] religious in character."[19] By such means even a society constituted of individuals can (if it puts itself to the task) spin an enveloping tradition, a power of suggestion, that can prompt its members to behave socially even when the law is not looking.

The technique pivots around what sociologists call "patterns of prestige." Every group has such patterns. In teenage gangs they may include toughness and outrageous floutings of convention; in monasteries, holiness and humility are valued. Whatever its content a pattern-of-prestige embodies the values the leaders of the group admire. Followers, taking their cues from leaders whom *they* admire, come to respect their values and are disposed to enact them—partly because they, too, have come to admire them, and partly to win peer approval.

It is a powerful routine, perhaps the only one by which distinctively human values ever permeate large groups. For nearly two thousand years the first sentence a Chinese child, living in the direct light of Confucius, was taught to read was not, "Look, look; look and see," but rather "Human beings are by nature good." We may smile at the undisguised moralizing, but every nation needs it. The United States has its story of George Washington and the cherry tree and the moralisms of the *McGuffey Reader*. The Romans' renown for discipline and obedience fed on their legend of the father who condemned his son to death for winning a victory against orders. Did Nelson actually say, "England expects every man to do his duty"? Did Francis I really exclaim, "All is lost save honor"? It doesn't much matter. The stories express national ideals, and shape peoples to their image. Similarly, the interminable anecdotes and maxims of Confucius' *Analects* were designed to create the prototype of what the Chinese hoped the Chinese character would become.

The Master said: "The true gentleman is friendly but not familiar; the inferior man is familiar but not friendly."

Tsu King asked: "What would you say of the person who is liked by all his fellow townsmen?" "That is not sufficient," was the reply. "What is better is that the good among his fellow townsmen like him, and the bad hate him."

The Master said: "The well-bred are dignified but not pompous. The ill-bred are pompous, but not dignified."

Once when Fan Ch'ih was rambling along with the Master under the trees at the Rain Altars, he remarked: "May I venture to ask how one may improve one's character, correct one's personal faults, and discriminate in what is irrational?"

"An excellent question," rejoined the Master. "If one puts duty first and success after, will not that improve one's character? If one attacks one's own failings instead of those of others, will that not remedy personal faults? For a morning's anger to forget one's own safety and that of one's relatives, is not this irrational?"

Confucius was creating for his countrymen their second nature which, to complete the statement of the social analyst that was begun several paragraphs back, is what people receive when they become civilized.

This second nature is made in the image of what [people are] living
for and should become. . . . Full allegiance to the community can
be given only by a man's second nature, ruling over his first and
primitive nature, and treating it as not finally himself. Then the
disciplines and the necessities and the constraints of a civilized life
have ceased to be alien to him, and imposed from without. They
have become his own inner imperatives.

The Content of Deliberate Tradition

Deliberate tradition differs from spontaneous tradition in requiring
attention. It requires attention first to maintain its force in the face of
the increased individualism that threatens to erode it. This Confucius regarded as the main responsibility of education in its
broadest sense. But, second, it requires that attention be given to the
content of that education. What is the character of the social life it
should engender? The main outlines of Confucius' answer can be
gathered under five key terms.

1. Jen.   *Jen,* etymologically a combination of the character for
"human being" and for "two," names the ideal relationship that
should pertain between people. Variously translated as goodness,
man-to-man-ness, benevolence, and love, it is perhaps best rendered
as human-heartedness. *Jen* was the virtue of virtues in Confucius'
view of life. It was a sublime, even transcendental, perfection that he
confessed he had never seen fully incarnated. Involving as it does the
display of human capacities at their best, it is a virtue so exalted that
one "cannot but be chary in speaking of it."[20] To the noble it is
dearer than life itself. "The determined scholar and the man of
jen . . . will even sacrifice their lives to preserve their *jen* complete."
Jen involves simultaneously a feeling of humanity toward others
and respect for oneself, an indivisible sense of the dignity of human
life wherever it appears. Subsidiary attitudes follow automatically:
magnanimity, good faith, and charity. In the direction of *jen* lies the
perfection of everything that would make one supremely human. In
public life it prompts untiring diligence. In private life it is expressed
in courtesy, unselfishness, and empathy, the capacity to "measure the
feelings of others by one's own." Stated negatively, this empathy leads
to what has been called the Silver Rule —"Do not do unto others what

you would not want others to do unto you,"[21] but there is no reason to stop with this negative wording for Confucius put the point positively as well. "The person of *jen*, desiring self-affirmation, seeks to affirm as well." Such largeness of heart knows no national boundaries for those who are *jen*-endowed know that "within the four seas all men are brothers and sisters."

2. *Chun tzu*.   The second concept is *chun tzu*. If *jen* is the ideal relationship between human beings, *chun tzu* refers to the ideal term in such relations. It has been translated the Superior Person and Humanity-at-its-Best. Perhaps the Mature Person is as faithful a rendering of the term as any.

The *chun tzu* is the opposite of a petty person, a mean person, a small-spirited person. Fully adequate, poised, the *chun tzu* has toward life as a whole the approach of an ideal hostess who is so at home in her surroundings that she is completely relaxed, and, being so, can turn full attention to putting others at their ease. Or to switch genders, having come to the point where he is at home in the universe at large, the *chun tzu* carries these qualities of the ideal host with him through life generally. Armed with a self-respect that generates respect for others, he approaches them wondering, not, "What can I get from them?" but "What can I do to accommodate them?"

With the hostess's adequacy go a pleasant air and good grace. Poised, confident, and competent, she is a person of perfect address. Her movements are free of brusqueness and violence; her expression is open, her speech free of coarseness and vulgarity. Or to switch genders again, the gentleman does not talk too much. He does not boast, push himself forward, or in any way display his superiority, "except perhaps at sports." Holding always to his own standards, however others may forget theirs, he is never at a loss as to how to behave and can keep a gracious initiative where others resort to conventions. Schooled to meet any contingency "without fret or fear," his head is not turned by success nor his temper soured by adversity.

It is only the person who is entirely real, Confucius thought, who can establish the great foundations of civilized society. Only as those who make up society are transformed into *chun tzus* can the world move toward peace.

If there is righteousness in the heart, there will be
   beauty in the character.
If there is beauty in the character, there will be
   harmony in the home.
If there is harmony in the home, there will be order
   in the nation.
If there is order in the nation, there will be peace
   in the world.

3. *Li.* The third concept, *li*, has two meanings.

Its first meaning is propriety, the way things should be done. Confucius thought it unrealistic to think that people could wisely determine on their own what those ways should be. They needed models, and Confucius wanted to direct their attention to the finest models their social history offered, so all could gaze, and memorize, and duplicate. The French, whose culture not only in its regard for cooking but in its attention to the art of life generally is China's nearest counterpart in the West, have several idioms that capture this idea so well that they have made their way into the Western vocabulary; *savoir faire*, the knowledge of how to comport oneself with grace and urbanity whatever the circumstance; *comme il faut*, the way things should be done; *apropos*, that which is appropriate; and *esprit*, the right feel for things. Confucius wanted to cultivate the Chinese character in precisely these directions. Through maxims (burlesqued in the West by parodies of "Confucius say . . ."), anecdotes (*The Analects* are full of them), and his own example ("Confucius, in his village, looked simple and sincere; when in court he spoke circumspectly"), he sought to order an entire way of life, so that no one who was properly raised would ever be in doubt as to how to behave. "Manners maketh man," a medieval bishop observed. Confucius anticipated that insight.

Propriety covers a wide range, but we can get the gist of what Confucius was concerned with if we look at his teachings on the Rectification of Names, the Doctrine of the Mean, the Five Constant Relationships, the Family, and Age.

"If terms be not correct," Confucius pointed out,

language is not in accordance with the truth of things. If language is not in accordance with the truth of things, affairs cannot be

*carried out to success. . . . Therefore a superior man considers it
necessary that the names he uses be spoken appropriately, and
also that what he speaks may be carried out appropriately. What
the superior man requires is that in his words there be nothing
that is incorrect.*

This may sound commonsensical, but Confucius was grappling
here with a problem that in our time has spawned a whole new discipline: semantics — the inquiry into the relation between words,
thought, and objective reality. All human thought proceeds through
words, so if words are askew, thought cannot proceed aright. When
Confucius says that nothing is more important than that a father be a
father, that a ruler be a ruler, he is saying that we must know what we
mean when we use those words. But equally important, the words
must mean the right things. Rectification of Names is the call for a
normative semantics — the creation of a language in which key nouns
carry the meanings they should carry if life is to be well ordered.

So important was the Doctrine of the Mean in Confucius' vision
that a book by that title is central to the Confucian canon. The two
Chinese words for mean are *chun yung*, literally "middle" and "constant." The Mean, therefore, is the way that is "constantly in the middle" between unworkable extremes. With "nothing in excess" as its
guiding principle, its closest Western counterpart is the Golden
Mean of Aristotle. The Mean balances a sensitive temperament
against overdose and indulgence, and in so doing checks depravity in
the bud. "Pride," the *Book of Li* admonishes, "should not be indulged.
The will should not be gratified to the full. Pleasure should not be
carried to excess." Respect for the Mean brings harmony and balance. It encourages compromise, and fosters a becoming reserve.
Wary of excess, toward pure values "equally removed from enthusiasm as from indifference," China's regard for the Mean has typically,
but not universally, protected her from fanaticism.

The Five Constant Relationships that constitute the warp and
woof of social life are, in the Confucian scheme, those between parent and child, husband and wife, elder sibling and junior sibling,
elder friend and junior friend, and ruler and subject.[22] It is vital to
the health of society that these key relationships be rightly constituted. None of them are transitive; in each, different responses are
appropriate to the two terms. Parents should be loving, children

reverential; elder siblings gentle, younger siblings respectful; husbands good, wives "listening"; elder friends considerate, younger friends deferential; rulers benevolent, subjects loyal. In effect Confucius is saying that you are never alone when you act. Every action affects someone else. Here, in these five relationships, is a frame within which you may achieve the maximum selfhood without damaging the web of life on which your life depends.

That three of the Five Relationships pertain within the family is indicative of how important Confucius considered this institution to be. In this he was not inventing but continuing the Chinese assumption that the family is the basic unit of society. This assumption is graphically embedded in Chinese legend, which credits the hero who "invented" the family with elevating the Chinese from animal to human level. Within the family, in turn, it is the children's respect for their parents that holds the key; hence the concept of filial piety. When the meanings of the parents are no longer meaningful to their children, someone has recently written, civilization is in danger. Confucius could not have agreed more. "The duty of children to their parents is the fountain from which all virtues spring." Accounts of devoted children pepper Confucian literature. They are outlandish stories, many of them, as for example that of the woman whose aged mother-in-law was pining for fish in the depth of winter. The young woman prostrated herself on the ice of a pond and bared her bosom to melt the ice so she might catch the fish that surfaced in the hole.

This regard for one's elders was not to stop with one's parents; it tied in with Confucius' Respect for Age generally. Two points locked together here. On purely utilitarian grounds it would be good to have a society in which (after a certain age) the young would tend the old, for soon enough the young would be old themselves and would need to draw on their investment. But more than this utilitarian argument was at work. Confucius clearly thought that the young should honor and serve the old not simply to repay a contractual debt. He saw age as deserving veneration by reason of its intrinsic worth. For on balance, he believed, years bring not only experience and seasoning, but a ripening of wisdom and mellowing of spirit; on counts that matter most the old are ahead of us. This view is so contrary to the West's, which venerates youth, that it is almost impossible for us to imagine how life would feel if one could look forward to being served and respected more with each passing year. After childhood, in each successive year proportionately more people would jump up from the table to fill the teapot instead of expecting you to do so, and you would be listened to with increasing attention and respect. Three of the Five Great Relations focus on looking up to one's elders.

In the Rectification of Names, the Doctrine of the Mean, the Five Great Relationships, and Regard for Age and the Family we have sketched important particulars of *li* in its first meaning, which is propriety or what's right. The other meaning of the word is ritual, which changes right — in the sense of what it is right to do — into rite. Or rather, it infuses the first meaning with the second; for when right behavior is detailed to Confucian lengths, the individual's entire life becomes stylized in a sacred dance. Social life has been choreographed. Its basic steps have been worked out, leaving little need for improvisation. There is a pattern for every act, from the way thrice-yearly the Emperor renders to Heaven an account of his mandate, right down to the way you entertain the humblest guest in your home and bring out the tea. Alfred North Whitehead's wife reported a Cambridge vicar who concluded his sermon by saying, "Finally, my brethren, for well-conducted people life presents no problems." *Li* was Confucius' blueprint for the well-conducted life.

4. Te.   The fourth pivotal concept Confucius sought to devise for his countrymen was *te*.

Literally this word meant power, specifically the power by which men are ruled. But this is only the beginning of its definition. What is this power? We have noted Confucius' rejection of the Realists' claim that the only effective rule is by physical might. How right he was in his judgment, history demonstrates through the one dynasty, the Ch'in, that fashioned its policy on Realist lines. Stunningly successful at the start, it united China for the first time and bequeathed to it its name as "Ch'in" became "China." But it collapsed in less than a generation — vivid witness to Talleyrand's dictum that "You can do everything with bayonets except sit on them." One of the best known of all Confucian stories is of how on the lonely side of Mount T'ai he heard the mourning wail of a woman. Asked why she wept, she replied, "My husband's father was killed here by a tiger, my husband also, and now my son has met the same fate."

"Then why do you dwell in such a dreadful place?" Confucius asked.

"Because here there is no oppressive ruler," the woman replied.

"Never forget, scholars," said Confucius to his disciples, "that an oppressive rule is more cruel than a tiger."

No state, Confucius was convinced, can constrain all its citizens all the time, nor even any large fraction of them a large part of the time. It must rely on an acceptance of its will, an appreciable confidence in what it is doing. Noting that the three essentials of government were economic sufficiency, military sufficiency, and the confidence of its people, Confucius added that popular trust is by far the most important, for "if the people have no confidence in their government, it cannot stand."

This spontaneous consent from its citizens, this morale without which nations cannot survive, arises only when people sense their leaders to be people of capacity, sincerely devoted to the common good and possessed of the kind of character that compels respect. Real *te*, therefore, is the power of moral example. In the final analysis, goodness becomes embodied in society neither through might nor through law, but through the impress of persons we admire. Everything turns on the head of state. If he or she is crafty or worthless, there is no hope for society. But if the leader is a true King of Consent whose sanction springs from inherent righteousness, such a person will gather a cabinet of "unpurchaseable allies." Their complete devotion to the public welfare will quicken in turn the public conscience of local leaders and seep down from there to inspire citizens at large. For the process to work, however, rulers must have no personal ambitions, which accounts for the Confucian saying, "only those are worthy to govern who would rather be excused."

The following statements epitomize Confucius' idea of *te*:

He who exercises government by means of his virtue [te] *may be compared to the north polar star, which keeps its place and all the stars turn toward it.*

Asked by the Baron of Lu how to rule, Confucius replied: "To govern is to keep straight. If you, Sir, lead the people straight, which of your subjects will venture to fall out of line?"

When on another occasion the same ruler asked him whether the lawless should be executed, Confucius answered: "What need is there of the death penalty in government? If you showed a sincere desire to be good, your people would likewise be good. The virtue of the prince is like the wind; the virtue of the people like grass. It is the nature of grass to bend when the wind blows upon it."

Justice Holmes used to say that he liked to pay taxes because he felt he was buying civilization. Where this positive attitude exists, things will go well politically. But how is the positive attitude to be elicited? Among Western theorists, Confucius would have found his spokesman in Plato:

Then tell me, Critias, how will a man choose the ruler that shall rule over him? Will he not choose a man who has first established order in himself, knowing that any decision that has its spring from anger or pride or vanity can be multiplied a thousandfold in its effects upon the citizens?

Confucius would also have seconded Thomas Jefferson, who thought that "the whole art of government consists in the art of being honest."

5. Wen.   The final concept in the Confucian gestalt is *wen*. This refers to "the arts of peace" as contrasted to "the arts of war"; to music, art, poetry, the sum of culture in its aesthetic and spiritual mode.

Confucius valued the arts tremendously. A simple refrain once cast such a spell over him that for three months he became indifferent to what he ate. He considered people who are indifferent to art only half human. Still, it was not art for art's sake that drew his regard. It was art's power to transform human nature in the direction of virtue that impressed him—its power to make easy (by ennobling the heart) a regard for others that would otherwise be difficult.

By poetry the mind is aroused; from music the finish is received. The odes stimulate the mind. They induce self-contemplation. They teach the art of sensibility. They help to restrain resentment. They bring home the duty of serving one's parents and one's prince.[23]

There is an added, political dimension to Confucius' notion of *wen*. What succeeds in international relations? Here again the Realists answered in terms of physical might; it was the answer Stalin echoed in our century when, asked how the Pope figured in a move he was contemplating against Poland, asked in return, "How many battalions does he have?" Confucius' thrust was characteristically different. Ultimately, the victory goes to the state that develops the highest *wen*, the most exalted culture—the state that has the finest art, the noblest philosophy, the grandest poetry, and gives evidence of realizing that "it is the moral character of a neighborhood that constitutes its excellence." For in the end it is these things that elicit the spontaneous admiration of women and men everywhere. The Gauls were fierce fighters, and so crude of culture that they were considered barbarians; but once they experienced what Roman civilization meant, its superiority was so evident that they never, after Caesar's conquest, had any general uprising against Roman rule. Confucius would not have been surprised.

The Confucian Project

Let us assume that the deliberate tradition Confucius sought to fashion was in place. How would life appear to a Chinese, set within it?

It would beckon as a never-ending project of self-cultivation toward the end of becoming more fully human. The good man or woman in the Confucian scheme is the one who is always trying to become better.

The project is not attempted in a vacuum—this is not *yogis* retiring to mountain caves to discover the God within. Quite the contrary; a Confucian who is bent on self-cultivation positions himself or herself squarely in the center of ever-shifting, never-ending crosscurrents of human relationships and would not wish things otherwise; saintliness in isolation had no meaning for Confucius. The point is not merely that human relationships are fulfilling; the Confucian claim runs deeper than that. It is rather that apart from human relationships there is no self. The self *is* a center of relationships. It is constructed through its interactions with others and is defined by the sum of its social roles.

This notion of the self is so different from Western individualism that we need to circle it for a paragraph. Confucius saw the human self as a node, not an entity; it is a meeting place where lives converge. In this it resembles a sea anemone, which is little more than a net through which tides and currents wash, leaving deposits that build what little substance the plant itself possesses. But though it is accurate in ways, this image is too passive; we do better to switch from sea currents to air currents that assail an eagle in flight. Those currents assault the eagle, but the eagle uses them to control its altitude by adjusting the tilt of its wings. Like an eagle in flight, our human life too is in motion, but in its case human *relationships* are the atmosphere through which it plows. The Confucian project is to master the art of adjusting one's wings in order to ascend toward the elusive but approachable goal of human perfection. Or as Confucius would have said, toward the goal of becoming more completely human.

In this analogy Confucius' Five Constant Relationships present themselves as relatively stable currents in atmospheric conditions that in other respects can fluctuate wildly. We have seen that all five relationships are asymmetrical in that behavior that is appropriate to one person in each pair is not identical with what is appropriate for the other person. This asymmetry presupposes role differentiation and details its specifics.

The crucial question here is whether the specifics Confucius proposed tilt the relationships, positioning one person in each pair above the other person. In one sense they definitely do. It seemed altogether natural to Confucius that children should look up to their parents, wives to husbands, subjects to rulers, and younger friends and siblings to their older counterparts, for the latter, generally older, are more experienced and provide natural role models. But this is where wingslants must be adjusted precisely, for a hair's-breadth difference puts the Confucian project into a nose dive. The danger is greatest for the "top" partner in each pair, who could be tempted to assume that the position carries built-in perquisites rather than ones that must be merited. Unquestionably, human nature being what it is, the Chinese succumbed to this temptation—to what extent defies calculation, but enough to make this the sinister side of the Confucian scheme. But Confucius himself tried to forestall abuse by insisting that authority—due authority—is not automatic; it must be earned. The loyalty that is due the husband from the wife is contingent on the husband's being the kind of husband who warrants— instinctively inspires—such loyalty, and comparably with the other four relationships, although the nuances of loyalty differ in each case. In the ruler-subject relationship, for example, the ruler retains the Mandate of Heaven—his right to his subjects' loyalty—only insofar as their welfare is in truth his chief concern and he possesses the talents needed to promote it. More than two thousand years before the

Magna Carta and the Rights of Man, two millennia before the West separated divine right from the office of kingship, the Chinese (through Confucius and his disciples) built the Right of Revolution solidly into their political philosophy: "Heaven sees as the people see; Heaven wills as the people will." Far from being enjoined, complicity in the face of unwarranted authority is, in the Confucian project, a human failing.

As a metaphor for the Confucian project, we introduced the image of an eagle adjusting its wings to maneuver the atmosphere — analogue for the Five Constant Relationships — in ways that enable it to ascend. If we round off this metaphor by asking what ascent means here, we find that the answer was begun in the preceding section. It means becoming a *chun tzu*, a fully realized human being, through expanding one's sympathy and empathy indefinitely. The Chinese character for this empathy/sympathy is *hsin*. Pictorially, *hsin* is a stylized drawing of the human heart, but in meaning it denotes both mind and heart, for in Confucian learning the two go together — sundered from each other, thought runs dry, feeling is rudderless, and the Confucian project gets grounded. As for the increase of this heart-mind that is *hsin*, it expands in concentric circles that begin with oneself and spread from there to include successively one's family, one's face-to-face community, one's nation, and finally all humanity. In shifting the center of one's empathic concern from oneself to one's family one transcends selfishness. The move from family to community transcends nepotism. The move from community to nation overcomes parochialism, and the move to all humanity counters chauvinistic nationalism.

This broadening process is accompanied by one that is deepening; for when it was suggested above that Confucius saw the self as the sum of its social roles, that overstates the case if it suggests that he denied that the self has an internal, subjective center. His repeated calls to self-examination and introspection generally show that he not only recognized an interior side to the self but considered it important. Confucian learning pivots on the self and is for the sake of the self, though (to be sure) as the self expands, its separation from others attenuates. Interior life grows richer as empathy increases, for it is the breadth and depth of one's *hsin* that shapes the contours of subjectivity and provides it with its primary food for thought.

So inside and outside work together in the Confucian scheme. The inner world deepens and grows more satisfying and refined as *jen* and *hsin* expand and the possibilities of *li* are progressively realized. The project is never attempted alone. It proceeds in the sea of humanity, alongside others who likewise (with varying degrees of seriousness) are trying to become fully human. Always the practice field is the Five Constant Relationships. In the course of one's training, one finds that mastering a role in one of the five sheds light on the other roles. To improve as a parent throws light on what being a good child (of one's own parents) entails. The nuances of the other roles likewise illuminate one another.

Ethics or Religion?

Is Confucianism a religion, or is it an ethic? The answer depends on how one defines religion. With its close attention to personal conduct and the moral order, Confucianism approaches life from a different angle than do other religions, but that does not necessarily disqualify it religiously. If religion is taken in its widest sense, as a way of life woven around a people's ultimate concerns, Confucianism clearly qualifies. Even if religion is taken in a narrower sense, as a concern to align humanity with the transcendental ground of its existence, Confucianism is still a religion, albeit a muted one. For though we have thus far spoken only of Confucius' social concerns, these, while definitely the focus, did not exhaust his outlook.

To see the transcendent dimension of Confucianism in perspective, we need to set it against the religious background of the ancient China in which Confucius lived. Until the first millennium B.C., the unquestioned outlook was a compound of three related ingredients:

First, Heaven and Earth were considered a continuum. The terms referred not primarily to places but to the people who dwelt in those places, as the House of Lords refers to the people who sit in that House. The people who comprised Heaven were the ancestors (*ti*) who were ruled over by a supreme ancestor (Shang Ti). They were the forefathers who had gone ahead and soon would be joined by the present retinue of Earth — the whole was one unbroken procession in which death spelled no more than promotion to a more honorable estate. The two realms were mutually implicated and in constant touch. Heaven held control of Earth's welfare—the weather for example was "Heaven's mood"—while depending on the current inhabitants of Earth to supply some of her needs through sacrifice. Of the two realms Heaven was by far the more important. Her inhabitants were more venerable and august and their authority was greater. Consequently, they commanded Earth's reverence and dominated her imaginings.

Being mutually dependent, Heaven and Earth would have needed to communicate for reasons of need even if not affection. The most concrete way by which Earth spoke to Heaven was through sacrifices. Earth's residents thought it both wise and natural to share their goods with their departed ancestors, and the essences of their earthly goods were carried to Heaven on the ascending smoke of the sacrificial fire. A mound for such offerings was the focus of every ancient village. When the Chinese nation arose, its ruler, the Son of Heaven, affirmed his right to that proud title by overseeing the nation's sacrifices to its ancestors. Even as late as Confucius' day, an administration that lapsed in its worship of the ancestors was considered to have lost its right to rule.

If sacrifice was the principal way Earth spoke to Heaven, augury was the channel through which Heaven responded. As the ancestors knew the entire past of their people, they were equipped to calculate its future. Augury was the device by which the present generation might tap into that knowledge. Being pleasantly disposed toward their descendants, the ancestors would naturally want to share with them their knowledge of things to come. They no longer possessed vocal cords, however, and therefore needed to resort to signs. It followed that everything that happened on Earth fell into two classes. Things people did intentionally were ordinary, but things that "happened of themselves"—we should read that phrase with a tinge of apprehension—were to be noticed with care. They were ominous, for one never knew when they might constitute the ancestors' efforts to get peoples' attention, most urgently to warn them of impending danger. Some of these omens occurred within or to the body: itchings, sneezings, twitchings, stumblings, buzzings in the ears, tremblings of the eyelids. Others were external: thunder, lightning, the courses of the stars, the doings of insects, birds, and animals. It was also possible for people to take the initiative and actively seek out

Heaven's prescience. They could throw yarrow stalks on the ground and observe their pattern; they could apply a hot iron to a tortoise shell and examine the cracks that appeared. Whatever the occasion — a trip, a war, a birth, a marriage — it was prudent to look for heavenly tips. An ancient record tells of a visitor who was asked by his host to prolong his stay into the evening. He answered, "I have divined about the day. I have not divined about the night. I dare not."

In each of these great features of early Chinese religion — its sense of continuity with the ancestors, its sacrifice, and its augury — there was a common emphasis. The emphasis was on Heaven instead of Earth. To understand the total dimension of Confucianism as a religion it is important to see Confucius shifting his people's attention from Heaven to Earth without dropping Heaven from the picture entirely.

The first of these twin aspects of Confucianism can be documented easily. On a much debated issue of his day—which should come first, the claims of earthly people or those of the spirit world through sacrifices?—he answered that though the spirits should not be neglected, people should come first. The worldliness and practical concern by which the Chinese were later to be known was coming to the fore, and Confucius did much to crystallize their this-world orientation.

"I do not say that the social as we know it *is* the whole," wrote John Dewey, "but I do emphatically suggest that it is the widest and richest manifestation of the whole accessible to our observation." Confucius would have agreed. His philosophy was a blend of common sense and practical wisdom. It contained no depth of metaphysical thought, no flights of speculation, no soul-stirring calls to cosmic piety. Normally, he "did not talk about spirits." "Recognize that you know what you know, and that you are ignorant of what you do not know," he said.[24] "Hear much, leave to one side that which is doubtful, and speak with due caution concerning the remainder. See much, leave to one side that of which the meaning is not clear, and act carefully with regard to the rest." Consequently, whenever he was questioned about other-worldly matters, Confucius drew the focus back to human beings. Asked about serving the spirits of the dead, he answered, "You are not even able to serve people. How can you serve the spirits?" Asked about death itself, he replied, "You do not understand even life. How can you understand death?"[25] In short: one world at a time.

One specific illustration of the way in which Confucius shifted the focus from Heaven to Earth is seen in his change of emphasis from ancestor worship to filial piety. In ancient China the dead were actually worshiped. True to the conservative component in his nature, Confucius did nothing to interrupt the ancestral rites themselves. He did not deny that the spirits of the dead exist; on the contrary he advised treating them "as if they were present." At the same time his own emphasis was directed toward the living family. He stressed that the most sacred tie is the tie among blood relatives. For him the obligations of present members of a family to one another were more important than their duties to the departed.

The extent to which Confucius shifted emphasis from Heaven to Earth should not lead us to think that he sundered Earth from Heaven entirely. He did not repudiate the main outlines of the world-view of his time, composed of Heaven and Earth, the divine creative pair, half physical and half more-than-physical, ruled over by the supreme Shang Ti. Reserved as he was about the supernatural, he was not without it; somewhere in the universe there was a power that was on the side of right. The spread of righteousness was, therefore, a cosmic demand, and "the Will of Heaven" the first thing a *chun tzu* would respect. Confucius believed that he had a mandate to spread his teachings. When during the "long trek" he was attacked in the town of Kwang, he reassured his followers by saying, "Heaven has appointed me to teach this doctrine, and until I have done so, what can the people of Kwang do to me?"[26] Feeling neglected by his people, he consoled himself with the thought: "There is Heaven—that knows me!" One of the most quoted religious sayings of all times came from his pen. "He who offends the gods has no one to pray to."[27]

This restrained and somewhat attenuated theism enables us to understand why a contemporary Confucian scholar can write that "the highest Confucian ideal is the unity of Man and Heaven," adding that in the *Doctrine of the Mean* this is described as "man forming a trinity with Heaven and Earth."[28] With this unity or trinity established as the consummating goal of the Confucian project, we can pick up on its successive steps, which in our earlier enumeration stopped short of the final goal. The project of becoming fully human involves transcending, sequentially, egoism, nepotism, parochialism, ethnocentrism, and chauvinistic nationalism, and (we should now add) isolating, self-sufficient humanism. To continue with the words of the Confucian scholar just quoted:

> To make ourselves deserving partners of Heaven, we must be constantly in touch with that silent illumination that makes the rightness and principle in our heart-minds shine forth brilliantly. If we cannot go beyond the constraints of our own species, the most we can hope for is an exclusive, secular humanism advocating man as the measure of all things. By contrast, Confucian humanism is inclusive; it is predicated on an "anthropocosmic" vision. Humanity in its all-embracing fullness "forms one body with Heaven, Earth, and the myriad things" and enables us to embody the cosmos in our sensitivity.[29]

Impact on China

In his book *The Next Million Years*, Charles Galton Darwin notes that anyone who wishes to make a sizable impact on human history has the choice of three levels at which to work. The agent may choose direct political action, or create a creed, or attempt to change the genetic composition of the human species. The first method is the weakest because the effects of political action seldom outlast their agent. The third is not feasible, for even if we had the knowledge and technique, a genetic policy would be difficult to enforce for even a short period and would almost certainly be dropped before any perceptible effects were achieved. "That is why," Darwin concludes, "a creed gives the best practical hope that man can have for really controlling his future fate."[30]

History affords no clearer support for this contention than the work of Confucius. For over two thousand years his teachings have profoundly affected a quarter of the population of this globe. Their advance reads like a success story, for the unbelievable upshot of Confucius' outwardly undistinguished career was the founding of a class of scholars who were to become China's ruling elite and the emergence of Confucius himself as the most important figure in China's history. In 130 B.C. the Confucian texts were made the basic discipline for the training of government officials, a pattern that continued (with interruption during the political fragmentation of A.D. 200–600) until the Empire collapsed in 1905. In that same Han

Dynasty Confucianism became, in effect, China's state religion; in A.D. 59 sacrifices were ordered for Confucius in all urban schools, and in the seventh and eighth centuries temples were erected in every prefecture of the empire as shrines to him and his principal disciples. China's famous civil service examinations, which democratized public office centuries before the rest of the world dreamed of doing so, had the Confucian corpus at their heart. The Sung Dynasty (late tenth through late thirteenth centuries) perfected that system, which remained in place into the opening years of our own century.

Darwin follows his general point about the power of "creed" by saying that "the Chinese civilization [which Confucius' creed did so much to shape] is to be accepted as the model type to a greater degree than any of the other civilizations of the world." We shall not go this far. As there is no measure by which to rank-order civilizations qualitatively, we shall content ourselves with quantity, where numbers do tell an objective story. Unlike Europe or even India, China held together, forging a political structure which at its height embraced a third of the human race. The Chinese Empire lasted under a succession of dynasties for over two thousand years, a stretch of time that makes the empires of Alexander, Caesar, and Napoleon look ephemeral. If we multiply the number of years that empire lasted by the number of people it embraced in an average year, it emerges quantitatively as the most impressive social institution human beings have devised.

It is not easy to say what Confucius contributed to this institution, because in time Confucian values merged with the generic values of the Chinese people to the point where it is difficult to separate the two. What we shall do here, therefore, is take note of some features of the Chinese character that Confucius and his disciples reinforced where they did not originate them. The features we shall mention pretty much blanket East Asia as a whole, for Japan, Korea, and much of Southeast Asia deliberately imported the Confucian ethic.

We can begin with East Asia's emphatic social emphasis, which Confucius helped to fix in place. Virtually every sinologist has remarked on this emphasis, but two verdicts will suffice here. "All Chinese philosophy is preeminently social philosophy," Etienne Balazs observed, and Wing-tsit Chan concurs: "Chinese philosophers have been interested primarily in ethical, social, and political

problems." To catch an immediate glimpse of how this social emphasis translates into practice, we can note that though China is as large
as the continental United States, it has a single time zone. Apparently, the Chinese feel that it is more important that they be syn-
chronized among themselves in their time sense than that their
clocks conform to impersonal nature.

This is a small point, to be sure, but small signs can reflect deep-
lying attitudes, and in any case larger evidence is at hand. Confucius'
social emphasis produced, in the Chinese, a conspicuous social
effectiveness—a capacity to get things done on a large scale when
need arose. Historians have speculated that the social emphasis we
are looking at may have gotten its start in China's early need for mas-
sive irrigation projects on the one hand, and titanic dikes to contain
her unruly rivers on the other; and we should not overlook the fact
that social effectiveness (as we are calling it here) can be wrongly
applied; there has been a lot of despostism in China. But, for good or
for ill, effectiveness seems to be a fact. Facing up to its population
problem in the third quarter of this century, China halved her birth-
rate in a single decade. And in the thirty years from 1949 to 1979, she
put famine, flood, and epidemic disease behind a quarter of the
world's population, seemingly forever. As the *Scientific American*
pointed out in its September 1980 issue, "this is a great event in
history."[31]

Directly related to the subject of this book is the way, unique
among the world's civilizations, that China syncretized her religions.
In India and the West religions are exclusive, if not competitive—it
makes no sense to think of someone as being simultaneously a Christian, a Muslim, and a Jew, or even a Buddhist and a Hindu simultaneously. China arranged things differently. Traditionally, every
Chinese was Confucian in ethics and public life, Taoist in private life
and hygiene, and Buddhist at the time of death, with a healthy dash
of shamanistic folk religion thrown in along the way. As someone has
put the point: Every Chinese wears a Confucian hat, Taoist robes,
and Buddhist sandals. In Japan Shinto was added to the mix.

The importance of the family in China—three of Confucius' Five
Constant Relationships pertain to it—scarcely requires comment.
Some sinologists argue that when ancestor worship and filial piety
are included, the family emerges as the real religion of the Chinese
people. The family surname comes first in China; only thereafter are

given names added. The Chinese extended family survived well into the twentieth century, as the following report attests: "A single family may embrace eight generations, including brothers, uncles, great-uncles, sons, nephews and nephews' sons. As many as thirty male parents with their offspring, each with their ancestors and offspring even unto grandparents and grandchildren, may live in a single joint family home comprising but one single family."[32] The Chinese vocabulary for family relationships is equally complex. A single word for brother is too clumsy; there must be two words to designate whether he is older or younger than the sibling who speaks. Likewise with sister, and with aunt, uncle, and grandparent, where different words are required to indicate whether these relations are on the father's or the mother's side. In all, there are titles for one hundred fifteen different relationships in the Chinese extended family.[33] Strong family bonds can smother, but they also bring benefits, and these work for East Asians right down to the present. One thinks of low crime at home—the burglary rate in Japan is 1 percent of that in the United States—and the impressive record of East Asian immigrants to other lands; their delinquency rate is low, and achievement and upward mobility are high. Relatives regularly pitch in to further the education of even distant kin.

The upward tilt toward the elder partner in three of Confucius' Five Constant Relationships helped to elevate East Asia's respect for age to an attitude that borders on veneration. In the West when someone confesses to being fifty, the response is likely to be, "You don't look a year over forty." In traditional China courtesy would have reached for a response more like, "You look every bit of sixty." In the mid-1980s an elderly visitor to Japan was asked by a Japanese friend how wise he was. The confusion the question generated caused the Japanese to realize that he had made a mistake. Apologizing for his faulty English, the Japanese explained that he had intended to ask how old his friend was. When we compare this with the Western attitude toward age—"You're over the hill at forty, and over the hill you pick up speed"—the contrast is glaring. Facing up to the inevitability of the body's decline, China created social structures that buoyed the spirit. With each passing year one could count on more solicitude from one's family and associates, and (as we have noted) more attentive, listening respect.

Confucius' Doctrine of the Mean continues to this day in the Chinese preference for negotiation, mediation, and the "middle man" as against resorting to rigid, impersonal statutes. Until recently, legal action has been regarded as something of a disgrace, a confession of human failure in the inability to work things out by compromises that typically involve family and associates. Figures are not available for China, but in the mid-1980s Japan in ratio to its population had one lawyer for every twenty-four in the United States. The issue of negotiation ties in with the peculiar oriental phenomenon of "face," for in the win/lose context of a legal verdict the party the judgment goes against loses face. This is serious, because if you are going to have to live on intimate terms with your associates, no long-term good can come from mashing them psychologically.

And there is *wen:* Confucius' conviction that learning and the arts are not mere veneer but are powers that transform societies and the human heart. China honored his conviction here: She placed the scholar-bureaucrat at the top of her social scale and soldiers at the bottom. One wonders whether anywhere other than Tibet, and during the brief early years of Islam there has been such an attempt to effect Plato's ideal of the philosopher king. It was only an attempt, yet here and there, now and again, it bore fruit. There have been golden ages in China when the arts have flourished as nowhere else in their time and deep learning was achieved: calligraphy, Sung landscape painting, and the life-giving dance of *tai chi chuan* come quickly to mind. Paper was invented. Four centuries before Gutenberg, movable type was discovered. A fifteenth-century encyclopedia, climax of the research of two thousand scholars, reached a total of 11,095 volumes. There has been great poetry, magnificent scroll painting, and ceramics, which "because of the fineness of their material and decoration, and because of the elegance of their shapes, may be considered the best pottery of all countries and of all times."[34]

Blending with the Confucian art of life itself, these objects of *wen* produced a culture with a flavor all its own. A compound of subtlety, brilliance, and restrained good taste, it endowed the Chinese with a power of assimilation that at its peak was unrivaled. Having the most open frontier of all the great civilizations, China was subject to wave after wave of invasions by cavalried barbarians who were always ready to fall on the Earthbound agriculturalists. To their gates came the Tartars, whose one long-range raid inflicted a mortal wound on the Roman Empire. But what the Chinese could not fend off, they absorbed. Each wave of invaders tended to lose its identity through voluntary assimilation; they admired what they saw. Time after time an illiterate invader, entering solely for plunder, succumbs. Within a few years his foremost hope is to write a copy of Chinese verse that his teacher, who is likewise his conquered slave, might acknowledge as not altogether unworthy of a gentleman, and his highest hope is to be mistaken for Chinese. Kublai Khan is the most striking example. He conquered China but was himself conquered by Chinese civilization, for his victory enabled him to realize his lasting ambition, which was to become an authentic Son of Heaven.

The magic did not last. In the fifteenth century Chinese civilization was still unrivaled throughout the world, but stagnation then set in and the last two centuries must be discounted because the West, armed with superior military technology, snatched China's fate from her own hands. There is little point in discussing Confucianism in the context of a Western-instigated war that forced opium on the Chinese and the subsequent division of China into European spheres of influence. Even the twentieth-century importation of Marxism must be seen as an act of desperation to regain a lost autonomy.

For the enduring constructive Confucian influence we must look not to China's twentieth-century politics but to the East Asian economic miracle of the last forty years. Taken together, Japan, Korea, Taiwan, and Singapore, all shaped by the Confucian ethic, constitute the dynamic center of economic growth in the latter twentieth century—impressive witness to what can happen when scientific technology links up with what might here be referred to as the social technology of East Asians. A single statistic, followed by a reporter's account of a routine episode, provide clues to what makes that social technology work. In 1982 Japanese workers took an average of only 5.1 of the 12 vacation days they were entitled to, for (by their own accounts) "longer vacations would have imposed burdens on their colleagues."[35] As for the report, it reads as follows:

Six o'clock on a spring morning. In front of the Kyoto Central Station six men are standing in a circle singing. They are all dressed in white shirts, black ties, black pants, and shiny black shoes. One of them reads a pledge in which they affirm their intention to serve their customers, their company, the city of Kyoto, Japan, and the world. They are taxi drivers beginning their work day as usual.[36]

It does not relate to the issue of productivity, but another report from Kyoto points up the courtesy for which orientals have been famous: "In the cyclonic mess of Kyoto traffic, two cars scrape bumpers. Both drivers leap out. Each bows, apologizing profusely for his carelessness."

These are lingering echoes of the Confucian spirit, but one must wonder if they are not fading ones. In a Westernizing world, what is the future of this religion?

No one knows the answer. It may be that we are looking at a religion that is dying. If so, it would be appropriate to close this chapter with the words Confucius applied to himself when on his deathbed his eyes rested for the last time on the majestic dome of T'ai Shan, China's sacred mountain:

The Sacred Mountain is falling,
The beam is breaking.
The wise man is withering away.

On the other hand, prophets have a way of outlasting politicians. Gandhi has outlasted Nehru, and it appears that Confucius will outlast Mao Tse-tung.

Suggestions for Further Reading

Laurence G. Thompson's *Chinese Religion* (Belmont, CA: Wadsworth, Inc., 1989) provides a good overview of the religious dimension of China generally.

For translations of the most important Confucian texts, Arthur Waley's *The Analects of Confucius* (New York: Random House, 1989), and D. C. Lau's *Mencius* (New York: Penguin Books, 1970) can be recommended. For the philosophically inclined, A. C. Graham's *Disputers of the Tao* (La Salle, IL: Open Court, 1989) offers the best general history of Chinese thought during its formative period.

The section on "The Confucian Project" in this chapter was prompted largely by the writings of the contemporary Confucian scholar Tu Wei-ming, especially his *Confucian Thought: Selfhood as Creative Transformation* (Albany: State University of New York Press, 1985), and *Humanity and Self-Cultivation: Essays in Confucian Thought* (Fremont, CA: Jain Publishing, 1980).

I did not single out Neo-Confucianism for separate treatment in my presentation. As an important movement that recast Confucianism in the light of Taoist and Buddhist influences, it began in the eighth century, flourished vigorously in the eleventh and twelfth centuries, and has produced notable interpreters right down to the present. Specifically, the Neo-Confucian scholars worked out a world view that paralleled the Buddhist cosmology, and a system of moral philosophy to explain Confucian ethics in metaphysical terms. Their story is presented in overview in Carsun Chang, *The Development of Neo-Confucian Thought* (Albany: State University of New York Press, 1957).

Confucius—The Secular as Sacred by Herbert Fingarette (New York: Harper & Row, 1972) is exceptional in being written by a ranking contemporary philosopher who discusses Confucius' ideas not for reasons of their historical importance, but because (in Fingarette's own words) he is "a thinker with an imaginative vision of man equal in its grandeur to any I know."

Notes

1. *The Analects of Confucius,* VII:1.
2. *The Doctrine of the Mean,* chapter 13. A statement comparable in spirit is found in *The Analects,* XIV:28.
3. *The Analects,* VII:33.
4. *The Analects, passim.*
5. As reported by Ruth Benedict.
6. Arthur Waley, *The Way and Its Power,* 1934. Reprint. (London: Allen & Unwin, 1958), 32.
7. The position of the Realists I shall present comes to us primarily through the eyes of orthodox Confucian historians. Scholars wonder if their characterization slips into caricature at times, but the general thrust of their depiction is not disputed.
8. Quoted in Arthur Waley, *Three Ways of Thought in Ancient China,* 1939. Reprint. (London: Allen & Unwin, 1963), 199.
9. Han Fei Tzu, as quoted in Waley, *The Way,* 74.
10. Waley, *The Way,* 162.
11. Though love is the literal meaning of *ai,* A. C. Graham uses "mutual concern," or "concern for everyone," to translate the phrase, arguing that this fits better with Mohism's pragmatic, utilitarian bent.
12. Yi-pao Mei, *Motse, the Neglected Rival of Confucius,* 1929. Reprint. (Westport, CT: Hyperion Press, 1973), 80f.

13. Yi-pao Mei, *Motse*, 89, 145.
14. Yi-pao Mei, *Motse*, 83.
15. I am treating these answers schematically rather than chronologically. Only after Confucius' death were the answers that he rejected put forward systematically. It remained for his disciples, following their master's guidelines, to argue explicitly against them.
16. A. C. Graham, *Disputers of the Tao* (La Salle, IL: Open Court, 1989), p. 43.
17. Walter Lippmann, *The Public Philosophy* (Boston: Little, Brown & Co., 1955).
18. Waley, *The Way*, 161.
19. Chiang Molin, *Tides from the West* (New Haven, CT: Yale University Press, 1947), 9, 19.
20. Confucius, as quoted by Arthur Waley, *The Analects of Confucius*, 1938. Reprint. (London: Allen & Unwin, 1956), 28.
21. *The Analects*, XII:2; XV:24.
22. I have broadened Confucius' "father/son," "elder-brother/junior-brother" wording to make it fit better with modern sensibilities. I do not think this violates Confucius' actual intent.
23. *The Analects*, XVII:9.
24. *The Analects*, II:17.
25. *The Analects*, XI:11.
26. *The Analects*, IX:5.
27. *The Analects*, III:13.
28. Tu Wei-ming, *The World and I* (August 1989): 484.
29. Tu Wei-ming, *The World and I*, 485.
30. Charles Galton Darwin, *The Next Million Years* (Garden City, NY: Doubleday, 1953).
31. Ding Chen, "The Economic Development of China," *Scientific American* (September 1980): 152.
32. F. C. S. Northrop, *The Taming of the Nations* (New York: Macmillan, 1953), 117.
33. Maxine Hong Kingston, *The Woman Warrior* (New York: Random House, 1989), 12.
34. The opinion of a knowledgeable collector as quoted in Rene Grousset, *The Rise and Splendour of the Chinese Empire*, 1953. Reprint. (Berkeley: University of California Press, 1965), 207.
35. Newspaper columnist Georgie Anne Geyer, from Tokyo, August 13, 1983.
36. *East West Journal* (December 1979).

V. Taoism

No civilization is monochrome. In China the classical tones of Confucianism have been balanced not only by the spiritual shades of Buddhism but also by the romantic hues of Taoism.

The Old Master

According to tradition Taoism (pronounced Dowism) originated with a man named Lao Tzu, said to have been born about 604 B.C. He is a shadowy figure. We know nothing for certain about him and scholars wonder if there ever was such a man. We do not even know his name, for Lao Tzu—which can be translated "the Old Boy," "the Old Fellow," or "the Grand Old Master"—is obviously a title of endearment and respect. All we really have is a mosaic of legends. Some of these are fantastic: that he was conceived by a shooting star, carried in his mother's womb for eighty-two years, and born already a wise old man with white hair. Other parts of the story do not tax our credulity: that he kept the archives in his native western state, and that around this occupation he wove a simple and unassertive life. Inferences concerning his personality derive almost entirely from a single slim volume that is attributed to him. From this some conclude that he was probably a solitary recluse who was absorbed in occult meditations; others picture him as down to earth—a genial neighbor with a lively sense of humor.

The only purportedly contemporary portrait, reported by China's first historian, Ssu-ma Ch'ien, speaks only of the enigmatic impression he left—the sense that he possessed depths of understanding that defied ready comprehension. According to this account Confucius, intrigued by what he had heard of Lao Tzu, once visited him. His description suggests that the strange man baffled him while leaving him respectful. "I know a bird can fly; I know a fish can swim; I know animals can run. Creatures that run can be caught in nets; those that swim can be caught in wicker traps; those that fly can be hit by arrows. But the dragon is beyond my knowledge; it ascends into heaven on the clouds and the wind. Today I have seen Lao Tzu, and he is like the dragon!"

The traditional portrait concludes with the report that Lao Tzu, saddened by his people's disinclination to cultivate the natural goodness he advocated and seeking greater personal solitude for his closing years, climbed on a water buffalo and rode westward toward what is now Tibet. At the Hankao Pass a gatekeeper, sensing the unusual character of the truant, tried to persuade him to turn back. Failing this, he asked if the "Old Boy" would not at least leave a record of his beliefs to the civilization he was abandoning. This Lao Tzu consented to do. He retired for three days and returned with a slim volume of five thousand characters titled *Tao Te Ching*, or *The Way and Its Power*. A testament to humanity's at-home-ness in the universe, it can be read in half an hour or a lifetime, and remains to this day the basic text of Taoist thought.

What a curious portrait this is for the supposed founder of a religion. The Old Boy didn't preach. He didn't organize or promote. He wrote a few pages on request, rode off on a water buffalo, and that was it as far as he was concerned. How unlike the Buddha, who trudged the dusty roads of India for forty-five years to make his point. How unlike Confucius, who pestered dukes and princes, trying to gain an administrative foothold (or at least a hearing) for his ideas. Here was a man so little concerned with the success of his surmises, to say nothing of fame and fortune, that he didn't even stay around to answer questions. And yet, whether the story of his life is fact or fiction, it is so true to Taoist attitudes that it will remain a part of Taoism forever. Emperors would claim this shadowy figure as their ancestor, and even scholars — though they do not see the *Tao Te Ching* as having been written by a single hand and do not think it attained the form in which we have it until the second half of the third century B.C. — concede that its ideas cohere to the point where we must posit the existence of *someone* under whose influence the book took shape, and have no objection to our calling him Lao Tzu.

The Three Meanings of Tao

On opening Taoism's bible, the *Tao Te Ching,* we sense at once that everything revolves around the pivotal concept of *Tao* itself. Literally, this word means path, or way. There are three senses, however, in which this "way" can be understood.

First, *Tao* is the *way of ultimate reality.* This *Tao* cannot be perceived or even clearly conceived, for it is too vast for human rationality to fathom. The *Tao Te Ching* announces in its opening line that words are not equal to it: "The *Tao* that can be spoken is not the true *Tao.*" Nevertheless, this ineffable and transcendent *Tao* is the ground of all that follows. Above all, behind all, beneath all is the Womb from which all life springs and to which it returns. Awed by the thought of it, the author/editor of the *Tao Te Ching* bursts recurrently into praise, for this primal *Tao* confronts him with life's basic mystery, the mystery of all mysteries. "How clear it is! How quiet it is! It must be something eternally existing!" "Of all great things, surely *Tao* is the greatest." But its ineffability cannot be denied, so we are taunted, time and again, by Taoism's teasing epigram: "Those who know don't say. Those who say don't know."[1]

Though *Tao* is ultimately transcendent, it is also immanent. In this secondary sense it is the *way of the universe,* the norm, the rhythm, the driving power in all nature, the ordering principle behind all life. Behind, but also in the midst of all life, for when *Tao* enters this second mode it "assumes flesh" and informs all things. It "adapts its vivid essence, clarifies its manifold fullness, subdues its resplendent luster, and assumes the likeness of dust." Basically spirit rather than matter, it cannot be exhausted; the more it is drawn upon, the more it flows, for it is "that fountain ever on," as Plotinus said of his counterpart to the *Tao,* his One. There are about it marks of inevitability, for when autumn comes "no leaf is spared because of its beauty, no flower because of its fragrance." Yet, ultimately, it is benign. Graceful instead of abrupt, flowing rather than hesitant, it is infinitely generous. Giving life to all things, it may be called "the Mother of the World." As nature's agent *Tao* in this second form resembles Bergson's *elan vital;* as nature's orderer, it resembles the *lex aeterna* of the Classical West, the eternal law that structures the world. Charles Darwin's colleague, George Romanes, could have been speaking of it when he referred to "the integrating principle of the whole—the Spirit, as it were, of the universe—instinct without contrivance, which flows with purpose."

In its third sense *Tao* refers to *the way of human life* when it meshes with the *Tao* of the universe as just described. Most of what follows in this chapter will detail what the Taoists propose that this way of life should be. First, however, it is necessary to point out that there have been in China not one but three Taoisms.

Three Approaches to Power and the Taoisms That Follow

Tao Te Ching, the title of Taoism's basic text, has been translated *The Way and Its Power*. We have seen that the first of these substantive terms, the Way, can be taken in three senses. Now we must add that this is also true of the second substantive term, power. Corresponding to the three ways *te* or power can be approached, there have arisen in China three species of Taoism so dissimilar that initially they seem to have no more in common than homonyms, like blew/blue or sun/son, that sound alike but have different meanings. We shall find that this is not the case, but first the three species must be distinguished. Two have standard designations, Philosophical Taoism and Religious Taoism respectively; and because many more people were involved with Religious Taoism it is often called Popular Taoism as well. The third school (which will come second in our order of presentation) is too heterogeneous to have acquired a single title. Its population constitutes an identifiable cluster, however, by virtue of sharing a common objective. All were engaged in vitalizing programs that were intended to facilitate *Tao*'s power, its *te,* as it flows through human beings.

Efficient Power: Philosophical Taoism

Unlike Religious Taoism, which became a full-fledged church, Philosophical Taoism and the "vitalizing Taoisms," as we shall clumsily refer to the second group, remain relatively unorganized. Philosophical Taoism is reflective and the vitalizing programs active, but no more than the Transcendentalist movement in New England or contemporary physical fitness programs are they formally institutionalized.

They share a second similarity in that both are self-help programs. Teachers are involved, but they are better thought of as coaches who train their students — guiding them in what they should understand, in the case of Philosophical Taoism, and in what they should do in the vitalizing regimens. In decided contrast to Religious Taoists, those in these first two camps work primarily on themselves.

The differences between them have to do with their respective stances toward the power of the *Tao* on which life feeds. To put the difference pointedly, Philosophical Taoists try to conserve their *te* by expending it efficiently, whereas "vitality" Taoists work to increase its available supply.

Because Philosophical Taoism is essentially an attitude toward life, it is the most "exportable" Taoism of the three, the one that has the most to say to the world at large, and as such will receive the longest treatment — not until the second half of this chapter, however. Here we shall only identify it to place it in its logical position before proceeding with its two sister Taoisms.

Called School Taoism in China, Philosophical Taoism is associated with the names of Lao Tzu, Chuang Tzu, and the *Tao Te Ching*. We can connect it with power by remembering that philosophy seeks knowledge and, as Bacon told the world pointedly, "knowledge is power"; to know how to repair a car is to have power over it. Obviously, the Taoists' eyes were not on machines; it was life that they wanted to repair. Knowledge that empowers life we call wisdom; and to live wisely, the Taoist philosophers argued, is to live in a way that conserves life's vitality by not expending it in useless, draining ways, the chief of which are friction and conflict. We shall examine Lao Tzu and Chuang Tzu's prescriptions for avoiding such dissipations in the second half of this chapter, but we can anticipate a single point here. Their recommendations revolve around the concept of *wu wei*, a phrase that translates literally as inaction but in Taoism means pure effectiveness. Action in the mode of *wu wei* is action in which friction — in interpersonal relationships, in intrapsychic conflict, and in relation to nature — is reduced to the minimum.

We turn now to the vitality cults as our second species of Taoism.

Augmented Power: Taoist Hygiene and Yoga

Taoist "adepts" — as we shall call the practitioners of this second kind of Taoism because all were engaged in training programs of some sort, many of them demanding — were not willing to settle for the philosophers' goal of managing their allotments of the *Tao* efficiently. They wanted to go beyond conserving to increasing the quota of the *Tao* they had to work with. In accounting terms we can say that if Philosophical Taoists worked at increasing net profits by cutting costs (reducing needless energy expenditures), Taoist adepts wanted to increase gross income.

The word *ch'i* cries out to be recognized as the rightful entry to this second school, for though it literally means breath, it actually means vital energy. The Taoists used it to refer to the power of the *Tao* that they experienced coursing through them — or not coursing because it was blocked — and their main object was to further its flow. *Ch'i* fascinated these Taoists. Blake registered their feelings precisely when he exclaimed, "Energy is delight," for energy is the life force and the Taoists loved life. To be alive is good; to be more alive is better; to be always alive is best, hence the Taoist immortality cults.

To accomplish their end of maximizing *ch'i*, these Taoists worked with three things: matter, movement, and their minds.

Respecting *matter*, they tried eating things — virtually everything, it would seem — to see if *ch'i* could be augmented nutritionally. In the course of this experimentation, they developed a remarkable pharmacopia of medicinal herbs,[2] but in a way this was incidental. What they really wanted was not cure but increase — increase and extension of the life force, the ultimate guarantor of which would be the much-sought elixir of life that would insure physical immortality.[3] Sexual experiments were also performed. In one such experiment men hypothesized that if they retained their semen during intercourse by pressing the ball of the thumb against the base of the penis at the moment of ejaculation, thereby diverting the semen into their own bodies,[4] they would absorb the *yin* of their female partners without dissipating their own *yang* energy. Breathing exercises were also developed. Working with air, the subtlest form of matter, they sought to draw *ch'i* from the atmosphere.

These efforts to extract *ch'i* from matter in its solid, liquid, and gaseous forms were supplemented by programs of bodily *movement* such as *t'ai chi chuan,* which gathers calisthenics, dance, meditation, *yin/yang* philosophy, and martial art into a synthesis that in this case was designed to draw *ch'i* from the cosmos and dislodge blocks to its internal flow. This last was the object of acupuncture as well.

Finally, turning to the *mind* itself, contemplatives, many of them hermits, developed Taoist meditation. This practice involved shutting out distractions and emptying the mind to the point where the power of the *Tao* might bypass bodily filters and enter the self directly.

This third way of increasing *ch'i* is more abstract than the others, so more needs to be said about it. For the reader who has read this book's chapter on Hinduism, the quickest gateway to meditational Taoism is to recollect what was said there about *raja yoga*, the way to God through psychophysical exercises. Whether or not China borrowed from India on this score, the physical postures and concentration techniques of Taoist meditation are so reminiscent of *raja yoga* that sinologists import the Sanskrit term and call it Taoist *yoga*. Still, the Chinese gave their *yoga* a distinctive twist. Their ubiquitous social concern led them to press the possibility that the *ch'i* that *yogis* accumulated through meditation could be transmitted psychically to the community to enhance its vitality and harmonize its affairs. Side by side with the Confucianists, who were working on the socializing *te* of moral example and ritualized etiquette, Taoist *yogis* sought to harness the *Tao* directly, drawing it first into their own heart-minds and then beaming it to others. *Yogis* who managed this feat would for the most part be unnoticed, but their life-giving enterprise did more for the community than the works of other benefactors.

We border on Philosophical Taoism here because animating this *yogic* Taoism was a dawning fascination in China with the inner as opposed to the outer self. Children do not separate these two sides of their being, and neither did early peoples. *Yogic* or meditational Taoism arose as the advancing self-consciousness of the Chinese brought subjective experience to full view. Novel, momentous, exciting, this world of the inner self invited exploration. So enthralling did it appear to its early explorers that matter suffered by comparison; it was mere shell and accretion. Still, the inner world housed a problem. Successive deposits of worry and distraction so silted the soul that their deposits had to be removed until "the self as it was meant to be" could surface. Pure consciousness would then appear, and the individual would see not merely "things perceived" but "that by which we perceive."

To arrive at this inwardness it was necessary to reverse all self-seeking and cultivate perfect cleanliness of thought and body. Pure spirit can be known only in a life that is "garnished and swept." Only where all is clean will it reveal itself; therefore "put self aside." Perturbing emotions must likewise be quelled. Ruffling the surface of the mind, they prevent introspection from seeing past them to the springs of consciousness beneath. (The proximity to Philosophical Taoism is becoming strong.) Desire and revulsion, grief and joy, delight and annoyance — each must subside if the mind is to return to its original purity, for in the end only peace and stillness are good for it. Let anxiety be dispelled and harmony between the mind and its cosmic source will come unsought.

> It is close at hand, stands indeed at our very side; yet is intangible, a thing that by reaching for cannot be got. Remote it seems as the furthest limit of the Infinite. Yet it is not far off; every day we use its power. For the Way of the Vital Spirit fills our whole frames, yet man cannot keep track of it. It goes, yet has not departed. It comes, yet is not here. It is muted, makes no note that can be heard, yet of a sudden we find that it is there in the mind. It is dim and dark, showing no outward form, yet in a great stream it flowed into us at our birth.[5]

Selflessness, cleanliness, and emotional calm are the preliminaries to arriving at full self-knowledge, but they must be climaxed by deep meditation. "Bide in silence, and the radiance of the spirit shall come in and make its home." For this to happen all outward impressions must be stilled and the senses withdrawn to a completely interior point of focus. Postures paralleling the Indian *asanas* were recommended, and the breath must be similarly controlled; it must be as soft and light as that of an infant, or even an embryo in the womb. The result will be a condition of alert waiting known as "sitting with a blank mind."

And when the realization arrives, what then? With it come truth, joy, and power. The climactic insight of meditational Taoism came with the impact of finality, everything at last having fallen into place. The condition could not be described as merely pleasurable. The direct perception of the source of one's awareness as "serene and immovable, like a monarch on a throne," brought joy unlike any hitherto known. The social utility of the condition, however, lay in the extraordinary power it provided over people and things, a power in fact which "could shift Heaven and Earth." "To the mind that is still, the whole universe surrenders." We have spoken of India in connection with this psychic power, but St. John of the Cross offers an identical promise: "Without labor you shall subject the peoples, and things shall be subject to you." Without lifting a finger overtly, a ruler who was adept in "stillness" could order a whole people with his mystical-moral power. A ruler who is desireless himself and has this much psychic power automatically turns his subjects from their unruly desires. He rules without even being known to rule.

> The sage relies on actionless activity;
> Puts himself in the background; but is always to the fore.
> Remains outside; but is always there.
> Is it not just because he does not strive for any personal end
> That all his personal ends are fulfilled? [6]

The Taoist *yogis* recognized that they could not hope for much understanding from the masses, and they made no attempt to publicize their position. When they did write their words tended to be veiled and cryptic, open to one interpretation by initiates and another by the general public. Part of the reason they wrote this way doubtless stemmed from their sensitivity to the lampooning that mysticism attracts from the uncongenial. We find even Chuang Tzu burlesquing their breathing exercises, reporting that these people "expel the used air with great energy and inhale the fresh air. Like bears, they climb trees in order to breathe with greater ease." Mencius joined in the fun. He likened those who sought psychic shortcuts to social harmony to impatient farmers who tug gently on their crops each night to speed their growth. Despite such satire Taoist *yoga* had an appreciable core of practitioners. Some sinologists consider it the basic perspective from which the *Tao Te Ching* was written. If this is true it is a testament to the veiled language of the book, for it is usually read in the philosophical way we shall come to. Before we turn to that way, however, we must introduce the third major branch of Taoism, which is religious.

Vicarious Power: Religious Taoism

Philosophical Taoism sought to manage life's normal quotient of the *Tao* efficiently, and energizing Taoism sought to boost its base supply, but something was lacking. Reflection and health programs take time, and the average Chinese lacked that commodity. Yet they too needed help; there were epidemics to be checked, marauding ghosts to be reckoned with, and rains to be induced or stopped as occasions demanded. Taoists responded to such problems. The measures they devised paralleled many of the doings of free-lance soothsayers, psychics, shamans, and faith healers who came by their powers naturally and constituted the unchanging landscape of Chinese folk religion. Religious Taoism institutionalized such activities. Influenced by Buddhism, which entered China around the time of Christ, the Taoist church — in Chinese the *Tao Chiao*, "Church Taoism" or "Taoist Teachings"— took shape in the second century A.D. It was anchored in a pantheon whose three originating deities included Lao Tzu. From these divinities sacred texts derived, which (by virtue of their divinely revealed origin) were accepted as true without reservation. The line of "papal" succession in the Taoist church continues down to the present in Taiwan.

Popular, Religious Taoism is a murky affair. Much of it looks — from the outside, we must always keep in mind — like crude superstition; but we must remember that we have little idea what energy is, how it proceeds, or the means by which (and extent to which) it can be augmented. We do know that faith healing can import or release energies, as does faith itself, including faith in oneself. Placebos likewise have effects. When we add to these the energies that magnetic personalities, rabble-rousers, and even pep rallies can generate, to say nothing of mysterious reserves that hypnotists tap into, concerning which we haven't an explanatory clue — if all this is borne in mind, it may temper our superciliousness and allow us to give religious Taoism a fair hearing. In any case its intent is clear. "The Taoist priesthood made cosmic life-power available for ordinary villagers."[7]

The texts of this school are crammed with descriptions of rituals that, if exactly performed, have magical effects, and the word *magic* here holds the key to sacerdotal, specifically religious, Taoism. The word must be freed, however, from the conventional meaning that has encrusted it. In its modern meaning, magic is trickery; it refers to performers who deceive audiences in ways that create the illusion that preternatural powers are at work. Traditionally, by contrast, magic was highly regarded. Jacob Boehme went so far as to assert that "magic is the best theology, for in it true faith is grounded. He is a fool that reviles it, for he knows it not and is more a juggler than a theologian of understanding." Traditionally, magic was understood as the means by which higher, occult powers are tapped for use in the visible world. Proceeding on the assumption that higher powers exist—the subtle rules the dense; energy rules matter, consciousness rules energy, and superconsciousness rules consciousness —magic made these powers available. When a hypnotist tells a subject that when his shoulder is touched his body will become rigid, and that happens—assistants can then place the subject's feet on one chair and his head on another without his body slumping—we come close to magic in the traditional sense, for the hypnotist calls into play powers that are not only astonishing but mysterious. Still, hypnotism falls short of magic in that the hypnotist is neither in an exceptional state of consciousness nor belongs to a sacerdotal order that is believed to be divinely empowered. For a genuine instance of magic in its traditional sense, we must turn to something like Peter's healing of Aeneas as reported in Acts 9:32–34.

> *Now as Peter went here and there among all the believers, he came down also to the saints living in Lydia. There he found a man named Aeneas, who had been bedridden for eight years, for he was paralyzed. Peter said to him, "Aeneas, Jesus Christ heals you; get up and make your bed!" And immediately he got up.*

Note that this was not a miracle. It would have been a miracle if Christ had empowered the paralytic Aeneas to climb out of bed without Peter's help, effecting thereby an instance of what clinicians refer to as spontaneous remission. As it was, Peter had a role in the cure, a necessary role we may assume, and we are confronted with magic; sacred magic, as it happens, for if a demon had been invoked for malevolent purposes, sorcery would have been at work.

It was under the rubric of magic as thus traditionally conceived that the Taoist church—dividing the territory with freelance wizards, exorcists, and shamans—devised ways to harness higher powers for humane ends.

The Mingling of the Powers

Philosophical Taoism, vitalizing programs for increasing one's individual *ch'i*, and the Taoist church: the three branches of Taoism, which at first seemed to have little in common, now show their family resemblances. All have the same concern—how to maximize the *Tao*'s animating *te*—and the specifics of their concerns fall on a continuum. The continuum begins with interest in how life's normal allotment of *ch'i* can be deployed to best effect (Philosophical Taoism). From there it moves on to ask if that normal quotient can be increased (Taoist vitalizing programs). Finally, it asks if cosmic energies can be gathered, as if by a burning glass, to be deployed vicariously for the welfare of people who need help (popular or Religious Taoism).

The danger in this arrangement is that in the interest of clarity the lines between the three divisions have been drawn too sharply. No solid walls separate them; the three are better regarded as currents in a common river. Throughout history each has interacted with the other two, right down to Taoism in Hong Kong and Taiwan today. John Blofeld, who lived in China for the twenty years preceding the Communist revolution, reported that he had never met a Taoist who was not involved to some degree with all three schools.

We can summarize. To *be* something, to *know* something, and *to be capable of* something is to rise above the superficial. A life has substance to the degree that it incorporates the profundity of mysticism (Taoist *yoga*), the direct wisdom of gnosis (Philosophical Taoism), and the productive power of magic (Religious Taoism). Where these three things come together there is a "school," and in China the school this chapter describes is Taoism.

It is now time to return to Philosophical Taoism and give it its due hearing.

Creative Quietude

The object of Philosophical Taoism is to align one's daily life to the *Tao*, to ride its boundless tide and delight in its flow. The basic way to do this, we earlier noted, is to perfect a life of *wu wei*. We have seen that *wu wei* should not be translated as do-nothingness or inaction, for those words suggest a vacant attitude of idleness or abstention. Better renderings are pure effectiveness and creative quietude.

Creative quietude combines within a single individual two seemingly incompatible conditions—supreme activity and supreme relaxation. These seeming incompatibles can coexist because human beings are not self-enclosed entities. They ride an unbounded sea of *Tao* that sustains them, as we would say, through their subliminal minds. One way to create is through following the calculated directives of the conscious mind. The results of this mode of action, however, are seldom impressive; they tend to smack more of sorting and arranging than of inspiration. Genuine creation, as every artist knows, comes when the more abundant resources of the subliminal self are somehow tapped. But for this to happen a certain dissociation from the surface self is needed. The conscious mind must relax, stop standing in its own light, let go. Only so is it possible to break through the law of reversed effort in which the more we try the more our efforts boomerang.

Wu wei is the supreme action, the precious suppleness, simplicity, and freedom that flows from us, or rather through us, when our private egos and conscious efforts yield to a power not their own. In a way it is virtue approached from a direction diametrically opposite to that of Confucius. Confucius turned every effort to building a pattern of ideal responses that might be consciously imitated. Taoism's approach is the opposite—to get the foundations of the self in tune with *Tao* and let behavior flow spontaneously. Action follows being; new action will follow new being, wiser being, stronger being. The *Tao Te Ching* puts this point without wasting a word. "The way to do," it says, "is to be."

How are we to describe the action that flows from a life that is grounded directly in *Tao?* Nurtured by a force that is infinitely subtle, infinitely intricate, it is a consummate gracefulness born from an abundant vitality that has no need for abruptness or violence. One simply lets the *Tao* flow in and flow out again until all life becomes a dance in which there is neither feverishness nor imbalance. *Wu wei* is life lived above tension:

> *Keep stretching a bow*
> *You repent of the pull,*
> *A whetted saw*
> *Grows thin and dull.*   (ch. 9)[8]

Far from inaction, however, it is the embodiment of suppleness, simplicity, and freedom—a kind of pure effectiveness in which no motion is wasted on bickering or outward show.

One may move so well that a foot-print never shows,
Speak so well that the tongue never slips,
Reckon so well that no counter is needed.   (ch. 27)

Effectiveness of this order obviously requires an extraordinary skill, a point conveyed in the Taoist story of the fisherman who was able to land enormous fish with a thread because it was so delicately made that it had no weakest point at which to break. But Taoist skill is seldom noticed, for viewed externally *wu wei*—never forcing, never under strain—seems quite effortless. The secret here lies in the way it seeks out the empty spaces in life and nature and moves through these. Chuang Tzu, the greatest popularizer of Philosophical Taoism, makes this point with his story of Prince Wen Hui's cook whose cleaver seemed never to lose its edge. When he cut up an ox, out went a hand, down went a shoulder. He planted a foot, he pressed with a knee, and the ox fell apart with a whisper. The bright cleaver murmured like a gentle wind. Rhythm! Timing! Like a sacred dance. Like "The Mulberry Grove," like ancient harmonies! Pressed for his secret, the cook replied: "There are spaces in the joints; the blade is thin and keen. When this thinness finds that space, there is all the room you need! It goes like a breeze! Hence I have this cleaver nineteen years as if newly sharpened![9]

The natural phenomenon that the Taoists saw as bearing the closest resemblance to *Tao* was water. They were struck by the way it would support objects and carry them effortlessly on its tide. The Chinese characters for swimmer, deciphered, mean literally "one who knows the nature of water." Similarly, one who understands the basic life force knows that it will sustain one if one stops thrashing and flailing and trusts oneself to its support.

Do you have the patience to wait
till your mud settles and the water is clear?
Can you remain unmoving
till the right action arises by itself?   (ch. 15)

Water, then, was the closest parallel to the *Tao* in the natural world. But it was also the prototype of *wu wei*. They noticed the way water adapts itself to its surroundings and seeks out the lowest places. So too,

> *The supreme good is like water,*
> *which nourishes all things without trying to.*
> *It is content with the low places that people disdain.*
> *Thus it is like the Tao.*   (ch. 8)

Yet despite its accommodation, water holds a power unknown to hard and brittle things. In a stream it follows the stones' sharp edges, only to turn them into pebbles, rounded to conform to its streamlined flow. It works its way past frontiers and under dividing walls. Its gentle current melts rocks and carries away the proud hills we call eternal.

> *Nothing in the world*
> *is as soft and yielding as water.*
> *Yet for dissolving the hard and inflexible,*
> *nothing can surpass it.*
>
> *The soft overcomes the hard;*
> *the gentle overcomes the rigid.*
> *Everyone knows this is true,*
> *but few can put it into practice.*   (ch. 78)

Infinitely supple, yet incomparably strong—these virtues of water are precisely those of *wu wei* as well. The person who embodies this condition, says the *Tao Te Ching*, "works without working." Such a one acts without strain, persuades without argument, is eloquent without flourish, and achieves results without violence, coercion, or pressure. Though the agent may be scarcely noticed, his or her influence is in fact decisive.

> *A leader is best*
> *When people barely know that he exists.*
> *Of a good leader, who talks little,*
> *When his work is done, his aim fulfilled,*
> *They will say, "We did this ourselves."*   (ch. 17)

A final characteristic of water that makes it an appropriate analogue to *wu wei* is the clarity it attains through being still. "Muddy water let stand," says the *Tao Te Ching*, "will clear." If you want to study the stars after being in a brightly lit room, you must wait twenty minutes for your eyes to dilate for their new assignment. There must be similar periods of waiting if the focal length of the mind is to readjust, withdrawing from the world's glare to the internal recesses of the soul.

> *The five colors can blind,*
> *The five tones deafen,*
> *The five tastes cloy.*
> *The race, the hunt, can drive men mad*
> *And their booty leave them no peace.*
> *Therefore a sensible man*
> *Prefers the inner to the outer eye.*   (ch. 12)

Clarity can come to the inner eye, however, only insofar as life attains a quiet that equals that of a deep and silent pool.

Other Taoist Values

Still following the analogy of water, the Taoists rejected all forms of self-assertiveness and competition. The world is full of people who are determined to be somebody or give trouble. They want to get ahead, to stand out. Taoism has little use for such ambitions. "The ax falls first on the tallest tree."

> *He who stands on tiptoe*
> *doesn't stand firm.*
> *He who rushes ahead*
> *doesn't go far.*
> *He who tries to shine*
> *dims his own light.*   (ch. 24)

Their almost reverential attitude toward humility led the Taoists to honor hunchbacks and cripples because of the way they typified meekness and self-effacement. They were fond of pointing out that the value of cups, windows, and doorways lies in the parts of them that are not there. "Selfless as melting ice" is one of their descriptive figures. The Taoists' refusal to clamber for position sprang from a profound disinterest in the things the world prizes. The point comes out in the story of Chuang Tzu's visit to the minister of a neighboring state. Someone told the minister that Chuang Tzu was coming in the hope of replacing him. The minister was alarmed. But when Chuang Tzu heard of the rumor he said to the minister:

In the South there is a bird. It is called yuan-ch'u. *Have you heard of it? This* yuan ch'u *starts from the southern ocean and flies to the northern ocean. During its whole journey it perches on no tree save the sacred Wo-tung, eats no fruit save that of the Persian Lilac, drinks only at the Magic Well. It happened that an owl that had got hold of the rotting carcass of a rat looked up as this bird flew by, and terrified lest the* yuan ch'u *should stop and snatch at the succulent morsel, it screamed, "Shoo! Shoo!" And now I am told that you are trying to "shoo" me off from this precious Ministry of yours.* [10]

So it is with most of the world's prides. They are not the true values they are thought to be. What is the point of competition or assertiveness? The *Tao* seems to get along very well without them.

Nature does not have to insist,
Can blow for only half a morning,
Rain for only half a day.   (ch. 23)

People should avoid being strident and aggressive not only toward other people but also toward nature. On the whole, the modern Western attitude has been to regard nature as an antagonist, an object to be squared off against, dominated, controlled, conquered. Taoism's attitude is the opposite of this. There is a profound naturalism in Taoist thought, but it is the naturalism of a Rousseau, a Wordsworth, a Thoreau, not that of a Galileo or Bacon.

Those who would take over the earth
And shape it to their will
Never, I notice, succeed.
The earth is like a vessel so sacred
That at the mere approach of the profane
It is marred
And when they reach out their fingers it is gone.   (ch. 29)

Nature is to be befriended. When the British scaled earth's highest peak, the exploit was widely hailed as "the conquest of Everest." D. T. Suzuki remarked: "We orientals would have spoken of befriending Everest." The Japanese team that scaled Anapurna, the second highest peak, climbed to within fifty feet of the summit and deliberately stopped, provoking a Western mountaineer to exclaim in disbelief, "That's class!" Taoism seeks attunement with nature, not dominance. Its approach is ecological, a characteristic that led Joseph Needham to point out that despite China's backwardness in scientific theory she early developed "an organic philosophy of nature closely resembling that which modern science has been forced to adopt after three centuries of mechanical materialism." The ecological approach of Taoism has inspired many Western architects, most notably Frank Lloyd Wright. Taoist temples do not stand out from their surroundings. They nestle against the hills, back under the trees, blending in with the environment. At best, human beings do likewise. Their highest achievement is to identify themselves with the *Tao* and let it work its magic through them.

This Taoist approach to nature deeply affected Chinese art. It is no accident that the greatest periods of Chinese art have coincided with upsurges of Taoist influence. Before assuming brush and silk, painters would go out to nature and lose themselves in it, to become, say, the bamboo that they would paint. They would sit for half a day or fourteen years before making a stroke. The Chinese word for landscape painting is composed of the radicals for mountain and water, one of which suggests vastness and solitude, the other pliability, endurance, and continuous movement. The human part in the vastness is small, so we have to look closely for human beings in the paintings if we find them at all. Usually, they are climbing with their bundles, riding a buffalo, or poling a boat—the self with its journey to make, its burden to carry, its hill to climb, but surrounded by beauty on every side. People are not as formidable as mountains; they do not live as long as the pines. Yet they too belong in the scheme of things as surely as do the birds and the clouds. And through them, as through the rest of the world, flows the everlasting *Tao*.

Taoist naturalism combined with a propensity for naturalness as well. Pomp and extravagance were regarded as silly. When Chuang Tzu's followers asked permission to give him a grand funeral, he replied: "Heaven and earth are my inner and outer coffins. The sun, moon, and stars are my drapery, and the whole creation my funeral procession. What more do I want?" Civilization was ridiculed and the primitive idealized. "Let us have a small country with few inhabitants," Lao Tzu proposed. "Let the people return to the use of knotted cords [for keeping records]. Let them obtain their food sweet, their clothing beautiful, their homes comfortable, their rustic tasks pleasurable." Travel was discouraged as pointless and conducive to idle curiosity. "The neighboring state might be so near at hand that one could hear the cocks crowing in it and dogs barking. But the people would grow old and die without ever having been there."[11]

It was this preference for naturalness and simplicity that most separated the Taoist from the Confucian. The basic objectives of the two schools did not differ widely, but the Taoists had small patience with the Confucian approach to them. All formalism, show, and ceremony left them cold. What could be hoped for from punctiliousness or the meticulous observance of propriety? The whole approach was artificial, a lacquered surface that was bound to prove brittle and repressive. Confucianism here was but one instance of the human tendency to approach life in regulated mode. All calculated systems, the very attempt to arrange life in shipshape order, is pointless. As different ways of slicing the same reality, none of them amounts to more than Three in the Morning. And what is Three in the Morning? Once, in the state of Sung, hard times forced a keeper of monkeys to reduce their rations. "From now on," he announced, "it will be three in the morning and four in the evening." Faced with howls of rebellion, the keeper agreed to negotiate, and eventually accepted his monkeys' demand that it be four in the morning and three in the evening. The monkeys gloried in their triumph.

Another feature of Taoism is its notion of the relativity of all values and, as its correlative, the identity of opposites. Here Taoism tied in with the traditional Chinese *yin/yang* symbol, which is pictured thus:

This polarity sums up all of life's basic oppositions: good/evil, active/passive, positive/negative, light/dark, summer/winter, male/female. But though the halves are in tension, they are not flatly opposed; they complement and balance each other. Each invades the other's hemisphere and takes up its abode in the deepest recess of its partner's domain. And in the end both find themselves resolved by the circle that surrounds them, the *Tao* in its eternal wholeness. In the context of that wholeness, the opposites appear as no more than phases in an endless cycling process, for each turns incessantly into its opposite, exchanging places with it. Life does not move onward and upward toward a fixed pinnacle or pole. It bends back upon itself to come, full circle, to the realization that all is one and all is well.

Those who meditate on this profound symbol, Taoists maintain, will find that it affords better access to the world's secrets than any length of words and discussion. Faithful to its import, Taoism eschews all sharp dichotomies. No perspective in this relative world can be considered as absolute. Who knows when the longest way 'round might not prove to be the shortest way home? Or consider the relativity of dream and wakefulness. Chuang Tzu dreamed that he was a butterfly, and during the dream had no notion that he had ever been anything else. When he awoke, however, he was astonished to find that he was Chuang Tzu. But this left him with a question. Was he really Chuang Tzu who had dreamed that he was a butterfly, or was he a butterfly that was now dreaming that it was Chuang Tzu?

All values and concepts, then, are ultimately relative to the mind that entertains them. When it was suggested to the wren and the cicada that there are birds that fly hundreds of miles without alighting, both quickly agreed that such a thing was impossible. "You and I know very well," they nodded, "that the furthest one can ever get, even by the most tremendous effort, is to that elm tree over there, and even this one cannot be sure of reaching every time. Often one finds oneself dragged back to earth long before one gets there. All these stories about flying hundreds of miles at a stretch are sheer nonsense."

In the Taoist perspective even good and evil are not head-on opposites. The West has tended to dichotomize the two, but Taoists are less categorical. They buttress their reserve with the story of a farmer whose horse ran away. His neighbor commiserated, only to be told, "Who knows what's good or bad?" It was true, for the next day the horse returned, bringing with it a drove of wild horses it had befriended. The neighbor reappeared, this time with congratulations for the windfall. He received the same response: "Who knows what is good or bad?" Again this proved true, for the next day the farmer's son tried to mount one of the wild horses and fell, breaking his leg. More commiserations from the neighbor, which elicited the question: "Who knows what is good or bad?" And for a fourth time the farmer's point prevailed, for the following day soldiers came by commandeering for the army, and the son was exempted because of his injury. If this all sounds very much like Zen, it should; for Buddhism processed through Taoism became Zen.

Taoism follows its principle of relativity to its logical limit by positioning life and death as complementing cycles in the *Tao's* rhythm. When Chuang Tzu's wife died, his friend Hui-tzu visited him to express his condolences, only to find Chuang Tzu sitting on the ground with his legs spread wide apart, singing away and whacking out a tune on the back of a wooden bowl.

"After all," said his friend, "she lived with you devotedly all these years, watched your eldest son grow to manhood, and grew old along with you. For you not to have shed a tear over her remains would have been bad enough, but singing and drumming away on a bowl — this is just too much!"

"You misjudge," said Chuang Tzu. "When she died I was in despair, as any man well might be. But then I realized that before she was born she had no body, and it became clear to me that the same process of change that brought her to birth eventually brought her to death. If someone is tired and has gone to lie down, we do not pursue her with hooting and bawling. She whom I have lost has lain down to sleep for a while in the chamber between heaven and earth. To wail and groan while my wife is sleeping would be to deny nature's sovereign law. So I refrain."

Elsewhere Chuang Tzu expressed his confidence in the face of death directly:

> *There is the globe,*
> *The foundation of my bodily existence.*
> *It wears me out with work and duties,*
> *It gives me rest in old age,*
> *It gives me peace in death.*
> *For the one who supplied me with what I needed in life*
> *Will also give me what I need in death.*[12]

It is no surprise to find an outlook as averse to violence as Taoism verging on pacifism. There are passages in the *Tao Te Ching* that read almost like the Sermon on the Mount.

One who would guide a leader of men in the uses of life
Will warn him against the use of arms for conquest.
Even the finest arms are an instrument of evil:
An army's harvest is a waste of thorns.   (ch. 30)

Weapons are the tools of violence;
all decent men detest them.
Weapons are the tools of fear;
a decent man will avoid them
except in the direst necessity
and, if compelled, will use them
only with the utmost restraint.
Peace is the highest value. . . .
He enters a battle gravely,
with sorrow and with great compassion,
as if he were attending a funeral.   (ch. 31)

That in China the scholar ranked at the top of the social scale may
have been Confucius' doing, but Taoism is fully as responsible for
placing the soldier at the bottom. "The way for a vital person to go is
not the way of a soldier." Only one "who recognizes all people as
members of his or her own body is qualified to guard them. . . .
Heaven arms with compassion those whom she would not see
destroyed."

War is a somber matter, and Taoism spoke to life's solemn, somber issues. Yet it always retained a quality of lightness verging on gai-
ety. There is a sophistication, an urbanity, a charm about the
perspective that is infectious. "He who feels punctured," notes the
Tao Te Ching, "must once have been a bubble." The economy, directness, and good humor in such a statement is typical of its entire outlook. In its freedom from a heavy-booted approach to life, Taoism is
at one with the rest of China; but it is also, as we have seen, free of the
Confucian tendency toward rigidity and formalism. Taoist literature
is full of dialogues with Confucianists in which the latter come off as
stuffy and pompous. An instance is the story of the Taoist Chuang Tzu
and the Confucian Hui Tzu, who on an afternoon's stroll came to a
bridge over the Hao River. "Look how the minnows dart hither and
thither at will. Such is the pleasure fish enjoy," Chuang Tzu
remarked.

"You are not a fish," responded Hui Tzu. "How do you know what gives pleasure to fish?"

"You are not I," said Chuang Tzu. "How do you know I don't know what gives pleasure to fish?"

Conclusion

Circling around each other like *yin* and *yang* themselves, Taoism and Confucianism represent the two indigenous poles of the Chinese character. Confucius represents the classical, Lao Tzu the romantic. Confucius stresses social responsibility, Lao Tzu praises spontaneity and naturalness. Confucius' focus is on the human, Lao Tzu's on what transcends the human. As the Chinese themselves say, Confucius roams within society, Lao Tzu wanders beyond. Something in life reaches out in each of these directions, and Chinese civilization would certainly have been poorer if either had not appeared.

There are books whose first reading casts a spell that is never quite undone, the reason being that they speak to the deepest "me" in the reader. For all who quicken at the thought that anywhere, at every time, the *Tao* is within us, the *Tao Te Ching* is such a book. Mostly it has been so for the Chinese, but an American poet can equally find it "the straightest, most logical explanation as yet advanced for the continuance of life, the most logical use yet advised for enjoying it."[13] Though obviously never practiced to perfection, its lessons of simplicity, openness, and wisdom have been for millions of Chinese a joyful guide.

> There is a being, wonderful, perfect;
> It existed before heaven and earth.
> How quiet it is!
> How spiritual it is!
> It stands alone and it does not change.
> It moves around and around, but does not on this account
>   suffer.
> All life comes from it.
> It wraps everything with its love as in a garment, and
> yet it claims no honor, it does not demand to be Lord.
> I do not know its name, and so I call it Tao, the Way,
> and I rejoice in its power.[14]

Suggestions for Further Reading

No rendering of Taoism's primary text can be definitive, but Stephen Mitchell's *Tao Te Ching* (Harper & Row, 1989) comes as close to being definitive for our time as any I know. D. C. Lau's translation (New York: Penguin Books, 1963) includes scholarly notes and a useful introduction. The Gia-fu Feng/Jane English edition (New York: Random House, 1972) includes photographs and the Chinese text in handsome calligraphy, and, in addition to being reliable, is a work of art.

Thomas Merton's *The Way of Chuang Tzu* (New York: New Directions, 1965) presents the outlook of this engaging and important thinker admirably. Chuang Tzu's full corpus is available in Burton Watson (tr.), *The Complete Works of Chuang Tzu* (New York: Columbia University Press, 1968).

Max Kaltenmark's *Lao Tzu and Taoism* (Stanford, CA: Stanford University Press, 1969) presents a good overview of the Taoist tradition as a whole.

One of the most interesting and original discussions of Philosophical Taoism is to be found in Part II of Toshihiko Izutsu's *Sufism and Taoism* (Berkeley: University of California Press, 1984).

Notes

1. *Tao Te Ching*, chapter 56.
2. "Any list of the drugs used by the ancient Chinese doctors, for many of which there is ample historical if not laboratory evidence of efficacy, leaves the entire Western world of medicine open to accusations of negligence and haughtiness." Richard Selzer, *Mortal Lessons: Notes on the Art of Surgery* (New York: Simon & Schuster, 1987), 116.
3. Immortality had both crude and subtle readings in Taoism. Michael Saso writes that "a Taoist is by definition a man who seeks immortality in the present life," but he goes on to add that for many this immortality "is not so much a longevity whereby man does not die but a state wherein he does not descend to the punishments of a fiery underworld after death." *Taoism and the Rite of Cosmic Renewal* (Pullman: Washington State University Press, 1989), 3.
4. In actuality the semen then entered the bladder, where it was expelled with the urine, but the Chinese did not know this.
5. Quoted by Arthur Waley, *The Way and Its Power*, 1934. Reprint. (London: Allen & Unwin, 1958), 48–49.

6. *Tao Te Ching*, chapters 2 and 7, Arthur Waley's translation.

7. Daniel Overmyer, *Religions of China* (New York: Harper & Row, 1986), 39.

8. Unless otherwise specified, quotations in this section and the next are from the *Tao Te Ching*. Those from chapters 8, 15, 24, 31, and 78 are from Stephen Mitchell's renderings in his *Tao Te Ching* (New York: Harper & Row, 1988); those from chapters 9, 12, 17, 23, 27, 29, and 30 are from Witter Bynner's *The Way of Life According to Laotzu*, 1944. Reprint. (New York: Putnam, 1986.)

9. Adapted from Thomas Merton's translation in his *The Way of Chuang Tzu* (New York: New Directions, 1965), 45–47.

10. Burton Watson (tr.), *Chuang Tzu: The Basic Writings* (New York: Columbia University Press, 1964), 109–10.

11. Fung Yu-lan's translation of the *Tao Te Ching*, chapter 80, in his *A Short History of Chinese Philosophy* (Princeton, NJ: Princeton University Press, 1953), 20.

12. Quoted in K. L. Reichelt's translation of the twenty-fifth chapter of the *Tao Te Ching* in his *Meditation and Piety in the Far East* (New York: Harper and Brothers, 1954), 102.

13. Bynner, *The Way of Life*, 12–13.

14. Adapted from K. L. Reichelt's translation of the twenty-fifth chapter of the *Tao Te Ching* in his *Meditation and Piety*, 41.

VI. Islam

We can begin with an anomaly. Of all the non-Western religions, Islam stands closest to the West—closest geographically, and also closest ideologically; for religiously it stands in the Abrahamic family of religions, while philosophically it builds on the Greeks. Yet despite this mental and spatial proximity, Islam is the most difficult religion for the West to understand. "No part of the world," an American columnist has written, "is more hopelessly and systematically and stubbornly misunderstood by us than that complex of religion, culture and geography known as Islam."[1]

This is ironic, but the irony is easily explained. Proximity is no guarantee of concord—tragically, more homicides occur within families than anywhere else. Islam and the West are neighbors. Common borders have given rise to border disputes, which, beginning with raids and counterraids, have escalated into vendettas, blood feuds, and all-out war. There is a happier side; in times and places Christians, Muslims, and Jews have lived together harmoniously—one thinks of Moorish Spain. But for a good part of the last fourteen hundred years, Islam and Europe have been at war, and people seldom have a fair picture of their enemies.[2] Islam is going to be an interesting religion for this book to negotiate.

Mistakes begin with its very name. Until recently it was called Muhammadanism by the West, which is not only inaccurate but offensive. It is inaccurate, Muslims say, because Muhammad didn't create this religion; God did—Muhammad was merely God's mouthpiece. Beyond this, the title is offensive because it conveys the impression that Islam focuses on a man rather than on God. To name

Christianity after Christ is appropriate, they say, for Christians believe that Christ was God. But to call Islam Muhammadanism is like calling Christianity St. Paulism. The proper name of this religion is Islam. Derived from the root *s-l-m*, which means primarily "peace" but in a secondary sense "surrender," its full connotation is "the peace that comes when one's life is surrendered to God." This makes Islam — together with Buddhism, from *budh*, awakening — one of the two religions that is named after the attribute it seeks to cultivate; in Islam's case, life's total surrender to God. Those who adhere to Islam are known as Muslims.

Background

"Around the name of the Arabs," writes Philip Hitti, "gleams that halo which belongs to the world-conquerors. Within a century after their rise this people became the masters of an empire extending from the shores of the Atlantic Ocean to the confines of China, an empire greater than that of Rome at its zenith. In this period of unprecedented expansion, they assimilated to their creed, speech, and even physical type, more aliens than any stock before or since, not excepting the Hellenic, the Roman, the Anglo-Saxon, or the Russian."[3]

Central in this Arab rise to greatness was their religion, Islam. If we ask how it came into being, the outsider's answer points to socioreligious currents that were playing over Arabia in Muhammad's day and uses them to explain what happened. The Muslims' answer is different. Islam begins not with Muhammad in sixth-century Arabia, they say, but with God. "In the beginning God . . ." the book of Genesis tells us. The Koran agrees. It differs only in using the word *Allah*. Allah is formed by joining the definite article *al* (meaning "the") with *Ilah* (God). Literally, Allah means "the God." Not *a* god, for there is only one. *The* God. When the masculine plural ending *im* is dropped from the Hebrew word for God, *Elohim*, the two words sound much alike.

God created the world, and after it human beings. The name of the first man was Adam. The descendants of Adam led to Noah, who had a son named Shem. This is where the word Semite comes from; literally a Semite is a descendant of Shem. Like the Jews, the Arabs consider themselves a Semitic people. The descendants of Shem led to Abraham, and so far we are still in the tradition of Judaism and

Christianity. Indeed, it was the submission of Abraham in his supreme test—would he be willing to sacrifice his son Ishmael?—that appears to have provided Islam with its name. Abraham married Sarah. Sarah had no son, so Abraham, wanting to continue his line, took Hagar for his second wife. Hagar bore him a son, Ishmael, whereupon Sarah conceived and likewise had a son, named Isaac. Sarah then demanded that Abraham banish Ishmael and Hagar from the tribe. Here we come to the first divergence between the koranic and biblical accounts. According to the Koran, Ishmael went to the place where Mecca was to rise. His descendants, flourishing in Arabia, become Muslims; whereas those of Isaac, who remained in Palestine, were Hebrews and became Jews.

The Seal of the Prophets

Following Ishmael's line in Arabia, we come in the latter half of the sixth century A.D. to Muhammad, the prophet through whom Islam reached its definitive form, Muslims believe. There had been authentic prophets of God before him, but he was their culmination; hence he is called "The Seal of the Prophets." No valid prophets will follow him.

The world into which Muhammad was born is described by subsequent Muslims in a single word: ignorant. Life under the conditions of the desert had never been serene. People felt almost no obligation to anyone outside their tribes. Scarcity of material goods made brigandage a regional institution and the proof of virility. In the sixth century political deadlock and the collapse of the magistrate in the leading city of Mecca aggravated this generally chaotic situation. Drunken orgies were commonplace, and the gaming impulse uncontrolled. The prevailing religion watched from the sidelines, providing no check. Best described as an animistic polytheism, it peopled the sandy wastes with beastly sprites called *jinn* or demons. Fantastic personifications of desert terrors, they inspired neither exalted sentiments nor moral restraint. Conditions could hardly have been better calculated to produce a smoldering undercurrent, which erupted in sudden affrays and blood feuds, some of which extended for half a century. The times called for a deliverer.

He was born into the leading tribe of Mecca, the Koreish, in approximately A.D. 570, and was named Muhammad, "highly praised," which name has since been borne by more male children than any other in the world. His early life was cradled in tragedy, for his father died a few days before he was born, his mother when he was six, and his grandfather, who cared for him after his mother's death, when he was eight. Thereafter he was adopted into his uncle's home. Though the latter's declining fortunes forced the young orphan to work hard minding his uncle's flocks, he was warmly received by his new family. The angels of God, we are told, had opened Muhammad's heart and filled it with light.

The description epitomizes his early character as this comes down to us by tradition. Pure-hearted and beloved in his circle, he was, it is said, of sweet and gentle disposition. His bereavements having made him sensitive to human suffering in every form, he was always ready to help others, especially the poor and the weak. His sense of honor, duty, and fidelity won him, as he grew older, the high and enviable titles of "The True," "The Upright," "The Trustworthy One." Yet despite his concern for others, he remained removed from them in outlook and ways, isolated in a corrupt and degenerate society. As he grew from childhood to youth and from youth to manhood, the lawless strife of his contemporaries, the repeated outbursts of pointless quarrels among tribes frequenting the Meccan fairs, and the general immorality and cynicism of his day combined to produce in the prophet-to-be a reaction of horror and disgust. Silently, broodingly, his thoughts were turning inward.

Upon reaching maturity he took up the caravan business, and at the age of twenty-five entered the service of a wealthy widow named Khadija. His prudence and integrity impressed her greatly, and gradually their relation deepened into affection, then love. Though she was fifteen years his senior, they were married and the match proved happy in every respect. During a long, desolate period that lay ahead, in which no one would believe in him, not even himself, Khadija was to remain steadfastly by his side, consoling him and tending hope's thin flame. "God," tradition was to record, "comforted him through her, for she made his burden light."

Following his marriage were fifteen years of preparation before his ministry was to begin. A mountain on the outskirts of Mecca, known as Mount Hira, contained a cave, and Muhammad, needing solitude, began to frequent it. Peering into the mysteries of good and evil, unable to accept the crudeness, superstition, and fratricide that were accepted as normal, "this great fiery heart, seething, simmering like a great furnace of thoughts," was reaching out for God.[4]

The desert *jinn* were irrelevant to this quest, but one deity was not. Named Allah,[5] he was worshiped by the Meccans not as the only God but as an impressive one nonetheless. Creator, supreme provider, and determiner of human destiny, he was capable of inspiring authentic religious feeling and genuine devotion. Certain contemplatives of the time, called *hanifs*, worshiped Allah exclusively, and Muhammad was one of their number. Through vigils, often lasting the entire night, Allah's reality became for Muhammad increasingly evident and awesome. Fearful and wonderful, real as life, real as death, real as the universe he had ordained, Allah (Muhammad was convinced) was far greater than his countrymen supposed. This God, whose majesty overflowed a desert cave to fill all heaven and earth, was surely not a god or even the greatest of gods. He was what his name literally claimed: He was *the* God, One and only, One without rival. Soon from this mountain cave was to sound the greatest phrase of the Arabic language; the deep, electrifying cry that was to rally a people and explode their power to the limits of the known world: *La ilaha illa 'llah!* There is no god but God!

But first the prophet must receive, around 610, his commission. Gradually, as Muhammad's visits to the cave became more compelling, the command that he later saw as predestined took form. It was the same command that had fallen earlier on Abraham, Moses, Samuel, Isaiah, and Jesus. Wherever, whenever, this call comes, its form may differ but its essence is the same. A voice falls from heaven saying, "You are the appointed one." On the Night of Power, as a strange peace pervaded creation and all nature was turned toward its Lord, in the middle of that night, say the Muslims, the Book was opened to a ready soul. Some add that on the anniversary of that Night it is possible to hear the grass grow and the trees speak, and that those who do so become saints or sages, for on the annual return of that Night one can see through the fingers of God.[6]

On that first Night of Power, as Muhammad lay on the floor of the cave, his mind locked in deepest contemplation, there came to him an angel in the form of a man. The angel said to him: "Proclaim!"[7]

and he said: "I am not a proclaimer"; whereupon, as Muhammad was himself to report, "the Angel took me and whelmed me in his embrace until he had reached the limit of my endurance. Then he released me and said again, 'Proclaim!' Again I said: 'I am not a proclaimer,' and again he whelmed me in his embrace. When again he had reached the limit of my endurance he said 'Proclaim!', and when I again protested, he whelmed me for a third time, this time saying:

> Proclaim in the name of your Lord who created!
> Created man from a clot of blood.
> Proclaim: Your Lord is the Most Generous,
> Who teaches by the pen;
> Teaches man what he knew not."   (Koran 96:1–3)

Arousing from his trance, Muhammad felt as if the words he had heard had been branded on his soul. Terrified, he rushed home and fell into paroxysms. Coming to himself, he told Khadija that he had become either a prophet or "one possessed—mad." At first she resisted this disjunction, but on hearing his full story she became his first convert—which, Muslims often remark, in itself speaks well for his authenticity, for if anyone understands a man's true character it is his wife. "Rejoice, O dear husband, and be of good cheer," she said. "You will be the Prophet of this people."

We can imagine the spiritual anguish, the mental doubts, the waves of misgivings that followed in the wake of the experience. Was the voice really God's? Would it come again? Above all, what would it require?

It returned repeatedly, and its command was always the same—to proclaim. "O thou, inwrapped in thy mantle, arise and warn, and glorify thy Lord." Muhammad's life was no more his own. From that time forth it was given to God and to humanity, preaching with unswerving purpose in the face of relentless persecution, insult, and outrage, the words that God was to transmit for twenty-three years.

The content of the revelation will be reserved for later sections. Here we need only speak of the response it drew and note that its appeal throughout was to human reason as vectored by religious discernment.

In an age charged with supernaturalism, when miracles were accepted as the stock-in-trade of the most ordinary saint, Muhammad refused to pander to human credulity. To miracle-hungry idolaters seeking signs and portents, he cut the issue clean: "God has not sent me to work wonders; He has sent me to preach to you. My Lord; be praised! Am I more than a man sent as an apostle?"[8] From first to last he resisted every impulse to inflate his own image. "I never said that God's treasures are in my hand, that I knew the hidden things, or that I was an angel. I am only a preacher of God's words, the bringer of God's message to mankind."[9] If signs be sought, let them be not of Muhammad's greatness but of God's, and for these one need only open one's eyes. The heavenly bodies holding their swift, silent course in the vault of heaven, the incredible order of the universe, the rain that falls to relieve the parched earth, palms bending with golden fruit, ships that glide across the seas laden with goodness — can these be the handiwork of gods of stone? What fools to cry for signs when creation tokens nothing else! In an age of credulity, Muhammad taught respect for the world's incontrovertible order, a respect that was to bring Muslims to science before it did Christians. Apart from his nocturnal ascent through the heavens, which will be mentioned, he claimed only one miracle, that of the Koran itself. That he with his own resources could have produced such truth — this was the one naturalistic hypothesis he could not accept.

As for the reaction to his message, it was (for all but a few) violently hostile. The reasons for the hostility can be reduced to three: (1) Its uncompromising monotheism threatened polytheistic beliefs and the considerable revenue that was coming to Mecca from pilgrimages to its 360 shrines (one for every day of the lunar year); (2) its moral teachings demanded an end to the licentiousness that citizens clung to; and (3) its social content challenged an unjust order. In a society riven with class distinctions, the new Prophet was preaching a message that was intensely democratic. He was insisting that in the sight of his Lord all people were equal.

As such a teaching suited neither their tastes nor their privileges, the Meccan leaders were determined to have none of it. They began their attack with ridicule: pinpricks of laughter, petty insults, and hoots of derision. When these proved ineffective, their words turned uglier — to abuse, calumny, vilification, and then overt threats. When these too failed, they resorted to open persecution. They covered Muhammad and his followers with dirt and filth as they were praying. They pelted them with stones, beat them with sticks, threw them in prison, and tried to starve them out by refusing to sell to them. To no avail; persecution only steeled the will of Muhammad's followers. "Never since the days when primitive Christianity startled the world from its sleep," wrote a scholar whose words assume added weight because he was on the whole a severe critic of Islam, "had men seen the like arousing of spiritual life—of faith that suffers sacrifices."[10] Muhammad himself set the pattern for their fidelity. Under the most perilous of circumstances, he continued to throw heart and soul into his preaching, adjuring listeners wherever he could find them to abandon their evil ways and prepare for the day of reckoning.

At first the odds were so heavily against him that he made few converts; three long years of heartbreaking effort yielded less than forty. But his enemies could do nothing to forever seal the hearts of the Meccans against his words. Slowly but steadily, people of energy, talent, and worth became convinced of the truth of his message until, by the end of a decade, several hundred families were acclaiming him as God's authentic spokesman.

The Migration That Led to Victory

By this time the Meccan nobility was alarmed. What had begun as a pretentious prophetic claim on the part of a half-crazed camel driver had turned into a serious revolutionary movement that was threatening their very existence. They were determined to rid themselves of the troublemaker for good.

As he faced this severest crisis of his career, Muhammad was suddenly waited on by a delegation of the leading citizens of Yathrib, a city 280 miles to Mecca's north. Through pilgrims and other visitors to Mecca, Muhammad's teachings had won a firm hold in Yathrib. The city was facing internal rivalries that put it in need of a strong leader from without, and Muhammad looked like the man. After receiving a delegation's pledge that they would worship Allah only, that they would observe the precepts of Islam, and that they would obey its prophet in all that was right and defend him and his adherents as they would their women and children, Muhammad received a sign from God to accept the charge. About seventy families preceded him. When the Meccan leaders got wind of the exodus they did everything in their power to prevent his going; but, together with his close companion Abu Bakr, he eluded their watch and set out for Yathrib, taking refuge on the way in a crevice south of the city. Horsemen scouring the countryside came so close to discovering them that Muhammad's companion was moved to despair. "We are only two," he murmured. "No, we are three," Muhammad answered, "for God is with us." The Koran agrees. "He was with them," it observes, for they were not discovered. After three days, when the search had slackened, they managed to procure two camels and make their hazardous way by unfrequented paths to the city of their destination.

The year was 622. The migration, known in Arabic as the *Hijra,* is regarded by Muslims as the turning point in world history and is the year from which they date their calendar. Yathrib soon came to be known as Medinat al-Nabi, the City of the Prophet, and then by contraction simply to Medina, "the city."

From the moment of his arrival at Medina, Muhammad assumed a different role. From prophecy he was pressed into administration. The despised preacher became a masterful politician; the prophet was transformed into statesman. We see him as the master not merely of the hearts of a handful of devotees but of the collective life of a city, its judge and general as well as its teacher.

Even his detractors concede that he played his new role brilliantly. Faced with problems of extraordinary complexity, he proved to be a remarkable statesman. As the supreme magistrate, he continued to lead as unpretentious a life as he had in the days of his obscurity. He lived in an ordinary clay house, milked his own goats, and was accessible day and night to the humblest in his community. Often seen mending his own clothes, "no emperor with his tiaras was obeyed as this man in a cloak of his own clouting."[11] God, say Muslim historians, put before him the key to the treasures of this world, but he refused it.

Tradition depicts his administration as an ideal blend of justice and mercy. As chief of state and trustee of the life and liberty of his people, he exercised the justice necessary for order, meting out punishment to those who were guilty. When the injury was toward himself, on the other hand, he was gentle and merciful even to his enemies. In all, the Medinese found him a master whom it was as difficult not to love as not to obey. For he had, as one biographer has written, "the gift of influencing men, and he had the nobility only to influence for the good." [12]

For the remaining ten years of his life, his personal history merged with that of the Medinese commonwealth of which he was the center. Exercising superb statecraft, he welded the five heterogeneous and conflicting tribes of the city, three of which were Jewish, into an orderly confederation. The task was not an easy one, but in the end he succeeded in awakening in the citizens a spirit of cooperation unknown in the city's history. His reputation spread and people began to flock from every part of Arabia to see the man who had wrought this "miracle."

There followed the struggle with the Meccans for the mind of Arabia as a whole. In the second year of the *Hijra* the Medinese won a spectacular victory over a Meccan army many times larger, and they interpreted the victory as a clear sign that the angels of heaven were battling on their side. The following year, however, witnessed a reversal during which Muhammad himself was wounded. The Meccans did not follow up their victory until two years later, when they laid siege to Medina in a last desperate effort to force the Muslims to capitulate. The failure of this effort turned the tide permanently in Muhammad's favor; and within three years—eight years after his Migration from Mecca—he who had left as a fugitive returned as conqueror. The city that had treated him cruelly now lay at his feet, with his former persecutors at his mercy. Typically, however, he did not press his victory. In the hour of his triumph the past was forgiven. Making his way to the famous Ka'ba, a cubical temple (said to have been built by Abraham) that Muhammad rededicated to Allah and adopted as Islam's focus, he accepted the virtual mass conversion of the city. Himself, he returned to Medina.

Two years later, in A.D. 632 (10 A.H., After the *Hijra*), Muhammad died with virtually all of Arabia under his control. With all the power of armies and police, no other Arab had ever succeeded in uniting his countrymen as he had. Before the century closed his followers had conquered Armenia, Persia, Syria, Palestine, Iraq, North Africa, and Spain, and had crossed the Pyrenees into France. But for their defeat by Charles Martel in the Battle of Tours in 733, the entire Western world might today be Muslim. Within a brief span of mortal life, Muhammad had "called forth out of unpromising material a nation never united before, in a country that was hitherto but a geographical expression; established a religion which in vast areas superseded Christianity and Judaism and still claims the adherence of a goodly portion of the human race; and laid the basis of an empire that was soon to embrace within its far-flung boundaries the fairest provinces of the then civilized world." [13]

In *The 100: A Ranking of the Most Influential Persons in History,* Michael Hart places Muhammad first. His "unparalleled combination of secular and religious influence entitles Muhammad to be considered the most influential single figure in human history," Hart writes. [14] The explanation that Muslims give for that verdict is simple. The entire work, they say, was the work of God.

The Standing Miracle

The blend of admiration, respect, and affection that the Muslim feels for Muhammad is an impressive fact of history. They see him as a man who experienced life in exceptional range. Not only was he a shepherd, merchant, hermit, exile, soldier, lawmaker, prophet-priest-king, and mystic; he was also an orphan, for many years the husband of one wife much older than himself, a many times bereaved father, a widower, and finally the husband of many wives, some much younger than himself. In all of these roles he was exemplary. All this is in the minds of Muslims as they add to the mention of his name the benediction, "Blessings and peace be upon him." Even so, they never mistake him for the earthly center of their faith. That place is reserved for the bible of Islam, the Koran.

Literally, the word *al-qur'an* in Arabic (and hence "koran,") means a recitation. Fulfilling that purpose, the Koran is perhaps the most recited (as well as read) book in the world. Certainly, it is the world's most memorized book, and possibly the one that exerts the most influence on those who read it. So great was Muhammad's regard for its contents that (as we have seen) he considered it the only major miracle God worked through him — God's "standing miracle," as he called it. That he himself, unschooled to the extent that he was unlettered *(ummi)* and could barely write his name, could have produced a book that provides the ground plan of all knowledge and at the same time is grammatically perfect and without poetic peer — this, Muhammad, and with him all Muslims, are convinced defies belief. He put the point in a rhetorical question: "Do you ask for a greater miracle than this, O unbelieving people, than to have your language chosen as the language of that incomparable Book, one piece of which puts all your golden poetry to shame?"

Four-fifths the length of the New Testament, the Koran is divided into 114 chapters or *surahs,* which (with the exception of the short first chapter that figures in the Muslim's daily prayers) are arranged in order of decreasing length. Thus Surah Two has 286 verses, Surah Three has 200, down to Surah One Hundred Fourteen, which has only six.

Muslims tend to read the Koran literally. They consider it the earthly facsimile of an Uncreated Koran in almost exactly the way that Christians consider Jesus to have been the human incarnation of God. The comparison that reads, "If Christ is God incarnate, the Koran is God inlibrate" (from *liber,* Latin for book) is inelegant but not inaccurate. The created Koran is the instantiation, in letters and sounds, of the Koran's limitless essence in its Uncreated Form. Not that there are two Korans, of course. Rather, the created Koran is the formal crystallization of the infinite reality of the Uncreated Koran. Two levels of reality are operative here. There is the Divine Reality of the Uncreated Koran, and there is the earthly reality of the created Koran. When the created Koran is said to be a miracle, the miracle referred to is the presence of the Uncreated Koran within the letters and sounds of its created (and therefore necessarily in certain ways circumscribed) manifestation.

The words of the Koran came to Muhammad in manageable segments over twenty-three years through voices that seemed at first to vary and sometimes sounded like "the reverberating of bells," but which gradually condensed into a single voice that identified itself as Gabriel's. Muhammad had no control over the flow of the revelation; it descended on him independent of his will. When it arrived he was changed into a special state that was externally discernible. Both his appearance and the sound of his voice would change. He reported that the words assaulted him as if they were solid and heavy: "For We shall charge thee with a word of weight" (73:5; all such references in this chapter are to *surah* and verse[s] in the Koran). Once they descended while he was riding a camel. The animal sought vainly to support the added weight by adjusting its legs. By the time the revelation ceased, its belly was pressed against the earth and its legs splayed out. The words that Muhammad exclaimed in these often trance-like states were memorized by his followers and recorded on bones, bark, leaves, and scraps of parchment, with God preserving their accuracy throughout.

The Koran continues the Old and New Testaments, God's earlier revelations, and presents itself as their culmination: "We made a covenant of old with the Children of Israel [and] you have nothing of guidance until you observe the Torah and the Gospel" (5:70, 68). This entitles Jews and Christians to be included with Muslims as "People of the Book." (Because the context of the koranic revelation is the Middle East, religions of other lands are not mentioned, but their existence is implied and in principle validated, as in the following verses: "To every people we have sent a messenger. . . . [Some] We have mentioned to you, and [some] we have not mentioned to you" [10:47, 4:164]). Nevertheless, Muslims regard the Old and New Testaments as sharing two defects from which the Koran is free. For circumstantial reasons they record only portions of Truth. Second, the Jewish and Christian Bibles were partially corrupted in transmission, a fact that explains the occasional discrepancies that occur between their accounts and parallel ones in the Koran. Exemption from these two limitations makes the Koran the final and infallible revelation of God's will. Its second chapter says explicitly: "This is the Scripture whereof there is no doubt."

From the outside things look otherwise, for from without the Koran is all but impenetrable. No one has ever curled up on a rainy weekend to read the Koran. Carlyle confessed that it was "as toilsome reading as I ever undertook; a wearisome, confused jumble, crude, incondite. Nothing but a sense of duty could carry any European through the Koran." Sir Edward Gibbon said much the same: "The European will peruse with impatience its endless incoherent rhapsody of fable and precept, and declamation, which seldom excites a sentiment or an idea, which sometimes crawls in the dust, and is sometimes lost in the clouds." [15] How are we to understand the discrepancy of the Koran as read from within and from without?

The language in which it was proclaimed, Arabic, provides an initial clue. "No people in the world," writes Philip Hitti, "are so moved by the word, spoken or written, as the Arabs. Hardly any language seems capable of exercising over the minds of its users such irresistible influence as Arabic." Crowds in Cairo, Damascus, or

Baghdad can be stirred to the highest emotional pitch by statements that, when translated, seem banal. The rhythm, melodic cadence, the rhyme produce a powerful hypnotic effect. Thus the power of the koranic revelation lies not only in the literal meaning of its words but also in the language in which this meaning incorporated, including its sound. The Koran was from the first a vocal phenomenon; we remember that we are to "recite" in the name of the Lord! Because content and container are here inseparably fused, translations cannot possibly convey the emotion, the fervor, and the mystery that the Koran holds in the original. This is why, in sharp contrast to Christians, who have translated their Bible into every known script, Muslims have preferred to teach others the language in which they believe God spoke finally with incomparable force and directness.[16]

Language, however, is not the only barrier the Koran presents to outsiders, for in content too it is like no other religious text. Unlike the Upanishads, it is not explicitly metaphysical. It does not ground its theology in dramatic narratives as the Indian epics do, nor in historical ones as do the Hebrew scriptures; nor is God revealed in human form as in the Gospels and the *Bhagavad-Gita*. Confining ourselves to the Semitic scriptures, we can say that whereas the Old and New Testaments are directly historical and indirectly doctrinal, the Koran is directly doctrinal and indirectly historical. Because the overwhelming thrust of the Koran is to proclaim the unity, omnipotence, omniscience, and mercy of God—and correlatively the total dependence of human life upon him—historical facts are in its case merely reference points that have scarcely any interest in themselves. This explains why the prophets are cited without any chronological order; why historical occurrences are sometimes recounted so elliptically as to be unintelligible without commentaries; and why the biblical stories that the Koran refers to are presented in an unexpected, abbreviated, and dry manner. They are stripped of their epic character and inserted as didactic examples of the infinitely various things that declare God's praise. When the Lord-servant relationship is the essential point to get across, all else is but commentary and allusion.

Perhaps we shall be less inclined to fault the Koran for the strange face it presents to foreigners if we note that foreign scriptures present their own problems to Muslims. To speak only of the Old and

New Testaments, Muslims express disappointment in finding that those texts do not take the form of Divine speech and merely report things that happened. In the Koran God speaks in the first person. Allah describes himself and makes known his laws. The Muslim is therefore inclined to consider each individual sentence of the Holy Book as a separate revelation and to experience the words themselves, even their sounds, as a means of grace. "The Qur'an does not document what is other than itself. It is not about the truth: it is the truth."[17] By contrast the Jewish and Christian Bibles seem more distant from God for placing religious meaning in reports of events instead of God's direct pronouncements.

The Koran's direct delivery creates, for the reader, a final problem that in other scriptures is eased by greater use of narrative and myth. One discerning commentator on the Koran puts this point as follows: "The seeming incoherence of the text has its cause in the incommensurable disproportion between the Spirit [Uncreated Koran] and the limited resources of human language. It is as though the poverty-stricken coagulation which is the language of mortal man were under the formidable pressure of the Heavenly Word broken into a thousand fragments, or as if God in order to express a thousand truths, had but a dozen words at his command and so was compelled to make use of allusions heavy with meaning, of ellipses, abridgements and symbolical syntheses."[18]

Putting comparisons behind us, it is impossible to overemphasize the central position of the Koran in the elaboration of any Islamic doctrine. With large portions memorized in childhood, it regulates the interpretation and evaluation of every event. It is a memorandum for the faithful, a reminder for daily doings, and a repository of revealed truth. It is a manual of definitions and guarantees, and at the same time a road map for the will. Finally, it is a collection of maxims to meditate on in private, deepening endlessly one's sense of the divine glory. "Perfect is the Word of your Lord in truth and justice" (6:115).

Basic Theological Concepts

With a few striking exceptions, which will be noted, the basic theological concepts of Islam are virtually identical with those of Judaism and Christianity, its forerunners. We shall confine our attention in this section to four that are the most important: God, Creation, the Human Self, and the Day of Judgment.

As in the other historical religions, everything in Islam centers on its religious Ultimate, God. God is immaterial and therefore invisible. For the Arabs this cast no doubt on his reality, for they never succumbed to the temptation — sorely reinforced by modern materialistic attitudes — to regard only the visible as the real; one of the tributes the Koran pays to Muhammad is that "he did not begrudge the Unseen." As desert dwellers, the notion of invisible hands that drove the blasts that swept the desert and formed the deceptive mirages that lured the traveler to his destruction was always with them.

Thus the Koran did not introduce the Arab to the unseen world of spirit, nor even to monotheism, since certain sensitive souls known as *hanifs* had already moved to that position before Muhammad. Its innovation was to remove idols from the religious scene and focus the divine in a single invisible God for everyone. It is in this sense that the indelible contribution of Islam to Arabic religion was monotheism.

We must immediately add that Muslims see monotheism as Islam's contribution not simply to the Arabs but to religion in its entirety. Hinduism's prolific images are taken as proof that it never arrived at the worship of the single God. Judaism was correctly instructed through its *Shema* — "Hear O Israel, the Lord our God, the Lord is One" — but its teachings were confined to the people of Israel. Christians, for their part, compromised their monotheism by deifying Christ. Islam honors Jesus as a prophet and accepts his virgin birth; Adam's and Jesus' souls are the only two that God created directly.[19] The Koran draws the line at the doctrine of the Incarnation and the Trinity, however, seeing these as inventions that blur the Divine/human distinction. In the words of the Koran: "They say the God of mercy has begotten a son. Now have you uttered a grievous thing. . . . It is not proper for God to have children" (3:78, 19:93). Muslims are not fond of parental images for God, even when employed metaphorically. To speak of human beings as "God's children" casts God in too human a mode. It is anthropomorphic.

Turning to the koranic depiction of God's nature, the first thing that strikes us is its awesomeness, its fear-inspiring power. Verse 7:143 contains the koranic account of Moses' request to see God.

When God showed himself instead to a neighboring mountain, thereby "sending it crashing down, Moses fell down senseless."[20]

Power of this order—it is infinite, for God is omnipotent—inspires fear, and it is fair to say that Muslims fear Allah. This, however, is not cringing fear in the face of a capricious tyrant. Rather, Muslims argue, it is the only appropriate emotion—any other involves denial in the technical, psychological sense of the word—when human beings face up to the magnitude of the consequences that follow from being on the right or wrong side of an uncompromisingly moral universe; one, moreover, in which beliefs and convictions are decisive because they generate actions. If nihilism is the dissipation of difference, a kind of moral leveling-out through entropy, Allah's universe is its exact opposite. Good and evil matter. Choices have consequences, and to disregard them would be as disastrous as climbing a mountain blindfolded. Belief in the Koran occupies the decisive place it does because it is the analogue to a mountaineer's assessment of Mount Everest: Its majesty is evident, but so are the dangers it presents. Mistakes could be disastrous. Koranic images of heaven and hell are pressed into full service here; but once we come to terms with the fear that life's inbuilt precariousness inspires, other lesser fears subside. The second, supporting root of the word *islam* is peace.

It is important to remember this last point, because the holy dread that Allah inspires led early Western students of the Koran to think that it outstrips God's mercy. Allah was seen to be a stern and wrathful judge, domineering and ruthless. This is a clear misreading; God's compassion and mercy are cited 192 times in the Koran, as against 17 references to his wrath and vengeance. He who is Lord of the worlds is also

> the Holy, the Peaceful, the Faithful, the Guardian over His servants, the Shelterer of the orphan, the Guide of the erring, the Deliverer from every affliction, the Friend of the bereaved, the Consoler of the afflicted; in His hand is good, and He is the generous Lord, the gracious, the Hearer, the Near-at-Hand, the Compassionate, the Merciful, the Very-forgiving, whose love for man is more tender than that of the mother-bird for her young.[21]

Thanks to Allah's mercy, the world of the Koran is finally a world of joy. There is air, and sun, and confidence—not only in ultimate justice but also in help along the way and pardon for the contrite.

By the noonday brightness, and by the night when it darkens,
your Lord has not forsaken you, neither has He been displeased.
Surely the Hereafter shall be better for you than the past; and in
the end He will be bounteous to you, and you will be satisfied. Did
He not find you an orphan, and give you a home; erring, and
guided you; needy, and enriched you?   (93:1–8)

Standing beneath God's gracious skies, the Muslim can at any
moment lift heart and soul directly into the divine presence, there to
receive both strength and guidance for life's troubled course. The
access is open because, though the human and the divine are
infinitely different, no barrier separates them.

Is He not closer than the vein of your neck? You need not raise
your voice, for he knows the secret whisper, and what is yet more
hidden. . . . He knows what is in the land and in the sea; no leaf
falls but He knows it; nor is there a grain in the darkness under the
earth, nor a thing, green or sere, but it is recorded.   (6:12, 59)

From God we can turn to Creation as our second theological
concept. The Koran abounds in lyrical descriptions of the natural
world. Here, though, the point is that that world is not presented as
emerging from the divine by some process of inbuilt emanation, as
Hindu texts suggest. It was created by a deliberate act of Allah's will:
"He has created the heavens and the earth" (16:3). This fact carries
two important consequences. First, the world of matter is both real
and important. Herein lies one of the sources of Islamic science,
which during Europe's Dark Ages flourished as nowhere else on
earth. Second, being the handiwork of Allah, who is perfect in both
goodness and power, the material world must likewise be good. "You
do not see in the creation of the All-merciful any imperfection.
Return your gaze. . . . It comes back to you dazzled" (67:4). Here we
meet a confidence in the material aspects of life and existence that
we will find shared by the other two Semitically originated religions,
Judaism and Christianity.

Foremost among God's creations is the human self, whose
nature, koranically defined, is our third doctrinal subject. "He has
created man," we read in Surah 16:3, and the first thing that we note
about this creation is its sound constitution. This could have been
inferred, given its Maker, but the Koran states it explicitly: "Surely

We have created humanity of the best stature" (95:4). The koranic word for human nature in its God-established original is *fitra*, and it has been stained by no catastrophic fall. The closest Islam comes to the Christian doctrine of original sin is in its concept of *ghaflah*, or forgetting. People do forget their divine origin, and this mistake needs repeatedly to be corrected. But their fundamental nature is unalterably good, so they are entitled to self-respect and a healthy self-image.

With life acknowledged as a gift from its Creator, we can turn to its obligations, which are two. The first of these is gratitude for the life that has been received. The Arabic word "infidel" is actually shaded more toward "one who lacks thankfulness" than one who disbelieves. The more gratitude one feels, the more natural it feels to let the bounty that has entered flow through one's life and on to others, for to hoard it would be as unnatural as trying to dam a waterfall. The ingrate, the Koran tells us, "covers" or "hides" God's blessings and thereby fails to enjoy the link with the Creator that every moment provides.

The second standing human obligation recalls us to the name of this religion. The opening paragraphs of this chapter informed us that *islam* means surrender, but we now need to probe this attribute more deeply.

Thoughts of surrender are so freighted with military connotations that it requires conscious effort to notice that surrender can mean a wholehearted giving of oneself—to a cause, or in friendship and love. William James shows how central surrender is to all religion.

> When all is said and done, we are in the end absolutely dependent on the universe; and into sacrifices and surrenders of some sort, deliberately looked at and accepted, we are drawn and pressed as into our only permanent positions of repose. Now in those states of mind which fall short of religion, the surrender is submitted to as an imposition of necessity, and the sacrifice is undergone at the very best without complaint. In the religious life, on the contrary, surrender and sacrifice are positively espoused: even unnecessary givings-up are added in order that the happiness may increase. Religion thus makes easy and felicitous what in any case is necessary.[22]

To this account of surrender's virtues we can add in Islamic parlance that to be a slave to Allah is to be freed from other forms of slavery—ones that are degrading, such as slavery to greed, or to anxiety, or to the desire for personal status. It also helps here if we alternate the word "surrender" with "commitment"; for in addition to being exempt from military associations, commitment suggests moving toward rather than giving up. In this reading Islam emerges as a religion that aims at total commitment; commitment in which nothing is withheld from the Divine. This explains why Abraham is by far the most important figure in the Koran, for he passed the ultimate test of willingness to sacrifice his own son if that was required.

Two final features of the human self provide a fitting transition to our final theological doctrine, the Day of Judgment, for it is there that they come into sharpest relief. The two are the soul's individuality and its freedom.

To begin with the first of these: Coming to Islam (as we do in this book) from the "no self" of Buddhism and the social self of Confucianism, we are struck by the stress the Koran places on the self's individuality: its uniqueness and the responsibility that devolves on it alone. In India the all-pervading cosmic spirit comes close to swallowing the individual self, and in China the self is so ecological that where it begins and ends is hard to determine. Islam and its Semitic allies reverse this drift, regarding individuality as not only real but good in principle. Value, virtue, and spiritual fulfillment come through realizing the potentialities that are uniquely one's own; in ways that are not inconsequential, those possibilities differ from those of every other soul that ever has lived, or ever will live in the future. As an important Muslim philosopher has written, "This inexplicable finite centre of experience is the fundamental fact of the universe. All life is individual; there is no such thing as universal life. God Himself is an individual; He is the most unique individual."[23]

The individuality of the human soul is everlasting, for once it is created it never dies. Never, though, is its distinctness more acutely sensed than on the Day of Judgment. "O son of Adam, you will die alone, and enter the tomb alone, and be resurrected alone, and it is with you alone that the reckoning will be made" (Hasan al-Basri).

This reckoning and its correlate, responsibility, lead directly to the issue of the soul's freedom, and it must be admitted that in Islam human freedom stands in tension with God's omnipotence, which

points toward predestination. Islamic theology has wrestled inter-
minably with this tension without rationally resolving it. It concludes
that the workings of the Divine Decree remain a mystery to humans,
who nevertheless are granted sufficient freedom and responsibility
to make genuine moral and spiritual decisions. "Whoever gets to
himself a sin, gets it solely on his own responsibility. . . . Whoever
goes astray, he himself bears the whole responsibility of wandering"
(4:111, 10:103).

As for the issue of judgment itself, Muslims consider it to be one
of the illusions of modernity that we can, as it were, slip quietly away
and not be noticed so long as we live (according to our own opinion)
decent and harmless lives and do not draw attention to ourselves. It
is the tearing away of all such illusions of security that characterizes
the doctrine of the Last Judgment and its anticipation in the Koran.
"When the sun shall be folded up, and the stars shall fall, and when
the mountains shall be set in motion . . . and the seas shall boil. . . .
Then shall every soul know what it has done" (81, *passim*). It is against
this background that the Koran presents life as a brief but immensely
precious opportunity, offering a once-and-for-all choice. Herein lies
the urgency that informs the entire book. The chance to return to life
for even a single day to make good use of their opportunities is something "the losers," facing their Reckoning, would treasure beyond
anything they desired while they were still alive (14:14).

Depending on how it fares in its Reckoning, the soul will repair
to either the heavens or the hells, which in the Koran are described
in vivid, concrete, and sensual imagery. The masses of the faithful consider them to be actual places, which is perhaps the inevitable consequence of such depiction. In the heavens we are treated to fountains,
cool shades, and chaste *houris* in gardens beneath which rivers flow;
to carpets, cushions, goblets of gold, and sumptuous food and drink.
In the hells there are burning garments, molten drinks, maces of iron,
and fire that splits rocks into fragments. To say that these are nothing
but symbols of the posthumous worlds — more rightly regarded as
posthumous conditions of experience — is not to explain them away;
but the object of the book is to present the hereafter in images of such
vividness "that the hearts of those who do not believe in the Hereafter
may incline to it" (6:113). The sharpness of the contrast between heaven
and hell is intended to pull the hearer/reader of the Koran out of the
spiritual lethargy that *ghaflah*, forgetfulness, induces.

The device works in periods of spiritual awareness and rebirth. In modern times it may be less effective for worldly-minded Muslims. In defense of allegorical interpretations of the images, liberal Muslims quote the Koran itself: "Some of the signs are firm—these are the basis of the book—and others are figurative" (3:5). Also supporting less materialistic views of paradise is Muhammad's statement that for the favored, "to see God's face night and morning [is] a felicity which will surpass all the pleasures of the body, as the ocean surpasses a drop of sweat."[24] Underlying the differences of interpretation, the belief that unites all Muslims concerning the afterlife is that each soul will be held accountable for its actions on earth with its future thereafter dependent upon how well it has observed God's commands. "We have hung every man's actions around his neck, and on the last day a wide-open book will be laid before him" (17:13).

As a final point: If all this talk of judgment still seems to cast God too much in the role of punisher, we can resort to verses in the Koran that remove Allah from direct involvement altogether. There souls judge themselves. What death burns away is self-serving defenses, forcing one to see with total objectivity how one has lived one's life. In the uncompromising light of that vision, where no dark and hidden corners are allowed, it is one's own actions that rise up to accuse or confirm. Once the self is extracted from the realm of lies, the falsities by which it armored itself become like flames, and the life it there led like a shirt of Nessus.

God, Creation, the Human Self, and the Day of Judgment—these are the chief theological pegs on which the Koran's teachings hang. In spite of their importance, however, the Koran is "a book which emphasizes deed rather than idea" (Muhammad Iqbal). It is to these deeds that we turn in the next two sections.

The Five Pillars

If a Muslim were asked to summarize the way Islam counsels people to live, the answer might be: It teaches them to walk the straight path. The phrase comes from the opening *surah* of the Koran, which is repeated many times in the Muslim's five daily prayers.

> *In the Name of Allah the Merciful, the Compassionate:*
> *Praise be to Allah, Creator of the worlds,*

The Merciful, the Compassionate,
Ruler of the day of Judgment.
Thee do we worship, and Thee do we ask for aid.
Guide us in the straight path,
The path of those on whom Thou hast poured forth Thy grace.
Not the path of those who have incurred Thy wrath and gone
    astray.

This *surah* has been called the heartbeat of the Muslim's response to God. At the moment, though, the question is why "the straight path"? One meaning is obvious; a straight path is one that is not crooked or corrupt. The phrase contains another meaning, however, which addresses something that in Islam is distinctive. The straight path is one that is straightforward; it is direct and explicit. Compared with other religions, Islam spells out the way of life it proposes; it pinpoints it, nailing it down through clear injunctions. Every major type of action is classified on a sliding scale from the "forbidden," through the "indifferent," to the "obligatory." This gives the religion a flavor of definiteness that is quite its own. Muslims know where they stand.

They claim this as one of their religion's strengths. God's revelation to humankind, they say, has proceeded through four great stages. First, God revealed the truth of monotheism, God's oneness, through Abraham. Second, God revealed the Ten Commandments through Moses. Third, God revealed the Golden Rule — that we are to do unto others as we would have them do unto us — through Jesus. All three of these prophets were authentic messengers; each introduced important features of the God-directed life. One question yet remained, however: *How* should we love our neighbor? Once life became complicated, instructions were needed to answer that question, and the Koran provides them. "The glory of Islam consists in having embodied the beautiful sentiments of Jesus in definite laws."[25]

What, then, is the content of this straight path that spells out human duties? We shall divide our presentation into two parts. In this section we shall consider the Five Pillars of Islam, the principles that regulate the private life of Muslims in their dealings with God. In the next section we shall consider the Koran's social teachings.

The first of the Five Pillars is Islam's creed, or confession of faith known as the *Shahadah*. Every religion contains professions that orient its adherents' lives. Islam's wastes no words. Brief, simple, and explicit, it consists of a single sentence: "There is no god but God, and Muhammad is His Prophet." The first half of the proclamation announces the cardinal principle of monotheism. "There is no god but Allah." There is no god but *the* God. More directly still, there is no God but *God*, for the word is not a common noun embracing a class of objects; it is a proper name designating a unique being and him only. The second affirmation—that "Muhammad is God's prophet"—registers the Muslim's faith in the authenticity of Muhammad and in the validity of the book he transmitted.

At least once during his or her lifetime a Muslim must say the *Shahadah* correctly, slowly, thoughtfully, aloud, with full understanding and with heartfelt conviction. In actuality Muslims pronounce it often, especially its first half, *La ilaha illa 'llah*. In every crisis and at every moment when the world threatens to overwhelm them, not excepting the approach of death, "There is no god but God" will spring to their lips. "A pious man, seized by rage, will appear suddenly to have been stopped in his tracks as he remembers the *Shahadah* and, as it were, withdraws, putting a great distance between himself and his turbulent emotions. A woman crying out in childbirth will as suddenly fall silent, remembering; and a student, bowed anxiously over his desk in an examination hall, will raise his head and speak these words, and a barely audible sigh of relief passes through the whole assembly. This is the ultimate answer to all questions."[26]

The second pillar of Islam is the canonical prayer, in which the Koran adjures the faithful to "be constant" (29:45).

Muslims are admonished to be constant in prayer to keep their lives in perspective. The Koran considers this the most difficult lesson people must learn. Though they are obviously creatures, having created neither themselves nor their worlds, they can't seem to get this straight and keep placing themselves at the center of things, living as if they were laws unto themselves. This produces havoc. When we ask, then, why Muslims pray, a partial answer is: in response to life's natural impulse to give thanks for its existence. The deeper answer, however, is the one with which this paragraph opened: to keep life in perspective—to see it objectively, which involves acknowledging human creatureliness before its Creator. In practice this comes down to submitting one's will to God's *(islam)* as its rightful sovereign.

How often should Muslims pray? There is an account in the Koran that speaks to this point.

One of the crucial events in Muhammad's life, we are told, was his renowned Night Journey to Heaven. On a certain night in the month of Ramadan, he was spirited on a wondrous white steed with wings to Jerusalem and upward from there through the seven heavens to the presence of God, who instructed him that Muslims were to pray fifty times each day. On his way back to earth, he stopped in the sixth heaven, where he reported the instruction to Moses, who was incredulous. "Fifty times a day!" he said in effect. "You've got to be kidding. That will never work. Go back and negotiate." Muhammad did so and returned with the number reduced to forty, but Moses was not satisfied. "I know those people," he said. "Go back." This routine was repeated four more times, with the number reduced successively to thirty, twenty, ten, and then five. Even this last figure struck Moses as excessive. "Your people are not capable of observing five daily prayers," he said. "I have tested men before your time and have labored most earnestly to prevail over the [sons of] Isra'il, so go back to your Lord and ask Him to make things lighter for your people." This time, however, Muhammad refused. "I have asked my Lord till I am ashamed, but now I am satisfied and I submit." The number remained fixed at five.[27]

The times of the five prayers are likewise stipulated: on arising, when the sun reaches its zenith, its mid-decline, sunset, and before retiring. The schedule is not absolutely binding. The Koran says explicitly, for example, that "When you journey about the earth it is no crime that you come short in prayer if you fear that those who disbelieve will attack you." Under normal conditions, however, the fivefold pattern should be maintained. While in Islam no day of the week is as sharply set apart from the others as is the Sabbath for the Jews or Sunday for the Christians, Friday most nearly approximates a weekly holy day. Congregational worship is not stressed as much in Islam as it is in Judaism and Christianity; even so, Muslims are expected to pray in mosques when they can, and the Friday noon prayer is emphasized in this respect. Visitors to Muslim lands testify that one of the impressive religious sights in the world comes to view when, in a dimly lighted mosque, hundreds of Muslims stand shoulder to shoulder, then repeatedly kneel and prostrate themselves toward Mecca.

Although Muslims first prayed in the direction of Jerusalem, a koranic revelation later instructed them to pray in the direction of Mecca; and the realization that Muslims throughout the world do this creates a sense of participating in a worldwide fellowship, even when one prays in solitude. Beyond this matter of direction the Koran says almost nothing, but Muhammad's teachings and practices moved in to structure the void. Washing, to purify the body and symbolically the soul, precedes the prayer, which begins in dignified, upright posture but climaxes when the supplicant has sunk to his or her knees with forehead touching the floor. This is the prayer's holiest moment, for it carries a twofold symbolism. On the one hand, the body is in a fetal position, ready to be reborn. At the same time it is crouched in the smallest possible space, signifying human nothingness in the face of the divine.

As for prayer's content, its standard themes are praise, gratitude, and supplication. There is a Muslim saying that every time a bird drinks a drop of water it lifts its eyes in gratitude toward heaven. At least five times each day, Muslims do likewise.

The third pillar of Islam is charity. Material things are important in life, but some people have more than others. Why? Islam is not concerned with this theoretical question. Instead, it turns to the practical issue of what should be done about the disparity. Its answer is simple. Those who have much should help lift the burden of those who are less fortunate. It is a principle that twentieth-century democracies have embraced in secular mode in their concept of the welfare state. The Koran introduced its basic principle in the seventh century by prescribing a graduated tax on the haves to relieve the circumstances of the have-nots.

Details aside, the figure the Koran set for this tax was 2½ percent. Alongside the tithe of Judaism and Christianity (which, being directed more to the maintenance of religious institutions than to the direct relief of human need, is not strictly comparable), this looks modest until we discover that it refers not just to income but to holdings. Poorer people owe nothing, but those in the middle and upper income brackets should annually distribute among the poor one-fortieth of the value of all they possess.

And to whom among the poor should this money be given? This too is prescribed: to those in immediate need; to slaves in the process of buying their freedom; to debtors unable to meet their obligations;

to strangers and wayfarers; and to those who collect and distribute the alms.

The fourth pillar of Islam is the observance of Ramadan. Ramadan is a month in the Islamic calendar—Islam's holy month, because during it Muhammad received his initial revelation and (ten years later) made his historic *Hijrah* (migration) from Mecca to Medina. To commemorate these two great occasions, able-bodied Muslims (who are not ill or involved in crises like war or unavoidable journeys) fast during Ramadan. From the first moment of dawn to the setting of the sun, neither food nor drink nor smoke passes their lips; after sundown they may partake in moderation. As the Muslim calendar is lunar, Ramadan rotates around the year. When it falls in the winter its demands are not excessive. When, on the other hand, it falls during the scorching heat of the summer, to remain active during the long days without so much as a drop of water is an ordeal.

Why, then, does the Koran require it? For one thing, fasting makes one think, as every Jew who has observed the fast of Yom Kippur will attest. For another thing, fasting teaches self-discipline; one who can endure its demands will have less difficulty controlling the demands of appetites at other times. Fasting underscores the creature's dependence on God. Human beings, it is said, are as frail as rose petals; nevertheless, they assume airs and pretensions. Fasting calls one back to one's frailty and dependence. Finally, fasting sensitizes compassion. Only those who have been hungry can know what hunger means. People who have fasted for twenty-nine days within the year will be apt to listen more carefully when next approached by someone who is hungry.

Islam's fifth pillar is pilgrimage. Once during his or her lifetime every Muslim who is physically and economically in a position to do so is expected to journey to Mecca, where God's climactic revelation was first disclosed. The basic purpose of the pilgrimage is to heighten the pilgrim's devotion to God and his revealed will, but the practice has fringe benefits as well. It is, for example, a reminder of human equality. Upon reaching Mecca, pilgrims remove their normal attire, which carries marks of social status, and don two simple sheet-like garments. Thus everyone, on approaching Islam's earthly focus, wears the same thing. Distinctions of rank and hierarchy are removed, and prince and pauper stand before God in their undivided humanity. Pilgrimage also provides a useful service in international

relations. It brings together people from various countries, demon-
strating thereby that they share a loyalty that transcends loyalty to
their nations and ethnic groupings. Pilgrims pick up information
about other lands and peoples, and return to their homes with better
understanding of one another.

The Five Pillars of Islam consist of things Muslims do to keep the
house of Islam erect. There are also things they should not do. Gambling, thieving, lying, eating pork, drinking intoxicants, and being
sexually promiscuous are some of these. Even Muslims who transgress these rulings acknowledge their acts as transgressions.

With the exception of charity, the precepts we have considered
in this section pertain to the Muslim's personal life. We turn now to
the social teachings of Islam.

Social Teachings

"O men! listen to my words and take them to heart! Know ye that
every Muslim is a brother to every other Muslim, and that you are
now one brotherhood." These notable words, spoken by the Prophet
during his "farewell pilgrimage" to Mecca shortly before his death,
epitomize one of Islam's loftiest ideals and strongest emphases. The
intrusion of nationalism in the last two centuries has played havoc
with this ideal on the political level, but on the communal level it has
remained discernibly intact. "There is something in the religious
culture of Islam which inspired, in even the humblest peasant or
peddler, a dignity and a courtesy toward others never exceeded and
rarely equalled in other civilizations," a leading Islamicist has
written.[28]

Looking at the difference between pre- and post-Islamic Arabia,
we are forced to ask whether history has ever witnessed a comparable moral advance among so many people in so short a time. Before
Muhammad there was virtually no restraint on intertribal violence.
Glaring inequities in wealth and possession were accepted as the
natural order of things. Women were regarded more as possessions
than as human beings. Rather than say that a man could marry an
unlimited number of wives, it would be more accurate to say that his
relations with women were so casual that beyond the first wife or two
they scarcely approximated marriage at all. Infanticide was common,
especially of girls. Drunkenness and large-scale gambling have

already been remarked upon. Within a half-century there was effected a remarkable change in the moral climate on all of these counts.

Something that helped it to accomplish this near-miracle is a feature of Islam that we have already alluded to, namely its explicitness. Its basic objective in interpersonal relations, Muslims will say, is precisely that of Jesus and the other prophets: brotherly and sisterly love. The distinctive thing about Islam is not its ideal but the detailed prescriptions it sets forth for achieving it. We have already encountered its theory on this point. If Jesus had had a longer career, or if the Jews had not been so socially powerless at the time, Jesus might have systematized his teachings more. As it was, his work "was left unfinished. It was reserved for another Teacher to systematize the laws of morality."[29] The Koran is this later teacher. In addition to being a spiritual guide, it is a legal compendium. When its innumerable prescriptions are supplemented by the only slightly less authoritative *hadith*—traditions based on what Muhammad did or said on his own initiative—we are not surprised to find Islam the most socially explicit of the Semitic religions. Westerners who define religion in terms of personal experience would never be understood by Muslims, whose religion calls them to establish a specific kind of social order. Islam joins faith to politics, religion to society, inseparably.

Islamic law is of enormous scope. It will be enough for our purposes if we summarize its provisions in four areas of collective life.

1. Economics.   Islam is acutely aware of the physical foundations of life. Until bodily needs are met, higher concerns cannot flower. When one of Muhammad's followers ran up to him crying, "My Mother is dead; what is the best alms I can give away for the good of her soul?" the Prophet, thinking of the heat of the desert, answered instantly, "Water! Dig a well for her, and give water to the thirsty."

Just as the health of an organism requires that nourishment be fed to its every segment, so too a society's health requires that material goods be widely and appropriately distributed. These are the basic principles of Islamic economics, and nowhere do Islam's democratic impulses speak with greater force and clarity. The Koran, supplemented by *hadith*, propounded measures that broke the barriers of economic caste and enormously reduced the injustices of special interest groups.

The model that animates Muslim economics is the body's circulatory system. Health requires that blood flow freely and vigorously; sluggishness can bring on illness, blood clots occasion death. It is not different with the body politic, in which wealth takes the place of blood as the life-giving substance. As long as this analogy is honored and laws are in place to insure that wealth is in vigorous circulation, Islam does not object to the profit motive, economic competition, or entrepreneurial ventures—the more imaginative the latter, the better. So freely are these allowed that some have gone so far as to characterize the Koran as "a businessman's book." It does not discourage people from working harder than their neighbors, nor object to such people being rewarded with larger returns. It simply insists that acquisitiveness and competition be balanced by the fair play that "keeps arteries open," and by compassion that is strong enough to pump life-giving blood—material resources—into the circulatory system's smallest capillaries. These "capillaries" are fed by the Poor Due, which (as has been noted) stipulates that annually a portion of one's holdings be distributed to the poor.

As for the way to prevent "clotting," the Koran went after the severest economic curse of the day—primogeniture—and flatly outlawed it. By restricting inheritance to the oldest son, this institution had concentrated wealth in a limited number of enormous estates. In banning the practice, the Koran sees to it that inheritance is shared by all heirs, daughters as well as sons. F. S. C. Northrop describes the settlement of a Muslim's estate that he chanced to witness. The application of Islamic law that afternoon resulted in the division of some $53,000 among no less than seventy heirs.

One verse in the Koran prohibits the taking of interest. At the time this was not only humane but eminently just, for loans were used then to tide the unfortunate over in times of disaster. With the rise of capitalism, however, money has taken on a new meaning. It now functions importantly as venture capital, and in this setting borrowed money multiplies. This benefits the borrower, and it is patently unjust to exclude the lender from his or her gain. The way Muslims have accommodated to this change is by making lenders in some way partners in the venture for which their monies are used. When capitalism is approached in this manner, Muslims find no incompatibility between its central feature, venture capital, and Islam. Capitalism's excesses—which Muslims consider to be glaringly exhibited in the secular West—are another matter. The equalizing provisos of the Koran would, if duly applied, offset them.

2. The Status of Women.   Chiefly because it permits a plurality of wives, the West has accused Islam of degrading women.

If we approach the question historically, comparing the status of Arabian women before and after Muhammad, the charge is patently false. In the pre-Islamic "days of ignorance," marriage arrangements were so loose as to be scarcely recognizable. Women were regarded as little more than chattel, to be done with as fathers or husbands pleased. Daughters had no inheritance rights and were often buried alive in their infancy.

Addressing conditions in which the very birth of a daughter was regarded as a calamity, the koranic reforms improved woman's status incalculably. They forbade infanticide. They required that daughters be included in inheritance—not equally, it is true, but to half the proportion of sons, which seems just, in view of the fact that unlike sons, daughters would not assume financial responsibility for their households. In her rights as citizen—education, suffrage, and vocation—the Koran leaves open the possibility of woman's full equality with man, an equality that is being approximated as the customs of Muslim nations become modernized.[30] If in another century women under Islam do not attain the social position of their Western sisters, a position to which the latter have been brought by industrialism and democracy rather than religion, it will then be time, Muslims say, to hold Islam accountable.

It was in the institution of marriage, however, that Islam made its greatest contribution to women. It sanctified marriage, first, by making it the sole lawful locus of the sexual act.[31]

To the adherents of a religion in which the punishment for adultery is death by stoning and social dancing is proscribed, Western indictments of Islam as a lascivious religion sound ill-directed. Second, the Koran requires that a woman give her free consent before she may be wed; not even a sultan may marry without his bride's express approval. Third, Islam tightened the wedding bond enormously. Though Muhammad did not forbid divorce, he countenanced it only as a last resort. Asserting repeatedly that nothing displeased God more than the disruption of marital vows, he instituted legal provisions to keep marriages intact. At the time of marriage husbands are required to provide the wife with a sum on which both agree and which she retains in its entirety should a divorce ensue. Divorce proceedings call for three distinct and separate periods, in each of which arbiters drawn from both families try to reconcile the two parties. Though such devices are intended to keep divorces to a minimum, wives no less than husbands are permitted to instigate them.

There remains, however, the issue of polygamy, or more precisely polygyny. It is true that the Koran permits a man to have up to four wives simultaneously, but there is a growing consensus that a careful reading of its regulations on the matter point toward monogamy as the ideal. Supporting this view is the Koran's statement that "if you cannot deal equitably and justly with [more than one wife], you shall marry only one." Other passages make it clear that "equality" here refers not only to material perquisites but to love and esteem. In physical arrangements each wife must have private quarters, and this in itself is a limiting factor. It is the second proviso, though—equality of love and esteem—that leads jurists to argue that the Koran virtually enjoins monogamy, for it is almost impossible to distribute affection and regard with exact equality. This interpretation has been in the Muslim picture since the third century of the *Hijrah,* and it is gaining increasing acceptance. To avoid any possible misunderstanding, many Muslims now insert in the marriage deed a clause by which the husband formally renounces his supposed right to a second concurrent spouse, and in point of fact—with the exception of African tribes where polygyny is customary—multiple wives are seldom found in Islam today.

Nevertheless, the fact remains that the Koran does permit polygyny: "You may marry two, three, or four wives, but not more." And what are we to make of Muhammad's own multiple marriages? Muslims take both items as instances of Islam's versatility in addressing diverse circumstances.

There are circumstances in the imperfect condition we know as human existence when polygyny is morally preferable to its alternative. Individually, such a condition might arise if, early in marriage, the wife were to contract paralysis or another disability that would prevent sexual union. Collectively, a war that decimated the male population could provide an example, forcing (as this would) the option between polygyny and depriving a large proportion of women of motherhood and a nuclear family of any sort. Idealists may call for the exercise of heroic continence in such circumstances, but heroism is never a mass option. The actual choice is between a legalized polygyny in which sex is tightly joined to responsibility, and alternatively monogamy, which, being unrealistic, fosters prostitution, where men disclaim responsibility for their sexual partners and their progeny. Pressing their case, Muslims point out that multiple marriages are at least as common in the West; the difference is that they are successive. Is "serial polygyny," the Western version, self-evidently superior to its coeval form, when women have the right to opt out of the arrangement (through divorce) if they want to? Finally, Muslims, though they have spoken frankly from the first of female sexual fulfillment as a marital right, do not skirt the volatile question of whether the male sexual drive is stronger than the female's. "Hoggledy higamous, men are polygamous; /Higgledy hogamus, women monogamous," Dorothy Parker wrote flippantly. If there is biological truth in her limerick, "rather than allowing this sensuality in the male to run riot, obeying nothing but its own impulses, the Law of Islam sets down a polygynous framework that provides a modicum of control. [It] confers a conscious mold on the formless instinct of man in order to keep him within the structures of religion."[32]

As for the veiling of women and their seclusion generally, the koranic injunction is restrained. It says only to "Tell your wives and your daughters and the women of the believers to draw their cloaks closely round them (when they go abroad). That will be better, so that they may be recognised and not annoyed" (33:59). Extremes that have evolved from this ruling are matters of local custom and are not religiously binding.

Somewhere in this section on social issues the subject of penalties should be mentioned, for the impression is widespread that Islamic law imposes ones that are excessively harsh. This is a reasonable place to address this issue, for one of the most frequently cited examples is the punishment for adultery, which repeats the Jewish law of death by stoning—two others that are typically mentioned are severance of the thief's hand, and flogging for a number of offenses. These stipulations are indeed severe, but (as Muslims see matters) this is to make the point that the injuries that occasion these penalties are likewise severe and will not be tolerated. Once this juridical point is in place, mercy moves in to temper the decrees. "Avert penalties by doubt," Muhammad told his people, and Islamic jurisprudence legitimizes any stratagem that averts the penalty without outright impugning the Law. Stoning for adultery is made almost impossible by the proviso that four unimpeachable witnesses must have observed the act in detail. "Flogging" can be technically fulfilled by using a light sandal or even the hem of a garment, and thieves may retain their hands if the theft was from genuine need.

3. Race Relations. Islam stresses racial equality and "has achieved a remarkable degree of interracial coexistence."[33] The ultimate test in this area is willingness to intermarry, and Muslims see Abraham as modeling this willingness in marrying Hagar, a black woman whom they regard as his second wife rather than a concubine. Under Elijah Muhammad the Black Muslim movement in America—it has had various names—was militant toward the whites; but when Malcolm X made his 1964 pilgrimage to Mecca, he discovered that racism had no precedent in Islam and could not be accommodated to it.[34] Muslims like to recall that the first *muezzin*, Bilal, was an Ethiopian who prayed regularly for the conversion of the Koreish—"whites" who were persecuting the early believers, many of whom were black. The advances that Islam continues to make in Africa is not unrelated to this religion's principled record on this issue.

4. The Use of Force.   Muslims report that the standard Western stereotype that they encounter is that of a man marching with sword outstretched, followed by a long train of wives. Not surprisingly, inasmuch as from the beginning (a historian reports) Christians have believed that "the two most important aspects of Muhammad's life . . . are his sexual licence and his use of force to establish religion."[35] Muslims feel that both Muhammad and the Koran have been maligned on these counts. License was discussed above. Here we turn to force.

Admit, they say, that the Koran does not counsel turning the other cheek, or pacifism. It teaches forgiveness and the return of good for evil when the circumstances warrant—"turn away evil with that which is better" (42:37)—but this is different from not resisting evil. Far from requiring the Muslim to turn himself into a doormat for the ruthless, the Koran allows punishment of wanton wrongdoers to the full extent of the injury they impart (22:39–40). Justice requires this, they believe; abrogate reciprocity, which the principle of fair play requires, and morality descends to impractical idealism if not sheer sentimentality. Extend this principle of justice to collective life and we have as one instance *jihad,* the Muslim concept of a holy war, in which the martyrs who die are assured of heaven. All this the Muslim will affirm as integral to Islam, but we are still a far cry from the familiar charge that Islam spread primarily by the sword and was upheld by the sword.

As an outstanding general, Muhammad left many traditions regarding the decent conduct of war. Agreements are to be honored and treachery avoided; the wounded are not to be mutilated, nor the dead disfigured. Women, children, and the old are to be spared, as are orchards, crops, and sacred objects. These, however, are not the point. The important question is the definition of a righteous war. According to prevailing interpretations of the Koran, a righteous war must either be defensive or to right a wrong. "Defend yourself against your enemies, but do not attack them first: God hates the aggressor" (2:190). The aggressive and unrelenting hostility of the idolaters forced Muhammad to seize the sword in self-defense, or, together with his entire community and his God-entrusted faith, be wiped from the face of the earth. That other teachers succumbed under force and became martyrs was to Muhammad no reason that he should do the same. Having seized the sword in self-defense he held onto it to the end. This much Muslims acknowledge; but they insist that while Islam has at times spread by the sword, it has mostly spread by persuasion and example.

The crucial verses in the Koran bearing on conversion read as follows:

> *Let there be no compulsion in religion*   (2:257).
>
> *To every one have We given a law and a way. . . . And if God had pleased, he would have made [all humankind] one people [people of one religion]. But he hath done otherwise, that He might try you in that which He hath severally given unto you: wherefore press forward in good works. Unto God shall ye return, and He will tell you that concerning which ye disagree*   (5:48).

Muslims point out that Muhammad incorporated into his charter for Medina the principle of religious toleration that these verses announce. They regard that document as the first charter of freedom of conscience in human history and the authoritative model for those of every subsequent Muslim state. It decreed that "the Jews who attach themselves to our commonwealth [similar rights were later mentioned for Christians, these two being the only non-Muslim religions on the scene] shall be protected from all insults and vexations; they shall have an equal right with our own people to our assistance and good offices: the Jews . . . and all others domiciled in Yathrib, shall . . . practice their religion as freely as the Muslims." Even conquered nations were permitted freedom of worship contingent only on the payment of a special tax in lieu of the Poor Due, from which they were exempt; thereafter every interference with their liberty of conscience was regarded as a direct contravention of Islamic law. If clearer indication than this of Islam's stand on religious tolerance be asked, we have the direct words of Muhammad: "Will you then force men to believe when belief can come only from God?"[36] Once, when a deputy of Christians visited him, Muhammad invited them to conduct their service in his mosque, adding, "It is a place consecrated to God."

This much for theory and Muhammad's personal example. How well Muslims have lived up to his principles of toleration is a question of history that is far too complex to admit of a simple, objective, and definitive answer. On the positive side Muslims point to the long centuries during which, in India, Spain, and the Near East, Christians, Jews, and Hindus lived quietly and in freedom under Muslim rule. Even under the worst rulers Christians and Jews held positions of influence and in general retained their religious freedom. It was Christians, not Muslims, we are reminded, who in the fifteenth century expelled the Jews from Spain where, under Islamic rule, they had enjoyed one of their golden ages. To press this example, Spain and Anatolia changed hands at about the same time—Christians expelled the Moors from Spain, while Muslims conquered what is now Turkey. Every Muslim was driven from Spain, put to the sword, or forced to convert, whereas the seat of the Eastern Orthodox church remains in Istanbul to this day. Indeed, if comparisons are what we want, Muslims consider Christianity's record as the darker of the two. Who was it, they ask, who preached the Crusades in the name of the Prince of Peace? Who instituted the Inquisition, invented the rack and the stake as instruments of religion, and plunged Europe into its devastating wars of religion? Objective historians are of one mind in their verdict that, to put the matter minimally, Islam's record on the use of force is no darker than that of Christianity.

Laying aside comparisons, Muslims admit that their own record respecting force is not exemplary. Every religion at some stages in its career has been used by its professed adherents to mask aggression, and Islam is no exception. Time and again it has provided designing chieftains, caliphs, and now heads of state with pretexts for gratifying their ambitions. What Muslims deny can be summarized in three points.

First, they deny that Islam's record of intolerance and aggression is greater than that of the other major religions. (Buddhism may be an exception here.)

Second, they deny that Western histories are fair to Islam in their accounts of its use of force.[37] *Jihad*, they say, is a case in point. To Westerners it conjures scenes of screaming fanatics being egged into war by promises that they will be instantly transported to heaven if they are slain. In actuality: (a) *jihad* literally means exertion, though because war requires exertion in exceptional degree the word is often, by extension, attached thereto. (b) The definition of a holy war in Islam is virtually identical with that of a just war in Christianity, where too it is sometimes called a holy war. (c) Christianity, too, considers those who die in such wars to be martyrs, and promises them salvation. (d) A *hadith* (canonical saying) of Muhammad ranks the battle against evil within one's own heart above battles against external enemies. "We have returned from the lesser *jihad*," the Prophet observed, following an encounter with the Meccans, "to face the greater *jihad*," the battle with the enemy within oneself.

Third, Muslims deny that the blots in their record should be charged against their religion whose presiding ideal they affirm in their standard greeting, *as-salamu 'alaykum* ("Peace be upon you").

Sufism

We have been treating Islam as if it were monolithic, which of course it is not. Like every religious tradition it divides. Its main historical division is between the mainstream Sunnis ("Traditionalists" [from *sunnah*, tradition] who comprise 87 percent of all Muslims) and the Shi'ites (literally "partisans" of Ali, Muhammad's son-in-law, whom Shi'ites believe should have directly succeeded Muhammad but who was thrice passed over and who, when he was finally appointed leader of the Muslims, was assassinated). Geographically, the Shi'ites cluster in and around Iraq and Iran, while the Sunnis flank them to the West (the Middle East, Turkey, and Africa) and to the East (through the Indian subcontinent, which includes Pakistan and Bangladesh, on through Malaysia, and into Indonesia, where alone there are more Muslims than in the entire Arab world). We shall pass over this historical split, which turns on an in-house dispute, and take up instead a division that has universal overtones. It is the vertical division between the mystics of Islam, called Sufis, and the remaining majority of the faith, who are equally good Muslims but are not mystics.

The root meaning of the word Sufi is wool, *suf*. A century or two after Muhammad's death, those within the Islamic community who bore the inner message of Islam came to be known as Sufis. Many of them donned coarse woolen garments to protest the silks and satins of sultans and califs. Alarmed by the worldliness they saw overtaking Islam, they sought to purify and spiritualize it from within. They wanted to recover its liberty and love, and to restore to it its deeper, mystical tone. Externals should yield to internals, matter to meaning, outward symbol to inner reality. "Love the pitcher less," they cried, "and the water more."

Sufis saw this distinction between the inner and the outer, the pitcher and what it contains, as deriving from the Koran itself, where Allah presents himself as both "the Outward [*al-zahir*] and the Inward [*al-batin*]" (57:3). Exoteric Muslims—we shall call them such because they were satisfied with the explicit meanings of the Koran's teachings—passed over this distinction, but the Sufis (esoteric Muslims) found it important. Contemplation of God occupies a significant place in every Muslim's life, but for most it must compete, pretty much on a par, with life's other demands. When we add to this that life is demanding—people tend to be busy—it stands to reason that not many Muslims will have the time, if the inclination, to do more than keep up with the Divine Law that orders their lives. Their fidelity is not in vain; in the end their reward will be as great as the

Sufis'. But the Sufis were impatient for their reward, if we may put the matter thus. They wanted to encounter God directly in this very life-time. Now.

This called for special methods, and to develop and practice them the Sufis gathered around spiritual masters (shaikhs), form-ing circles that, from the twelfth century onward, crystallized into Sufi orders (*tariqahs*). The word for the members of these orders is *faqir*—pronounced *fakir*; literally poor, but with the connotation of one who is "poor in spirit." In some ways, however, they constituted a spiritual elite, aspiring higher than other Muslims, and willing to assume the heavier disciplines their extravagant goals required. We can liken their *tariqahs* to the contemplative orders of Roman Catholicism, with the difference that Sufis generally marry and are not cloistered. They engage in normal occupations and repair to their gathering places (*zawiyahs*, Arabic; *khanaqahs*, Persian) to sing, dance, pray, recite their rosaries in concert, and listen to the dis-courses of their Master, all to the end of reaching God directly. Some-one who was ignorant of fire, they observe, could come to know it by degrees: first by hearing of it, then by seeing it, and finally by being burned by its heat. The Sufis wanted to be "burned" by God.

This required drawing close to him, and they developed three overlapping but distinguishable routes. We can call these the mysti-cisms of love, of ecstasy, and of intuition.

To begin with the first of these, Sufi love poetry is world famous. A remarkable eighth-century woman saint, Rabi'a, discovered in her solitary vigils, often lasting all night, that God's love was at the core of the universe; not to steep oneself in that love and reflect it to others was to forfeit life's supreme beatitude. Because love is never more evi-dent than when its object is absent, that being the time when the beloved's importance cannot be overlooked, Persian poets in particu-lar dwelt on the pangs of separation to deepen their love of God and thereby draw close to him. Jalal ad-Din Rumi used the plaintive sound of the reed flute to typify this theme.

> *Listen to the story told by the reed, of being separated.*
> *"Since I was cut from the reedbed, I have made this crying*
>   *sound.*
> *Anyone separated from someone he loves understands what I*
>   *say, anyone pulled from a source longs to go back."*

The lament of the flute, torn from its riverbank and symbol therefore
for the soul's severance from the divine, threw the Sufis into states of
agitation and bewilderment. Nothing created could assuage those
states; but its beloved, Allah, is so sublime, so dissimilar, that human
love for him is like the nightingale's for the rose, or the moth's for the
flame. Even so, Rumi assures us, that human love is returned:

> *Never does the lover seek without being sought by his beloved.*
> *When the lightning of love has shot into this heart, know that*
>   *there is love in that heart. . . .*
> *Mark well the text: "He loves them and they love Him."*
> (Koran, 5:59).

But the full truth has still not been grasped, for Allah loves his
creatures *more* than they love him. "God saith: Whoso seeketh to
approach Me one span, I approach him one cubit; and whoso seeketh
to approach Me one cubit, I approach him two fathoms; and whoever
walks towards Me, I run towards him."[38] Rabi'a celebrates the eventual meeting of the two souls, one finite, the other Infinite, in her
famous night prayer:

> *My God and my Lord: eyes are at rest, the stars are setting,*
> *hushed are the movements of birds in their nests, of monsters in*
> *the deep. And you are the Just who knows no change, the Equity*
> *that does not swerve, the Everlasting that never passes away. The*
> *doors of kings are locked and guarded by their henchmen, but*
> *your door is open to those who call upon you. My Lord, each lover*
> *is now alone with his beloved. And I am alone with you.*

We are calling the second Sufi approach to the divine presence
ecstatic (literally, "to stand outside oneself") because it turns on
experiences that differ, not just in degree but in kind, from usual
ones. The presiding metaphor for ecstatic Sufis was the Prophet's
Night Journey through the seven heavens into the Divine Presence.
What he perceived in those heavens no one can say, but we can be
sure the visions were extraordinary—increasingly so with each level
of ascent. Ecstatic Sufis do not claim that they come to see what
Muhammad saw that night, but they move in his direction. At times
the content of what they are experiencing engrosses them so completely that their states become trancelike because of their total
abstraction from self. No attention remains for who they are, where

they are, or what is happening to them. In psychological parlance they are "dissociated" from themselves, losing consciousness of the world as it is normally perceived. Journeying to meet such adepts, pilgrims reported finding themselves ignored—not out of discourtesy, but because literally they were not seen. Deliberate inducement of such states required practice; a pilgrim who sought out a revered ecstatic named Nuri reported finding him in such an intense state of concentration that not a hair of his body moved. "When I later asked him, 'From whom did you learn this deep concentration?' he replied, 'From a cat watching by a mouse hole. But its concentration is much more intense than mine.'"[39] Nevertheless, when the altered state arrives, it feels like a gift rather than an acquisition. The phrase that mystical theology uses, "infused grace," feels right here; for Sufis report that as their consciousness begins to change, it feels as if their wills were placed in abeyance and a superior will takes over.

Sufis honor their ecstatics, but in calling them "drunken" they serve notice that they must bring the substance of their visions back with them when they find themselves "sober" again. In plain language, transcendence must be made immanent; the God who is encountered apart from the world must also be encountered within it. This latter does not require ecstasy as its preliminary, and the direct route to cultivating it carries us to the third Sufi approach: the way of intuitive discernment.

Like the other two methods this one brings knowledge, but of a distinct sort. Love mysticism yields "heart knowledge," and ecstasy "visual or visionary knowledge," because extraterrestrial realities are seen; but intuitive mysticism brings "mental knowledge," which Sufis call *ma'rifah*, obtained through an organ of discernment called "the eye of the heart."[40] Because the realities attained through *ma'rifah* are immaterial, the eye of the heart is immaterial as well. It does not compete with the physical eye whose objects, the world's normal objects, remain fully in view. What it does is clothe those objects in celestial light. Or to reverse the metaphor: It recognizes the world's objects as garments that God dons to create a world. These garments become progressively more transparent as the eye of the heart gains strength. It would be false to say that the world is *God*—that would be pantheism. But to the eye of the heart, the world *is* God-in-disguise, God veiled.

The principal method the Sufis employed for penetrating the disguise is symbolism. In using visible objects to speak of invisible things, symbolism is the language of religion generally; it is to religion what numbers are to science. Mystics, however, employ it to exceptional degree; for instead of stopping with the first spiritual object a symbol points to, they use it as stepping stone to a more exalted object. This led al-Ghazali to define symbolism as "the science of the relation between multiple levels of reality." Every verse of the Koran, the Sufis say, conceals a minimum of seven hidden significations, and the number can sometimes reach to seventy.

To illustrate this point: For all Muslims removing one's shoes before stepping into a mosque is a mark of reverence; it signifies checking the clamoring world at the door and not admitting it into sacred precincts. The Sufi accepts this symbolism fully, but goes on to see in the act the additional meaning of removing everything that separates the soul from God. Or the act of asking forgiveness. All Muslims pray to be forgiven for specific transgressions, but when the Sufi pronounces the formula *astaghfiru'llah,* I ask forgiveness of God, he or she reads into the petition an added request: to be forgiven for his or her separate existence. This sounds strange, and indeed, exoteric Muslims find it incomprehensible. But the Sufis see it as an extension of Rabi'a's teaching that "Your existence is a sin with which no other can be compared." Because *ex*-istence is a standing *out* from something, which in this case is God, existence involves separation.

To avoid it Sufis developed their doctrine of *fana* — extinction — as the logical term of their quest. Not that their *consciousness* was to be extinguished. It was their *self*-consciousness — their consciousness of themselves as separate selves replete with their private personal agendas — that was to be ended. If the ending was complete, they argued, when they looked inside the dry shells of their now-emptied selves they would find nothing but God. A Christian mystic put this point by writing:

> God, whose boundless love and joy
> Are present everywhere;
> He cannot come to visit you
> Unless you are not there.   (Angelus Silesius)

Al-Hallaj's version was: "I saw my Lord with the eye of the Heart. I said: 'Who are you?' He answered: 'You.'"

As a final example of the Sufis' extravagant use of symbolism, we can note the way they tightened the creedal assertion "There is no god but God" to read, "There is *nothing* but God." To exoteric Muslims this again sounded silly, if not blasphemous: silly because there are obviously lots of things—tables and chairs—that are not God; blasphemous because the mystic reading seemed to deny God as Creator. But the Sufis' intent was to challenge the independence that people normally ascribe to things. Monotheism to them meant more than the theoretical point that there are not two Gods; that they considered obvious. Picking up on the existential meaning of theism—God is that to which we give (or should give) ourselves—they agreed that the initial meaning of "no god but God" is that we should give ourselves to nothing but God. But we do not catch the full significance of the phrase, they argued, until we see that we *do* give ourselves to other things when we let them occupy us as objects in their own right; objects that have the power to interest or repel us by being simply what they are. To think of light as caused by electricity—by electricity only and sufficiently, without asking where electricity comes from—is in principle to commit *shirk;* for because only God is self-sufficient, to consider other things as such is to liken them to God and thereby ascribe to him rivals.

Symbolism, though powerful, works somewhat abstractly, so the Sufis supplement it with *dhikr* (to remember), the practice of remembering Allah through repeating his Name. "There is a means of polishing all things whereby rust may be removed," a *hadith* asserts, adding: "That which polishes the heart is the invocation of Allah." Remembrance of God is at the same time a forgetting of self, so Sufis consider the repetition of Allah's Name the best way of directing their attention Godward. Whether they utter God's Name alone or with others, silently or aloud, accenting its first syllable sharply or prolonging its second syllable as long as breath allows, they try to fill every free moment of the day with its music. Eventually, this practice kneads the syllables into the subconscious mind, from which it bubbles up with the spontaneity of a birdsong.

The foregoing paragraphs sketch what Sufism is at heart, but they do not explain why this section opened by associating it with a division within Islam. The answer is that Muslims are of two minds about Sufism. This is partly because Sufism is itself a mixed bag. By the principle that the higher attracts the lower, Sufi orders have at times attracted riffraff who are Sufis in little more than name. For example, certain mendicant orders of Sufism have used poverty as a discipline, but it is only a step from authentic Sufis of this stripe to beggars who do no more than claim to be Sufis. Politics too has at times intruded. Most recently, groups have arisen in the West that call themselves Sufis, while professing no allegiance whatsoever to Islamic orthodoxy.

It is not surprising that these aberrations raise eyebrows, but even authentic Sufism (as we have tried to describe it) is controversial. Why? It is because Sufis take certain liberties that exoteric Muslims cannot in conscience condone. Having seen the sky through the skylight of Islamic orthodoxy, Sufis become persuaded that there is more sky than the aperture allows. When Rumi asserted, "I am neither Muslim nor Christian, Jew nor Zoroastrian; I am neither of the earth nor of the heavens, I am neither body nor soul," we can understand the exoterics' fear that orthodoxy was being strained beyond permissible limits. Ibn 'Arabi's declaration was even more unsettling:

> *My heart has opened unto every form. It is a pasture for gazelles, a cloister for Christian monks, a temple for idols, the Ka'ba of the pilgrim, the tablets of the Torah and the book of the Koran. I practice the religion of Love; in whatsoever directions its caravans advance, the religion of Love shall be my religion and my faith.*

As for Al-Hallaj's assertion that he was God,[41] no explanation from the Sufis to the effect that he was referring to the divine Essence that was within him could keep exoterics from hearing this as outright blasphemy.

Mysticism breaks through the boundaries that protect the faith of the typical believer. In doing so it moves into an unconfined region that, fulfilling though it is for some, carries dangers for those who are unqualified for its teachings. Without their literal meaning being denied, dogmas and prescriptions that the ordinary believer sees as absolute are interpreted allegorically, or used as points of reference that may eventually be transcended. Particularly shocking to some is the fact that the Sufi often claims, if only by implication, an authority derived directly from God and a knowledge given from above rather than learned in the schools.

Sufis have their rights, but—if we may venture the verdict of Islam as a whole—so have ordinary believers whose faith in unambiguous principles, fully adequate for salvation, could be undermined by teachings that seem to tamper with them. For this reason many spiritual Masters have been discreet in their teachings, reserving parts of their doctrine for those who are suited to receive them. This is also why the exoteric authorities have regarded Sufism with understandable suspicion. Control has been exercised, partly by public opinion and partly by means of a kind of dynamic tension, maintained through the centuries, between the exoteric religious authorities on the one hand and Sufi *shaikhs* on the other. An undercurrent of opposition to Sufism within sections of the Islamic community has served as a necessary curb on the mystics, without this undercurrent having been strong enough to prevent those who have had a genuine vocation for a Sufi path from following their destiny.

On the whole, esoterism and exoterism have achieved a healthy balance in Islam, but in this section we shall let the esoterics have the last word. One of the teaching devices for which they are famous has not yet been mentioned; it is the Sufi tale. This one, "The Tale of the Sands," relates to their doctrine of *fana*, the transcending, in God, of the finite self.

A stream, from its source in far-off mountains, passing through every kind and description of countryside, at last reached the sands of the desert. Just as it had crossed every other barrier, the stream tried to cross this one, but it found that as fast as it ran into the sand, its waters disappeared.

It was convinced, however, that its destiny was to cross this desert, and yet there was no way. Now a hidden voice, coming from the desert itself, whispered: "The Wind crosses the desert, and so can the stream."

The stream objected that it was dashing itself against the sand, and only getting absorbed: that the wind could fly, and this was why it could cross a desert.

"By hurtling in your own accustomed way you cannot get across. You will either disappear or become a marsh. You must allow the wind to carry you over, to your destination."

But how could this happen? "By allowing yourself to be absorbed in the wind."

This idea was not acceptable to the stream. After all, it had never been absorbed before. It did not want to lose its individuality.

And, once having lost it, how was one to know that it could ever be regained?

"The wind," said the sand, "performs this function. It takes up water, carries it over the desert, and then lets it fall again. Falling as rain, the water again becomes a river."

"How can I know that this is true?" "It is so, and if you do not believe it, you cannot become more than a quagmire, and even that could take many, many years. And it certainly is not the same as a stream."

"But can I not remain the same stream that I am today?"

"You cannot in either case remain so," the whisper said. "Your essential part is carried away and forms a stream again. You are called what you are even today because you do not know which part of you is the essential one."

When it heard this, certain echoes began to arise in the thoughts of the stream. Dimly it remembered a state in which it— or some part of it?— had been held in the arms of a wind. It also remembered— or did it?— that this was the real thing, not necessarily the obvious thing, to do.

And the stream raised its vapor into the welcoming arms of the wind, which gently and easily bore it upwards and along, letting it fall softly as soon as they reached the roof of a mountain, many, many, miles away. And because it had its doubts, the stream was able to remember and record more strongly in its mind the details of the experience. It reflected, "Yes, now I have learned my true identity."

The stream was learning. But the sands whispered: "We know, because we see it happen day after day: and because we, the sands, extend from the riverside all the way to the mountain."

And that is why it is said that the way in which the stream of Life is to continue on its journey is written in the Sands.[42]

Whither Islam?

For long periods since Muhammad called his people to God's oneness, Muslims have wandered from the spirit of the Prophet. Their leaders are the first to admit that practice has often been replaced by mere profession, and that fervor has waned.

Viewed as a whole, however, Islam unrolls before us one of the most remarkable panoramas in all history. We have spoken of its early greatness. Had we pursued its history there would have been sections on the Muslim empire, which, a century after Muhammad's death, stretched from the bay of Biscay to the Indus and the frontiers of China, from the Aral Sea to the upper Nile. More important would have been the sections describing the spread of Muslim ideas: the development of a fabulous culture, the rise of literature, science, medicine, art, and architecture; the glory of Damascus, Baghdad, and Egypt, and the splendor of Spain under the Moors. There would have been the story of how, during Europe's Dark Ages, Muslim philosophers and scientists kept the lamp of learning bright, ready to spark the Western mind when it roused from its long sleep.

Nor would the story have been entirely confined to the past, for there are indications that Islam is emerging from several centuries of stagnation, which colonization no doubt exacerbated. It faces enormous problems: how to distinguish industrial modernization (which on balance it welcomes), from Westernization (which on balance it doesn't); how to realize the unity that is latent in Islam when the forces of nationalism work powerfully against it; how to hold on to Truth in a pluralistic, relativizing age. But having thrown off the colonial yoke, Islam is stirring with some of the vigor of its former youth. From Morocco across from Gibraltar on the Atlantic, eastward across North Africa, through the Indian subcontinent (which includes Pakistan and Bangladesh), on to the near-tip of Indonesia, Islam is a vital force in the contemporary world. Numbering in the order of 900 million adherents in a global population of 5 billion, one person out of every five or six belongs today to this religion which guides human thought and practice in unparalleled detail. And the proportion is increasing. Read these words at any hour of day or night and somewhere from a minaret (or now by radio) a *muezzin* will be calling the faithful to prayer, announcing:

> *God is most great.*
> *God is most great.*
> *I testify that there is no god but God.*
> *I testify that Muhammad is the Prophet of God.*
> *Arise and pray;*

God is most great.
God is most great.
There is no god but God.

Suggestions for Further Reading

Granting the Muslim's contention that the Koran suffers incomparably in translation, Mohammed Pickthall's *The Meaning of the Glorious Koran* (New York: New American Library, 1953) may be recommended as being as serviceable as any.

Kenneth Cragg's *The House of Islam* (Belmont, CA: Wadsworth, 1988) and Victor Danner's *The Islamic Tradition* (Amity, NY: Amity House, 1988) offer admirable overviews of this tradition, as do Seyyed Hossein Nasr's, *Ideals and Realities of Islam* (San Francisco: Harper-Collins, 1989) and Abdel Halim Mahmud's *The Creed of Islam* (London: World of Islam Festival Trust, 1978; distributed by Thorsons Publishers, Denington Estate, Wellingborough, Northants, England).

The best metaphysical discussion of Sufi doctrines is to be found in Frithjof Schuon's *Understanding Islam* (New York: Penguin Books, 1972), which a leading Muslim scholar has hailed as "the best work in English on the meaning of Islam and why Muslims believe in it." It is a demanding book, however. More accessible to the general reader are William Stoddart's *Sufism* (New York: Paragon Press, 1986) and Martin Lings' *What Is Sufism?* (London: Unwin Hyman, 1975, 1988).

For the writings of the greatest Sufi poet, Rumi, John Moyne and Coleman Barks' *Open Secret* (Putney, VT: Threshold Books, 1984) and Coleman Barks' *Delicious Laughter* (Athens, GA: Maypop Press, 1989) are recommended.

My thirty minute video cassette on "Islamic Mysticism: The Sufi Way" is available from Hartley Film Foundation, Cat Rock Road, Cos Cob, CT 06807.

The pleasures of Sufi tales can be sampled through Idries Shah's collection, *Tales of the Dervishes* (New York: E. P. Dutton, 1970).

Notes

1. Meg Greenfield, *Newsweek* (March 26, 1979): 116.
2. Norman Daniel, *Islam and the West: The Making of an Image*, 1960. Rev. ed. (Edinburgh: Edinburgh University Press, 1966) details the emergence of

the distorted picture of Islam that has dominated the West for over a thousand years.

3. Philip Hitti, *History of the Arabs*, 1937. Rev. ed. (New York: St. Martin's Press, 1970), 3–4.

4. Thomas Carlyle's description in "The Hero as Prophet," in *Heroes and Hero-Worship*, 1840. Reprint. (New York: Oxford University Press, 1974.)

5. Arabic has no neuter gender. As its nouns are invariably masculine or feminine, its pronouns are as well. In fidelity to the grammar of the Koran, therefore, I shall, when referring to Allah who possesses a masculine proper name, use the masculine pronoun.

6. See Charles Le Gai Eaton, *Islam and the Destiny of Man* (Albany: State University of New York Press, 1985), 103.

7. The literal meaning of the word *iqra'* is "recite," but here, where Muhammad was given his commission, I have followed the trajectory of Victor Danner's "preach" (*The Islamic Tradition* [Amity, NY: Amity House, 1988], 35), but changed his word to "proclaim."

8. As rendered by Ameer Ali in *The Spirit of Islam*, 1902. Rev. ed. (London: Christophers, 1923), 18.

9. Ali, *Spirit of Islam*, 32.

10. Sir William Muir, quoted in Ali, *Spirit of Islam*, 32.

11. Quoted without source in Ali, *Spirit of Islam*, 52.

12. Ali, *Spirit of Islam*, 52.

13. Philip Hitti, *The Arabs: A Short History*, 1949. Rev. ed. (New York: St. Martin's Press, 1968), 32.

14. Michael H. Hart, *The 100: A Ranking of the Most Influential Persons in History* (New York: Citadel Press, 1989), 40.

15. Edward Gibbon, *The Decline and Fall of the Roman Empire*, 1845. Reprint. (New York: Modern Library, 1977), vol. 2, 162.

16. Today the language of Islam is a matter of sharp controversy. While all orthodox Muslims agree that the ritual use of the Koran in canonical prayers, and so on, must be in Arabic, there are many, including some among the *ulama* (religious scholars), who believe that on other occasions those who do not know Arabic should read the Koran in translation.

17. Kenneth Cragg, trans., *Readings in the Qur'an* (London: Collins, 1988), 18.

18. Frithjof Schuon, *Understanding Islam* (New York: Penguin Books, 1972), 44–45.

19. "She [Mary] said: My Lord! How can I have a child when no mortal hath touched me? He [the angel] said: So. Allah createth what He will. If He decreeth a thing, He saith unto it only: Be! and it is" (3:47).

20. Tabari relates traditions on this episode that have God flattening the mountain with just his little finger.

21. Ali, *Spirit of Islam*, 150.

22. William James, *The Varieties of Religious Experience* (New York: Macmillan, 1961), 57.

23. Sir Muhammad Iqbal, *The Secrets of the Self*, 1920. Reprint. (Lahore: Muhammad Ashraf, 1979), xxi.

24. Quoted in Ali, *Spirit of Islam*, 199.

25. Ali, *Spirit of Islam*, 170.

26. Gai Eaton, *Islam and the Destiny of Man*, 55.

27. A *hadith* of the Prophet, reported in *Mishkat al-Masabih*, James Robson, trans. (Lahore: Sh. Muhammad Ashraf, 1965), 1264–67.

28. Bernard Lewis, *The Atlantic Monthly* (September 1990): 59.

29. Ali, *Spirit of Islam*, 173.

30. As of this writing the Prime Minister of Pakistan and the leader of the opposition party in Bangladesh are both women. Muslim women could hold property in their own names from the start, whereas married women in the United States did not win that right until the twentieth century.

31. Outside slavery, we must add—a subject that, due to the variety of its local and historical forms, is too complex to consider here. See Bernard Lewis, *Race and Slavery in the Middle East* (New York: Oxford University Press, 1990).

32. Victor Danner, *The Islamic Tradition* (Amity, NY: Amity House, 1988), 131.

33. Kenneth Cragg, *The House of Islam* (Belmont, CA: Wadsworth, 1975), 122.

34. See Malcolm X, *The Autobiography of Malcolm X* (New York: Grove Press, 1964), 338–47.

35. Daniel, *Islam and the West*, 274.

36. Quoted by Ali, *Spirit of Islam*, 212.

37. Norman Daniel's *Islam and the West* supports them on this point.

38. *Hadith qudsi*, an extra-Koranic canonical saying of the Prophet, in which Allah speaks in the first person.

39. Cyprian Rice, *The Persian Sufis* (London: Allen & Unwin, 1964), 57.

40. The relation between mental and visionary knowledge is brought out in an exchange between the great Muslim philosopher, Ibn Sina (Avicenna), and a contemporary ecstatic named Abu Sa'id. Ibn Sina said of Abu Sa'id, "What I know, he sees." Abu Sa'id returned the compliment. "What I see," he said, "he knows."

41. His actual words were, "I am the Truth," but Truth used here as one of the Ninety-nine Beautiful Names of Allah.

42. Idries Shah, *Tales of the Dervishes* (New York: E. P. Dutton, 1970), 23–24.

VII. *Judaism*

In has been estimated that one-third of our Western civilization bears the marks of its Jewish ancestry. We feel its force in the names we give to our children: Adam Smith, Noah Webster, Abraham Lincoln, Isaac Newton, Rebecca West, Sarah Teasdale, Grandma Moses. Michelangelo felt it when he chiseled his "David" and painted the Sistine Ceiling; Dante when he wrote the *Divine Comedy* and Milton, *Paradise Lost.* The United States carries the indelible stamp of its Jewish heritage in its collective life: the phrase "by their Creator" in the Declaration of Independence; the words "Proclaim Liberty throughout the land" on the Liberty Bell. The real impact of the ancient Jews, however, lies in the extent to which Western civilization took over their angle of vision on the deepest questions life poses.

When, mindful of the impact the Jewish perspective has had on Western culture, we go back to the land, the people, and the history that made this impact, we are in for a shock. We might expect these to be as impressive as their influence, but they are not. In time span the Hebrews were latecomers on the stage of history. By 3000 B.C.E. (Before the Common Era, as Jews prefer to render the period B.C.), Egypt already had her pyramids, and Sumer and Akkad were world empires. By 1400 Phoenicia was colonizing. And where were the Jews in the midst of these mighty eddies? They were overlooked. A tiny band of nomads milling around the upper regions of the Arabian desert, they were too inconspicuous for the great powers even to notice.

When they finally settled down, the land they chose was equally unimpressive. One hundred and fifty miles in length from Dan to Beersheba, about fifty miles across at Jerusalem but much less at most places, Canaan was a postage stamp of a country, about one-eighth the size of Illinois. Nor does the terrain make up for what the region lacks in size. Visitors to Greece who climb Mount Olympus find it easy to imagine that the gods chose to live there. Canaan, by contrast, was a "mild and monotonous land. Did the Prophets flash their lightning of conviction from these quiet hills where everything is open to the sky?" Edmund Wilson asked on a visit to the Holy Land. "Were the savage wars of Scripture fought here? How very unlikely it seems that [the Bible emerged] from the history of these calm little hills, dotted with stones and flocks, under pale and trans-parent skies."[1] Even Jewish history, when viewed from without, amounts to little. It is certainly not dull history, but by external stan-dards it is very much like the histories of countless other little peo-ples, the people of the Balkans, say, or possibly the Native tribes of North America. Small peoples are always getting pushed around. They get shoved out of their lands and try desperately to scramble back into them. Compared with the histories of Assyria, Babylon, Egypt, and Syria, Jewish history is strictly minor league.

If the key to the achievement of the Jews lies neither in their antiquity nor in the proportions of their land and history, where does it lie? This is one of the greatest puzzles of history, and a number of answers have been proposed. The lead that we shall follow is this: What lifted the Jews from obscurity to permanent religious greatness was their passion for meaning.

Meaning in God

"In the beginning God. . . ." From beginning to end, the Jewish quest for meaning was rooted in their understanding of God.

Whatever a peoples' philosophy, it must take account of the "other." There are two reasons for this. First, no one seriously claims to be self-created; and as they are not, other people (being likewise human) did not bring themselves into being either. From this it fol-lows that humankind has issued from something other than itself. Second, everyone at some point finds his or her power limited. It may be a rock too large to lift, or a tidal wave that sweeps one's village away. Add therefore to the Other from which one has issued, a generalized Other that underscores one's limitations.

Merging these two ineluctable "others," people wonder if it is meaningful. Four characteristics could keep it from being so; if it were prosaic, chaotic, amoral, or hostile. The triumph of Jewish thought lies in its refusal to surrender meaning to any of these alternatives.

The Jews resisted the prosaic by personifying the "Other." In this they were at one with their ancient contemporaries. The concept of the inanimate — brute dead matter governed by blind, impersonal laws — is a late projection. For early peoples the sun that could bless or scorch, the earth that gave of its fertility, the gentle rains and the terrible storms, the mystery of birth and the reality of death were not to be explained as clots of matter regulated by mechanical laws. They were parts of a world that was pervaded by feeling and purpose throughout.

It is easy to smile at the anthropomorphism of the early Hebrews, who could imagine ultimate reality as a person walking in the garden of Eden in the cool of the morning. But when we make our way through the poetic concreteness of the perspective to its underlying claim — that in the final analysis ultimate reality is more like a person than like a thing, more like a mind than like a machine — we must ask ourselves two questions. First, what is the evidence against this hypothesis? It seems to be so completely lacking that as knowledgeable a philosopher-scientist as Alfred North Whitehead could embrace the hypothesis without reserve. Second, is the concept intrinsically less exalted than its alternative? The Jews were reaching out for the most exalted concept of the Other that they could conceive, an Other that embodied such inexhaustible worth that human beings would never begin to fathom its fullness. The Jews found greater depth and mystery in people than in any of the other wonders at hand. How could they be true to this conviction of the Other's worth except by extending and deepening the category of the personal to include it?

Where the Jews differed from their neighbors was not in envisioning the Other as personal but in focusing its personalism in a single, supreme, nature-transcending will. For the Egyptians, Babylonians, Syrians, and lesser Mediterranean peoples of the day, each major power of nature was a distinct deity. The storm was the storm-god, the sun the sun-god, the rain the rain-god. When we turn to the Hebrew Bible we find ourselves in a completely different atmosphere. Nature here is an expression of a single Lord of all being. As an authority on polytheism in the ancient Middle East has written:

> When we read in Psalm 19 that "The heavens declare the glory of God; and the firmament showeth his handiwork," we hear a voice which mocks the beliefs of Egyptians and Babylonians. The heavens, which were to the psalmist a witness of God's greatness, were to the Mesopotamians the very majesty of godhead, the highest ruler, Anu. To the Egyptians the heavens signified the mystery of the divine mother through whom man was reborn. In Egypt and Mesopotamia the divine was comprehended as immanent: the gods were in nature. The Egyptians saw in the sun all that a man may know of the creator; the Mesopotamians viewed the sun as the god Shamash, the guarantor of justice. But to the psalmist the sun was God's devoted servant who is as a bridegroom coming out of his chamber, and "rejoiceth as a strong man to run a race." The God of the psalmists and the prophets was not in nature. He transcended nature. . . . It would seem that the Hebrews, no less than the Greeks, broke with the mode of speculation which had prevailed up to their time.[2]

Though the Hebrew Bible contains references to gods other than Yahweh (misread Jehovah in many translations), this does not upset the claim that the basic contribution of Judaism to the religious thought of the Middle East was monotheism. For a close reading of the text shows that these other gods differed from Yahweh in two respects. First, they owed their origin to Yahweh—"You are gods, children of the Most High, all of you" (Psalm 82:6). Second, unlike Yahweh, they were mortal—"You shall die like mortals, and fall like any prince" (Psalm 82:7). These differences are clearly of sufficient importance to place the God of Israel in a category that differs from that of the other gods, not merely in degree but in kind. They are not Yahweh's rivals; they are God's subordinates. From a very early date, possibly from the very beginning of the biblical record, the Jews were monotheists.

The significance of this achievement in religious thought lies ultimately in the focus it introduces into life. If God is that to which one gives oneself unreservedly, to have more than one God is to live a life of divided loyalties. If life is to be whole; if one is not to spend one's days darting from one cosmic bureaucrat to another to discover who's in charge that day; if, in short, there is a consistent way in which life is to be lived if it is to move toward fulfillment, a way that can be searched out and approximated, there must be a singleness to the Other that supports this way. That there is, has been the foundation of Jewish belief. "Hear, O Israel, the Lord our God, the Lord is One" (Deuteronomy 6:4).

There remains the question of whether the Other, now seen as personal and ultimately one, was either amoral or hostile. If it were either, this too could frustrate meaning. Interpersonal life obviously flows more smoothly when people behave morally; but if ultimate reality does not support such behavior, if the world is such that morality does not pay, people face an impasse as to how to live. As to the Other's disposition toward people, its power so obviously outweighs human power that if its intents run counter to human well-being, human life, far from being fully meaningful, can be nothing but a game of cat-and-mouse. This insight caused Lucretius, a short distance around the Mediterranean in Rome, to preach atheism on grounds that were actually religious. If the gods are as the Roman believed them to be—immoral, vindictive, and capricious—meaningful existence requires that they be opposed or rejected.

The God of the Jews possessed none of these traits, which in greater or lesser degree characterized the gods of their neighbors. It is here that we come to the supreme achievement of Jewish thought— not in its monotheism as such, but in the character it ascribed to the God it intuited as One. The Greeks, the Romans, the Syrians, and most of the other Mediterranean peoples would have said two things about their gods' characters. First, they tend to be amoral; second, toward humankind they are preponderantly indifferent. The Jews reversed the thinking of their contemporaries on both these counts. Whereas the gods of Olympus tirelessly pursued beautiful women, the God of Sinai watched over widows and orphans. While Mesopotamia's Anu and Canaan's El were pursuing their aloof ways, Yahweh speaks the name of Abraham, lifting his people out of slavery, and (in Ezekiel's vision) seeks out the lonely, heartsick Jewish exiles in Babylon. God is a God of righteousness, whose loving-kindness is from everlasting to everlasting and whose tender mercies are in all his works.

Such, then, was the Hebrews' conception of the Other that confronts human beings. It is not prosaic, for at its center sits enthroned a Being of awesome majesty. It is not chaotic, for it coheres in a divine unity. The reverse of amoral or indifferent, it centers in a God of righteousness and love. Are we surprised, then, to find the Jew exclaiming with the exultation of frontier discovery: "Who is like you among the gods, O Yahweh?" "What great nation has a God like the Lord?"

Meaning in Creation

In *The Brothers Karamazov* Dostoevsky has Ivan blurt out: "I don't accept this world of God's, and although I know it exists, I don't accept it at all. It's not that I don't accept God, you must understand, it's the world created by Him I don't and cannot accept."

Ivan is not alone in finding God, perhaps, good, but the world not. Entire philosophies have done the same — Cynicism in Greece, Jainism in India. Judaism, by contrast, affirms the world's goodness, arriving at that conclusion through its assumption that God created it. "In the beginning God created the heavens and the earth" (Genesis 1:1) and pronounced it to be good.

What does it mean to say that the universe, the entire realm of natural existence as we know it, is God-created? Philosophers might look to such a statement as explanation for the means by which the world came into being, but that is a purely cosmogonic question that has no bearing on how we live. Did the world have a first cause or not? Our answer to that question seems unrelated to the way life feels to us.

There is another side to the affirmation that the universe is God-created, however. Approached from this second angle, the assertion speaks not to the way the earth originated but to the character of its agent. Unlike the first issue, this one affects us profoundly. Everyone at times finds himself or herself asking whether life is worthwhile, which amounts to asking whether, when the going gets rough, it makes sense to continue to live. Those who conclude that it does not make sense give up, if not once and for all by suicide, then piecemeal, by surrendering daily to the encroaching desolation of the years. Whatever else the word God may mean, it means a being in whom power and value converge, a being whose will cannot be thwarted and whose will is good. In this sense, to affirm that existence is God-created is to affirm its unimpeachable worth.

There is a passage in T. S. Eliot's *The Cocktail Party* that speaks to this point. Celia, who has been not just disappointed but disillusioned in love, goes to a psychiatrist for help and begins her first session with this surprising statement:

> *I must tell you*
> *That I should really like to think there's something*
>   *wrong with me—*
> *Because, if there isn't, then there's something*
>   *wrong*
> *With the world itself—and that's much more*
>   *frightening!*
> *That would be terrible. So I'd rather believe*
> *There is something wrong with me, that could be put*
>   *right.*

These lines speak to the most basic decision life demands. Things repeatedly go wrong in life. When they do, what are we to conclude? Ultimately, the options come down to two. One possibility is that the fault lies in the stars, dear Brutus. Many have so concluded. They range all the way from quipsters who propose that the best educational toy we could give to children is jigsaw puzzles in which no two pieces fit together, to Thomas Hardy, who inferred that the power that spawned a universe so inherently tragic must be some sort of dumb vegetable. In Somerset Maugham's *Of Human Bondage* the principal character, Philip, was given a Persian rug by a Bohemian roué who assured him that by studying the carpet he would be able to comprehend life's meaning. The donor died, and Philip was still in the dark. How could the involved pattern of a Persian rug solve the problem of life's meaning? When the answer finally dawned on him, it seemed obvious: Life has no meaning. "For nothing was there a why and a wherefore."

This is one possibility. The other possibility is that when things go wrong the fault lies not in the stars but in ourselves. Neither answer can be objectively validated, but there is no doubt as to which elicits the more creative response. In the one case human beings are helpless, for their troubles stem from the botched character of existence itself, which is beyond their power to remedy. The other possibility challenges people to look closer to home—to search for causes of their problems in places where they can effect changes. Seen in this light, the Jewish affirmation that the world is God-created equipped them with a constructive premise. However desperate their lot, however deep the valley of the shadow of death they found themselves in, they never despaired of life itself. Meaning was always waiting to be won; the opportunity to respond creatively was never absent. For the world had been fashioned by the God who not only meted out the heavens with a span, but whose goodness endured forever.

Thus far we have been speaking of the Jewish estimate of creation as a whole, but one element in the biblical account deserves special attention: its regard for nature — the physical, material component of existence.

Much of Greek thought takes a dim view of matter. Likewise Indian philosophy, which considers matter a barbarian, spoiling everything it touches. Salvation in such contexts involves freeing the soul from its material container.

How different the first chapter of Genesis, which (as we have seen) opens with the words "In the beginning God created the heavens *and the earth*," emphasis now added, and climaxes with God reviewing "everything that he had made, and behold, it was very good." We ought to let our minds dwell on that adjective "very," for it gives a lilt to the entire Jewish, and subsequently Western, view of nature. Pressing for meaning in every direction, the Jews refused to abandon the physical aspects of existence as illusory, defective, or unimportant. Fresh as the morning of Creation, nature was to be relished. The abundance of food made the Promised Land "a good land, a land with flowing streams, with springs and underground waters welling up in valleys and hills, a land of wheat and barley, of vines and fig trees and pomegranates, a land of olive trees and honey, a land where you may eat bread without scarcity" (Deuteronomy 8:7–8). Sex, too, was good. An occasional minority movement like the Essenes might have concluded the opposite, but Jews as a whole hold marriage in high regard. The entire assumption behind the prophets' denunciation of the inequalities of wealth that confronted them was the reverse of the opinion that possessions are bad. They are so good that more people should have more of them.

Such an affirmative and buoyant attitude toward nature does seem to set Judaism off from India's basic outlook. It does not, however, distinguish it from East Asia, where the appreciation of nature is profound. What divides the Hebraic from the Chinese view of nature does not come out until we note a third verse in this crucial first chapter of Genesis. In verse 26 God says of the people he intends to create: "Let them have dominion . . . over all the earth." How much this differs from the Chinese attitude toward nature can be seen by recalling its opposite sentiment in the *Tao Te Ching:*

> *Those who would take over the earth*
> *And shape it to their will*
> *Never, I notice, succeed.*

If we propositionalize the three key assertions about nature in the opening chapter of Genesis —

> *God created the earth;*
> *let [human beings] have dominion over the earth;*
> *behold, it was very good . . .*

—we find an appreciation of nature, blended with confidence in human powers to work with it for the good, that in its time was exceptional. It was, as we well know, an attitude that was destined to bear fruit, for it is no accident that modern science first emerged in the Western world. Archbishop William Temple used to say that Judaism and its offspring, Christianity, are the most materialistic religions in the world. When Islam is added to the list, the Semitically originated religions emerge as exceptional in insisting that human beings are ineradicably body as well as spirit and that this coupling is not a liability. From this basic premise three corollaries follow: (1) that the material aspects of life are important (hence the strong emphasis in the West on humanitarianism and social service); (2) that matter can participate in the condition of salvation itself (affirmed by the doctrine of the Resurrection of the Body); and (3) that nature can host the Divine (the Kingdom of God is to come "on Earth," to which Christianity adds its doctrine of the Incarnation).

Meaning in Human Existence

The most crucial element in human thinking is self-directed. What does it mean to be a human self, to live a human life?

Here, too, the Jews looked for meaning. They were intensely interested in human nature, but not for the brute facts of the case.

They wanted truth-for-life. They wanted to understand the human condition so as to avail themselves of its highest reaches.

The Jews were acutely aware of human limitations. Compared with the majesty of the heavens, people are "dust" (Psalm 103:14); facing the forces of nature they can be "crushed like a moth" (Job 4:19). Their time upon the earth is swiftly spent, like grass that in the morning flourishes, but "in the evening fades and withers" (Psalm 90:6). Even this brief span is laced with pain that causes our years to end "as a sigh" (Psalm 90:9). Not once but repeatedly the Jews were forced to the rhetorical question: "What are human beings" that God should give them a second thought? (Psalm 8:4).

Considering the freedom of Israel's thought and her refusal to repress doubts when she felt them, it is not surprising to find that there were moments when they suspected that "human beings . . . are only animals. For the fate of humans and the fate of animals is the same; as one dies, so dies the other" (Ecclesiastes 3:18–19). Here is a biological interpretation of the human species as uncompromising as any the nineteenth century ever produced. The significant point, however, is that this passing thought did not prevail. The striking feature of the Jewish view of human nature is that without blinking its frailty, it went on to affirm its unspeakable grandeur. We are a blend of dust and divinity.

The word *unspeakable* two sentence above is not hyperbole. The King James Version translates the central Jewish claim concerning the human station as follows: "Thou hast made him a little lower than the angels" (Psalm 8:5). That last word is a straight mistranslation, for the original Hebrew plainly reads "a little lower than the gods [or God]"— the number of the Hebrew word *'elohim* is indeterminate. Why did the translators reduce deity to angels? The answer seems obvious: It was not erudition that they lacked, but rather the boldness — one is tempted to say nerve — of the Hebrews. We can respect their reserve. It is one thing to write a Hollywood script in which everyone seems wonderful; it is another thing to make such characters seem real. The one charge that has never been leveled against the Bible is that its characters are not real people. Even its greatest heroes, like David, are presented so unvarnished, so "warts and all," that the Book of Samuel has been called the most honest historical writing of the ancient world. Yet no amount of realism could dampen the aspiration of the Jews. Human beings who on occasion so justly deserve the epithets "maggot and worm" (Job 25:6) are equally the beings whom God has "crowned with glory and honor" (Psalm 8:6). There is a rabbinic saying to the effect that whenever a man or woman walks down the street he or she is preceded by an invisible choir of angels crying, "Make way, make way! Make way for the image of God."

In speaking of the realism of the Jewish view of human nature we have thus far emphasized its recognition of physical limitations: weakness, susceptibility to pain, life's brevity. We shall not have plumbed the full scope of its realism, however, until we add that they saw the basic human limitation as moral rather than physical. Human beings are not only frail; they are sinners: "I was born guilty, a sinner when my mother conceived me" (Psalm 51:5). It is totally false to claim this verse for the defense of either the doctrine of total human depravity or the notion that sex is evil. These are both imported notions that have nothing to do with Judaism. The verse does, however, contribute something of great importance to Jewish anthropology. The word sin comes from a root meaning "to miss the mark," and this people (despite their high origin) manage continually to do. Meant to be noble, they are usually something less; meant to be generous, they withhold from others. Created more than animal, they often sink to being nothing else.

Yet never in these "missings" is the misstep required. Jews have never questioned human freedom. The first recorded human act involved free choice. In eating Eden's forbidden fruit, Adam and Eve were, it is true, seduced by the snake, but they could have resisted. The snake merely tempted them; it is clearly a story of a human lapse. Inanimate objects cannot be other than they are; they do what nature and circumstance decree. Human beings, once created, make or break themselves, forging their own destinies through their decisions. "Cease to do evil, learn to do good" (Isaiah 1:16–17) — only for human beings does this injunction hold. "I have set before you life and death . . . therefore choose life" (Deuteronomy 30:19).

Finally, it followed from the Jewish concept of their God as a loving God that people are God's beloved children. In one of the tenderest metaphors of the entire Bible, Hosea pictures God yearning over people as though they were toddling infants:

> *It was I who taught Ephraim to walk,*
> *I took them up in my arms;*

I led them with cords of human kindness,
     with bands of love.
I was to them like those who lift infants to their cheeks.
How can I give you up, Ephraim?
     How can I hand you over, O Israel?
My heart recoils within me,
     my compassion grows warm and tender.   (Hosea 11:3–4,8)

Even in this world, immense as it is and woven of the mighty powers of nature, men and women can walk with the confidence of children in a home in which they are fully accepted.

What are the ingredients of the most creatively meaningful image of human existence that the mind can conceive? Remove human frailty — as grass, as a sigh, as dust, as moth-crushed — and the estimate becomes romantic. Remove grandeur — a little lower than God — and aspiration recedes. Remove sin — the tendency to miss the mark — and sentimentality threatens. Remove freedom — choose ye this day! — and responsibility goes by the board. Remove, finally, divine parentage and life becomes estranged, cut loose and adrift on a cold, indifferent sea. With all that has been discovered about human life in the intervening 2,500 years, it is difficult to find a flaw in this assessment.

Meaning in History

Let us begin with a contrast. "According to most classical philosophies and religions," a historian writes, "ultimate reality is disclosed when man, either by rational contemplation or mystic ascent, goes beyond the flow of events which we call 'history.' The goal is the apprehension of an order of reality unaffected by the unpredictable fortunes of mankind. In Hinduism, for instance, the world of sense experience is regarded as *maya*, illusion; the religious man, therefore, seeks release from the wheel of life in order that his individuality may fade out into the World-Soul, Brahma. Or, Greek philosophers looked upon the world as a natural process which, like the rotation of the seasons, always follows the same rational scheme. The philosopher, however, could soar above the recurring cycles of history by fixing his mind upon the unchanging absolute which belongs to the eternal order. Both of these views are vastly different from the

Biblical claim that God is found within the limitations of the world of change and struggle, and especially that he reveals himself in events which are unique, particular, and unrepeatable. For the Bible, history is neither *maya* nor a circular process of nature; it is the arena of God's purposive activity."[3]

What is at stake when we ask if there is meaning in history? At stake is our whole attitude toward the social order and collective life within it. If we decide that history is meaningless, it follows that the social, political, and cultural contexts of life do not warrant active concern. Life's pivotal problems will be judged to lie elsewhere, in the extent to which we can rise above circumstances and triumph over them. To the extent that we see things this way, we shall take little interest in, and feel little responsibility for, the problems that beset societies, cultures, and civilizations.

The Hebrew estimate of history was the exact opposite of this attitude of indifference. To the Jews history was of towering significance. It was important, first, because they were convinced that the context in which life is lived affects that life in every way, setting up its problems, delineating its opportunities, conditioning its outcomes. It is impossible to talk about Adam and Noah (the same may be said of every major biblical character) apart from the particular circumstances — in this case Eden and the Flood — that enveloped them and in response to which their lives took form. The events the Hebrew Bible relates are profoundly contextual.

Second, if contexts are crucial for life, so is collective action; social action as we usually call it. There are times when the only way to get things changed is by working together — planning, organizing, and then acting in concert. The destiny of the Hebrew slaves in Egypt is not depicted as depending on the extent to which they individually "rose above" their slavery by cultivating a liberty of spirit that could tolerate physical chains. They needed to stand up collectively and break for the desert.

Third, history was important for the Jews because they saw it as a field of opportunity. As it was ruled by God — the "theater of God's glory," John Calvin claimed, extrapolating from this Old Testament base — nothing in history happens accidentally. Yahweh's hand was at work in every event — in Eden, the Flood, the Exodus, the Babylonian Exile — shaping each sequence into a teaching experience for his people.

Finally, history was important because life's opportunities are not monotnously alike. Events, all of them important, are not equally important. It is not the case that anyone, anywhere and at any time, can turn to history and find awaiting an opportunity equivalent to all others in time and place. Each opportunity is unique, but some are decisive: "There is a tide in the affairs of men which, taken at the flood, leads on to fortune." History must, therefore, be attended to carefully, for when opportunities pass they are gone forever.

This uniqueness of events is epitomized in the Hebrew notions (a) of God's direct intervention in history at certain critical points, and (b) of a chosen people as recipients of God's unique challenges. Both are vividly illustrated in the epic of Abraham. This epic is introduced by a remarkable prologue, Genesis 1–11, which describes the steady deterioration of the world from its original, pristine goodness. Disobedience (eating the forbidden fruit) is followed by murder (Cain of Abel), promiscuity (the sons of God and the daughters of men), incest (the sons of Noah), until a flood is needed to sluice out the mess. In the midst of the corruption, God is not inactive. Against its backdrop, in the last days of the Sumeric universal state, God calls Abraham. He is to go forth into a new land to establish a new people. The moment is decisive. Because Abraham answers its call, he ceases to be anonymous. He becomes the first Hebrew, the first of a "chosen people."

We shall need to return to this "chosen people" theme, but for the present we must ask what gave the Jews their insight into history's significance. We have noted the *kind* of meaning they found in history. What enabled them to see history as *embodying* this meaning?

For India, human destiny lies outside history altogether. There the world that houses humanity is (as we have seen) the "middle world." Good and evil, pleasure and pain, right and wrong are woven into it in relatively equal proportions as its warp and weft. And so things will remain. All thought of cleaning up the world and changing its character appreciably is mistaken in principle. The nature religions of Israel's neighbors reached the same conclusion by a different route. For them, human destiny lay within history all right, but in history as currently constituted, not as it might become. We can see why change — specifically change for the better — did not suggest itself to nature religionists. If one's eye is on nature preeminently, one does not look beyond it for fulfillment elsewhere. But neither—and this is the point—does one dream of improving nature or the social order that is its extension, for these are assumed to be ingrained in the nature of things and not subject to human alteration. The Egyptian no more asked whether the sun god Ra was shining as he should shine than the modern astronomer asks whether the sun is expending itself at a proper rate; for in nature the accent is on what is, not what should be—the *is* rather than the *ought*.

The Israelites' historical outlook differed from that of India and Middle Eastern polytheism because they had a different idea of God. Had the issue been raised to the level of conscious debate, they would have argued against India that God would not have created people as material beings if matter were adventitious to their destiny. Against the nature polytheists the Jews would have argued that nature is not self-sufficient. Because nature was created by God, God cannot be assimilated to it. The consequence of keeping God and nature distinct is momentous, for it means that the "ought" cannot be assimilated to the "is"—God's will transcends (and can differ from) immanent actuality. By the double stroke of involving human life with the natural order but not confining it to that order, Judaism established history as both important and subject to critique. Those who do not learn from history are doomed to repeat it.

The nature polytheisms that surrounded Judaism all buttressed the status quo. Conditions might not be all the heart desired, but what impressed the polytheist was that they could be a lot worse. For if the powers of nature reside in many gods—in Mesopotamia their number reached into the thousands—there was always the danger that these gods might fall out among themselves with resulting chaos. So religion's attention was directed toward keeping things as they were. Egyptian religion repeatedly contrasted "passionate people" to "silent people," extolling the latter because they didn't cause trouble. Small wonder that no nature polytheism ever spawned a principled revolution. Traditionally, Indian religion likewise had a conservative cast; for if polytheisms feared change, Hinduism considered substantive social change to be impossible.

In Judaism, by contrast, history is in tension between its divine possibilities and its manifest frustrations. A sharp tension exists between the ought and the is. Consequently, Judaism laid the groundwork for social protest. When things are not as they should be, change in some form is in order. The idea bore fruit. It is in the lands that have been affected by the Jewish historical perspective, one that influenced Christianity and to some extent Islam, that the chief thrusts for social betterment have occurred. The prophets set the pattern. "Protected by religious sanctions, the prophets of Judah were a reforming political force which has never been surpassed and perhaps never equalled in subsequent world history." On fire with the conviction that things were not as they should be, they created in the name of the God for whom they spoke an atmosphere of reform that "put Hyde Park and the best days of muckraking newspapers to shame."[4]

Meaning in Morality

Human beings are social creatures. Separated from their kind at birth, they never become human; yet living with others, they are often barbaric. The need for morality stems from this double fact. Nobody likes moral rules any more than they like stop lights or "no left turn" signs. But without moral constraints, human relations would become as snarled as traffic in the Chicago loop if everyone drove at will.

The Jewish formulation of "those wise restraints that make men free" is contained in her Law. We shall have occasion to note that this Law contains ritualistic as well as ethical prescriptions, but for the present we are concerned with the latter. According to the rabbinic view, the Hebrew Bible contains no less than 613 commandments that regulate human behavior. Four of these will suffice for our purposes: the four ethical precepts of the Ten Commandments, for it is through these that Hebraic morality has had its greatest impact. Appropriated by Christianity and Islam, the Ten Commandments constitute the moral foundation of most of the Western world.

There are four danger zones in human life that can cause unlimited trouble if they get out of hand: force, wealth, sex, and speech. On the animal level these are well contained. Two scarcely surface as problems at all. The spoken word does not, for animals cannot communicate enough to seriously deceive. Neither, really, does wealth, for to become a serious social problem the drive for possessions requires foresight and sustained greed at levels unknown in the animal kingdom. As for sex and force, they too pose no serious problems. Periodicity keeps sex from becoming obsessive, and inbuilt restraints hold violence in check. With the curious exception of ants, intraspecial warfare is seldom found. Where it has broken out, the species has usually destroyed itself.

With human beings things are different. Jealousies, hatreds, and revenge can lead to violence that, unless checked, rips communities to pieces. Murder instigates blood feuds that drag on indefinitely. Sex, if it violates certain restraints, can rouse passions so intense as to destroy entire communities. Similarly with theft and prevarication. We can imagine societies in which people do exactly as they please on these counts, but none have been found and anthropologists have now covered the globe. Apparently, if total permissiveness has ever been tried, its inventors have not survived for anthropologists to study. Perhaps here, more than anywhere else, we encounter human constants. Parisians are cousins to Bongolanders; twentieth-century sophisticates are related to aborigines. All must contain their appetites if history is to continue.

What the Ten Commandments prescribe in these areas are the minimum standards that make collective life possible. In this sense the Ten Commandments are to the social order what the opening chapter of Genesis is to the natural order; without each there is only a formless void. Whereas Genesis structures (and thereby creates) the physical world, the Ten Commandments structure (and thereby make possible) a social world. Regarding force, they say in effect: You can bicker and fight, but killing within the in-group will not be permitted, for it instigates blood feuds that shred community. Therefore *thou shalt not murder.* Similarly with sex. You can be a rounder, flirtatious, even promiscuous, and though we do not commend such behavior, we will not get the law after you. But at one point we draw the line: Sexual indulgence of married persons outside the nuptial bond will not be allowed, for it rouses passions the community cannot tolerate. Therefore *thou shalt not commit adultery.* As for possessions, you may make your pile as large as you please and be shrewd and cunning in the enterprise. One thing, though, you may not do, and that is pilfer directly off someone else's pile, for this outrages the sense of fair play and builds animosities that become ungovernable. Therefore *thou shalt not steal.* Finally, regarding the spoken word, you may dissemble and equivocate, but there is one time when we require that you tell the truth, the whole truth, and nothing but the truth. If a dispute reaches such proportions as to be brought before a tribunal, on such occasions the judges must know what happened. If you lie then, while under oath to tell the truth, the penalty will be severe. *Thou shalt not bear false witness.*

The importance of the Ten Commandments in their ethical dimensions lies not in their uniqueness but in their universality, not in their finality but in their foundational priority. They do not speak the final word on the topics they touch; they speak the words that must be spoken if other words are to follow. This is why, over three thousand years after Mount Sinai, they continue as the "moral esperanto" of the world. This led Heine to exclaim of the man who received them: "How tiny does Sinai appear when Moses stands upon it," and the biblical writers to assert categorically, "There arose not in Israel [another] prophet like Moses" (Deuteronomy 34:10).

Meaning in Justice

It is to a remarkable group of men whom we call the prophets more than to any others that Western civilization owes its convictions (1) that the future of any people depends in large part on the justice of its social order, and (2) that individuals are responsible for the social structures of their society as well as for their direct personal dealings.

When someone today is referred to as a prophet or is said to prophesy, we think of a soothsayer—someone who foretells the future. This was not the original meaning of the world. "Prophet" comes from the Greek word *prophetes*, in which *pro* means "for" and *phetes* means "to speak." Thus, in its original Greek, a prophet is someone who "speaks for" someone else. This meaning is faithful to the original Hebrew. When God commissions Moses to demand from Pharaoh the release of his people and Moses protests that he cannot speak, God says, "Your brother Aaron shall be your prophet" (Exodus 7:1).

If for the Hebrews the generic meaning of the word prophet was "one who speaks on the authority of another," its specific meaning (as used to refer to a distinctive group of people in the biblical period) was "one who speaks for God." A prophet differed from other men in that his mind, his speech, and occasionally even his body could become a conduit through which God addressed immediate historical conditions.

A review of the prophetic movement in Israel shows it not to have been a single phenomenon. Moses stands in a class by himself, but the prophetic movement passed through three stages, with the divine working differently in each of them.

The first is the stage of the Prophetic Guilds, of which the ninth and tenth chapters of First Samuel provide one of the best glimpses. In this stage prophecy is a group phenomenon. Prophets are not here identified as individuals because their talent is not an individual possession. Traveling in bands or schools, prophecy for them was a field phenomenon that required a critical mass. Contemporary psychologists would consider it a form of collective, self-induced ecstasy. With the help of music and dancing, a prophetic band would work itself into a state of frenzy. Its members would lose their self-consciousness in a collective sea of divine intoxication.

There was no ethical dimension to prophecy in this guild stage. The prophets assumed that they were possessed by the divine only because the experience brought an inrush of ecstatic power. In the second stage, ethics entered. This was the stage of the Individual Pre-Writing Prophets. Being alive and in motion, prophecy now began to launch individuals like rockets from the bands that formed their base. Their names have come down to us—Elijah, Elisha, Nathan, Micaiah, Ahijah, and others—but as they were still in the pre-writing stage, no books of the Bible carry their names. Ecstasy still figured large in their prophetic experience, and power, too, for when "the hand of the Lord" visited these men they outran chariots for thirty miles and were caught up from the plains and cast on mountaintops.[5] But two things were different. Though these prophets too had a guild base, they could receive the divine visitation while they were alone. And second, the divine spoke through them more clearly. No longer did it manifest itself as an overpowering emotion only. Emotion backed God's demand for justice.

Two episodes from the Bible may be drawn from many to make this point. One is the story of Naboth who, because he refused to turn over his family vineyard to King Ahab, was framed on false charges of blasphemy and subversion and then stoned; as blasphemy was a capital crime, his property then reverted to the throne. When news of this travesty reached Elijah, the word of the Lord came to him, saying, "Go down to meet Ahab king of Israel. Say to him, 'Thus says the Lord. You have killed and taken possession. In the place where dogs

licked up the blood of Naboth, dogs will also lick up your blood'"
(1 Kings 21:18–19).

The story carries revolutionary significance for human history,
for it is the story of how someone without official position took the
side of a wronged man and denounced a king to his face on grounds
of injustice. One will search the annals of history in vain for its parallel. Elijah was not a priest. He had no formal authority for the terrible
judgment he delivered. The normal pattern of the day would have
called for him to be struck down by bodyguards on the spot. But the
fact that he was "speaking for" an authority not his own was so transparent that the king accepted Elijah's pronouncement as just.

The same striking sequence recurred in the incident of David
and Bathsheba. From the top of his roof David glimpsed Bathsheba
bathing and wanted her. There was an obstacle, however: she was
married. To the royalty of those days this was a small matter; David
simply moved to get rid of her husband. Uriah was ordered to the
front lines, carrying instructions that he be placed in the thick of the
fighting and support withdrawn so he would be killed. Everything
went as planned; indeed, the procedure seemed routine until
Nathan the prophet got wind of it. Sensing immediately that "the
thing that David had done displeased the Lord," he went straight to
the king, who had absolute power over his life, and said to him:

> *Thus says the Lord, the God of Israel: "You have struck down
> Uriah with the sword, and have taken his wife to be your wife, [so]
> I will raise up trouble against you within your own house; and I
> will take your wives before your eyes, and give them to your neigh-
> bor, and he shall lie with your wives in the sight of this very sun.
> For you did it secretly; but I will do this thing before all Israel.
> Because you have utterly scorned the Lord, the child that is born
> to you shall die."*   (2 Samuel 12:7, 9, 11–12, 14)

The surprising point in each of these accounts is not what the
kings do, for they were merely exercising the universally accepted
prerogatives of royalty in their day. The revolutionary and unprecedented fact is the way the prophets challenged their actions.

We have spoken of the Prophetic Guilds and the Individual Pre-
Writing Prophets. The third and climactic phase of the prophetic
movement arrived with the great Writing Prophets: Amos, Hosea,
Micah, Jeremiah, Isaiah, and the rest. Again at this stage, ecstasy was

not absent from the prophetic experience; Ezekiel 1–3, Jeremiah 1, and Isaiah 6 (where the prophet "saw the Lord, high and exalted") are among the most impressive theophanies on record. The Pre-Writing Prophets' ethical emphasis, too, continued, but here there was an important development. Whereas a Nathan or an Elijah perceived God's displeasure at individual acts of flagrant injustice, an Amos or an Isaiah could sense God's disapproval of injustices that were less conspicuous because they were perpetrated not by individuals through specific acts but were concealed in the social fabric. Whereas the Pre-Writing Prophets challenged individuals, the Writing Prophets challenged corruptions in the social order and oppressive institutions.

The Writing Prophets found themselves in a time that was shot through with inequities, special privilege, and injustices of the most flagrant sort. Wealth was concentrated in the hands of rich grandees, paupers were branded like cattle and sold as slaves, and debtors were traded for a pair of shoes. It was a world in which masters punished their slaves at will, women were subjugated to men, and unwanted children were abandoned to die in lonely places.

As a threat to the contemporary social health of the body politic, this moral delinquency was one important fact of Jewish political life at the time, but there was another. Danger within was matched by danger from without; for, sandwiched between the colossal empires of Assyria and Babylonia to the east, Egypt to the south, and Phoenicia and Syria to the north, Israel and Judah were in danger of being crushed. In similar situations the other peoples of the region assumed that outcomes rested on the relative strengths of the national gods involved—in other words, on a simple calculus of power in which questions of morality were irrelevant. Such an interpretation, however, drains opportunity, and hence meaning, from such situations. If eventualities are strictly determined by power, there is little that a small nation can do. The Jews resisted this reading, out of what we have targeted as their unquenchable passion for meaning. Even where it seemed almost impossible to do otherwise, they refused to concede that any event was meaningless in the sense of leaving no room for a creative response involving a moral choice. Thus, what other nations would have interpreted as simply a power squeeze, they saw as God's warning to clean up their national life: establish justice throughout the land, or be destroyed.

Stated abstractly, the Prophetic Principle can be put as follows: The prerequisite of political stability is social justice, for it is in the nature of things that injustice will not endure. Stated theologically the point reads: God has high standards. Divinity will not put up forever with exploitation, corruption, and mediocrity. This principle does not contradict what was said earlier about Yahweh's love. On the whole the prophets join the psalmists in speaking more of love than of justice. Later, a Rabbi was to describe the relationship between the two as follows:

> A king had some empty glasses. He said: "If I pour hot water into them they will crack; if I pour ice-cold water into them they will also crack!" What did the king do? He mixed the hot and the cold water together and poured it into them and they did not crack. Even so did the Holy One, blessed be He, say: "If I create the world on the basis of the attribute of mercy alone, the world's sins will greatly multiply. If I create it on the basis of the attribute of justice alone, how could the world endure? I will therefore create it with both the attributes of mercy and justice, and may it endure!"[6]

The prophets of Israel and Judah are one of the most amazing groups of individuals in all history. In the midst of the moral desert in which they found themselves, they spoke words the world has never been able to forget. Amos, a simple shepherd but no straw blown north by accident; instead, a man with a mission, stern and rugged as the desert from which he came; a man with all his wits about him and every faculty alert, crying in the crass marketplace of Bethel, "Let justice roll down like waters, and righteousness like a mighty stream." Isaiah, city-bred, stately, urbane, eloquent, but no less aflame with moral passion, crying out for one "who will bring forth justice in all the earth." Hosea, Micah, Jeremiah—what a company they make! The prophets come from all classes. Some are sophisticated, others as plain and natural as the hillsides from which they come. Some hear God roaring like a lion; others hear the divine decree in the ghostly stillness that follows the storm.

Yet one thing is common to them all: the conviction that every human being, simply by virtue of his or her humanity, is a child of God and therefore in possession of rights that even kings must respect. The prophets enter the stage of history like a strange, elemental, explosive force. They live in a vaster world than their compatriots, a world in which pomp and ceremony, wealth and splendor count for nothing, where kings seem small and the power of the mighty is as nothing compared with purity, justice, and mercy. So it is that wherever men and women have gone to history for encouragement and inspiration in the age-long struggle for justice, they have found it more than anywhere else in the ringing proclamations of the prophets.

Meaning in Suffering

From the eighth to the sixth centuries B.C.E., during which Israel and Judah tottered before the aggressive power of Syria, Assyria, Egypt, and Babylon, the prophets found meaning in their predicament by seeing it as God's way of underscoring the demand for righteousness. God was engaged in a great controversy with his people, a controversy involving moral issues not evident to the secular observer. To correct a wayward child a parent may coax and cajole, but if words fail action may prove to be necessary. Similarly, in the face of Israel's indifference to God's commands and pleadings, Yahweh had no alternative but to let the Israelites know who was God—whose will must prevail. It was to make this point that God was using Israel's enemies against her.

> *Thus says the Lord:*
> *For three transgressions of Israel,*
> *   and for four, I will not revoke the punishment;*
> *because they sell the righteous for silver,*
> *   and the needy for a pair of sandals—*
> *Therefore an adversary shall surround the land,*
> *   and strip you of your defense;*
> *and your strongholds shall be plundered.*   (Amos 2:6; 3:11)

Jeremiah takes up the refrain. Because the Jews had forsaken righteousness, it is God's decision to "make this city a curse for all the nations of the earth" (Jeremiah 26:6).

We can appreciate the moral courage required to come up with this interpretation of impending doom. How much easier to assume that God is on our side, or resign oneself to defeat.

The climax, however, is yet to come. Defeat was not averted. In 721 B.C.E. Assyria "came down like a wolf on the fold" and wiped the

Northern Kingdom from the map forever, converting its people into
"the Ten Lost Tribes of Israel." In 586 Judah, the Southern Kingdom,
was conquered, though in this case its leadership remained intact as
Nebuchadnezzar marched it collectively into captivity in Babylonia.

If ever there was a time when the possibility of meaning seemed
unlikely, this was it. The Jews had bungled their opportunity and in
consequence had been brought low. Surely now the prophets might
be expected to concede their people's doom with a self-serving "I
told you so."

This retort, a blend of vindictiveness and despair, was not in the
prophets' vocabulary. The most staggering fact in the Jewish quest
for meaning is the way in which in this blackest hour, when meaning
had been exhausted in the deepest strata the Jews had yet mined, the
prophets dug deeper still to uncover an entirely new vein. Not to
have done so would have amounted to accepting the prevailing view
that the victors' god was stronger than the god of the defeated, a logic
that would have ended the biblical faith and the Jewish people along
with it. The rejection of that logic rescued the Jewish future. A
prophet who wrote in sixth century Babylonia where his people were
captives—his name has been lost, but his words come down to us in
the latter chapters of the book of Isaiah—argued that Yahweh had not
been worsted by the Babylonian god Marduk; history was still Yahweh's province. This meant that there must have been point in the
Israelites' defeat; the challenge was again to see it. The point that
"Second Isaiah" saw was not this time punishment. The Israelites
needed to *learn* something that their defeat would teach, but their
experience would also be *redemptive* for the world.

On the learning side, there are lessons and insights that suffering
illumines as nothing else can. In this case the experience of defeat
and exile was teaching the Jews the true worth of freedom, which,
despite their early Egyptian captivity, they had come to hold too
lightly. Lines have come down to us that disclose the spiritual agony
of the Israelites as displaced persons—how heavily they felt the yoke
of captivity, how fervently they longed for their homeland.

> *By the rivers of Babylon—there we sat down*
> *and there we wept when we remembered Zion.*
> *On the willows there we hung up our harps.*
> *For there our captors asked us for songs,*

> *and our tormentors asked for mirth, saying,*
> *"Sing us one of the songs of Zion!"*
> *How could we sing the Lord's song in a foreign land?*
> *If I forget you, O Jerusalem, let my right hand wither!*
> *Let my tongue cling to the roof of my mouth.*   (Psalm 137:1–6)

Sometimes a single phrase is enough to convey the poignancy and pathos of their plight: "Is it nothing to you, oh you who pass by"; or "How long, O Lord, how long?"

When Cyrus, King of Persia, conquered Babylon in 538 and permitted the Jews to return to Palestine, the prophets saw another lesson that only suffering can fully impart: the lesson that those who remain faithful in adversity will be vindicated. In the end their rights will be restored.

> *Go out from Babylon, declare this*
> *with a shout of joy, proclaim it,*
> *send it forth to the end of the earth;*
> *say, "The Lord has redeemed His servant Jacob."*
> (Isaiah 48:20–22)

But what the Jews might themselves learn from their captivity was not the only meaning of their ordeal. God was using them to introduce into history insights that all peoples need but to which they are blinded by ease and complacency. God was burning into the hearts of the Jews through their suffering a passion for freedom and justice that would affect all humankind.

> *I have given you as a light to the nations,*
> *to open the eyes that are blind,*
> *to bring out the prisoners from the dungeon,*
> *from the prison those who sit in darkness.*   (Isaiah 42:6–7)

Stated abstractly, the deepest meaning the Jews found in their Exile was the meaning of vicarious suffering: meaning that enters lives that are willing to endure pain that others might be spared it. Second Isaiah related this general principle to the experience of his people by envisioning a day when the nations of the earth would see that the tiny nation they once scorned (here personified as an individual) had actually been suffering on their behalf:

> *Surely he has borne our infirmities*
> *and carried our diseases;*
> *yet we accounted him stricken,*
> *struck down by God, and afflicted.*
> *But he was wounded for our transgressions,*
> *crushed for our iniquities;*
> *upon him was the punishment that made us whole,*
> *and by his bruises we are healed.*
> *All we like sheep have gone astray;*
> *we have all turned to our own way;*
> *and the Lord has laid on him*
> *the iniquity of us all.* (Isaiah 53:4–6)

Meaning in Messianism

Though the Jews were able to find their suffering meaningful, meaning for them did not end there. It climaxed in Messianism.

We can work our way into this concept by way of an arresting fact. The idea of progress—belief that the conditions of life can improve, and that history can in this sense get somewhere—originated in the West. Insofar as other peoples have come to this notion, they have acquired it from the West.

Striking as this fact is, it seems explicable. If we confine ourselves to the two other enduring civilizations—South Asian, centering in India, and East Asian, centering in China and its cultural offshoots[7]—we find that their presiding outlooks were forged by people who were in power; in India these were the *brahmins,* and in China the literati. By contrast, the West's outlook was decisively shaped in this matter by the Jews, who for most of their formative period were underdogs. Ruling classes may be satisfied with the *status quo,* but underdogs are not. Unless their spirits have been crushed, which the Jewish spirit never was, oppressed people hope for improvement. This hope gave the biblical Jews a forward and upward looking cast of mind. They were an expectant people—a people who were waiting, if not to throw off the yoke of the oppressor, then to cross over into the promised land.

> *Sweet, sweet the open spreading fields*
> *Lay decked in shining green;*

So to the Jews fair Canaan stood,
While Jordan rolled between.

To sum up the matter: Underdogs have only one direction to look, and it was the upward tilt of the Jewish imagination that eventually led the West to conclude that the conditions of life as a whole might improve.

Hope has more purchase on the human heart when it is rendered concrete, so eventually Jewish hope came to be personified in the figure of a coming Messiah. Literally, Messiah (from the Hebrew *mashiah*) means "anointed"; but as kings and high priests were anointed with oil, the terms became a title of honor, signifying someone who had been elevated or "chosen." During the Babylonian Exile the Jews began to hope for a redeemer who would effect the "ingathering of the exiles" to their native homeland. After the second destruction of the Temple (70 C.E.), the honorific title "Messiah" was used to designate the person who would rescue them from that diaspora.

Things, though, are never this simple, and in the course of time the messianic idea became complex. Its animating concept was always hope, and this hope always had two sides to it: the politico-national side (which foresaw the triumph of the Jews over their enemies and their elevation to a position of importance in world affairs), and a spiritual-universal side (in which their political triumph would be attended by a moral advance of worldwide proportions).

They shall beat their swords into plowshares, and their spears
*   into pruning hooks;*
nation shall not lift up sword against nation,
*   neither shall they learn war any more.*   (Isaiah 2:4)

These three features of the messianic idea — hope, national restitution, and world upgrade — remained constant, but within this stable framework differing scenarios were scripted.

One important difference concerned the way the messianic age would arrive. Some expected an actual Messiah to appear — a priest or king who, as God's deputy, would effect the new order. On the other side were those who thought God would dispense with a human agent and intervene directly. The latter view, appropriately called *the messianic expectation*, hoped for "an age in which there would be political freedom, moral perfection, and earthly bliss for the people of Israel in their own land, and also for the entire human race."[8] The first concept includes everything in the second, but adds the figure of a lofty and exalted political and spiritual human personality, who comes to prepare the world for the Almighty's kingdom.

A second tension reflected the restorative and utopian impulses within Judaism generally. Restorative Messianism looked for the recreation of past conditions, typically the Davidic monarchy but now idealized. Here hope turned backward to the reestablishment of an original state of things and to a "life lived with the ancestors." But Messianism also accommodated Judaism's forward-looking impulse, so there were versions that were utopian in envisioning a state of things that never before existed.

Finally, Messianists differed concerning whether the new order would be continuous with previous history or would shake the world to its foundations and replace it (in the End of Days) with an aeon that was supernaturally different in kind. As the power of the Jews dwindled in the face of a rising Europe, and hope of political restoration in Israel seemed increasingly impossible, the expectation of a miraculous redemption strangled political yearnings. Apocalypticism, elements of which are visible in the prophets themselves, replaced hopes for military victory. The Messianic Age would break in at any moment, abruptly and cataclysmically. Mountains would crumble and the seas boil. The laws of nature would be abrogated to make way for a divine order that was unimaginable save that the "birth pangs of the Messianic Age"—its fearful images excited by terrors the Jews were actually experiencing—would be followed by peace. Thus even this apocalyptic version contained a utopian element. Peril and dread were balanced by consolation and redemption.

In all three of these polarities the alternatives were deeply intertwined, while being contradictory by nature. The messianic idea crystallized and retained its vitality out of the tensions created by its ingredient opposites. Nowhere do we find a pure case of one without the other; only the proportions between them fluctuated, often wildly. The direction in which the pendulum swung was determined by historical events and the individual character of their proclaimers, a number of whom—the "false messiahs"—assumed the messianic title for themselves and in several instances attracted large followings. In periods when the Israelites were still living an independent political life in their own land, ethical perfection and earthly bliss were emphasized; whereas in periods of subjugation and exile the yearning for political freedom was more prominent. In times of national freedom the worldwide, universalistic part of the hope was basic; but in times of trouble and distress the nationalistic element came to the fore. Throughout, however, the political component went arm in arm with the ethical, and the nationalistic with the universal. Political and spiritual longings united, as did hopes for themselves and the world at large. Both themes figure in Zionism, the modern movement for political and spiritual renewal of the Jewish people, which helped the Jews return to Palestine and found the State of Israel in 1948.

So we return to the underlying messianic theme, which is hope. Moving into Christianity, it took the form of the Second Coming of Christ. In seventeenth-century Europe it surfaced as the idea of historical progress, and in the nineteenth century it assumed Marxist idiom in the vision of a coming classless society. But whether we read it in its Jewish, its Christian, its secular, or its heretical version, the underlying theme is the same. "There's going to be a great day!" That says it prosaically. Martin Luther King, Jr., drawing his images from the Prophet Isaiah, said it rhetorically in his address to the audience of 200,000 in the 1968 civil rights March on Washington.

> *I have a dream today.*
> *I have a dream that one day every valley shall be exalted,*
> *every hill and mountain shall be made low, the rough places will*
> *be made plain, and the crooked places will be made straight, and*
> *the glory of the Lord shall be revealed, and all flesh shall see it*
> *together.*

The Hallowing of Life

Up to this point in our effort to enter the Jewish perspective, we have been dealing with ideas as these occurred to the Jews in their struggle to make sense out of life. As an entrance to Judaism this serves a purpose, for ideas have a universality that makes them intelligible even to outsiders. We have reached a point, however, where (if we are to move deeper into the understanding of this faith) we must table further consideration of Jewish ideas and look at Jewish practices.

We must consider Jewish ceremonies and observances, for it is generally agreed that Judaism is less an orthodoxy than an orthopraxis; Jews are united more by what they do than by what they think. One evidence of this is that Jews have never promulgated an official creed that must be accepted to belong to this faith. Observance, on the other hand—the circumcision of males, for example—is decisive. This emphasis on practice gives Judaism something of an oriental flavor; for whereas the West, influenced by the Greek partiality for abstract reason, emphasizes theology and creed, the East has approached religion through ritual and narrative. The difference is between the abstract and the concrete. Does Plato or Dostoevsky get closer to reality? Is love better expressed through words or an embrace?

Before turning to Jewish ritual as such, it will be well to speak briefly of ritual in general, for despite its place in every religion we have thus far not addressed it directly. From a narrowly rational or utilitarian point of view, ritual is nonsense, a waste any way we look at it. All that money lavished on candles, cathedrals, prayer books, and incense; all the time spent in worship and sacrament; all the energy that goes into rising up and sitting down, kneeling and prostration, circumambulation and singing—to what end? It isn't cost effective, we say. Moreover, it has about it an arbitrariness that makes it almost incomprehensible from the outside. A popular magazine carries a photograph of a chief-of-state rubbing noses with an Eskimo. To Eskimos rubbing noses is a friendship ritual. To us it's simply funny.

Yet with all its arbitrariness and seeming waste, ritual plays a part in life that nothing else can fill, a part that is by no means confined to religion. For one thing, it eases us through tense situations and times of anxiety. Sometimes the anxiety is mild—during introductions, for example. I am introduced to a stranger. Not knowing how he or she will respond, I don't know how to proceed. What should I say? What should I do? Ritual covers my uncertainty and awkwardness. It tells me to extend my hand and say "How do you do?" or "I'm pleased to meet you." And in so doing it brings form out of chaos. It provides the moment I need to get my bearings. The awkwardness is over. I have recovered my balance and am ready to explore freer behavior.

If we need ritual to help us through situations as inconsequential as a casual introduction, how much more when we find ourselves really at a loss. Death is the glaring example. Stunned by tragic bereavement, we would founder completely if we were thrown on our own and had to think our way through the ordeal. This is why death, with its funerals and memorial services, its wakes and sitting *shiva*, is the most ritualized rite of passage. Ritual, with its prepared score to orchestrate the occasion, channels our actions and feelings at a time when solitude would be unbearable. And in the process it softens the blow. "Ashes to ashes, dust to dust"— the words don't say whose ashes, for this is everybody; all of us. Ritual also rouses courage: "The Lord giveth and the Lord taketh away; blessed be the name of the Lord!" Finally, ritual sets death in perspective, connecting this particular death with its universal archetype. The deceased takes his or her place in the company of humankind, one step in the endless march of life into death and death into life again, with the continuum stretching both ways toward eternity.

From the triviality of an introduction to the trauma of death, ritual smooths life's transitions as perhaps nothing else can. But it also serves another function. In times of happiness it can intensify experience and raise joy to celebration. Here the examples are birthdays, weddings, and most simply a family's evening meal. Here, in this best meal of the day, when perhaps for the first time the family is relaxed and together, a blessing can be something more than the starting line for a food race. It can hallow the occasion. The opposite of dead weight, it consecrates a daily pleasure.

Against these background observations concerning the place of ritual in life generally, we turn now to its place in Judaism, where it aims to hallow life — ideally, all life. The nineteenth chapter of Leviticus capsules the point when God says to Moses, "You shall be holy for I, your God, am holy!" What does holiness involve? To many moderns the word is empty; but those who feel the stir of wonder and can sense the ineffable pressing in on their lives from every side will know what Plato was talking about when he wrote, "First a shudder runs through you, and then the old awe creeps over you." Those who have had such experiences will know the blend of mystery, ecstasy, and the numinous, which received classic description in Rudolph Otto's *The Idea of the Holy*.

To speak of the hallowing of life in Judaism is to refer to its conviction that all life down to its smallest element can, if rightly approached, be seen as a reflection of the infinite source of holiness, which is God. The name for this right approach to life and the world is piety, carefully distinguished from piosity, its counterfeit. In Judaism piety prepares the way for the coming of God's kingdom on earth: the time when everything will be redeemed and sanctified and the holiness of all God's creation will be transparently evident.

The secret of piety consists in seeing the entire world as belonging to God and reflecting God's glory. To rise in the morning on seeing the light of a new day, to eat a simple meal, to see a stream running between mossy stones, to watch the day slowly turn into evening—even small things like these can mirror God's majesty. "To the religious man," writes Abraham Heschel, "it is as if things stood with *their backs to him, their faces turned to God.*" To accept the good things of life, most of which come to us quite apart from our own efforts, as if they were matters of course without relating them to God, is quite wrong. In the Talmud to eat or drink without first making a blessing over the meal is compared to robbing God of his property. Through all Judaism runs this double theme: We should enjoy life's goodness, and at the same time we should augment this joy by sharing it with God, just as any joy we feel is augmented when shared with friends. Jewish law sanctions all the good things of life—eating, marriage, children, nature, while elevating them all to holiness. It teaches that people should eat, that they should prepare their tables in the presence of the Lord. It teaches that people should drink, that they should use wine to consecrate the Sabbath. It teaches that people should be merry, that they should dance around the Torah.

If we ask how this sense of the sanctity of all things is to be preserved against the backwash of the world's routine, the Jew's chief answer is: through tradition. Without attention, the human sense of wonder and the holy will stir occasionally, but to become a steady flame it must be tended. One of the best ways to do this is to steep oneself in a history that cries aloud of God's providential acts and mercy in every generation. Against those who would throw the past away with both hands that they may grasp the present more firmly, Judaism accounts the memory of the past a priceless treasure. The most historically minded of all the religions, it finds holiness and history inseparable. In sinking the roots of their lives deep into the past, the Jews draw nourishment from events in which God's acts were clearly visible. The Sabbath eve with its candles and cup of sanctification, the Passover feast with its many symbols, the austere solemnity of the Day of Atonement, the ram's horn sounding the New Year, the scroll of the Torah adorned with breastplate and crown—the Jew finds nothing less than the meaning of life in these things, a meaning that spans the centuries in affirming God's great goodness to God's people. Even when Jews recall their tragedies and the price their survival has exacted of them, they are vividly aware of God's sustaining hand. "To live by the Law," writes a recent Jewish philosopher, "is to live within time the life of eternity."[9]

The basic manual for the hallowing of life is this Law, the first five books of the Bible, the Torah. When in the traditional synagogue service the time comes for returning the Torah to the Ark, the people recite a line from the Book of Proverbs: "It is a tree of life to those who grasp it." There is meaning in this simile, for a tree is symbolic of life itself, of the miracle whereby inert elements of sun and rain and soil are drawn into the mystery of growth. So, too, for the Jews, the Torah. It too is a creative power that can elicit and sustain holiness in the lives of those whose flowering world would otherwise become dry stones. "It is a tree of life to those who grasp it."

Revelation

We have followed the Jews in their interpretation of the major areas of human experience and found them arriving at a more profound grasp of meaning than any of their Mediterranean neighbors; indeed, a grasp that in its essentials has not been surpassed. This raises the question: What produced this achievement? Was it an accident? Did the Jews simply stumble by chance on this cache of insight? If they had struck profundity in one or two areas, this thesis might be plausible; but as they rose to genius on every basic question, it seems inadequate. Is the alternative, then, that the Jews were innately wiser than other peoples? The Jewish doctrine that humanity constitutes a single family—symbolically announced in the story of Adam and Eve—expressly precludes such a notion. The Jews' own answer is that they did not reach these insights on their own. They were revealed to them.

Revelation means disclosure. When someone says, "It came as a revelation to me," the meaning is that something hitherto obscure becomes clear. A veil has lifted, and what was concealed is now revealed. As a theological concept revelation shares this basic meaning, while focusing on disclosure of a specific sort: God's nature and will for humankind.

As the record of these disclosures is in a book, there has been a tendency to approach revelation as if it were primarily a verbal phenomenon; to think of it as what God said either to the prophets or to other biblical writers. This, however, puts the cart before the horse. For the Jews God revealed himself first and foremost in actions—not words but deeds. This comes out clearly in Moses' instruction to his people. "When your children ask you in time to come, 'What is the meaning of the testimonies and the statutes and the ordinances that the Lord our God has commanded you?' then you shall say to your son, 'We were Pharaoh's slaves in Egypt, but the Lord brought us out of Egypt with a mighty hand'"(Deuteronomy 6:21–22). The Exodus, that incredible event in which God liberated an unorganized, enslaved people from the mightiest power of the age, was not only the event that launched the Israelites as a nation. It was also the first clear act by which Yahweh's character was made known to them.

It is true that Genesis describes a number of divine revelations that preceded the Exodus, but the accounts of them were written later in the light of the decisive Exodus event. That God was a direct party to their escape from Pharaoh, the Jews did not doubt. "By every known sociological law," writes Carl Mayer, "the Jews should have perished long ago." The biblical writers would have gone further, contending that by every known sociological law the Jews should not have become a distinct people in the first place. Yet here was the fact: a tiny, loosely related group of people, who had no real collective identity and were in servitude to the great power of the day, had succeeded in making their getaway, eluding the chariots of their pursuers. As acutely aware of their own weakness as of Egypt's strength, it seemed to the Jews impossible that their liberation was their own doing. It was a miracle. "By the grace of God, Israel was saved from death and delivered from the power of the Egyptians" (Exodus 12:50).

Vividly cognizant of God's saving power in the Exodus, the Jews proceeded to review their earlier history in the light of this divine intervention. As their liberation had obviously been engineered by God, what of the sequence that led up to it? Had it been mere chance? The Jews saw God's initiative at work in every step of their corporate existence. It was no vagabond impulse that prompted Abraham to leave his home in Ur and assume the long, uncharted trek toward Canaan. Yahweh had called him to father a people of destiny. So it had been throughout: Isaac and Jacob had been providentially protected and Joseph exalted in Egypt for the express purpose of preserving God's people from famine. From the perspective of the Exodus, everything fell into place. From the beginning God had been leading, protecting, and shaping his people for the decisive Exodus event that made of the Israelites a nation.

The Exodus, we are saying, was more than a historical divide that turned a people into a nation. It was an episode in which this people became overwhelmingly aware of God's reality and character. But to put it this way, saying that the Jews *perceived* God's character, is again to put the matter backward. As God took the initiative, it was God who *showed* the Jews his nature. God should be the subject of the assertion, not its object.

And what was the nature of the God that the Exodus disclosed? First, Yahweh was powerful—able to outdo the mightiest power of the time and whatever gods might be backing it. But equally, Yahweh was a God of goodness and love. Though this might be less obvious to outsiders, it was overwhelmingly evident to the Jews who were its direct recipients. Repeatedly, their gratitude burst forth in song: "Happy are you, O Israel; who is like you—a people saved by Yahweh?" (Deuteronomy 33:29). Had they themselves done anything to deserve this miraculous release? Not as far as they could see. Freedom had come to them as an act of sheer, unmerited grace, a clear instance of Yahweh's unanticipated and astonishing love for them. It is of small moment whether the Jews recognized at once that this love was for all humanity, not just for themselves. Once the realization of God's love had taken root, the Jews soon came to see it as extended to everyone. By the eighth century B.C.E. the Jews would be hearing God saying, "Are you not like the Ethiopians to me?" But the fact of God's love had to be grasped before its range could be explored, and it was in the Exodus that this fact was brought home to them.

Besides God's power and love, the Exodus disclosed a God who was intensely concerned with human affairs. Whereas the surrounding gods were primarily nature deities, reifications of the numinous awe that people feel for nature's grand phenomena, the Israelites' God had come to them not through sun or storm or fertility but in a historical event. The difference in religious meaning was decisive.

The God that the Exodus disclosed cared enough about a human situation to step in and do something about it. That realization changed Israel's religious agenda forever. No longer would the Jews be party to cajoling nature's forces. They would rivet their attention on discerning Yahweh's will and trying to enact it.

Given these three basic disclosures of the Exodus—of God's power, goodness, and concern for history—the Jews' other insights into God's nature followed readily. From the goodness of that nature it followed that God would want people to be good as well; hence Mount Sinai, where the Ten Commandments were established as the Exodus's immediate corollary. The prophets' demand for justice extended God's requirements for virtue to the social sphere—institutional structures, too, are accountable. Finally, suffering must carry significance because it was unthinkable that a God who had miraculously saved his people would ever abandon them completely.

The entire gestalt, when it burst upon the Jews, took shape around the idea of the covenant. A covenant is a contract, but more. Whereas a contract (to build a house, for example) concerns only a part of the lives of those who enter into it, a covenant (such as marriage) involves the pledging of total selves. Another difference is that a contract usually has a termination date, whereas a covenant lasts till death. To the Jews, God's self-disclosure in the Exodus was the invitation to a covenant. Yahweh would continue to bless the Israelites if they, for their part, would honor the laws they had been given.

> You have seen what I did to the Egyptians, and how I bore you on eagle's wings and brought you to myself. Now therefore, if you obey my voice and keep my covenant, you shall be my treasured possession out of all the peoples. Indeed, the whole earth is mine, but you shall be for me a priestly kingdom and a holy nation.
> (Exodus 19:4–6)

Once the covenant relation was clearly formulated at Sinai, those who wrote the Bible saw the Abraham epic in its light as well. In the last days of the Sumerian universal state, from all the peoples of the Euphrates, God called Abraham and entered into covenant with him. If Abraham would be faithful to God's will, God would not only give him a goodly land as inheritance but would cause his descendants to be numbered as the sands of the sea.

We entered this chapter via the Jewish passion for meaning. As our understanding of the religion deepened, however, we came to see that the key had to be recast. Meaning was secured, but from the Jewish perspective, not because they sought it exceptionally. It was revealed to them—not told to them but shown to them through Yahweh's amazing actions. The sequence began with the Exodus-disclosure of Yahweh's power, goodness, and concern. From those we can understand how the rest followed.

But why was this disclosure made to the Jews? Their own answer has been: Because we were chosen. This sounds so simple as to seem ingenuous. Clearly, the answer needs scrutiny.

The Chosen People

There is a familiar quatrain that runs:

> *How odd*
> *Of God*
> *To choose*
> *The Jews.*

Certainly, the idea that a universal God decided that the divine nature should be uniquely and incomparably disclosed to a single people is among the most difficult notions to take seriously in the entire study of religion. It is awkward not only for seeming to violate principles of impartiality and fair play, but also because many early peoples considered themselves special; one thinks of the Japanese, whose creation myth presents them as direct descendants of the Sun Goddess Amaterasu. When Moses tells the Jews, "The Lord God has chosen you to be a people for His own possession, out of all the peoples that are on the face of the earth" (Deuteronomy 7:6), is there any reason to think that we are in the presence of anything more than routine religious chauvinism?

It is true that the Jewish doctrine of the election begins in a conventional mode, but almost at once it takes a surprising turn. For unlike other peoples, the Jews did not see themselves as singled out for privileges. They were chosen to serve, and to suffer the trials that service would often exact. By requiring that they "do and obey all that the Lord has spoken," their election imposed on them a far more demanding morality than was exacted of their peers. A rabbinic theory has it that God initially offered the Torah to the world at large, but only the Jews were willing to accept its rigors. And (the thesis whimsically concludes) even they did so on impulse, not realizing what they were getting into. For "You only have I known of all the families of the earth; therefore I will punish you for all your iniquities" (Amos 3:2). Nor was this all. We have seen that Second Isaiah's doctrine of vicarious suffering meant that the Jews were elected to shoulder a suffering that would otherwise have been distributed more widely.

How different from the usual doctrine of election this Jewish version turns out to be! How much more demanding; how unattractive to normal inclinations. Still, the problem is not resolved. For grant that God called the Jews to heroic ordeal, not sinecure; the fact that they were singled out for a special role in the redemption of the world still looks like favoritism. The Bible makes no attempt to avert this suspicion. "It was not because you were more in number than other people, . . . but because the Lord loves you [that he] has chosen you to be a people for his own" (Deuteronomy 7:6–8).

This rankles. Flying as it does in the face of democratic sentiments, it has provoked a special theological phrase to accommodate it: "the scandal of particularity." It is the doctrine that God's doings can focus like a burning glass on particular times, places, and people(s) — in the interest, to be sure, of intentions that embrace human beings universally.

We shall not be able to validate this doctrine, but there are two things that we can do. We can understand what led the Jews to adopt the concept, and what it did for them.

Our search for what led the Jews to believe that they were chosen will carry us past an obvious possibility — national arrogance — to the facts of their history that we have already rehearsed. Israel came into being as a nation through an extraordinary occurrence, in which a milling band of slaves broke the shackles of the tyrant of their day and were lifted to the status of a free and self-respecting people. Almost immediately afterwards they were brought to an understanding of God that was head and shoulders above that of their neighbors, and deduced from it standards of morality and justice that still challenge the world. Through the three thousand years that have followed, they have continued their existence in the face of unbelievable odds

and adversity, and have contributed to civilization out of all proportion to their numbers.

From beginning to end — this is the point that lies at the heart of
the matter — the story of the Jews is unique. According to expectations they should not have escaped from Pharaoh in the first place.
Why their God, Yahweh, became in their eyes a God of righteousness, whereas Chemosh, god of the Moabites, and other local deities
did not, is, as even such a protagonist of natural explanations as Well-
hausen admitted, "a question to which one can give no satisfactory
answer." The prophetic protest against social injustice is universally
conceded to be "without close parallel in the ancient world."[10] And
to the already quoted judgment that "by every sociological law the
Jews should have perished long ago," we can now add that of the philosopher Nicholas Berdyaev: "The continued existence of Jewry
down the centuries is rationally inexplicable."

If what these facts and judgments attest is true and Jewish history has been exceptional, there are two possibilities. Either the
credit belongs to the Jews themselves, or it belongs to God. Given
this alternative, the Jews instinctively turned the credit Godward.
One of the striking features of this people has been their persistent
refusal to see anything innately special about themselves as people.
According to a *midrashic* legend, when God took clay for the making
of Adam he gathered it from every part of the world and from every
color of earth to insure the universality and basic homogeneity of the
human race. So the specialness of the Jewish experience must have
derived from God's having chosen them. A concept that appears at
first to be arrogant turns out to be the humblest interpretation the
Jews could give to the facts of their origin and survival.

It is possible, of course, to resent particularism even here, but
one must ask whether in doing so we would not be resenting the kind
of world we have. For like it or not, this *is* a world of particulars, and
human minds are tuned thereto. Nothing registers on human attention until it obtrudes from its background. Apply this point to theology and what does it give us? God probably blesses us as much
through the air we breathe as through other gifts; but if piety had to
wait for people to infer God's goodness from the availability of oxygen, it would have been long in coming. The same holds for history.
If relief from oppression were routine, the Jews would have taken
their liberation for granted. Chalk it up to human obtuseness, the

fact remains that divine favors could envelop humanity as the sea envelops fish; were they automatic they would be dismissed as commonplace. This being so, perhaps only the individual, the unique, the particular could have brought the divine to human attention.

Today Jewish opinion is divided on the doctrine of the election. Some Jews believe that it has outgrown whatever usefulness or objective validity it may have had in biblical times. Other Jews believe that until the world's redemption is complete, God continues to need people who are set apart, peculiar in the sense of being God's task force in history. For those who think in this second way, the words of Isaiah speak not only of the past but with continuing, contemporary meaning.

> Listen to me, O coastlands,
>   pay attention, you peoples from far away!
> The Lord called me from before I was born,
>   while I was in my mother's womb he named me.
> He made my mouth like a sharp sword,
>   in his quiver he hid me away.
> And he said to me, "You are my servant,
>   Israel, in whom I will be glorified.   (Isaiah 49:1–3)

Israel

This chapter is about to conclude, and everything we have spoken of took place in the biblical period. There are reasons for this. First, it was in biblical times that most of the great formative ideas of Judaism took shape; second, those ideas constitute the side of Judaism that is most accessible to outsiders for whom this book is primarily intended. If, however, this chapter were to create the impression that Jewish creativity stopped with the closing of the Hebrew canon, that would be reductionism of the grossest sort. Judaism cannot be reduced to its biblical period. What happened was this. In 70 C.E. the Romans destroyed the Temple in Jerusalem that the Jews had rebuilt on returning from their Babylonian exile, and the focus of Judaism shifted from the sacrificial rite of the Temple to the study of the Torah and its accompanying Oral Tradition in academies and synagogues. Thenceforth it was not the priests, who were no longer functional, but the rabbis (literally teachers) who held Judaism together, for their synagogues became centers not only for study but for worship and congregational life in general. Rabbinic Judaism grounded itself in the commandment to make the study of the Torah a lifelong endeavor, and Judaism acquired a distinctly intellectual dimension and character. Through the tradition of Torah-study as it developed in the Talmud, the mind was made integral to religious life and mental energies were introduced into piety. Study, including the kind of constant, unceasing questioning and the rigid sense of logic that pervades the Talmud, became a way of worship. In this complex, the Bible became a revealed text inviting and requiring interpretation, and interpretation was raised to the status of revelation itself.

The rabbinic accomplishment of keeping Judaism alive for the two-thousand years of its diaspora is one of the wonders of history, but for the reasons that were given above we shall not pursue it here. Instead, having taken note of rabbinic Judaism, we shall jump the two millennia of the Common Era to close this chapter with a look at the twentieth century.

Judaism is the faith of a people. As such it contains, as one of its features, faith *in* a people—in the significance of the role the Jews have played and will play in human history. This faith calls for the preservation of the identity of the Jews as a distinct people. In the past Jewish self-identity posed no policy problem. During the biblical period the Jews *needed* to be separate to keep their distinctive viewpoint from being compromised by neighboring polytheisms. This was the basis of the repeated prophetic demand that the Jews remain a "peculiar" people. Later, especially in post-medieval Europe up to the French Revolution, the Jews were *forced* to be separate. Required to live in ghettos surrounded by walls whose gates were locked at night, they had no alternative but to live a life that largely turned inward.

Since the French Revolution the issue of Jewish identity has become something of a problem. With the emancipation of the Jews and their entry into the political, professional, and cultural life of the countries in which they live, the world no longer requires that their identity be retained. Nor is there the clear ethical discrepancy that once compelled Jews to remain aloof from their neighbors on moral grounds. Today, if Jewish distinctness is to continue, the case for it must be argued.

Within Judaism itself the arguments differ. Some Jews adhere to the religious thesis of the preceding section: as God has chosen

Israel to be a unique instrument for good, the shape and edge of that instrument should be retained. Other Jews argue for distinctiveness on grounds of cultural pluralism. A healthy individual identity depends on a sense of one's origins, one's roots. The inclusion of multiple heritages in a society is an advantage, for uniformity breeds sameness and diminishes creativity. Marx, Einstein, and Freud have contributed enormously to modern thought. It seems reasonable to assume that their Jewishness had something to do with making them great.

If the argument thus far has carried weight and we have been able to catch some of the Jews' sense of the importance of maintaining their identity, in what does this identity consist?

Not doctrine, for there is nothing one *has* to believe to be a Jew. Jews run the gamut, from those who believe that every letter and punctuation mark of the Torah was dictated by God, to those who do not believe in God at all. Indeed, it is impossible to name any one thing that of itself suffices to make one a Jew. Judaism is a complex. It is like a circle that is whole but divisible into sections that converge in a common center. There is no authority that says that a Jew must affirm all (or any one) of these sections or face excommunication. Still, the more sections one embodies, the more Jewish one will be.

Generally speaking, the four great sectors of Judaism that constitute its spiritual anatomy are faith, observance, culture, and nation. Its faith has already been described. Jews approach it from intellectual angles that range from fundamentalism to ultra-liberalism, but the direction in which their faith looks is much the same. This can also be said of Jewish observance. Different groups of Jews vary markedly in their interpretation and practice of basic rituals such as the Sabbath, dietary laws, daily prayers, and the like. But however great the difference in extent of observance, its intent is the same — the hallowing of life, as that has been described. What remains is to say a few words about the other two components of Judaism; namely, culture and nation.

Culture, denoting as it does a total way of life, defies exhaustive description. It includes mores, art forms, styles of humor, philosophy, a literature, and much else. Its ingredients are so numerous that we shall have to limit ourselves to three. Jewish culture includes a language, a lore, and an affinity for a land.

Its lore is apparent, for much of it has spilled over into Western culture generally. There is an aura that surrounds the Hebrew scriptures' characters and events that dwarfs Olympus, but for Judaism this is only the beginning. The Torah is followed by the Talmud, a vast compendium of history, law, folklore, and commentary that is the basis of post-biblical Judaism. This in turn is supplemented by the *midrashim*, an almost equal collection of legend, exegesis, and homily, which began to develop before the biblical canon was fixed and reached its completion in the late Middle Ages. The whole provides an inexhaustible mine for scholarship, anecdote, and cultural identity.

In addition to its lore, every people has its language and its land. For the Jews these are, respectively, Hebrew and Israel.[11] Both are sacred for their associations. As it was in Hebrew and the Holy Land that Revelation came to the Jews, regard for that Revelation extended to those contexts. Jews conduct all or part of their prayers in Hebrew, and consciousness of the Holy Land enlivens their reading of the Torah and their study of rabbinic literature. It is one of the paradoxes of Judaism that during the two thousand years in which it crossed every national boundary and had no habitation but human hearts, it retained its passion for the land of its birth. Prayers for their return to Zion figured in every public service and every private devotion, including the night prayer after retiring. The toast, "Next year in Jerusalem," carries so much hope and feeling that people other than Jews sometimes invoke it.

In the opening pages of this chapter we quoted Edmund Wilson as describing Palestine as "mild and monotonous." To the Jew this characterization seems incredible, for it is a wonderful land even physically. Much of its terrain is spectacular: the course from Jerusalem to the Dead Sea that falls 3,481 feet in thirty-five miles, the Jordan that cuts deeply through rock as it winds south from Mount Hermon, the spiny ridge that runs southward from Mount Carmel by the sea, the rough wilderness of Tekoah that runs southward into the desolation of the Negev in sharp contrast to the lush greenness along the banks of south Jordan. There are pinnacles of cypress that reach up like dark spires, "mountains that skip like rams, [and] hills like lambs" (Psalm 114:4), the Fields of Esdraelon that slope upward to Galilee in broad checkerboards of brown and green, and harbors deep with the blue of the Mediterranean, all bathed in a brilliant sunlight and limpid air that lifts the expectant spirit. History cries out from every city and hillside, storied in the past. A brooding sense of the ages is present everywhere, now as when the ancient Hebrew seer beheld, enthroned, the "Ancient of Days."

But to speak of this land is to enter the fourth component of total Judaism, its nation. For we live in a century when, for the first time since their compulsory dispersion in 70 C.E., Palestine has been restored to the Jews.

The reasons leading to the establishment of the modern state of Israel in 1948 are complex. Beyond the powerful religious pull toward return, the chief contributing motifs were four.

1. The argument from security. The 1938–1945 Nazi-instigated Holocaust in which six million Jews — one-third of their total number — were killed, confirmed for many a conviction that had been growing since the renewal of pogroms in Russia in 1881: that the Jews could not hope for security in European life and civilization. They needed a place where their wounded and terrorized, still fortunate to be among the living, might gather to breathe the air of freedom and security.

2. The psychological argument. Some were convinced that it was psychologically unhealthy for the Jews to be everywhere in minority status; that this was breeding in them a subservience and self-rejection that only a nation of their own could correct.

3. The cultural argument. The stuff of Judaism was running thin and its tradition was bleeding to death. Somewhere in the world there needed to be a land where Judaism was the dominant ethos.

4. The social, utopian argument. Somewhere in the world there should be a nation dedicated to the historical realization of prophetic ideals and ethics — a better way of life in its totality, including economic structures, than history had yet evinced. Long before the Holocaust, a small but determined number of Jewish dreamers, most of them in eastern Europe, longed for a chance to refashion society in more healthful ways. Beginning in the late eighteen hundreds, several generations of pioneers made their way to Palestine to forge a life in which they would be free to ordain all aspects of their existence. Debarred from agriculture in the lands they left, they hoped to give birth to a new humanity through a way of life built on the foundation of physical labor and life on the land. The *kibbutzim*, collective agriculture settlements, that they founded were an expression of that idealism.

Whatever the reasons that have gone into her creation, Israel is here. Her achievements have been impressive. Her land reclamation, her hospitality to Jewish immigrants (a true ingathering of exiles) her provisions for the laboring class, her new patterns of group living, her intellectual and cultural vitality—all have combined to make Israel an exciting social experiment.

But the twentieth century has also produced two agonizing problems for the Jews. The first relates to the Holocaust. What meaning can the concept of a Chosen People have in the face of a God who permitted this enormity, they wonder. Some go so far as to ask if even their postulate of a righteous God continues to make sense.

The other agonizing problem relates to the idealistic argument for the state of Israel that was mentioned. Having all but scripted the ideals of freedom and justice for Western civilization, if not for the entire world, Jews now find themselves withholding these rights—for security reasons, forced to withhold them, many Jews believe—from Palestinians whose territories they occupy as a result of the 1967 war. The tension between Palestinian national rights and Israeli security is acute and unresolved.

Without presuming to answer these problems, we can appreciate the burdens they place on the conscience of this exceptionally conscientious people. Facing their gravity, they take courage in the fact that at least they are now politically free to confront them. As the Star of David waves over their spiritual homeland, the first flag of their own in almost twenty centuries, the dominant thought in the minds of the Jews is: *Am Yisrael chai,* The people of Israel live! How wonderful to be living when all this is happening.

Suggestions for Further Reading

Robert M. Seltzer's *Jewish People, Jewish Thought* (New York: Macmillan, 1980) complements this chapter by giving proportionate attention to the post-biblical era. Barry W. Holz (ed.), *Back to the Sources* (New York: Simon and Schuster, 1986) introduces the reader to different kinds of Jewish texts.

Jewish Worship by Abraham Millgram (Philadelphia: Jewish Publication Society, 1971) describes and explains that aspect of this religion.

For the mystical dimension of Judaism, see David Ariel, *The Mystic Quest: An Introduction to Jewish Mysticism* (Northvale, NJ: Jason Aronson, 1988); Daniel Chanan Matt (trans.), *The Zohar* (New York: Paulist Press, 1983), and Adin Steinsaltz, *The Thirteen Petalled Rose* (New York: Basic Books, 1980).

On the Holocaust and its impact on Jewish thinking, Michael R. Marrus's *The Holocaust in History* (New York: New American Library, 1989) provides both a reliable introduction to the subject and an authoritative summary for the expert. Simpler and more compact is Nora Levin's, *The Holocaust* (New York: Schocken, 1973).

Notes

1. *The New Yorker* (December 4, 1954): 204–5.
2. Henri Frankfort, *The Intellectual Adventure of Ancient Man* (Chicago: University of Chicago Press, 1946), 363.
3. Bernard Anderson, *Rediscovering the Bible* (New York: Haddam House, 1957), 26–28.
4. W. F. Albright, in *Approaches to World Peace* (New York: Harper Bros. 1943), 9.
5. See 1 Kings 18:46 and 2 Kings 2:16.
6. Quoted by Aba Hillel Silver, *Where Judaism Differed*, 1956. Reprint. (Northvale, NJ: Jason Aronson, 1987), 109.
7. I am thinking of civilizations here as possessing large cities and cumulative written records. By this definition other parts of the world are rich in cultures — to be considered in chapter 9, "The Primal Religions"— but are not, strictly speaking, civilizations. My definition is descriptive, not normative.
8. Joseph Klausner, *The Messianic Idea in Israel* (New York: Macmillan, 1955), 9.
9. Abraham Heschel.
10. G. Ernest Wright, *The Old Testament Against Its Environment*, (Chicago: Alex R. Allenson, 1950), 60.
11. Respecting Hebrew, save for the fact that the canonical prayers are to be said in Hebrew, my statement oversimplifies things somewhat, for there are also other Jewish languages. The two Talmuds are written in Aramaic, and a whole family of languages (Yiddish, Ladino, Judeo-Arabic, Judeo-Persian, and so on) emerged as Jews adopted the language of the lands in which they lived but wrote that language using the Hebrew alphabet. In many cases a rich culture and literature evolved in which the specific language is a key element.

VIII. Christianity

Of all the great religions Christianity is the most widespread and has the largest number of adherents. The figure is probably inflated, but registries list almost one out of every three persons today as Christian, bringing the number into the neighborhood of one and one-half billion.[1]

Nearly two thousand years of history have brought an astonishing diversity to this religion. From the majestic pontifical High Mass in St. Peter's to the quiet simplicity of a Quaker meeting; from the intellectual sophistication of Saint Thomas Aquinas to the moving simplicity of spirituals such as "Lord, I want to be a Christian"; from St. Paul's in London, the parish Church of Great Britain, to Mother Teresa in the slums of Calcutta—all this is Christianity. From this dazzling and often bewildering complex, it will be our task to indicate first the central strands that unite this religion, and then its three major divisions: Roman Catholicism, Eastern Orthodoxy, and Protestantism.

The Historical Jesus

Christianity is basically a historical religion. That is to say, it is founded not on abstract principles but in concrete events, actual historical happenings. The most important of these is the life of a Jewish carpenter who, as has often been pointed out, was born in a stable, was executed as a criminal at age thirty-three, never traveled more than ninety miles from his birthplace, owned nothing, attended no college, marshaled no army, and instead of producing books did his

317

only writing in the sand. Nevertheless, his birthday is kept across the world and his death day sets a gallows against almost every skyline. Who was he?

The biographical details of Jesus' life are so meager that early in this century some investigators went so far as to suggest that he may never have lived. That possibility was soon rejected, but the impact of Albert Schweitzer's century-dominating *Quest for the Historical Jesus* reduced what the world was hearing about Jesus from biblical scholars to two points: We know almost nothing about him; and of the little we know, what is most certain is that he was wrong—this last referred to his putative belief that the world would quickly come to an end. As this is not much to build a Church on, it is fortunate that "the extreme historical skepticism that has marked most Jesus study in this century is abating."[2] Classicists have remarked that if the canons for historical reliability that have been erected for the Bible had been required in their studies, our view of the Greco-Roman world (which seems to be reasonably in place) would be in shambles.

Who, then, was this Jesus whom New Testament scholars are beginning to return to view? He was born in Palestine during the reign of Herod the Great, probably around 4 B.C.—our reckoning of the centuries that purports to date from his birth is almost certainly off by several years. He grew up in or near Nazareth, presumably after the fashion of other normal Jews of the time. He was baptized by John, a dedicated prophet who was electrifying the region with his proclamation of God's coming judgment. In his early thirties he had a teaching-healing career, which lasted between one and three years and was focused largely in Galilee. In time he incurred the hostility of some of his own compatriots and the suspicion of Rome, which led to his crucifixion on the outskirts of Jerusalem. From these facts that fix the framework of Jesus' life, we turn to the life that was lived within that framework.

Minimally stated, Jesus was a charismatic wonder-worker who stood in a tradition that stretched back to the beginnings of Hebrew history. The prophets and seers who comprised that tradition mediated between the everyday world, on the one hand, and a Spirit world that enveloped it. From the latter they drew power, which they used both to help people and to challenge their ways. We shall expand this capsule characterization by considering successively (a) the Spirit world, to which Jesus was exceptionally oriented and which powered his ministry; (b) his deployment of his Spirit-derived powers in the alleviation of human suffering; and (c) the new social order he sought to effect.

"The Spirit of the Lord Is Upon Me." According to Luke Jesus opened his ministry by quoting this statement from Isaiah and adding, "Today this scripture has been fulfilled." We must attend to this Spirit that Jesus experienced as empowering him, for there can be no understanding of his life and work if it is omitted.

In what has proved to be one of our century's most durable books about religion, *The Varieties of Religious Experience,* William James tells us that "in its broadest terms, religion says that there is an unseen order, and that our supreme good lies in rightful relations to it." Until recently, modern science seemed to question the reality of unseen entities; but with Eddington's observation that the world is more like a mind than a machine, and astrophysicists' reports that 90 percent of the "matter" in the universe is invisible in the sense that it impacts none of their instruments, scientific skepticism has begun to subside.[3] The point here, however, is that the biblical tradition in which Jesus stood can only be read as a continuous, sustained-and-demanding dialogue of the Hebrew people with the unseen order that William James emphasizes. They called that order Spirit (as in the opening verses of the Bible, where Spirit plays over primordial waters to create the world) and, sensing it as intensely alive, they populated it with beings such as angels, archangels, cherubim, and seraphim. Its center, however, was Yahweh, whom they viewed personally: as shepherd, king, lord, father (and less commonly, mother), and lover. Though Spirit was typically pictured as being above the earth—images of ladders to Heaven are routine—that was only to stress its distinctness from, and superiority over, the mundane world. The two were not spatially separated, and were in continuous interaction. God walked in the garden of Eden, and "the whole earth is full of God's glory," his radiant presence.

Not only was Spirit not spatially removed; though invisible, it could be known. Often it would take the initiative and announce itself. It did this supremely to Moses on Mount Sinai, but it also spoke in a still small voice to Elijah, in lions' roars to other prophets, and in dramatic events like the Exodus. Concurrently, human beings could take the initiative in contacting it. Fasting and solitude were means for doing so, and Jews who felt the call would periodically remove themselves from the world's distractions to commune with the divine through these aids. It will not be amiss to think of them as soaking themselves in Spirit during these vigils, for when they return to the world they often give evidence of having almost palpably absorbed something: Spirit and its attendant power.

That Jesus stood in the Jewish tradition of Spirit-filled mediators is the most important fact for understanding his historical career. His immediate predecessor in this tradition was John the Baptist; and it is a testament to his spiritual power that it was his initiation (baptism) of Jesus that opened his third or spiritual eye, as Asians would say, causing him to see "the heavens opened and the Spirit descending upon him like a dove." Having descended, the Spirit "drove" Jesus into the wilderness where, during forty days of prayer and fasting, he consolidated the Spirit that had entered him. Having done so he reentered the world, empowered.

"By the Spirit of God I Cast Out Demons." If science no longer discounts invisible realities, it has also grown open to the prospect that they may be powerful, for experiments now suggest that "the energy inherent in one cubic centimeter of empty space is greater than the energy of all the matter in the known universe."[4] Whatever the fate of that particular hypothesis, the Jews accepted the supremacy of Spirit over nature without question. The Spirit-filled personages of the Bible have power. To say that they were charismatic is to say they had power to attract people's attention, but that is only the beginning of the matter. The reason they attracted notice was the exceptional power they possessed. They "had something," as we say—something ordinary mortals lack. That something was Spirit. The Bible frequently depicts them as "filled with the power of the Spirit," a power that enabled them at times to influence the natural course of events. They healed diseases, cast out demons, and occasionally quelled storms, parted waters, and caused the dead to return to life. The Gospels attribute these powers to Jesus copiously. Again and again they report people flocking to him, drawn by his wonder-working reputation. "They brought to him all who were sick or possessed with demons," we read, "and the whole city was gathered together about the door." A New Testament scholar comments that "despite the difficulty which miracles pose for the modern mind, on historical grounds it is virtually indisputable that Jesus was a healer and exorcist."[5]

He could have been that—indeed, he could have been "the most extraordinary figure in . . . the stream of Jewish charismatic healers," as the same New Testament scholar goes on to say—without attracting more than local attention. What made him outlive his time and place was the way he used the Spirit that coursed through him not just to heal individuals but—this was his aspiration—to heal humanity, beginning with his own people.

"Thy Kingdom Come, on Earth."   Politically, the position of the Jews in Jesus' time was desperate. They had been in servitude to Rome for the better part of a century and, along with their loss of freedom, were being taxed almost beyond endurance. Existing responses to their predicament were four. The Sadducees, who were relatively well off, favored making the best of a bad situation and accommodated themselves to Hellenistic culture and Roman rule. The other positions hoped for change. All three recognized that the change would have to be effected by Yahweh, and all assumed that the Jews needed to do something that would prompt his intervention. Two of the three were renewal movements. The Essenes considered the world as too corrupt to allow for Judaism to renew itself within it, so they dropped out. Withdrawing into property-sharing communes, they devoted themselves to lives of disciplined piety. The Pharisees, on the other hand, remained within society and sought to revitalize Judaism through adhering strictly to the Mosaic law, especially its holiness code. Representatives of the fourth position have been referred to as Zealots, but it is doubtful that they were sufficiently organized to deserve a name. Despairing that any change could occur without brute force, they launched sporadic acts of resistance that culminated in the catastrophic revolt of 66–70 A.D., which led to the second destruction of the Temple in Jerusalem.

Into this political cauldron Jesus introduced a fifth option. Unlike the Sadducees, he wanted change. Unlike the Essenes, he stayed in the world. Unlike the advocates of the military option, he extolled peacemakers and urged that even enemies be loved. It was the Pharisees that Jesus stood closest to, for the difference between them was one of emphasis only. The Pharisees stressed Yahweh's holiness, while Jesus stressed Yahweh's compassion; but the Pharisees

would have been the first to insist that Yahweh was also compassionate, and Jesus that Yahweh was holy. The difference appears at first to
be small, but in actuality it proved to be too large for a single religion
to accommodate. We must understand why this was the case.

Grounding themselves in the understanding of Yahweh as majestic holiness, the Pharisees went on to affirm the accepted version of
Jewish self-understanding. Being holy himself, Yahweh wanted to hallow the world as well, and to accomplish this aim he selected the Jews
to plant for him, as it were, a beachhead of holiness in human history.
On Mount Sinai he had prescribed a holiness code, faithful observance
of which would make of the Hebrews "a nation of priests." Yahweh's dictum to them, "You shall be holy, as I the Lord your God am holy,"
became the Pharisees' watchword. It was laxity in the observance of
the holiness code that had reduced the Jews to their degraded state,
and only the wholehearted return to it would reverse that state.

Much of this Jesus subscribed to, but there was an important feature of the holiness program he found unacceptable: the lines that it
drew between people. Beginning by categorizing acts and things as
clean or unclean (foods and their preparation, for example), the holiness code went on to categorize people according to whether they
respected those distinctions. The result was a social structure that
was riven with barriers: between people who were clean and
unclean, pure and defiled, sacred and profane, Jew and Gentile, righteous and sinner. Having concluded that Yahweh's central attribute
was compassion, Jesus saw social barriers as an affront to that compassion. So he parleyed with tax collectors, dined with outcasts and
sinners, socialized with prostitutes, and healed on the sabbath when
compassion prompted doing so. This made him a social prophet,
challenging the boundaries of the existing order and advocating an
alternative vision of the human community.

Jesus was deeply Jewish; at the same time he stood in sharp tension with Judaism. (One is tempted to claim this as an important
aspect of his Jewishness, for no religion has manifest, and on the
whole encouraged, internal criticism to the extent that this one has.)
Jesus saw the holiness code and the distinctions that followed from it
as having been needed to lift the Jews to a purity that surpassed their
neighbors. His own encounter with God, however, led him to the
conviction that, as practiced in his time, the purity system had

created social divisions that compromised God's compassion, which compassion the Pharisees equally subscribed to in principle.

It is important to emphasize that the issue was not God's compassion; it was whether the social system that the holiness code in its outworkings had structured was compassionate. Jesus' conviction that it was not put him at odds with the Pharisees, but his protest did not prevail. It did, however, attract enough attention to alarm the Roman authorities, which led to Jesus' arrest and execution on charges of treason.

Thereafter the future of the "Jesus people" lay with the wider world. In time Christians came to read this development positively. To their eyes God's revelation to the Jews was too important to be confined to a single ethnic group. Jesus' mission had been to crack the shell of Judaism in which revelation was encased and release that revelation to a ready and waiting world. Putting it this way does not cancel the need for a continuing Jewish presence. Until the world is regenerated, the witness of a nation of priests remains relevant.

The Christ of Faith

How does one move from the Jesus of history, whose life and work have thus far occupied us, to the Christ whom his followers came to believe had been God in human form? His disciples did not reach that conclusion before Jesus' death, but even in his lifetime we can witness momentum building in its direction. Having tried in the preceding section to describe the facts of Jesus' life, we turn now to the way he appeared to his disciples. Here we are on firmer ground, for if the Gospels disclose little in the way of historical facts, they are transparent as to his impact on his associates. Our presentation will fall into three parts: what they saw Jesus do, what they heard him say, and what they sensed him to be.

"He Went About Doing Good."   We begin with what Jesus did. The Gospel accounts, written by members of the early Church, vibrate with wonder at his performances. Their pages, especially those of Mark, teem with miracles. We have seen that these impressed multitudes, but it would be a mistake to place our emphasis there. For one thing, Jesus did not emphasize his miracles. He never used them as devices to strong-arm people into believing in him. He was tempted to do so, but in the wilderness soul-searchings that prefaced his ministry he rejected this temptation. Almost all of his extraordinary deeds were performed quietly, apart from the crowds, and as a demonstration of the power of faith. Moreover, other writings of the times abound in miracles, but this didn't lead witnesses to deify their agents. They merely credited the miracle-workers with unusual powers.

We get a better perspective on Jesus' actions if we place the emphasis where one of his disciples did. Once, in addressing a group, Peter found it necessary to compress into short compass what Jesus did during his lifetime. His summary? "He went about doing good" (Acts 10:38). A simple epitaph, but a moving one. Circulating easily and without affectation among ordinary people and social misfits, healing them, counseling them, helping them out of chasms of despair, Jesus went about doing good. He did so with such single-mindedness and effectiveness that those who were with him constantly found their estimate of him modulating to a new key. They found themselves thinking that if divine goodness were to manifest itself in human form, this is how it would behave.

"Never Spoke Man Thus."   It was not only what Jesus did, however, that made his contemporaries think of him in new dimensions. It was also what he said.

There has been a great deal of controversy over the originality of Jesus' teachings. Possibly the most balanced view is that of the great Jewish scholar Joseph Klausner. If you take the teachings of Jesus separately, he wrote, you can find every one of them paralleled in either the Old Testament or its commentary, the Talmud. But if you take them as a whole, they have an urgency, an ardent, vivid quality, an abandon, and above all a complete absence of second-rate material that makes them refreshingly new.

The language of Jesus has proved to be a fascinating study in itself, quite apart from its content. If simplicity, concentration, and the sense of what is vital are marks of great religious literature, these qualities alone would make Jesus' words immortal. But this is just the beginning. They carry an extravagance of which wise men, tuned to the importance of balanced judgment, are incapable. Their passionate quality has led one poet to coin a special word for Jesus' language, calling it "gigantesque." If your hand offends you, cut if off. If your eye stands between you and the best, gouge it out. Jesus talks of camels that hump through needles' eyes, of people who fastidiously strain gnats from their drinks while oblivious of the camels that caravan down their gullets. His characters go around with timbers protruding from their eyes, looking for tiny specks in the eyes of others. He talks of people whose outer lives are stately mausoleums while their inner lives stink of decaying corpses. This is not language tooled for rhetorical effect. The language is part of the message itself, prompted by its driving urgency.

A second arresting feature of Jesus' language was its invitational style. Instead of telling people what to do or what to believe, he invited them to *see* things differently, confident that if they did so their behavior would change accordingly. This called for working with peoples' imaginations more than with their reason or their will. If listeners were to accept his invitation, the place to which they were being invited would have to seem real to them. So, because the reality his hearers were most familiar with consisted of concrete particulars, Jesus began with those particulars. He spoke of mustard seeds and rocky soil, of servants and masters, of weddings and of wine. These specifics gave his teachings an opening ring of reality; he was speaking of things that were very much a part of his hearers' worlds. But having gotten them that far, having roused in them a momentum of assent, Jesus would then ride that momentum while giving its trajectory a startling, subversive twist. That phrase, "momentum of assent," is important, for its deepest meaning is that Jesus located the authority for his teachings not in himself or in God-as-removed but in his hearers' hearts. My teachings are true, he said in effect, not because they come from me, or even from God through me, but because (against all conventionality) your own hearts attest to their truth.

So what did Jesus use his invitational, gigantesque language to say? Quantitatively, not a great deal, as far as the records report; everything that the New Testament records can be spoken in two hours. Yet his teachings may be the most repeated in history. "Love your neighbor as yourself." "Whatsoever you would that men should do unto you, do you also unto them." "Come unto me, all you that labor and are heavy laden, and I will give you rest." "You shall know the truth, and the truth shall make you free." Most of the time, however, he told stories that we call parables: of buried treasure, of sowers who went out to sow, of pearl merchants, of a good Samaritan, of a young man who blew his inheritance on a binge and found himself cadging scraps from the pigs, of a man who had two sons. The world knows them well. People who heard these stories were moved to exclaim, "This man speaks with authority. . . . Never spoke man thus!"

They were astonished, and with reason. If we are not it is because we have heard Jesus' teachings so often that their edges have been worn smooth, dulling their subversiveness. If we could recover their original impact, we too would be startled. Their beauty would not cover the fact that they are "hard sayings" for presenting a scheme of values so counter to the usual as to rock us like an earthquake.

We are told that we are not to resist evil but to turn the other cheek. The world assumes that evil must be resisted by every means available. We are told to love our enemies and bless those who curse us. The world assumes that friends are to be loved and enemies hated. We are told that the sun rises on the just and the unjust alike. The world considers this undiscriminating; it would like to see clouds over evil people and is offended when they go unpunished. We are told that outcasts and harlots enter the kingdom of God before many who are perfunctorily righteous. Again unfair, the world thinks; respectable people should head the procession. We are told that the gate to salvation is narrow. The world would prefer it to be broad. We are told to be as carefree as birds and flowers. The world counsels prudence. We are told that it is more difficult for the rich to enter the Kingdom than for a camel to pass through a needle's eye. The world admires wealth. We are told that the happy people are those who are meek, who weep, who are merciful and pure in heart. The world assumes that it is the rich, the powerful, and the wellborn who are happy. The great Russian philosopher Nikolai Berdyaev said that a wind of freedom blows through these teachings that frightens the world and makes us want to deflect them by postponement—not yet, not yet! H. G. Wells was evidently right: Either there was something mad about this man, or our hearts are still too small for his message.

Again we must come back to what those teachings were about. Everything that came from his lips formed the surface of a burning glass to focus human awareness on the two most important facts about life: God's overwhelming love of humanity, and the need for people to accept that love and let it flow through them to others. In experiencing God as infinite love bent on peoples' salvation, Jesus was an authentic child of Judaism; he differed, we have seen, only in not allowing the post-Exilic holiness code to impede God's compassion. Time after time, as in his story of the shepherd who risked ninety-nine sheep to go after the one that had strayed, Jesus tried to convey God's absolute love for every single human being. To perceive this love and to let it penetrate one's very marrow was to respond in the only way that was possible—in profound and total gratitude for the wonders of God's grace.

The only way to make sense of Jesus' extraordinary admonitions as to how people should live is to see them as cut from this understanding of the God who loves human beings absolutely, without pausing to calculate their worth or due. We are to give others our cloak as well as our coat if they need it. Why? Because God has given us what we need. We are to go with others the second mile. Why again? Because we know, deeply, overwhelmingly, that God has borne with us for far longer stretches. Why should we love not only our friends but our enemies, and pray for those who persecute us? "So that you may be children of your Father in heaven; for he makes his sun rise on the evil and on the good, and sends rain on the righteous and the unrighteous. . . . Be perfect, therefore, as your heavenly Father is perfect" (Matthew 5:45, 48). We say his ethic is perfectionistic—a polite word for unrealistic—because it asks that we love unreservedly. But the reason we consider that unrealistic, Jesus would have answered, is because we do not experience the constant, unstinted love that flows from God to us. If we did experience it, problems would still arise. To which of the innumerable needy should limited supplies of coats and cloaks be given? If the target of evil is someone other than myself, should I still not resist it? Jesus offered no rule book to obviate hard choices. What he argued was the stance from which they should be approached. All we can say in advance, as we face the demands of a tangled world, is that we should respond to our neighbors—all of them insofar as we can foresee the consequences of our acts—not in proportion to what we judge to be their due, but in proportion to their need. The cost to us personally should count for nothing.

We have spoken of what Jesus did and what he said. But these alone would not have been enough to edge his disciples toward the conclusion that he was divine had it not been for a third factor: what he was.

"*We Have Seen His Glory.*"

"There is in the world," writes Dostoevsky, "only one figure of absolute beauty: Christ. That infinitely lovely figure is . . . an infinite marvel."

Certainly, the most impressive thing about the teachings of Jesus is not that he taught them but that he appears to have lived them. From the accounts that we have, his entire life was one of humility, self-giving, and love that sought not its own. The supreme evidence of his humility is that it is impossible to discover precisely what Jesus thought of himself. His concern was what people thought of God— God's nature and God's will for their lives. True, by indirection this tells us something about Jesus' own self-image, but it is the obvious, that he esteemed himself to be less than God. "Why do you call me good? Don't you know that only God is good?" It is impossible to read what Jesus said about selflessness without sensing how free of pride he was himself. Similarly with sincerity. What he said on the subject could only have been said by someone whose life was uncluttered by deceit. Truth was like the air to him.

Through the pages of the Gospels Jesus emerges as a man of strength and integrity who bore about him, as someone has said, no strangeness at all save the strangeness of perfection. He liked people and they liked him in turn. They loved him; they loved him intensely and they loved him in numbers. Drawn to him not only for his charismatic powers but for the compassion they sensed in him as well, they surrounded him, flocked about him, followed him. He stands by the Sea of Galilee and they press so hard that he has to speak to them from a boat. He sets out for the day and a crowd of several thousand accumulates, missing their lunch, staying on until suddenly they discover that they are famished. People responded to Jesus, but equally he responded to them. He felt their appeal, whether they were rich or poor, young or old, saints or sinners. We have seen that he ignored the barriers that mores erected between people. He loved children. He hated injustice because of what it did to those he called, tenderly, "the least of these" (Matthew 25:40). Above all he hated hypocrisy, because it hid people from themselves and precluded the authenticity he sought to build into relationships. In the end it seemed to those who knew him best that here was a man in whom the human ego had disappeared, leaving his life so completely under the will of God that it was transparent to that will. It came to the point where they felt that as they looked at Jesus they were looking at something resembling God in human form. This is what lies behind the lyric cry of the early Church: "We have seen his glory, . . . full of grace and truth" (John 1:14). Centuries later, Shakespeare put it this way:

> Some say that ever 'gainst that season comes
> Wherein our Savior's birth is celebrated,
> The bird of dawning singeth all night long;
> And then, they say, no spirit can walk abroad;
> The nights are wholesome; then no planets strike,
> No fairy tales, nor witch hath power to charm,
> So hallow'd and so gracious is the time.

The End and the Beginning

The way that Jesus' earthly ministry ended is known to everyone. After mingling with his people and teaching them for a number of months, he was crucified.

That might well have been the end of the story. History abounds with visionaries who proposed schemes, died, and that is the last that is heard of them. In this case, however, it was just the beginning. Within a short time his followers were preaching the gospel of their Risen Lord.

We are given too few details to know exactly what happened after the crucifixion; virtually all that is certain is that his followers were convinced that death had not held him. They reported that beginning on Easter Sunday he "appeared to them" as the same person they had known during his ministry but in a new way. It is not possible to determine exactly what that new way was; certain accounts suggest corporeality—eating, and Thomas's touching the wound in his side—while others are more visionary, reporting him as passing through closed doors. Fidelity to the reports, all of which were entered by disciples who were convinced of Jesus' resurrection, make clear that he did not simply resume his former physical body; resurrection was not resuscitation. Instead, it was entry into another mode of being, a mode that was sometimes visible but usually was not. What is clear is that Jesus' followers began to experience him in a new way, namely as having the qualities of God. He could now be known anywhere, not just in physical proximity.

Faith in Jesus' resurrection produced the Church and its Christology. To grasp the power of the belief, we must see that it did not merely concern the fate of a worthy man. Its claim extended ultimately to the status of goodness in the universe, contending that it was all-powerful. If Golgotha's cross had been the end, the goodness Jesus embodied would have been beautiful, but how significant? A fragile blossom afloat on a torrential stream, soon to be dashed—how relevant is goodness if it has no purchase on reality, no power at its disposal? The resurrection reversed the cosmic position in which the cross had placed Jesus' goodness. Instead of being fragile, the compassion the disciples had encountered in him was powerful; victorious over everything, even the seeming end of everything, death itself. "Grave, where is your victory? Death, where is your sting?"

The way this message moved into, and eventually took over, the Mediterranean world is our next concern.

The Good News

The conviction that Jesus continued to live transformed a dozen or so disconsolate followers of a slain and discredited leader into one of the most dynamic groups in human history. We read that tongues of fire descended upon them. It was a fire destined to set the Mediterranean world aflame. People who were not speakers waxed eloquent. They exploded across the Greco-Roman world, preaching what has come to be called the Gospel but which, if translated literally, would be called the Good News. Starting in an upper room in Jerusalem, they spread their message with such fervor that in Jesus' very generation it took root in every major city of the region.

And what was this Good News that snapped Western history like a dry twig, into B.C. and A.D. and left its impact through the Christian Church? Was it Jesus' ethical teachings—the Golden Rule, the Sermon on the Mount? Not at all. We have already noted that every teaching of Jesus was already in the literature of his day. Paul, whose letters epitomize the concerns of the early Church, knew what Jesus had taught, but he almost never quotes him. Obviously, the news that transformed him was not Jesus' ethical precepts nor even the way his life embodied them. It was something quite different.

What this other something was may be approached through a symbol. If we had been living around the eastern Mediterranean in the early centuries of the Christian era, we might have noticed scratched here and there on the sides of walls and houses or simply on the ground the crude outline of a fish. Even if we had seen it in several places, we would probably have dismissed it as innocuous graffiti or a doodle, for these were mainly seaport towns where fishing was a part of daily life. Had we been Christians, however, we would have seen these drawings as the logo for the Good News. The heads of the fish would have pointed us toward the place where the local Christian group held its underground meetings. For in those years of catacombs and arenas, when to be known as a Christian meant that one might be thrown to the lions or turned into a human torch, Christians were forced to more cryptic symbols than the cross. The fish was one of their favorites, for the Greek letters for the word fish are also the first letters of the Greek words for "Jesus Christ, Son of God, Savior." *This* was the Good News, epitomized in the crude outline of an ordinary fish.

But what does the phrase itself mean: Jesus Christ, Son of God, Savior? Those who have grown up with it may know the answer well. Our task, however, is to go behind the immense history of the phrase and try to work our way into what it meant to the men and women who first uttered it, for the entire subsequent history of Christianity grew out of their understanding of its significance.

In doing so one is tempted to plunge at once into ideas, definitions, and theology, but it will be wise to begin in another way. Ideas are important in life, but of themselves they seldom provide starting points. They grow out of facts and experiences and, torn from this soil, lose their life like uprooted trees. We shall find ourselves quite incapable of understanding Christian theology unless we manage to see clearly the experience it tried to account for.

The people who first heard Jesus' disciples proclaiming the Good News were as impressed by what they saw as by what they heard. They saw lives that had been transformed — men and women who were ordinary in every way except for the fact that they seemed to have found the secret of living. They evinced a tranquility, simplicity, and cheerfulness that their hearers had nowhere else encountered. Here were people who seemed to be making a success of the enterprise everyone would like to succeed at — that of life itself.

Specifically, there seemed to be two qualities in which their lives abounded. The first of these was mutual regard. One of the earliest observations about Christians that we have by an outsider is, "See how these Christians love one another." Integral to this mutual regard was a total absence of social barriers; it was a "discipleship of equals," as one New Testament scholar puts it.[6] Here were men and women who not only said that everyone was equal in the sight of God but who lived as though they meant it. The conventional barriers of race, gender, and status meant nothing to them, for in Christ there was neither Jew nor Gentile, male nor female, slave nor free. As a consequence, in spite of differences in function or social position, their fellowship was marked by a sense of genuine equality.

E. Schillebeeckx tells us that "being sad in Jesus' presence [was] an existential impossibility,"[7] and this takes us to the second quality that early Christians exhibited. Jesus once told his followers that his teachings were to the end "that my joy may be in you, and that your joy may be complete" (John 15:11), and to a remarkable degree that object appears to have been realized. Outsiders found this baffling. These scattered Christians were not numerous. They were not wealthy or powerful. If anything, they faced more adversity than the average man or woman. Yet, in the midst of their trials, they had laid hold of an inner peace that found expression in a joy that seemed exuberant. Perhaps radiant would be a better word. Radiance is hardly the word used to characterize the average religious life, but none other fits as well the life of these early Christians. Paul is an example. Here was a man who had been ridiculed, driven from town to town, shipwrecked, imprisoned, flogged until his back was covered with stripes. Yet here was a life in which joy was the constant refrain: "Joy unspeakable and full of glory." "Thanks be to God who giveth us the victory." "In all things we are more than conquerors." "God who commanded the light to shine out of darkness has shined in our hearts." "Thanks be to God for his unspeakable gift." The joy of these early Christians *was* unspeakable. As the fifth chapter of Ephesians suggests, they sang not out of convention but from the irrepressible overflow of their direct experience. Life for them was no longer a matter of coping. It was glory discerned.

What produced this love and joy in these early Christians? The qualities themselves are universally desired; the problem is how they are to be obtained. The explanation, insofar as we are able to gather from the New Testament record, is that three intolerable burdens had suddenly and dramatically been lifted from their shoulders. The first of these was fear, including the fear of death. We have the word of Carl Jung that he never met a patient over forty whose problems did not root back to fear of approaching death. The reason the Christians could not be intimidated by the lions and even sang as they entered the arena was that Jesus' counsel, "Fear not, for I am with you," worked for them.

The second burden from which they had been released was guilt. Rationalists consider guilt a vanishing phenomenon, but psychologists do not agree. Recognized or repressed, guilt of some degree seems built into the human condition, for no one lives up to his or her ideals completely. It is not only that we behave less well toward others than conscience dictates; we also fail ourselves by leaving talents undeveloped and letting opportunities slip. We may manage to keep remorse at bay while the sun is up, but in sleepless hours of the night it visits us:

> . . . *the rending pain of re-enactment*
> *Of all that you have done, and been; the shame*
> *Of motives late revealed, and the awareness*
> *Of things ill done and done to other's harm*
> *Which once you took as exercise of virtue.*
> (T. S. Eliot, "Little Gidding")

Unrelieved guilt reduces creativity. In its acute form it can rise to a fury of self-condemnation that shuts life down. Paul had felt its force before he was released: "Wretched man that I am! Who will rescue me from this body of death?" (Romans 7:24).

The third release the Christians experienced was from the cramping confines of the ego. There is no reason to suppose that prior to their new life these men and women had been any more self-centered than the next person, but this was enough for them to know that their love was radically restricted. They knew that "the human curse is to love and sometimes to love well, but never well enough."[8] Now this curse had been dramatically lifted.

It is not difficult to see how release from guilt, fear, and self could feel like rebirth. If someone were to free us from these crippling impediments, we too would call that person savior. But this only pushes our question back a step. How did the Christians get free of these burdens? And what did a man named Jesus, now gone, have to do with the process that they should credit it as his doing?

The only power that can effect transformations of the order we have described is love. It remained for the twentieth century to discover that locked within the atom is the energy of the sun itself. For this energy to be released, however, the atom must be bombarded from without. So too, locked in every human being is a store of love that partakes of the divine — the *imago dei*, image of God, it is sometimes called. And it too can be activated only through bombardment, in its case love's bombardment. The process begins in infancy, where a mother's initially unilateral loving smile awakens love in her baby and, as coordination develops, elicits its answering smile. The process continues into childhood. A loving human being is not produced by exhortations, rules, and threats. Love only takes root in children when it comes to them — initially and most importantly from nurturing parents. Ontogenetically speaking, love is an answering phenomenon. It is literally a response.

An actual incident may help to bring this point home:

He was a diffident freshman in a small midwestern college when one morning the instructor, one he idolized in the way the young idolize their role models, opened the class by saying, "Last evening I read some of the most significant sentences that I can recall." As he proceeded to read them the boy's heart leapt into his throat, for he was hearing his own words being read back to him from the paper he had submitted the preceding week. As he relates the incident: "I don't remember another thing that occurred during that hour, but I shall never forget my feelings when the bell brought me to my senses. It was noon and October was never so beautiful. I was exultant. If anyone had asked me for anything, I would have given it gladly, for I wanted nothing. I ached only to give to the world that had given so much to me."

If a young man found himself changed to this extent by the interest a mere man had shown in him, it is not difficult to imagine the change that would have come over the early Christians if they knew that they were loved by God. Imagination may fail us here, but logic need not. If we too felt loved, not abstractly or in principle but vividly and personally, by one who unites all power and perfection, the experience could melt our fear, guilt, and self-concern permanently. As Kierkegaard said, if at every moment both present and future I were certain that nothing has happened or can ever happen that would separate us from the infinite love of the Infinite, that would be the reason for joy.

God's love is precisely what the first Christians did feel. They had experienced Jesus' love and had became convinced that Jesus was God incarnate. Once that love reached them it could not be stopped. Melting the barriers of fear, guilt, and self, it poured through them as if they were sluice gates, augmenting the love they had hitherto felt for others until the difference in degree became a difference in kind and a new quality, which the world has come to call Christian love, was born. Conventional love is evoked by lovable qualities in the beloved, but the love people encountered from Christ embraced sinners and outcasts, Samaritans and enemies. It gave, not prudentially in order to receive, but because giving was its nature. Paul's famous description of Christian love in the thirteenth chapter of First Corinthians ought not to be read as if he were commenting on an attitude we are already familiar with. His words point to the attribute of a specific person, Jesus Christ. In phrases of classic beauty it describes the divine love that Paul believed Christians would reflect toward others once they experienced Christ's love for them. The reader should approach Paul's words as if they define a novel capacity which, as it had been fully realized "in the flesh" only in Christ, Paul was describing for the first time.

> *Love is patient; love is kind; love is not envious or arrogant or rude. It does not insist on its own way; it is not irritable or resentful; it does not rejoice in wrongdoing, but rejoices in the truth. It bears all things, believes all things, hopes all things, endures all things. Love never ends.*   (1 Corinthians 13:4–8)

So astonishing did the first Christians find this love and the fact that it had actually entered their lives that they had to appeal for help in describing it. Paul, in closing one of the earliest recorded sermons on the Good News, turned back to the words of one of the prophets, who in turn was speaking for God: "Look at this, you scornful souls, and lose yourselves in wonder; for in your days I do such a deed that, if men were to tell you this story, you would not believe it" (Acts 13:41).

The Mystical Body of Christ

The first Christians who spread the Good News throughout the Mediterranean world did not feel themselves to be alone. They were not even alone together, for they believed that Jesus was in their midst as a concrete, energizing power. They remembered that he had said, "Where two or three are gathered in my name, I am there among them" (Matthew 18:20). So, while their contemporaries were nicknaming them Christ-ians (literally the Messiah-folk, because they believed Jesus to be the Redeemer the prophets foretold), they began to call themselves an *ekklesia*, a Greek word that means literally "called out," or "called apart." The choice of this name points up how unlike a self-help society the early Christian community thought it was. It was no human association in which people of goodwill banded together to encourage one another in good works and lift themselves by their collective bootstraps. Human members constituted it, but it was powered by Christ's — which is to say God's — presence within it, though that presence was now spiritual and no longer visible.

Completely convinced of this, the disciples went out to possess a world they believed God had already possessed for them. Images came to mind to characterize the intense corporate identity they felt. One of these came from Christ himself: "I am the vine, you are the branches." This is obviously a metaphor, but we shall miss its force unless we see the exact sense in which the early Church read it. Just as a physical substance flows through the vine, entering its branches, leaves, and fruit to bring life to them, so a spiritual substance, the Holy Spirit, was flowing from the resurrected Christ into his followers, empowering them with the love that bore good works as its fruit. (The earliest Christians regarded the Holy Spirit as Christ/God's empowering presence in the world. By the fourth century that presence had assumed a spiritual identity of its own and was identified as the third person of the triune God and was judged to be consubstantial and co-eternal with God the Father and God the Son, Christ.) This was the way Jesus' followers read his own statement of the matter: "I am the true vine. . . . Abide in me as I abide in you. Just as the branch cannot bear fruit by itself unless it abides in the vine, neither can you unless you abide in me" (John 15:1, 4).

Saint Paul adapted Christ's image by using the human body instead of a vine to symbolize the Church. This preserved the vine's image of a central life-substance that animated its parts, while allowing for greater diversity than branches and leaves suggest. Though the offices and talents of individual Christians might differ as much as eyes and feet, Paul argued, all are animated by a single source. "For as in one body we have many members, so we who are many, are one body in Christ"— Christ and Church being synonymous here (Romans 12:4–5).

This seemed to the early Christians to be the completely apposite image for their corporate life. The Church was the Mystical Body of Christ. Mystical here meant supernatural and mysterious, but not unreal. The human form of Christ had left the earth, but he was continuing his uncompleted mission through a new physical body, his Church, of which he remained the head. This Mystical Body came to life in the "upper room" in Jerusalem at Pentecost through the animating power of the Holy Spirit. For "what the soul is to the body of man," Saint Augustine was to write, "that the Holy Spirit is to the Body of Christ, which is the Church."

If Christ was the head of this body and the Holy Spirit its soul, individual Christians were its cells, few at first but increasing as the body came of age. The cells of an organism are not isolates; they draw their life from the enveloping vitality of their hosts, while at the same time contributing to that vitality. The analogy is exact. The aim of Christian worship was to say those words and do those things that kept the Mystical Body alive, while at the same time opening individual cells, souls, to its inflowing vitality. The transaction literally "incorporated" Christians into Christ's person, for in an important sense Christ now *was* the Church. In any given Christian the divine life might be flowing fully, partially, or not at all according to whether his or her faith was vital, perfunctory, or apostate, the latter condition being comparable to paralysis. Some cells might even turn cancerous and turn on their host—these are the Christians Paul speaks of as bringing disrepute upon the Church by falling into scandal. But to the degree that members were in Christian health, the pulse of the Holy Spirit coursed through them. This bound Christians to one another and at the same time placed them in the closest conceivable relation to Christ himself. "Do you not know that your bodies are members of Christ?" (1 Corinthians 6:15). "It is no longer I who live, but it is Christ who lives in me" (Galatians 2:20).

Building upon this early conception of the Church, Christians came to think of it as having a double aspect. Insofar as it consists of

Christ and the Holy Spirit dwelling in people and suffusing them with grace and love, it is perfect. Insofar as it consists of fallible human members, it always falls short of perfection.[9] The worldly face of the Church is always open to criticism. But its mistakes, Christians hold, have been due to the human material through which it works.

In what sense there is salvation apart from the Body of Christ is a question on which Christians differ. Some Protestant liberals reject completely Christianity's historic claim that "there is no salvation outside the Church" as indicative of religious imperialism. At the other extreme are fundamentalists who insist that no one but those who are knowingly and formally Christians will be saved. Other Christians, however, answer the question by drawing a distinction between the Church Visible and the Church Invisible. The Church Visible is composed of those who are formally members of the Church as an earthly institution. Pope Pius IX spoke the views of the majority of Christians when he rejected membership in the Church Visible as indispensable to salvation. "Those who are hampered by invincible ignorance about our Holy Religion," he said,

> and, keeping the natural law, with its commands that are written by God in every human heart, and being ready to obey him, live honorably and uprightly, can, with the power of Divine light and grace helping them, attain eternal life. For God, who clearly sees, searches out, and knows the minds, hearts, thoughts, and disposi-tions of all, in his great goodness and mercy does not by any means suffer a man to be punished with eternal torments, who is not guilty of voluntary faults.

This statement clearly allows for those who are not members of the Church Visible to be saved.[10] Beyond the Church Visible stands the Church Invisible, composed of all who, whatever their formal persua-sion, follow as best they are able the lights they have. Most Christians continue to affirm that in this second meaning of the Church there is no salvation apart from it. Most of them would add to this their belief that the divine life pulses more strongly through the Church Visible than through any alternative institution. For they concur with the thought John Donne put poetically in his sonnet on the Resurrec-tion, where he says of Christ,

> *He was all gold when He lay down, but rose*
> *All tincture. . . .*

Donne was referring to the alchemists, whose ultimate hope was to discover not a way of making gold but a tincture that would transmute into gold all the baser metals it touched. A Christian is someone who has found no tincture equal to Christ.

The Mind of the Church

It was not the disciples' minds that were first drawn to Jesus. Rather, we have seen, it was their experience — the experience of living in the presence of someone whose selfless love, crystalline joy, and preternatural power came together in a way his disciples found divinely mysterious. It was only a matter of time, however, before Christians felt the need to understand this mystery in order to explain it to themselves and to others. Christian theology was born, and from then on the Church was head as well as heart.

Forced in this brief survey to choose, we shall confine ourselves to Christianity's three most distinctive tenets: the Incarnation, the Atonement, and the Trinity. The very names of these doctrines warn that our discussion will be theological, so before going further we should say something about this discipline. The modern mind is more interested in psychology and ethics than theology and metaphysics. This means that people, Christians among them, tend to appreciate the ethical teachings of Jesus more than the theological arguments of Saint Paul. However little they may care to live by the Sermon on the Mount, they at least respect it. Doctrines like those we are about to discuss, on the other hand, seem tedious if not incredible and at times annoying. Even New Testament scholars sometimes fall into step with this mood to the extent of trying to draw a sharp line between the "religion of Jesus" and "the religion about Jesus," between the forthright ethics of Jesus and the convoluted theology of Paul, between the human Jesus and the cosmic Christ, with strong insinuations that in each case the former is the nobler.

Notwithstanding the fact that even scholars can succumb to the view that religion's essence is ethics, the view is mistaken. High religion always includes a summons to the upright life, but its eyes are not fixed primarily on that summons. Faith's focal attention is on a vision of reality that sets morality in motion, often as a by-product almost. Religion begins with experience; "belief, ritual, and spiritual experience, and the greatest of these is the last."[11] Because the experience is of things that are invisible, it gives rise to symbols as the mind tries to think about invisible things. Symbols are ambiguous, however, so eventually the mind introduces thoughts to resolve the ambiguities of symbols and systematize their intuitions. Reading this sequence backwards we can define theology as the systematization of thoughts about the symbols that religious experience gives rise to. The Christian Creeds are the bedrock of Christian theology for being the earliest attempts by Christians to understand systematically the events that had changed their lives.

We may begin with the doctrine of the Incarnation, which took several centuries to fix into place. Holding as it does that in Christ God assumed a human body, it affirms that Christ was God-Man; simultaneously both fully God and fully man. To say that such a contention is paradoxical seems a charitable way to put the matter—it looks more like a blatant contradiction. If the doctrine held that Christ was half human and half divine, or that he was divine in certain respects while being human in others, our minds would not balk. But such concessions are precisely what the Creeds refuse to grant. In the words of the Creed of Chalcedon, Jesus Christ was "at once complete in Godhead and complete in manhood, truly God and truly man . . . of one essence with the Father as regards his Godhead, and at the same time of one essence with us as regards his manhood, in all respects like us, apart from sin."

The Church has always admitted that such assertions are opaque; the question is whether this is the last word on the matter. Actually, we can ask the same question of science. The anomalies of frontier physics provoked Haldane to his famous mutterance that "the universe is not only queerer than we suppose, but queerer than we *can* suppose." In more than one field, it appears, reality can be too strange for logic to comprehend. And where logic and evidence clash, it seems prudent to stick with evidence, for this holds the prospect of leading to a wider logic, whereas the opposite approach closes the door to discovery.

In suggesting that it was evidence that forced Christians to their logic-taxing assertion that Christ was both human and divine, we are of course speaking of religious experience — intuitions of the soul concerning ultimate issues of existence. Such evidence cannot be presented with an obviousness that will compel assent, for it does not turn on sense reports. But if we try we can arrive at at least an intimation of the experiential leads that the Christians were following. When in the year 325 the Emperor Constantine convened the Council of Nicea to decide whether Christ was of the same substance as God or only of like substance, three hundred bishops and their attendants came rushing in a frenzy of excitement from all over the empire. They must have presented a strange sight, for many of them bore empty eye sockets, disfigured faces, and limbs that were twisted and paralyzed from the Diocletian persecution they had endured. Obviously, more than forensics was involved in their deliberations.

The Nicene decision that Christ was "of one substance with the Father" claimed something about both Jesus and God. Note first its initial claim about Jesus. Among the many possible meanings the word "God" carries, none is more important than "that to which one gives oneself without reservation." In saying that Jesus was God, one of the things the Church was saying was that his life provides the perfect model by which to order human life. Slavish imitation of details is never creative, but insofar as Christ's love, his freedom, and the daily beauty of his life can find their authentic parallels in our own we are carried Godward, for the traits are authentically divine.

This much is obvious. But as we enter more deeply into the doctrine of the Incarnation we must prepare ourselves for surprises.

To begin with, though the Christian announcement of the Incarnation — a God-man — was as startling to its day as it is to ours, the shock attaches to different poles. Because we find disturbing the thought that a human being can be divine, we find the shocking feature of the Incarnation to be what it says about Jesus, that he was God. But in its own world, where the dividing line between the human and the Divine was perforated to the point that even emperors routinely claimed to be divine, a struggling sect's claim that its founder was divine raised few eyebrows. What else is new? would have been the common retort.

The Incarnation claimed that there *was* something newsworthy in the Christian message; namely, its proclamation of the kind of God that God was, as demonstrated by God's willingness to assume a human life of the form that Jesus exemplified. That willingness, together with the character of Jesus' life, added up to a different understanding of divinity than the Mediterranean world had known. In the Christian view God was *concerned* about humanity; concerned enough to suffer in its behalf. This was unheard of, to the point that the reaction to it was disbelief followed by alarm. In the eyes of threatened conservatives, such blasphemy, coupled with the Christians' radically egalitarian social views, justified persecution to stamp out this new sect. That Christians were aware of the novelty of their theology is illustrated by the fact that they seldom referred to God without stipulating that it was "the God and Father of our Lord Jesus Christ" that they were talking about.

As for what the Incarnation asserts about Christ, here too we are surprised. For what we find is that instead of wasting many words on Jesus' divinity, the Creeds assume that their primary task is to argue his full humanity. This ties in with what was just said about the casual overlap of divine and human in Greco-Roman understanding—the Olympic deities, quasi-human, quasi-divine, formed the religious backdrop. The Christian Jesus did not fit into this framework. We have seen that in his case the divine/human overlap was not one of compromise—somewhat human, somewhat divine. It was the conjunction of stark opposites: absolute divinity overlapping complete humanity. And because in the Church's experience it was Jesus' full humanity that was in danger of slipping from their grasp, so rapidly was his divinity moving to the fore, it was that humanity that the Church's first Creed set out to affirm.

I believe in God the Father Almighty, Maker of heaven and earth; and in Jesus Christ our Lord, who was conceived *by the Holy Ghost,* born *of the Virgin Mary,* suffered *under Pontius Pilate, was* crucified, died, *and* buried. . . .

How casually this Apostles' Creed touches on Christ's divinity! As early as the second century this point no longer had to be argued; it was assumed. The burden of the Apostles' Creed, carried by the words we have romanized, was to insist that Christ was man as well. He *really was* born, it says; he really suffered, he really died and was buried. These incidents were not just make-believe, a sequence through which God merely feigned to brush with the human estate; that notion was later targeted as the Docetic Heresy. Christ endured these experiences as fully as we do. He was "truly man."

And is it true? And is it true,
This most tremendous tale of all . . .
That God was Man in Palestine
And lives today in Bread and Wine.
    (John Betjeman, *Christman*)

It is not difficult to see why (at cost of immense logical awkwardness) the Church felt that it needed to retain Christ's humanity. A
bridge must touch both banks, and Christ was the bridge that joined
humanity to God. "God became man that man might become God,"
was Irenaeus' way of putting the matter. To have said that Christ was
man but not God would have been to deny that his life was fully *normative* and to concede that other ways might be as good. To have said
that he was God but not man would have been to deny that his example was fully *relevant;* it might be a realistic standard for God but not
for human beings. The Christians could have relaxed one claim or
the other and salvaged logic, but at the cost of betraying their core
experience.

Turning to the doctrine of the Atonement, we know that its root
meaning is reconciliation, the recovery of wholeness or at-one-ment.
Christians were convinced that Christ's life and death had effected
an unparalleled rapprochement between God and humanity. In the
words of Saint Paul, "In Christ God was reconciling the world to
himself" (2 Corinthians 5:19). Two metaphors have dominated the
Church's understanding of this occurrence. One, legalistic, runs as
follows: By voluntarily disobeying God's order not to eat of the forbidden fruit in Eden, Adam sinned. As his sin was directed against God,
it was of infinite proportion. Sins must be compensated for, otherwise God's justice would be compromised. An infinite sin demands
infinite recompense, and this could only be effected by God's vicarious assumption of our guilt and payment of the ultimate penalty it
required, namely death. God made this payment through the Person
of Christ and the debt is canceled.

Where the mind had a different cast—in the Middle Ages especially—this understanding of the Atonement carried weight, but
Christendom's presiding metaphor on this topic has been release
from bondage. The bondage Christ released humanity from was sin,
which means that we have no choice but to tackle this unpalatable
subject.

We can begin by noting that though the word is usually used in the plural, suggesting thereby specific acts — a catalogue of misdeeds or rules that have been broken, perhaps those of the Ten Commandments — Christians find in its singular, "sin," something deeper: a disconnectedness or estrangement from God. It is the heart's misplacement; a disalignment of our affections. Augustine, making this point in a positive vein, said, "Love [God] and do what you will." When there is wholehearted love for the All, for the universal good we might say, then the will wants that good and needs no rules. For the most part matters are otherwise; concern for ourselves sabotages our love for others. And yet we do not truly like ourselves very much. Our hearts are drawn to something larger, beyond the narrow confines of the ego.

Thus the bondage that imprisons us is attachment to ourselves, with the fear and guilt that trail in its wake. Put the other way around, our bondage results from our estrangement, our sin or sunderment, from full participation in the divine life. Being excluded from such participation doesn't feel good. Paul had the openness and honesty first to see this and then to admit it: I feel wretched, he said. Prisoners always do. A good part of their wretchedness springs from their helplessness; by definition they can't free themselves. So Paul continues: "I do not do what I want, but I do the very thing I hate" (Romans 14:15). He is admitting that he is trapped, which realization leads to his desperate cry that we have already quoted, "Who will rescue me from this body of death?" (Romans 14:24). In whatever words it is the cry that every alcoholic has repeated. If there is to *be* a liberation, it will have to come from without, or better, from above: a higher power. It was the Christian witness that the Power that works the liberation, and restores the self to the ground of its being, is Christ. One could equally say that it is God, but Christians add that in this instance God's purpose was accomplished by Christ.

The third key Christian doctrine that we shall consider is the Trinity. It holds that while God is fully one, God is also three. The latter half of this claim leads Jews and Muslims to wonder if Christians are truly monotheists, but Christians are confident that they are. As water, ice, and steam, H_2O assumes states that are liquid, solid, and gaseous while retaining its chemical identity.

What prompted the Christians to this atypical view that God is Three-in-One? As always in such matters, the notion had an experiential base. The theological doctrine of the Trinity was not set in place until the fourth century, but the experiences that it impounds are those of the earliest Church; indeed, they generated that Church. As full-fledged Jews, Jesus' disciples affirmed Yahweh unquestioningly. But as we have seen, they came to see Jesus as Yahweh's extension in the world, and as his life and mission grew in vividness they began to accord to his person a distinct region within the divine. This meant that in their religious imagings they could now apprehend God either directly or by way of his Son, though in fact the two were so closely joined that the result was the same. And then came Pentecost, which brought a third visitation. While they were all together in one place,

> *suddenly from heaven there came a sound like the rush of a violent wind, and it filled the entire house where they were sitting. Divided tongues, as of fire, appeared among them, and a tongue rested on each of them. All of them were filled with the Holy Spirit.*   (Acts 2:1–4)

The secular mind would say that the disciples first reified this experience, turning it into a thing, the Holy Spirit, and then personified that reification, thereby generating the third Person of the Trinity, but the disciples would have rejected this explanation. Jesus may not have said, "the Father will give you another Counselor, to be with you forever, even the Spirit of truth"; the assertion appears in the last of the Gospels to be written, in John, and is therefore disputed. But if the words were attributed to Jesus, it was because they reflected the disciples' understanding of their Pentecost experience. What they there witnessed, they were persuaded, was the dramatic arrival of a third party to the divine assembly, the Holy Spirit.

This is how the disciples were brought to their understanding of God in three Persons; but once that understanding was in place, they projected it back to the beginning of time. If the divine "triangle" has three "sides" now, it must always have had three sides. The Son and the Holy Spirit had indeed proceeded principially from the Father, but not temporally. The three were together from the start; for after the multiplicity in the divine nature was brought home to them, Christians could no longer think of God as complete without it. We have noted that the other two Abrahamic religions, Judaism and Islam, object to this theology, but Christians love it. For love is a relationship, they say, and love is incomplete without others to love. If, then, love is not just one of God's attributes but instead God's very essence — and it may be the Christian mission in history to claim just this point — at no point could God have been truly God without having relationships, a requirement that was met "before the foundation of the world" (Ephesians 1:4) through the three Persons' of the Triune God loving one another. "The Godhead is a society of three divine persons, knowing and loving each other so entirely that not merely can none exist without the others, but in some mysterious way each *is* what the other is," a theologian has written.[12] The Nicene Creed put it this way:

> *We believe in one God the Father almighty, . . .*
> *and in one Lord Jesus Christ, the only-begotten Son of God, . . .*
> *and in the Holy Spirit, the Lord, the Life-giver, . . .*
> *who with the Father and the Son together*
>   *is worshipped and glorified.*

Roman Catholicism

We have been speaking of Christianity as a whole. This does not mean that every Christian will agree with all that has been said. Christianity is such a complex phenomenon that it is difficult to say anything significant about it that will carry the assent of all Christians. So it must be stressed that what has gone before is an interpretation. Nevertheless, it has sought to be an interpretation of the points that, substantially at least, Christians hold in common.

When we turn from the early Christianity we have been considering thus far to Christendom today, we find the Church divided into three great branches. Roman Catholicism focuses in the Vatican in Rome and spreads from there, being dominant, on the whole, through central and southern Europe, Ireland, and South America. Eastern Orthodoxy has its major influence in Greece, the Slavic countries, and the Soviet Union. Protestantism dominates Northern Europe, England, Scotland, and North America.

Up to 313 the Church struggled in the face of official Roman persecution. In that year it became legally recognized and enjoyed equal rights with other religions of the empire. Before the century was out, in 380, it became the official religion of the Roman Empire.

With a few minor splinterings, such as the Nestorians, it continued as
a united body up to 1054. This means that for roughly half its history
the Church remained substantially one institution. In 1054, however,
its first great division occurred, between the Eastern Orthodox
Church in the East and the Roman Catholic Church in the West. The
reasons for the break were complex—geography, culture, language,
and politics as well as religion were involved—but it is not our concern to detail them here. Instead we move to the next great division,
which occurred in the Western Church with the Protestant Reformation in the sixteenth century. Protestantism follows four main courses
—Baptist, Lutheran, Calvinists, and Anglican—which themselves
subdivide until the current census lists over 900 denominations in
the United States alone. Currently, the ecumenical movement is
bringing some of these denominations back together again. With
these minimum facts at our disposal, we can proceed to our real concern, which is to try to understand the central perspectives of
Christendom's three great branches. Beginning with the Roman
Catholic Church, we shall confine ourselves to what are perhaps the
two most important concepts for the understanding of this branch of
Christendom: the Church as teaching authority, and the Church as
sacramental agent.

The Church as Teaching Authority.   First, the Church as teaching authority. This concept begins with the premise that God came
to earth in the person of Jesus Christ to teach people the way to
salvation—how they should live in this world so as to inherit eternal
life in the next. If this is true, if his teachings really are the door to salvation and if the opening of this door was one of the prime reasons
why he came to earth, it seems unlikely that he would have held this
door ajar for his generation only. Would he not want his saving teachings to continue to be available to the world?

The reader might agree but add, "Do we not *have* his teachings
—in the Bible?" This, however, raises the question of interpretation.
The Constitution of the United States is a reasonably unambiguous
document, but our social life would be chaos without an authority,
the Supreme Court, to interpret it. Equally with the Bible. Leave it
to private interpretation and whirlwind is the sure harvest. Unguided
by the Church as teaching authority, Bible study is certain to lead
different students to different conclusions, even on subjects of the

highest moment. And since the net effect of proposing alternative answers to the same question is to make it impossible to believe any answer confidently, this approach would reduce the Christian faith to hesitation and stammer.

Let us take a specific issue for illustration. Is divorce moral? Surely, on a question as important as this, any religion that proposes to guide the conscience of its members may be expected to have a definite view. But suppose we try to draw that view directly from the Bible? Mark 10:11 tells us that "Whoever divorces his wife and marries another commits adultery." Luke 16:18 concurs. But Matthew 5:32 enters a reservation: "except on the ground of unchastity." What is the Christian to think? What are the probabilities that the Matthew text has been tampered with? May an unwronged party remarry or not?

The question is only a sample of the many that must remain forever in doubt if our only guides are the Bible and private conscience. Was Christ born of a virgin? Did his body ascend after death? Is the fourth Gospel authentic? Without a sure court of appeal, moral and theological disintegration seem inevitable. It was precisely to avert such disintegration that Christ established the Church to be his continuing representative on earth, that there might be one completely competent authority to adjudicate between truth and error on life-and-death matters. Only so could the "dead letter" of scripture be continually revivified by the living instinct of God's own person. This is the meaning of the words, attributed to Jesus, "I tell you, you are Peter, and on this rock I will build my Church. . . . I will give you the keys of the Kingdom of heaven, and whatever you bind on earth shall be bound in heaven, and whatever you loose on earth shall be loosed in heaven" (Matthew 16:18–19).

Ultimately, this idea of the Church as teaching authority shapes the idea of papal infallibility. Every nation has its ruler, be he emperor, king, or president. The earthly head of the Church is the pope, successor to St. Peter in the bishopric of Rome. The doctrine of papal infallibility asserts that when the pope speaks officially on matters of faith or morals, God stays him against error.

This doctrine is so often misunderstood that we must emphasize that infallibility is a strictly limited gift. It does not assert that the pope is endowed with extraordinary intelligence. It does not mean that God helps him to know the answer to every conceivable question. Emphatically, it does not mean that Catholics have to accept the pope's view on politics. The pope can make mistakes. He can fall into sin. The scientific or historical opinions he holds may be mistaken. He may write books that contain errors. Only in two limited spheres, faith and morals, is he infallible, and in these only when he speaks officially as the supreme teacher and lawgiver of the Church, defining a doctrine that should be held by all its members. When, after studying a problem that relates to faith or morals as carefully as possible and with all available help from expert consultants, he emerges with the Church's answer—on these rare occasions it is not strictly speaking *an* answer, it is *the* answer. For on such occasions the Holy Spirit protects him from the possibility of error. These answers constitute the infallible teachings of the Church and as such are binding on Roman Catholics.

The Church as Sacramental Agent.   The second idea central to Roman Catholicism is the idea of the Church as sacramental agent. This supplements the idea of the Church as teaching authority. It is one thing to know what we should do; it is quite another to be able to do it, which is why there is a need for the Sacraments. The Church helps with both problems. It points the way in which we should live, and empowers us to live accordingly.

The second gift is as important as the first. Christ called his followers to live lives far above the average in charity and service. No one would claim that this is easy. The Catholic, however, insists that we have not faced our situation squarely until we realize that without help such a life is impossible. For the life to which Christ called people is supernatural in the exact sense of being contrary to the pull of natural human instincts. By their own efforts people can no more live above human nature than an elephant can live a life of reason. Help, therefore, is needed. The Church, as God's representative on earth, is the agency to provide it, and the Sacraments its means for doing so.

Since the twelfth century the number of Sacraments in the Roman Catholic Church has been fixed at seven. In a striking way these parallel the great moments and needs of human life. People are born, they come of age, they marry or dedicate themselves completely to some life-purpose, and they die. Meanwhile, they must be reintegrated into society when they deviate, and they must eat. The Sacraments provide the spiritual counterparts of these natural events. As birth brings a child into the natural world, *Baptism* (by planting God's first special grace in its soul) draws the infant into the supernatural order of existence. When the child reaches the age of reason and needs to be strengthened for mature reflection and responsible action, it is *Confirmed*. Usually, there comes a solemn moment during which an adult is joined to a human companion in *Holy Matrimony*, or dedicates his or her life entirely to God in *Holy Orders*. At life's close *the Sacrament of the Sick* (extreme unction) closes earthly eyes and prepares the soul for its last passage.

Meanwhile two Sacraments need to be repeated frequently. One of these is *Reconciliation* (confession). Being what we are, people cannot live without falling into error and straying from the right. These aberrations make necessary definite steps by which they may be restored to the human community and divine fellowship. The Church teaches that if one confesses one's sin to God in the presence of one of God's delegates, a priest, and truly repents of the sin committed and honestly resolves (whether or not this resolve proves effective) to avoid it in the future, one will be forgiven. God's forgiveness depends on the sinner's penitence and resolve being genuine, but the priest has no infallible means for determining whether they are or not. If the penitent deceives himself or herself and the priest, the absolution pronounced is inoperative.

The central Sacrament of the Catholic Church is the *Mass*, known also as the Holy Eucharist, Holy Communion, or the Lord's Supper. The word Mass derives from the Latin *missa*, which is a form of the verb "to send." The ancient liturgy contained two dismissals, one for people interested in Christianity but not yet baptized, which preceded the sacrament of the Eucharist, and a second for fully initiated Christians after it had been celebrated. Coming as it did between these two dismissals, the rite came first to be called *missa* and then, by transliteration, the Mass.

The central feature of the Mass is the reenactment of Christ's Last Supper in which, as he gave his disciples bread and wine, he said, "This is my blood that is shed for you." It is false to the Catholic concept of this Sacrament to think of it as a commemoration through which priest and communicants elevate their spirits by symbolic remembrance of Christ's example. The Mass provides an actual transfusion of spiritual energy from God to human souls. In a general way this holds for all the Sacraments, but for the Mass it holds uniquely. For the Catholic Church teaches that in the host and the chalice, the consecrated bread and wine, Christ's human body and blood are actually present. They consider his words, "This is my body. . . . This is my blood," explicit on this point. When a priest utters these words of consecration, therefore, the change that they effect in the elements is not one of significance only. The elements may not appear different afterward; analysis would register no chemical change. In technical language this means that their "accidents" remain as they were, but their "substance" is transubstantiated. We might say the Eucharist conveys God's grace as a boat conveys its passengers, whereas the other sacraments convey grace as a letter conveys meaning. For the letter to have meaning, intelligence is required in addition to the paper and ink marks; so too in Sacraments other than the Eucharist God's power is necessary in addition to the instruments of the sacrament. But in the Mass spiritual nourishment is literally to be had from the elements themselves. It is exactly as important for the Christians' spiritual life to feast upon them as it is for their bodily lives to partake of food. Opening your mouth for the Bread of Life, writes Saint Francis de Sales,

> *full of faith, hope and charity, receive Him, in whom, by whom, and for whom, you believe, hope and love. . . . Represent to yourself that as the bee, after gathering from the flowers the dew of heaven and the choicest juice of the earth, reduces them into honey and carries it into her hive, so the priest, having taken from the altar the Savior of the world, the true Son of God, who, as the dew, is descended from heaven, and the true Son of the Virgin, who, as a flower is sprung from the earth of our humanity, puts him as delicious food into your mouth and into your body.*[13]

This personal presence of God in the elements of the Mass distinguishes it significantly from the other Sacraments, but it does not vitiate the common bond that unites them all. Each is a means by which God, through Christ's mystical body, literally infuses into human souls the supernatural power that enables them so to live in this world that in the world to come they may have life everlasting.

Catholics see Christ as having explicitly joined the sacramental agency of the Church to its teaching authority in his closing commission to his disciples. "Go and make disciples of all nations, baptizing them in the name of the Father and of the Son and of the Holy Spirit, teaching them to observe all that I have commanded you; and lo, I am with you always, to the close of the age" (Matthew 28:19–20).

Eastern Orthodoxy

The Eastern Orthodox Church, which today has somewhere in the neighborhood of 250 million communicants, broke officially with the Roman Catholic Church in 1054, each charging the other with responsibility for the break. Eastern Orthodoxy includes the Churches of Albania, Bulgaria, Georgia, Greece, Romania, Russia, Serbia, and Sinai. While each of these Churches is self-governing, they are in varying degrees in communion with one another, and their members think of themselves as belonging primarily to the Eastern Church and only secondarily to their particular divisions within it.

In most ways the Eastern Orthodox Church stands close to the Roman Catholic, for during more than half their histories they constituted a single body. It honors the same seven Sacraments and interprets them in fundamental respects exactly as does the Roman Church. On the teaching authority there is some difference, but even here the premise is the same. Left to private interpretation the Christian faith would disintegrate into conflicting claims and a mass of uncertainties. It is the Church's responsibility to insure against this, and God enables it to do so; the Holy Spirit preserves its official statements against error. This much is shared with Rome. The differences are two. One of these has to do with extent. The Eastern Church considers the issues on which unanimity is needed to be fewer than does the Roman Church. In principle only issues that are mentioned in scripture can qualify, which is to say that the Church can interpret doctrines but it cannot initiate them. In practice the Church has exercised her prerogative as interpreter only seven times, in the Seven Ecumenical Councils, all of which were held before 787. This means that the Eastern Church assumes that though the articles a Christian must believe are decisive, their number is relatively few. Strictly speaking, all the decisions that the Ecumenical Councils reached are embedded in the creeds themselves; beyond these there is no need for dogmatic pronouncements on such matters as purgatory, indulgences, the Immaculate Conception, or the bodily assumption of Mary, the last of which Orthodoxy introduced in practice but without proclaiming as dogma. Catholics regard these dogmas positively, as the development of doctrine, whereas the Orthodox consider them "innovations." Generalizing this difference, we can say that the Latin Church stresses the development of Christian doctrine, whereas the Greek Church stresses its continuity, contending that there has been no *need* for the Church to exercise its teaching authority outside the Ecumenical Councils. What is referred to as "the magisterium of the academy" enters into this difference, for nothing like the great university centers of Bologna and Paris characterize the Eastern experience. When we reach for an image to epitomize Roman Catholicism, we think of the Middle Ages. Its counterpart for Eastern Orthodoxy is the Church Fathers.

The other way in which the Eastern Church's understanding of its role as teaching authority differs from the Western pertains to the means by which its dogmas are reached. The Roman Church, as we have seen, holds that in the final analysis they come through the pope; it is the decisions that he announces that the Holy Spirit preserves from error. The Eastern Church has no pope—if we want to epitomize the difference between the two Churches, it is this. Instead, it holds that God's truth is disclosed through "the conscience of the Church," using this phrase to refer to the consensus of Christians generally. This consensus needs, of course, to be focused, which is what ecclesiastical councils are for. When the bishops of the entire Church are assembled in Ecumenical Council, their collective judgment establishes God's truth in unchangeable monuments.[14] It would be correct to say that the Holy Spirit preserves their decisions from error, but it would be truer to the spirit of the Eastern Church to say that the Holy Spirit preserves Christian minds as a whole from lapsing into error, for the bishops' decisions are assumed to do no more than focus the thought of the latter.

This brings us to one of the special emphases of the Eastern Church. Because in many ways it stands midway between Roman Catholicism and Protestantism, it is more difficult to put one's finger on features within it that are clearly distinctive; but if we were to select two (as we did in our sketch of Roman Catholicism), one of these would be its exceptionally corporate view of the Church.

Common to all Christians is the view of the Church as the mystical body of Christ. Just as the parts of the body are joined in common well-being or malaise, so too are the lives of Christians interrelated.

All Christians accept the doctrine that they are "members of one another"; but while matters of degree are notoriously difficult to determine, it could be argued that the Eastern Church has taken this notion more seriously than either Roman Catholicism or Protestantism. Each Christian is working out his or her salvation in conjunction with the rest of the Church, not individually to save a separate soul. The Russian branch of Orthodoxy has a saying to this effect: "One can be damned alone, but saved only with others." And Orthodoxy goes further. It takes seriously Saint Paul's theme of the entire universe as "groaning and in travail" as it awaits redemption. Not only is the destiny of the individual bound up with the entire Church; it is responsible for helping to sanctify the entire world of nature and history. The welfare of everything in creation is affected to some degree by what each individual contributes to or detracts from it.

Though the most important consequence of this strong corporate feeling is the spiritual one just stated—the downplaying of that "holy selfishness" that puts its own personal salvation before everything else—the concept comes out in two other quite practical ways. One of these has already been noted. In identifying the Church's teaching authority with Christian conscience as a whole— "the conscience of the people is the conscience of the Church"— Orthodoxy maintains that the Holy Spirit's truth enters the world diffused through the minds of Christians generally. Individual Christians, laity as well as clergy, are cells in "the mind of Christ," which functions through them collectively.

The other side of this point concerns administration. Whereas the administration of the Roman Church is avowedly hierarchical, the Eastern Church grounds more of its decisions in the laity. Congregations, for example, have more say in the selection of their clergy. The Roman Church may argue that this confuses the offices of laity with clergy; but the strong corporate feeling of the Eastern Church has led her to believe, again, that divine guidance, even when it reaches down to touch practical issues of Church administration, is more generally diffused among Christians than Rome allows. The clergy has its uninfringeable domain, the administration of the Sacraments; but outside that domain the line that separates clergy from the laity is thin. Priests need not be celibate. Even the titular head of the Eastern Church, the Patriarch of Constantinople, is no more than "first among equals," and the laity is known as the "royal priesthood."

In presenting the religions of Asia, it was suggested that union has counted for more there, and individuality less, than in the West; Hinduism sets the pace, with merger with the Absolute as its presiding goal. If this is roughly correct it helps to explain why it is the easternmost branch of Christianity that has most emphasized the corporate nature of the Church, both the ecclesiastical equality of its members (as against Catholicism), and their solidarity (as against Protestantism).[15] It is also possible that residing, as it does, on the outskirts of Europe, it may have acquired less of a modern, Western overlay, and in consequence stands somewhat closer to early Christianity. We shall not explore that possibility, however, but proceed to the second distinctive emphasis its geography may have fostered, its mysticism, which resonates in ways with that of Asia.

Like all the religions we have considered, Christianity believes reality to be composed of two realms, the natural and the supernatural. Following death, human life is fully translated into the supernatural domain. Even in the present world, however, it is not insulated from it. For one thing the Sacraments, as we have seen, are channels whereby supernatural grace is made available to people in their current state.

This much virtually all Christianity teaches. The differences come when we ask to what extent it should be a part of the Christian program to try to partake of supernatural life while here on earth. Roman Catholicism holds that the Trinity dwells in every Christian soul, but its presence is not normally felt. By a life of prayer and penance it is possible to dispose oneself for a special gift by which the Trinity discloses its presence and the seeker is lifted to a state of mystical ecstasy. But as human beings have no *right* to such states, the states being wholly in the nature of free gifts of grace, the Roman Church neither urges nor discourages their cultivation. The Eastern Church encourages the mystical life more actively. From very early times, when the deserts near Antioch and Alexandria were filled with hermits seeking illumination, the mystical enterprise has occupied a more prominent place in its life. As the supernatural world intersects and impregnates the world of sense throughout, it should be a part of Christian life in general to develop the capacity to experience directly the glories of God's presence.

> *Does the fish soar to find the ocean,*
> *The eagle plunge to find the air,*
> *That we ask of the stars in motion*
> *If they have rumour of thee there?*
>
> *Not where the wheeling systems darken,*
> *And our benumbed conceiving soars,*
> *The drift of pinions, would we harken,*
> *Beats at our own clay-shuttered doors.*
>
> *The angels keep their ancient places;*
> *Turn but a stone, and start a wing:*
> *'Tis ye, 'tis your estranged faces*
> *That miss the many-splendoured thing.*
> (Francis Thompson, "The Kingdom of God")

Mysticism is a practical program even for the laity. The aim of every life should be union with God—actual deification, by Grace, to the point of sharing the Divine Life; *theosis* is the Greek word for the doctrine that this sharing is possible. As our destiny is to enter creatively into the life of the Trinity, the love that circulates incessantly among the Father, Son, and Holy Spirit, movement toward this goal should be a part of every Christian life. For only as we advance toward increasing participation in the Trinity are we able to love God with our whole heart and soul and mind, and our neighbor as ourselves. The mystical graces are open to everyone, and it is incumbent for each to make of one's life a pilgrimage toward glory.

Protestantism

The causes that led to the break between Roman Catholicism and what came to be known as Protestant Christianity are complex and still in dispute. Political economy, nationalism, Renaissance individualism, and a rising concern over ecclesiastical abuses all played their part. They do not, however, camouflage the fact that the basic cause was religious, a difference in Christian perspective between Roman Catholicism and Protestantism. As we are concerned here with ideas rather than history, we shall say no more about the causes of the Protestant Reformation. Instead, we shall be content to treat the sixteenth century—Luther, Calvin, the Ninety-five Theses, the Diet of Worms, King Henry VIII, the Peace of Augsburg—as a vast tunnel.

The Western Church entered that tunnel whole; it emerged from it in two sections. More accurately, it emerged in several sections, for Protestantism is not so much a Church as a movement of Churches.

The deepest differences in Protestantism today are not denominational; they are emphases that cut across denominations and often combine in the same person: fundamentalist, conservative-evangelical, mainline, charismatic, and social activist. In this brief overview we shall not go into these differences, which tend to be of recent origin. Instead, without repeating the bulk of its faith and practice, which it shares with Catholicism and Orthodoxy— Protestantism is more Christian than Protestant—we shall proceed to its two great enduring themes with which we must here be content. They are (1) justification by faith and (2) the Protestant Principle.

Faith.   Faith, in the Protestant conception, is not simply a matter of belief, an acceptance of knowledge held with certainty yet not on evidence. It is a response of the entire self; in Emil Brunner's phrase, "a totality-act of the whole personality." As such it does *include* a movement of the mind in assent—specifically, a conviction of God's limitless, omnipresent creative power—but this is not its all. To be truly faith it must include as well a movement of the affections in love and trust, and a movement of the will in desire to be an instrument of God's redeeming love. When Protestantism says that human beings are justified—that is, restored to right relationship with the ground of their being, and with their associates—by faith, it is saying that such restoration requires a movement of the total self, in mind, will, and affections, all three. It is a mark of the strength of the ecumenical movement in our time that Roman Catholic theologians now increasingly understand faith in the same way.

Thus defined, faith is a personal phenomenon. "Right beliefs" or "sound doctrine" can be accepted secondhand and largely by rote, but service and love cannot. Faith is the response by which God, heretofore a postulate of philosophers or theologians, becomes God for me, my God. This is the meaning of Luther's statement that "Everyone must do his own believing as he will have to do his own dying."

To feel the force of the Protestant emphasis on faith as response of the entire self, we need to see it as a passionate repudiation of religious perfunctoriness. Luther's protest against indulgences, which were thought to help reduce their purchasers' time in purgatory, is only a symbol of this wider protest, which extended in a number of directions. No number of religious observances, no record of good deeds, no roster of doctrines believed could guarantee that an individual would reach his or her desired state. Such things were not irrelevant to the Christian life; but unless they helped to transform the believer's heart (his or her attitudes and response to life), they were inadequate. This is the meaning of the Protestant rallying cry, "Justification by faith alone." It does not mean that the Creeds or the Sacraments are unimportant. It means that unless these are accompanied by the experience of God's love and a returning love for God, they are insufficient. Similarly with good works. The Protestant position does not imply that good works are unimportant. It means that fully understood, they are correlatives of faith rather than its preludes. If one really does have faith, good works will flow from it naturally,[16] whereas the reverse cannot be assumed; that is, good works do not necessarily lead to faith. To a large extent both Paul and Luther had been driven to their emphasis on faith precisely because a respectable string of good works, doggedly performed, had not succeeded in transforming their hearts.

Once more we need to draw here on the analogy of the child in its home, an analogy that speaks so directly to one aspect of human religiousness that we have cited it several times already. After the child's physical needs have been met, or rather while they are being met, the child needs above all to feel the enveloping love and acceptance of its parents. Paul, Luther, and Protestants in general say something comparable for human beings throughout their lifespans. Since from first to last they are vulnerable before the powers that confront them, their lifelong need is to know that their basic environment, the ground of being from which they have derived and to which they will return, is *for* them rather than against them. If they can come to know this to the extent of really feeling it, they are released from the basic anxiety that causes them to try to elbow their way to security. This is why, just as the loved child is the cooperative child, the man or woman in whom God's love has awakened the answering response of faith is the one who can truly love other people. The key is inward. Given faith in God's goodness, everything of importance follows. In its absence, nothing can take its place.

The Protestant Principle.   The other controlling perspective in Protestantism has come to be called the Protestant Principle. Stated philosophically, it warns against absolutizing the relative. Stated theologically, it warns against idolatry.

The point is this. Human allegiance belongs to God—this all religions (with allowance for terminology) will affirm. God, however, is beyond nature and history. God is not removed from these, but the divine cannot be equated with either or any of their parts, for while the world is finite, God is infinite. With these truths all the great religions in principle agree. They are, however, very hard truths to keep in mind; so hard that people continually let them slip and proceed to equate God with something they can see or touch or at least conceptualize more precisely than the infinite. Early on they equated God with statues, until prophets—the first "protestants" or protesters on this score—rose up to denounce their transpositions, dubbing their pitiful substitutes idols, or "little pieces of form." Later, people stopped deifying wood and stone, but this did not mean that idolatry ended. While the secular world proceeded to absolutize the state, or the self, or human intellect, Christians fell to absolutizing dogmas, the Sacraments, the Church, the Bible, or personal religious experience. To think that Protestantism devalues these or doubts that God is involved in them is to misjudge it seriously. It does, however, insist that none of them is God. All, being involved in history, contain something of the human; and since the human is always imperfect, these instruments are to some degree imperfect as well. As long as they point beyond themselves to God, they can be invaluable. But let any of them claim absolute or unreserved allegiance—which is to say claim to be God—and it becomes diabolical. For this, according to tradition, is what the devil is: the highest angel who, not content to be second, was determined to be first.

In the name of the sovereign God, who transcends all the limitations and distortions of finite existence, therefore, every human claim to absolute truth or finality must be rejected. Some examples will indicate what this principle means in practice. Protestants cannot accept the dogma of papal infallibility because this would involve removing from criticism forever opinions that, having been channeled through human minds, can never (in the Protestant view) wholly escape the risk of limitation and partial error. Creeds and pronouncement can be believed; they can be believed fully and wholeheartedly. But to place them beyond the cleansing crossfire of challenge and criticism is to absolutize something finite—to elevate "a little piece of form" to the position that should be reserved for God alone.

Instances of what Protestants consider idolatry are not confined to other sects or religions. Protestants admit that the tendency to absolutize the relative is universal; it occurs among them as much as it does anywhere, bringing the need for continual self-criticism and reformation to the door of Protestantism itself. The chief Protestant idolatry has been Bibliolatry. Protestants do believe that God speaks to people through the Bible as in no other way. But to elevate it as a book to a point above criticism, to insist that every word and letter was dictated directly by God and so can contain no historical, scientific, or other inaccuracies, is again to forget that in entering the world, God's word must speak through human minds. Another common instance of idolatry within Protestantism has been the deification of private religious experience. Its insistence that faith must be a living experience has often led its constituents to assume that any vital experience must be the working of the Holy Spirit. Perhaps so, but again the experience is never pure Spirit. The Spirit must assume the contours of the human vessel, which means again that the whole is never uncompounded.

By rejecting all such absolutes, Protestantism tries to keep faith with the first Commandment, "You shall have no other gods before me" (Exodus 20:3). The injunction contains a negative, and for many the word Protestant too carries a predominantly negative ring. Is not a Protestant a person who protests against something? We have seen that this is certainly true; Protestants who are truly such protest without ceasing the usurpation of God's place by anything less than God. But the Protestant Principle can just as well be put positively, which is how it should be put if its full import is to be appropriated. It protests *against* idolatry because it testifies *for* (pro-testant = one who testifies for) God's sovereignty in human life.

But how is God to enter human life? To insist that God cannot be equated with anything in this tangible, visible world leaves people at sea in God's ocean. God doubtless surrounds us; but to gain access to human awareness, divinity needs to be condensed and focused.

This is where, for Protestants, the Bible figures. In its account of God working through Israel, through Christ, and through the early

Church, we find the clearest picture of God's great goodness, and how human beings may find new life in fellowship with the divine. In this sense the Bible is, for Protestants, ultimate. But note with care the sense in which this is so. It is ultimate in the sense that when human beings read this record of God's grace with true openness and longing for God, God stands at the supreme intersection between the divine and the human. There, more than anywhere else in the world of time and space, people have the prospect of catching, not with their minds alone but with their whole beings, the truth about God and the relation in which God stands to their lives. No derivative interpretation by councils, peoples, or theologians can replace or equal this. The Word of God must speak to each individual soul directly. It is this that accounts for the Protestant emphasis on the Bible as the *living* word of God.

Is not this concept of Christianity freighted with danger? The Protestant readily admits that it is. First, there is the danger of misconstruing God's word. If, as the Protestant Principle insists, all things human are imperfect, does it not follow that each individual's vision of God must at least be limited and possibly quite erroneous? It does. Protestantism not only admits this; it insists on it. But as the fact happens to be true, how much better to recognize it and open the door to the corrections of the Holy Spirit working through other minds than to saddle Christendom with what is in fact limited truth masquerading as finality. As Jesus himself says: "I still have many things to say to you, but you cannot bear them now. When the Spirit of truth comes, he will guide you into all the truth" (John 16:12). One very important reason for restricting final loyalty to the transcendent God is to keep the future open.

The other danger is that Christians will derive different truths from the Bible. The nine hundred-odd denominations of Protestantism in the United States alone prove not only that this danger exists, but that it could conceivably slope toward complete individualism. Protestantism admits this, but adds three points.

First, Protestant diversity is not as great as its hundreds of denominations, most of them more adequately termed sects, suggest. Most of these are of negligible size. Actually, 85 percent of all Protestants belong to twelve denominations. Considering the freedom of belief Protestantism affirms in principle, the wonder lies not in its diversity but in the extent to which Protestants have managed to stay together.

Second, Protestant divisions reflect differing national origins in Europe or differing social groupings in the United States more than they do differing theologies.

The third point, however, is the most important. Who is to say that diversity is bad? People differ, and historical circumstances, too, can occasion life-affecting differences that must be taken seriously: "New occasions teach new duties." Protestants believe that life and history are too fluid to allow God's redeeming Word to be enclosed in a single form, whether it be doctrinal *or* institutional. They are concerned about the brokenness of Christ's "body" and take steps to mend differences that are no longer meaningful; this is the so-called ecumenical movement, which is vigorous. But they do not believe that people should cuddle up to one another just to keep warm. Comforts of togetherness should not lead to structures that will restrict the dynamic character of God's continuing revelation. "The Spirit bloweth where it listeth" (John 3:8).

Protestants acknowledge, then, that their perspective is fraught with dangers—the danger of uncertainty as individuals wrestle inwardly (and at times in what seems like a frightening aloneness) to try to determine whether they have heard God's will correctly; the danger of schism as Christians find themselves apprehending God's will diversely. But they accept these dangers because, risk for risk, they prefer their precarious freedom to the security of doctrines or institutions that, even while looking toward God, remain fallible. It is their faith that, in the end, prevents these burdens from discouraging them. Asked where he would stand if the Church excommunicated him, Luther is said to have replied, "Under the sky."

Suggestions for Further Reading

For the general reader the most helpful book on Jesus' life and mission is Marcus Borg's *Jesus: A New Vision* (San Francisco: Harper & Row, 1988).

Those who wish to move more deeply into New Testament scholarship will find Edward Schillebeeckx's *Jesus* (New York: Crossroad, 1981) impressive. Elisabeth Schüssler Fiorenza's *In Memory of Her: A Feminist Theological Reconstruction of Christian Origins* (New York: Crossroad, 1984) reviews early materials responsibly from a feminine perspective. Gerd Theissen's *The Shadow of the Galilean*

(Philadelphia: Fortress Press, 1987) is an effective historical novel about Jesus and his movement by today's foremost German New Testament scholar.

Jaroslav Pelikan uses Jesus as a prism through which to provide an overview of Christian thought in his *Jesus Through the Centuries* (New York: Harper & Row, 1987). Hans Kung's *On Being a Christian* explains what Christianity means to an informed and thoughtful contemporary.

For the three major branches of Christendom, the following are recommended: Karl Adam, *The Spirit of Catholicism* (New York: Doubleday, 1954); Timothy Ware, *The Orthodox Church* (New York: Penguin Books, 1986); and George W. Forell, *The Protestant Faith* (Columbus, OH: Augsburg Fortress Publications, 1975).

For the Christian Mystics, see Louis Dupré and James Wiseman (eds.), *Light from Light: An Anthology of Christian Mysticism* (New York: Paulist Press, 1988).

Notes

1. The figures are from the 1989 *Encyclopedia Britannica Book of the Year.*
2. Marcus Borg, *Jesus: A New Vision* (San Francisco: Harper & Row, 1988), 15.
3. See the chapters on "Excluded Knowledge" and "Beyond the Modern Western Mindset," in Huston Smith, *Beyond the Post-Modern Mind* (Wheaton, IL: Quest Books, 1989).
4. B. Alan Wallace, *Choosing Reality* (Boston: Shambhala, 1989), 11. See also Smith, *Beyond the Post-Modern Mind,* 60; and his summary of David Bohm on this point, 76.
5. Borg, *Jesus,* 61.
6. Elisabeth Schüssler Fiorenza, *In Memory of Her: A Feminist Theological Reconstruction of Christian Origins* (New York: Crossroad, 1983), esp. 68–159.
7. E. Schillebeeckx, *Jesus* (New York: Crossroad, 1981), 201.
8. Robert Penn Warren, *Brother to Dragons,* 1953. Rev. ed., (New York: Random House, 1979).
9. Practically speaking, this distinction holds; but theologically, the divine and human aspects of the Mystical Body are regarded as inseparably united, paralleling the dual nature of Christ himself.
10. Meeting from 1962–1965, the Second Vatican Council reaffirmed this position. "Those also can attain to salvation who . . . strive by their deeds to do [God's] will as it is known to them through the dictates of conscience" (*Lumen Gentium,* The Church, paragraph 16).

11. I. M. Lewis, *Ecstatic Religion*, 1971. Reprint. (New York: Penguin, 1978), 11.
12. Thomas Corbishley, *Roman Catholicism* (London: Hutchinson House, 1950), 40.
13. Francis de Sales, *Introduction to the Devout Life* (New York: Harper & Row, 1966), 40–41.
14. The Roman Church agrees on this point with, of course, the pope as bishop of Rome included in such councils. It also holds that the bishops are infallible when, in the absence of formal definition, they nevertheless teach unanimously that a given doctrine is divinely revealed and to be believed by all the faithful. The differences lie in the sharp line the Roman Church draws between clergy and laity in the preaching of its doctrines and (as stated) in the absence in the Eastern Church of the final authoritative voice of a single individual.
15. It is interesting to reflect on how much both these emphases of Eastern Orthodoxy, its mysticism and it sensitivity to the interrelatedness of lives, figure in Russian novels, especially those of Dostoevsky and Tolstoy.
16. James is explicit on this point. "Faith without works is dead" (James 2:17, 20, 26).

IX. *The Primal Religions*

This book has dealt with the major historical religions. Historical religions have sacred texts and a cumulative tradition that builds and develops. The Christianity of the Middle Ages is not that of the Apostolic Church any more than NeoConfucianism is the Confucianism its founder taught, though in both cases strong continuities can be discerned.

The historical religions now pretty much blanket the earth, but chronologically they form only the tip of the religious iceberg; for they span less than four thousand years as compared with the three million years or so of the religions that preceded them. During that immense time span people lived their religion in an importantly different mode, which must have shaped their sensibilities significantly. We shall call their religious pattern primal because it came first, but alternatively we shall refer to it as tribal because its groupings were invariably small, or oral because writing was unknown to them. This mode of religiosity continues in Africa, Australia, Southeast Asia, the Pacific Islands, Siberia, and among the Indians of North and South America. Its numbers are diminishing, but we devote this final substantive chapter to them, partly to pay them tribute but also for the contrasting light they can throw on the historical religions that have engaged us. What was, and in the places just mentioned still is, the religion of peoples who live in small communities, on subsistent economies that are the direct product of their own efforts, and without depending on writing? Without hope of doing justice to the subject, and skirting almost entirely the continental and intracontinental differences among them, we shall try to catch a glimpse of human religiousness in its earliest mode. It is a more-than-academic exercise, for we can be sure that remnants of this mode survive as psychic traces in our deep unconscious. There is also the possibility that we might learn from them, for tribes may have retained insights and virtues that urbanized, industrial civilizations have allowed to fall by the wayside.

The Australian Experience

We can begin by putting behind us the nineteenth-century prejudice that later means better, a view that may hold for technology, but not for religion. History does show that social roles become more differentiated as societies grow in size and complexity. Lines between clergy and laity get drawn, and divisions between sacred and secular come to view; in this respect later societies resemble later biological species, which develop differentiated limbs and organs. But in both cases life was present from the start, and in the religious case it is a mistake to assume that later historical expressions are nobler than earlier ones. If God does not evolve, neither, it seems, does *homo religiosus,* not in any important respect. Mircea Eliade came to believe that archaic peoples are more spiritual than their descendants because, clothed as they are in leaves and skins and nourished directly by the fruits of the earth, they are unencumbered by external devices. However that may be, everything that we find flowering in the historical religions — monotheism, for example — is prefigured in the primal ones in faint but discernible patterns.

The muted character of distinctions in the primal religions — distinctions that in the historical religions explode into opposites, such as heaven and hell, or *samsara* and *nirvana* — provides a fitting entry into our subject and one that is nicely illustrated by the religion of the Australian aborigines. Australia is the only continent that did not undergo the Neolithic experience, which elsewhere began about 10,000 B.C. and witnessed the invention of farming and technically advanced stone implements. This exemption places the Australian aborigines closest among extant peoples to the earth's original human inhabitants, with the negligible exception of a tiny tribe in the Philippines, the Tassaday, whose authenticity is disputed. The world of aboriginal religion is a single one. We shall see that other primal religions resemble it in this respect, but the "antiquity" of the aborigines makes the sharpest division in their world—every world includes divisions of some sort—seem subdued in comparison to its counterparts in other primal cosmologies.

The distinction we have in mind is that between the aborigines' ordinary life and what anthropologists began by calling their "mythic world" (*le monde mythique;* Lēvy-Bruhl) but now refer to by the aborigines' own term, "the Dreaming." This latter term has the advantage of indicating that there are not two worlds, but instead a single world that can be experienced in different ways.

The world that the aborigines ordinarily experience is measured out by time; the seasons cycle, and generations come and go. Meanwhile, the backdrop for this unending procession is stable. Time does not touch it, for it is "everywhen." Legendary figures people this backdrop world. They are not gods; they are much like ourselves, while at the same time being larger than life. What gives them their exceptional status is that they originated, or better instituted, the paradigmatic acts of which daily life consists. They were geniuses for having molded and thereby modeled life's essential conditions—male and female; human, bird, fish, and the like—and its essential activities such as hunting, gathering, war, and love. We are inclined to say that when the Arunta go hunting they mime the exploits of the first and archetypal hunter, but this distinguishes them from their archetype too sharply. It is better to say that they enter the mold of their archetype so completely that each *becomes* the First Hunter; no distinction remains. Similarly for other activities, from basket weaving to lovemaking. Only while they are conforming their actions to the model of some archetypal hero do the Arunta feel that they are truly alive, for in those roles they are immortal. The occasions on which they slip from such molds are quite meaningless, for time immediately devours those occasions and reduces them to nothingness.

We can see from this that aboriginal religion turns not on worship but on identification, a "participation in," and acting out of, archetypal paradigms. The entire life of the aborigine, insofar as it rises above triviality and becomes authentic, is ritual. Mythic beings are not addressed, propitiated, or beseeched. The line that divides the human from those beings is broad in principle, but it can be easily erased, for it disappears in the moment of ritual merger when everywhen becomes now. Here there are no priests, no congregations, no mediating officiants, no spectators. There is only the Dreaming and conformance to it.

Parallels to the Dreaming motif abound, but nowhere with outlines quite as sharp as those in the Australian prototype. Though this difference is small, it is the only one in the population of the primal religions that we will mention. For the rest of the chapter we will be occupied with features that the primal religions share, and which set them apart as a group from the historical religions that have been this book's focus. The next section will consider their "orality"—a word invented to designate a mode of life in which words are spoken only, never written—and the distinctive ways they conceive of space and time. Other commonalities will emerge when their world view is outlined.

Orality, Place, and Time

Orality.   Literacy, we have noted, is unknown to the primal religions. To be sure, it has now visited some of them; but this changes little in our inquiry for, when it arrives, leaders usually shelter their tribe's sacred lore from its encroachments. To commit living myth and legend to lifeless script, they assume, would be to imprison it and sound its death knell. It is not easy for people who value writing to fathom their instinct here, but if we try we can perhaps catch a glimpse of why they consider writing to be not just a competitor to exclusive orality but one that threatens the virtues it bestows.

We can begin with the versatility of the spoken over the written word. Speech is a part of a speaker's life, and as such shares that life's vitality. This gives it a flexibility that can be tailored to speaker and hearer alike. Familiar themes can be enlivened by fresh diction. Rhythm can be introduced, together with intonations, pauses, and accentuations, until speaking borders on chanting, and storytelling emerges as a high art. Dialect and delivery can be added to flesh out characters that are being described, and when animal postures and gaits are mimed and their noises simulated, we are into theater. Silence can be invoked to heighten tension or suspense, and can even be used to indicate that the narrator has interrupted the story to engage in private prayer.

This much is obvious, but it scarcely touches on the distinctive genius of primal orality. For if we go no further than this, we leave the door open for advocates of writing to respond, "Fine; let's have both," which of course is what the historical religions do have; their scriptures share the stage with homilies, songs, pageants, and morality plays. We do not understand the distinctiveness of primal orality until we confront its exclusiveness, the way it views writing not as a supplement to speaking but its foe. For once introduced, writing does not leave the virtues of orality intact. In important ways it undercuts them.

Chief among the endowments that exclusive reliance on speech confers is human memory. Literate peoples grow slack in recall. "Why should I tax myself when I can find what I need written down somewhere?" is the lettered attitude toward memory. It is not difficult to see that things would be different if libraries were not available. The memories of blind people, for example, are legendary; and we can add this report from the New Hebrides: "The children are educated by listening and watching. . . . Without writing, memory is perfect, tradition exact. . . . The thousand myths which every child learns (often word perfect, and one story may last for hours) are a whole library." And what do they think of us? "The natives easily learn to write after white impact. They regard writing as a curious and useless performance. They say: 'Cannot a man remember and speak?'"[1]

To help us comprehend what life without writing would be like, we might try visualizing our forebears as bands of blind Homers who gather each evening around their fire after the day's work is accomplished. Everything that their ancestors learned with difficulty, from healing herbs to stirring legends, is now stored in their collective minds, and there only. Would they not cherish the heritage their conversation sustains? Would they not revere it and rehearse it endlessly, each supplementing and correcting the accounts of others?

What is important for us to understand here is the impact of this ongoing, empowering seminar on its participants. Everyone feeds the living reservoir of knowledge, while receiving in return its answering flow of information that shapes and stocks their lives. Each member of the tribe becomes its walking library. To see this as a genuine alternative to the advantages of reading, we can listen to an early adventurer in Africa who reported, "My trusted friend and companion was an old man who could not read or write, though well versed in stories of the past. The old chiefs listened enthralled.

Under the present system of [colonial] education there is grave risk that much of this may be lost."[2] Another traveler to Africa pointed out that "unlike the English system in which one could pass one's life without coming into contact with poetry, the Uraon tribal system uses poetry as a vital appendix to dancing, marriages and the cultivation of a crop—functions in which all Uraons join as a part of their tribal life. If we have to single out the factor which caused the decline of English village culture, we should have to say it was literacy."[3]

If exclusive orality protects human memory, it also guards against two other depletions. The first of these is the capacity to sense the sacred through nonverbal channels. Because writing can grapple with meanings explicitly, sacred texts tend to gravitate to positions of such eminence as to be considered the preeminent if not exclusive channel of revelation. This eclipses other means of divine disclosure. Oral traditions do not fall into this trap. The invisibility of their texts, which is to say their myths, leaves their eyes free to scan for other sacred portents, virgin nature and sacred art being the prime examples. In the Middle Ages, when Europe was even less lettered than China, "the ignorant and unlettered man could read the meaning of sculptures that now only trained archaeologists can interpret."[4]

Finally, because writing has no limits, it can proliferate to the point where people get lost in its endless corridors. Secondary material comes to blur what is important. Minds become waterlogged with information and narrowed through specialization. Memory is protected against such cripplings. Being embedded in life, life calls it to count at every turn, and what is useless and irrelevant is quickly weeded out.

We can summarize the gifts of exclusive orality by quoting anthropologist Paul Radin. "The disorientation in our whole psychic life and in our whole apperception of the external realities produced by the invention of the alphabet, the whole tendency of which has been to elevate thought and thinking to the rank of the exclusive proof of all verities, never occurred among [tribal] peoples."[5]

Place versus Space..   A second distinguishing feature of primal religion is its embeddedness in place. Place is not space. Whereas space is abstract, place is concrete. A cubic yard of space is identical wherever we calculate it, but no two places are alike, as Stephen Foster's refrain, "There's no place like home," attests.

Many historical religions are attached to places; Judaism and Shinto, both of which began as primal religions, come immediately to mind. No historical religion, however, is embedded in place to the extent that tribal religions are. Two anecdotes, both drawn from the Onondaga tribe of the *Hau de no sau nee* (the Six Nations in upstate New York), can serve to make this point.

Oren Lyons was the first Onondagan to enter college. When he returned to his reservation for his first vacation, his uncle proposed a fishing trip on a lake. Once he had his nephew in the middle of the lake where he wanted him, he began to interrogate him. "Well, Oren," he said, "you've been to college; you must be pretty smart now from all they've been teaching you. Let me ask you a question. Who are you?" Taken aback by the question, Oren fumbled for an answer. "What do you mean, who am I? Why, I'm your nephew, of course." His uncle rejected his answer and repeated his question. Successively, the nephew ventured that he was Oren Lyons, an Onondagan, a human being, a man, a young man, all to no avail. When his uncle had reduced him to silence and he asked to be informed as to who he was, his uncle said, "Do you see that bluff over there? Oren, you *are* that bluff. And that giant pine on the other shore? Oren, you are that pine. And this water that supports our boat? You are this water."[6]

The second anecdote comes from the same tribe. An outdoor ceremony in which this author was included opened with a prayer that lasted for fifty minutes. No eyes were closed; on the contrary, everyone seemed to be actively looking around. As the prayer was offered in native tongue, I could understand nothing of it. When I later asked its content, I was told that the entire prayer had been devoted to naming everything in sight, animate and "inanimate," with the invisible spirits of the area included, inviting them to join in the occasion and bless its proceedings.

It would be wrong to think that attention to detail (in this second anecdote) and to ancestral setting (in the first) makes this notion of place confining. When the Australian Kurnai go on walkabouts, the concreteness of place goes with them. The springs and major trees and rocks that they encounter are not interchangeable with others of their kind; each triggers memories of the legendary events they were a part of. The Navajos do not even need to leave home for their sense of place to balloon. By fashioning their dwellings to the world's shape, their buildings draw the world into their homes. The pillars that support their roofs are named for, and thus identified with, the deities that support the entire cosmos: Earth, Mountain Woman, Water Woman, and Corn Woman.

In the opening pages of *The Savage Mind,* Claude Lévi-Strauss quotes a native thinker as remarking, penetratingly, that "all sacred things must have their place." The observation argues that location in place—not any place, but in each and every instance the exact and rightful place—is a feature of sanctity. "Being in their place," Lévi-Strauss continues, "is what makes [objects] sacred; for if they were taken out of their place, even in thought, the entire order of the universe would be destroyed."[7]

Eternal time. In contrast to the historical religions of the West, which are messianically forward looking, primal religions give the appearance of looking toward the past. That is not altogether wrong, and from the Western perspective, where time is linear, there is no other way to put the matter. But primal time is not linear, a straight line that moves from the past, through the present, into the future. It is not even cyclical as the Asian religions tend to regard it, turning in the way the world turns and seasons cycle. Primal time is atemporal; an eternal now. To speak of atemporal or timeless time is paradoxical, but the paradox can be relieved if we see that primal time focuses on causal rather than chronological sequence; for primal peoples, "past" means preeminently closer to the originating Source of things. That the Source precedes the present is of secondary importance.

The word Source is used here to refer to the gods who, where they did not actually create the world, ordered it and gave it its viable structure. Those gods continue to exist, of course, but that does not shift interest to the present, for the past continues to be considered the Golden Age. When divine creation had suffered no ravages of time and mismanagement, the world was as it should be. That is no longer the case, for a certain enfeeblement has occurred; thus steps are needed to restore the world to its original condition. "For religious man of the archaic cultures," Mircea Eliade writes, "the world is renewed annually; in other words, with each new year it recovers its original sanctity, the sanctity that it possessed when it came from the Creator's hands."[8] Altars are erected that simulate the world's original shape, and the mandating words the gods uttered on the day the world was created are faithfully repeated. We can liken such rites of renewal to telephone poles that boost sagging cables. The annual

Sun Dance of the Plains Indians is called the Dance for World and Life Renewal. Individual tasks, too, need renewing. For example, the Polynesian Island of Tikopia has a ritual for repairing boats. In it a boat is repaired, not because it needs repair but ritualistically, "according to specifications," as we might say, which in this case means the way the gods demonstrated the repair of boats. The ritual recharges this important island activity with significance and at the same time reinstates standards that may have slipped.

If we stopped here we would have said nothing distinctive about the primal view of time, for historical religions too have renewal rites, these being a feature of their primal heritage that they have retained. All of them have solstice festivals of some sort to reverse the winter's darkness, as well as "easters" to abet nature's rebirth. In Taiwan the Taoist festival *Chiao* effects renewal through rituals that span a sixty-year cycle, for just as nature needs to be revived each spring, so too must the greater cosmos be renewed on the scale of a human lifespan. Everyone participates in these rites. Preparations for a given phase of the cycle can take years, and the financial outlay is enormous.

For a feature of the primal view of time that the historical religions have largely abandoned, we can turn to the way it tends to rank order beings according to their proximity to their divine source. Thus animals are often venerated for their "anteriority," and among animals the otter's relative stupidity leads the Winnebagos to infer that it was created last. This principle applies to the human species as well; its pioneers are revered over their descendants, who are regarded as something of epigones. Primal peoples respect their elders enormously.

East Asians do likewise with their filial piety and ancestor worship; and it can be remarked in passing that Taoism and its Japanese cousin Shinto are the historical religions that across the board have remained closest to their primal roots. But to stay with the primal religions, it is not going too far to say that they think of their gods in more or less ancestral terms. Human ancestors are viewed as prolongations of the tribe's earliest ancestors, who were divine. This makes them a bridge that connects the current generation with its first and supreme ancestor; one thinks again of Shinto, where the Emperor is the direct descendant of the Sun Goddess Amaterasu, and the Japanese people are her indirect descendants. Standing closer to the gods than does the present generation, ancestors are seen as inheriting more of their virtues, which makes them models for conduct. Exempt from the complications of life that devolution introduces, ancestors are thought to enjoy a wholeness of character that their offspring lack. The assumption probably arises not from Freud's postulate of subconscious idealizations of parental figures, but from deeper regions of intuition; from an instinctive ontological recognition that closer-to-the-source means to be in some sense better. In any case, all that has been said of the ancestors applies to some extent to elders of the current generation. Even the childlikeness and naivete of their later years tends to be regarded as an advance toward the state of paradisiacal rightness that preceded the world's decline. Toward the close of his life, Black Elk , a shaman of the Oglala Sioux, often fell to all fours to play with toddlers. "We have much in common," he said. "They have just come from the Great Mysterious and I am about to return to it."

We turn now to other features of primal religion that are embedded in its worldview. In sketching that view we continue to use broad strokes, confining ourselves to features that remain relatively constant beneath the variety of concrete cosmologies through which they find expression.

The Primal World

A useful place to begin is with the embeddedness of primal peoples in their world. This starts with their tribe, apart from which they sense little independent identity. The web of tribal relationships sustains them psychologically and energizes every aspect of their life. To be separated from the tribe threatens them with death, not only physically but psychologically as well. Other tribes might be viewed as alien and even hostile, but to their own tribe they are related in almost the way that a biological organ is related to its host's body.

As for the tribe, it is embedded in nature, and again so solidly that the line between the two is not easy to establish. Indeed, in the case of totemism it does not exist. We shall continue with totemism in a moment, but let us first note the route we shall be taking. The contrary of embeddedness is a world of scissions and segregations, so we shall approach the embeddedness of primal life by noticing the relative absence of these in its world. Totemism is a fitting place to begin, because it shows primal peoples disregarding altogether the division between animal and human.

In totemism a human tribe is joined to an animal species in a social and ceremonial whole that gives them a common life. The totem animal bonds the human members of its clan distinctively to one another, while acting as their mate, friend, guardian, and helper, for it is of their "flesh." They, in return, respect it and refuse to injure it unless in dire distress. The totem animal serves as the clan's emblem, and at the same time symbolizes the ancestor or hero whom the members commemorate. It also symbolizes the life force of the species, for the health of which the human members of the totem are ritually responsible. All this springs from the conviction that human beings and nature belong to a single order. Rituals for increasing the totem species do not stem from standing apart from nature and attempting to control it. They are, instead, expressions of human needs, specifically the need for the normal order of nature to be preserved. They are ways of cooperating with nature at those seasons when the increase of a particular species, or when rainfall for that matter, should occur. Rather than being attempts to produce extraordinary effects or control nature magically, primal rites work mainly to maintain the regular and normal; they are rituals of cooperation. As such they have both economic and psychological sides. While articulating economic facts and needs, they also sustain confidence in the processes of nature, spiritually conceived and determined, and renew hope for the future.

Totemism itself is not universal among tribal peoples, but they all share its nonchalance concerning the animal/human division. Animals and birds are frequently referred to as "peoples," and in certain circumstances animals and humans can exchange forms and convert to their opposite numbers. The division between animal and vegetable is equally muted, for plants have spirits like the rest of us. The following anecdote can illustrate this; it was related to the author by the father of a student who was involved. At one point the art department of Arizona State University decided to offer a course on basket weaving, and approached a neighboring Indian reservation for an instructor. The tribe proposed its masterweaver, an old woman, for the position. The entire course turned out to consist of trips to the plants that provided the fibers for her baskets, where myths involving the plants were recounted and supplicating songs and prayers were memorized. There was no weaving.

The progression of the preceding paragraph reaches its logical term when we note that even the line between animate and "inanimate" is perforated. Rocks are alive. Under certain conditions they are believed to be able to talk, and at times — as in the case of Ayers Rock in Australia — they are considered divine. It is easy to see how this absence of discontinuities produces embeddedness. Primal peoples are not blind to nature's differences; they are famous for their powers of observation. The point is rather that they see distinctions as bridges instead of barriers. Fertility cycles, along with the ceremonies that celebrate and sustain them, establish a creative harmony between humanity and its setting, with myths confirming the symbiosis at every turn. Male and female contribute equally to the cosmic life force. All beings, not overlooking heavenly bodies and the elements of wind and rain, are brothers and sisters. Everything is alive, and each depends in ways on all the others. As we continue this meditation on embeddedness, there comes a point where the order reverses itself and we begin to think, not of primal peoples as embedded in nature, but of nature, seeking itself, as extending itself to enter deeply into them, infusing them in order to be fathomed by them.

Turning from the world's structure to human activities, we are again struck by the relative absence of compartmentalizations between them. For example, "Among the languages of American Indians there is no word for 'art,' because for Indians everything is art."[9] Equally, everything is, in its way, religious. This means that to learn of primal religion, we can start anywhere, with paintings, dance, drama, poetry, songs, dwellings, or even utensils and other artifacts. Or we could study the daily doings of its peoples, which are also not separated in sacred and profane. A hunter, for example, does not set out simply to assuage his tribes' hunger. He launches on a complex of meditative acts, all of which — whether preparatory prayer and purification, pursuit of the quarry, or the sacramental manner by which the animal is slain and subsequently treated — are imbued with sanctity. An inquirer who lived with Black Elk for two years reported the latter's assertion that hunting is — Black Elk did not say represents, the reporter emphasized — life's quest for ultimate truth; the quest requires preparatory prayer and sacrificial purification. "The diligently followed tracks are signs or intimations of the goal, and the final contact or identity with the quarry is the realization of Truth, the ultimate goal of life."[10]

Thus far we have been noting the absence of sharp divisions within the primal world, but another absence is, if anything, more telling; namely, the absence of a line separating this world from another world that stands over and against it. In the historical religions this division emerges and much comes to be made of it.[11]

Plato, speaking philosophically for Greek religion, presents the body as a tomb. The Hebrew Scriptures contrast the created world with a holy, righteous, transcendent Lord. For Hinduism the world is *maya*, only marginally real. The Buddha likened the world to a burning house from which escape is imperative. An apocryphal account has Jesus saying, "The world is a bridge; pass over, but build no house upon it." The Koran compares the world to vegetation that will be quickly harvested or turn to straw. In Japan Master Taishi called the world a lie against which only the Buddha is true. World devaluation figures prominently in the historical religions.

In primal ones divisions of such severity never appear; there is, for example, nothing like the notion of creation *ex nihilo*. Primal peoples are, we are emphasizing, oriented to a single cosmos, which sustains them like a living womb. Because they assume that it exists to nurture them, they have no disposition to challenge it, defy it, refashion it, or escape from it. It is not a place of exile or pilgrimage, though pilgrimages take place within it. Its space is not homogeneous; the home has a number of rooms, we might say, some of which are normally invisible. But together they constitute a single domicile. Primal peoples are concerned with the maintenance of personal, social, and cosmic harmony, and with attaining specific goods—rain, harvest, children, health—as people always are. But the overriding goal of salvation that dominates the historical religions is virtually absent from them, and life after death tends to be a shadowy semi-existence in some vaguely designated place in their single domain.

The Symbolic Mind

A summary of the primal world as thus far sketched shows its internal divisions to be provisional and there to be no transcendent reality that relativizes it. All of this, however, would amount to a string of zeros without a digit to confer value on them were we not to introduce the divine source from which the world is believed to issue, or in other versions, divine arrangers who bring order out of chaos. The presence of these divinities raises the question of theism in the primal traditions, and it must be considered carefully, for the issue is a subtle one.

A common stereotype pegs primal religions as polytheistic, and this is not altogether wrong if the word tokens that the divine can congeal in hallowed places and alight on specific objects. But this has nothing to do with the flat, Olympian, and Mediterranean polytheism generally that the Bible had to contend with; nor does it militate against a single Ultimate of which the many gods are instantiations or expressions. Wilhelm Schmidt's twelve-volume *Ursprung der Gottesidee*,[12] concluded that every then-known tribe—the work was published between 1912 and 1955—had its High God who lives and works through its deputies. The Yoruba of West Africa, for example, never rank their Supreme Being, Olodimave, with lesser divinities *(orisa)*, nor do the Edo confuse Osanobuwa with the *ebo*. Even if Schmidt overstates the case, however, this scarcely matters; for the issue is not whether tribal peoples explicitly identify a Supreme Being who coordinates the gods but instead, whether they *sense* such a being whether they name and personify it or not. The evidence suggests that they do. As the Navajo artist Carl Gorman points out: "Some researchers into Navajo religion say that we have no supreme God because he is not named. This is not so. The Supreme Being is not named because he is unknowable. He is simply the Unknown Power. We worship him through his creation for he is everything in his creation. The various forms of creation have some of his spirit within them."[13] One can call this pan- or poly-monotheism if one wishes. The fact remains that though primal religions affirm the divine Unity less exclusively, and in some cases seem even to veil it, they contain nothing that is strictly comparable to the anthropomorphic polytheism of the early Europeans. It is just that the holy, the sacred, the *wakan* as the Sioux call it, need not be exclusively attached, or consciously attached at all, to a distinguishable Supreme Being.

Something may even be lost by so attaching it, that loss being the removal of holiness from things that are other than the God that is factored out. This brings us to what is probably the most important single feature of living primal spirituality; namely, what has been called its symbolist mentality.[14] The symbolist vision sees the things of the world as transparent to their divine source. Whether that source is specified or not, the world's objects are open to its light. Physical sight presents the water in a lake in existential isolation, for as far as the eye reports, the body of water exists as a reality in its own right. From there modern thought may go on to reason that the water is composed of oxygen and hydrogen, and if a spiritual gloss is desired it may attribute to the water allegorical significance. Normally, however, modernity recognizes no ontological connection between material things and their metaphysical, spiritual roots. In this respect primal peoples are better metaphysicians, though their metaphysics, where articulated—we have seen that it need not be—is naturally of mythic cast. When ethnologists declared that for the Algonquins "there is no *manitu* [spirit] outside the world of appearances," this simply meant that they were unaware that for the primal mind appearances never exist entirely on their own. As the friend of Black Elk whom we have already mentioned puts the point:

> *It is often difficult for those who look on the tradition of the Red Man from the outside or through the "educated" mind to understand that no object is what it appears to be, but it is simply the pale shadow of a Reality. It is for this reason that every created object is* wakan, *holy, and has a power according to the loftiness of the spiritual reality that it reflects. The Indian humbles himself before the whole of creation because all visible things were created before him and, being older than he, deserve respect.*[15]

A student of the Musicas in the high Andes of Columbia confirms this point: "All primordial men saw the 'more' in the 'less,' in the sense that the landscape was for them a reflection of a superior reality which 'contained' the physical reality; they added, may one say, to the latter, a 'spiritual dimension' which escapes modern man."[16]

Paul Radin, who was mentioned earlier, was as impatient as any anthropologist with the "erroneous impression" that primal people are mystics across the board. He insisted that we find among them, as among us, "two general types of temperament: the man of action and the thinker, the type which lives fairly exclusively on what might be called a motor level and the type that demands explanations and derives pleasure from some form of speculative thinking." Yet he would "not for a moment," he said, "deny that mysticism and symbolism are more frequently utilized among them than among Western Europeans today. . . . Only when we have fully grasped the mystic and symbolic meanings inherent in most of the activities of primitive man can we hope to understand him."[17] As an example of what he was referring to, we can cite the tribesman who pointed out that the circles in spider webs are sticky, whereas its radii are not. This means, he said, that if you wander from side to side in life you get stuck, but if you move toward its center you don't.

This section should not end without mentioning a distinctive personality type, the shaman—widespread but not universal in tribal societies—who can bypass symbolism and perceive spiritual realities directly. We can think of shamans as spiritual savants, savant being defined as a person whose talents, be they in music (Mozart), drama (Shakespeare), mathematics, or whatever domain, are exceptional to the point of belonging to a different order of magnitude. Subject to severe physical and emotional traumas in their early years, shamans are able to heal themselves and reintegrate their lives in ways that place psychic if not cosmic powers at their disposal. These powers enable them to engage with spirits, both good and evil, drawing power from the former and battling the latter where need be. They are heavily engaged in healing, and appear to have preternatural powers to foretell the future and discern lost objects.

Conclusion

As between the primal and the historical religions, time seems to be on the side of the latter, for though millions would now like to see the primal way of life continue, it seems unlikely that it will do so. "Civilization" is seductive where not imperious, and we cannot quarantine the primal peoples who remain, preserving them for anthropologists to study and the rest of us to romanticize as symbols of our lost paradise. How industrial peoples will comport themselves toward the primal in what seems to be the short time they have left on this planet will be the final topic of this chapter.

The historical religions have largely abandoned their earlier missionary designs on "the heathen," as they were once disparagingly referred to. If anything, the pendulum has swung in the opposite direction, toward romanticizing the primal. Dismayed by the relentless utilitarianism of technological society and its seeming inability to contain its power to destroy both people and planet, citified peoples have come to hope that a fundamentally different way of life is possible, and they latch onto primal peoples to support that hope. Guilt enters the picture too, as the descendants of those who had power face up to the ways their forbears looked down on, despoiled, and destroyed those who lacked it. Whether things could have gone differently, given what the conquerors then understood and the seemingly irresistible disposition of those who possess power to abuse it, we shall never know. What we do know, and it is at least to our credit that we now confess it, is that there was holocaust on a global scale.

On the positive side we can note that we now recognize that we were mistaken in our assessment of these people. Primal peoples are not primitive and uncivilized, much less savage. They are not backward; they are different. They are not impaired; they are apart. With this realization in place and disparagement of the primal behind us, we return for a moment to our current propensity to romanticize these people, for there is an aspect of that impulse that is not widely understood.

Disenchantment with the complexities and mistakes of industrial life, the scission between human beings and nature it has effected, and the bitter fruits that that scission has borne, have (as we were saying) produced by way of reaction the image of tribal peoples as wholly natural. We regard them as sons and daughters of the earth and sky, brothers and sisters of animals and plants, who live by nature's ways and do not upset the delicate balances of their ecological zones; gentle hunting folk who are still in touch with the magic and myth that we ourselves so badly need. Seeing them thus, we assume that our ancestors resembled them in these respects and we celebrate them as our heroes. There is a deep, unconscious reason for this bent of thought. Every people, ourselves not excepted, needs to think well of its origins; it is part of having a healthy self-image. So modern peoples, who are no longer confident that God created them, transfer some of God's nobility to the source from which they assume that they did derive, namely early humankind. This is the deepest impulse behind "the myth of the noble savage" that the eighteenth century invented.

What may be hoped is that we are now ready to put both prejudice and idealization behind us. If we are, perhaps we can live out our numbered years of planetary partnership in mutual respect, guided by the dream of one primal spokesman that "we may be brothers after all." If we succeed in doing this, there is still time for us to learn some things from them. For, tabling shortcomings that are not the issue here, it is not romantic to affirm what John Collier, one time United States Commissioner of Indian Affairs, said of his charges:

> *They had what the world has lost: the ancient, lost reverence and passion for human personality joined with the ancient, lost reverence and passion for the earth and its web of life. Since before the Stone Age they have tended that passion as a central, sacred fire. It should be our long hope to renew it in us all.*[18]

Suggestions for Further Reading

Robert Bellah's essay on "Religious Evolution" in his *Beyond Belief* (Berkeley and Los Angeles: University of California Press, 1991) does the best job of positioning the primal peoples in historical perspective. Sam Gill's *Beyond "The Primitive"* (Englewood Cliffs, NJ: Prentice-Hall, 1982) corrects a number of deep-seated errors that plague our approach to them and attempts to develop a more self-conscious approach to the study of their religions.

For African religions see Noel King, *African Cosmos: An Introduction to Religion in Africa* (Belmont, CA: Wadsworth Publishing Company, 1986) and John Mbiti, *Introduction to African Religion* (New York: Praeger, 1975).

Joseph Epes Brown's *The Spiritual Legacy of the American Indian* (New York: Crossroad, 1989) treats the Native American traditions comprehensively. Frithjof Schuon's *The Feathered Sun* (Bloomington, IN: World Wisdom Books, 1990) plumbs their metaphysical depths in words and paintings.

Notes

1. Tom Harrisson, *Savage Civilization* (New York: Alfred Knopf, 1937), 45, 344, 353.
2. R. St. Barbe Baker, *African Drums*, 145, as quoted in Ananda K. Coomaraswamy, *The Bugbear of Literacy* (Pates Manor, Bedfont, England: Perennial Books, 1949–1979), 38.
3. W. G. Archer, *Journal of the Bihar and Orissa Research Society*, 29:68.

4. Edward Prior and Arthur Gardner, *An Account of Medieval Figure-Sculpture in England* (Cambridge: Cambridge University Press, 1912), 25.

5. Paul Radin, *Primitive Man as Philosopher* (New York: Dover Publications, 1927/1957), 61.

6. Related to the author by Chief Oren Lyons.

7. Claude Levi-Strauss, *The Savage Mind* (Chicago: The University of Chicago Press, 1966), 10.

8. Mircea Eliade, *The Sacred and the Profane,* 1957. Reprint. (New York: Harcourt Brace Jovanovich, 1959), 75.

9. Jamake Highwater, *The Primal Mind* (New York: Harper & Row, 1981), 13.

10. Reported by Joseph Epes Brown, *The Spiritual Legacy of the American Indian,* 1987. Reprint. (New York: Crossroad, 1989), 73–74.

11. This paragraph and the next owe much to Robert Bellah's article on "Religious Evolution" in his collection of essays titled *Beyond Belief,* 1970. Reprint. (Los Angeles and Berkeley: University of California Press, 1991).

12. Abridged in English as Wilhelm Schmidt, *The Origin and Growth of Religion: Facts and Theories,* translated by H. J. Rose (London: Methuen & Co., 1931).

13. Quoted in Joseph Epes Brown, "Modes of Contemplation Through Action: North American Indians," in *Main Currents in Modern Thought* 30, no. 2 (November/December, 1973): 58–59.

14. As in Frithjof Schuon's chapter on "The Symbolist Mind" in his book *The Feathered Sun* (Bloomington, IN: World Wisdom Books, 1990).

15. From a letter written by Joseph Epes Brown, quoted in Schuon, *The Feathered Sun,* 47.

16. Francois Petitpierre, "The Symbolic Landscape of the Musicas," *Studies in Comparative Religion* (Winter 1975): 48.

17. Radin, *Primitive Man,* 230, 212, 208.

18. John Collier, *Indians of the Americas* (New York: New American Library, 1947). Slightly rearranged from pages 1 and 7.

X. A Final Examination

The most obvious question that suggests itself at the close of this inquiry is: What have we gotten out of it? Has it done any good?

It would be surprising if we had not picked up some facts along the way: what the *yogas* are, Buddha's analysis of the cause of life's dislocation, Confucius' ideal of the true gentleman, what the *yin/yang* symbol signifies, the literal meaning of "Islam," what the Exodus means to the Jews, what was the "good news" that excited the early Christians, and so on. Such facts are not to be belittled; a well-stocked mind adds interest to the world that comes its way. But is this all?

New questions may have emerged from the reading, or old ones assumed new urgency. Three such questions suggest themselves, and their consideration will round off this study. First, how are we to *gestalt* or pattern the religions we have considered? Having listened to them individually, what do we now take to be their relationships to one another? Second, have they anything to say collectively to the world at large? Granted their variety, do they speak with a concerted voice on any important matters? Third, how should we comport ourselves in a world that is religiously pluralistic where it is religious at all?

The Relation between Religions

To the question of how to pattern these religions, three answers suggest themselves. The first holds that one of the world's religions is superior to the others. Now that the peoples of the world are getting to know one another better, we hear this answer less often than we

384

used to; but even so it should not be dismissed out of hand. The opening chapter of this book quoted Arnold Toynbee as saying that no one alive knows enough to say with confidence whether or not one religion is superior to the others—the question remains an open one. True, this book has found nothing that privileges one tradition above the others, but that could be due to the kind of book it is: It eschews comparisons in principle. Nothing in the comparative study of religions requires that they cross the finishing line of the reader's regard in a dead heat.

A second position lies at the opposite end of the spectrum: It holds that the religions are all basically alike. Differences are acknowledged but, according to this second view, they are incidental in comparison to the great enduring truths on which the religions unite.

This appeals to our longing for human togetherness, but on inspection it proves to be the trickiest position of the three. For as soon as it moves beyond vague generalities—"every religion has some version of the Golden Rule"; or, "Surely we all believe in some sort of something," as a Member of Parliament once ventured following a bitter debate in the House of Commons over the Book of Common Prayer—it founders on the fact that the religions differ in what they consider essential and what negotiable. Hinduism and Buddhism split over this issue, as did Judaism, Christianity, and Islam. In the nineteenth century Alexander Campbell tried to unite Protestants on grounds of their common acceptance of the Bible as the model for faith and organization. To his surprise he discovered that denominational leaders were not prepared to concede that the uniting principle he proposed was more important than their distinctive tenets; his movement ended by adding another denomination—the Disciples of Christ (Christian Church)—to the Protestant roster. On a world scale Baha'u'llah's mission came to the same end. Baha'i, which originated in the hope of rallying the major religions around the beliefs they held in common, has settled into being another religion among many.

Because this second position is powered by the hope that there may someday be a single world religion, it is well to remind ourselves again of the human element in the religious equation. There are people who want to have their own followers. They would prefer to head their own flock, however small, than be second-in-command in the largest congregation. This suggests that if we were to find ourselves with a single religion tomorrow, it is likely that there would be two the day after.

A third conception of the way the religions are related likens them to a stained glass window whose sections divide the light of the sun into different colors. This analogy allows for significant differences between the religions without pronouncing on their relative worth. If the peoples of the world differ from one another temperamentally, these differences could well affect the way Spirit appears to them; it could be seen from different angles, so to speak. Stated in the language of revelation, for God to be heard and understood divine revelations would have had to be couched in the idioms of its respective hearers. The Koran comes close to saying just this in Surah 14:4: "We never sent a messenger except with the language of his people, so that he might make (the message) clear for them."

Having mentioned three obvious ways in which the world's religions might be configured, we turn to what they might have to say collectively to the world at large.

The Wisdom Traditions

The opening chapter of this book mentioned T. S. Eliot's rhetorical questions: "Where is the knowledge that is lost in information? Where is the wisdom that is lost in knowledge?" And even earlier, in one of the book's epigraphs, we encountered E. F. Schumacher's assertion that "we need the courage to consult and profit from the 'wisdom traditions of mankind.'" Those traditions have been the subject of this book. What wisdom do they offer the world?[1]

In traditional times it was assumed that they disclosed the ultimate nature of reality. In the sixteenth and seventeenth centuries science began to cast doubt on that assumption; for Scriptures only assert their truths, whereas controlled experiments can prove scientific hypotheses. After three centuries of confusion on this point, however, we now see that such proofs hold only for the empirical world. The worthful aspects of reality—its values, meaning, and purpose—slip through the devices of science in the way that the sea slips through the nets of fishermen.

Where then can we turn for counsel concerning things that matter most? Our realization that science cannot help us reopens the door to looking seriously again at what the wisdom traditions propose. Not all of their contents are enduringly wise. Modern science has superseded their cosmologies, and the social mores of their day, which they reflect—gender relations, class structures, and the like—must be reassessed in the light of changing times and the continuing struggle for justice. But if we pass a strainer through the world's religions to lift out their conclusions about reality and how life should be lived, those conclusions begin to look like the winnowed wisdom of the human race.

What are the specifics of that wisdom? In the realm of *ethics* the Decalogue pretty much tells the cross-cultural story. We should avoid murder, thieving, lying, and adultery. These are minimum guidelines (the chapter on Judaism expands them slightly) but they are not nothing, as we realize if we reflect on how much better the world would be if they were universally honored.

Proceeding from this ethical base to the kind of people we should strive to become, we encounter the *virtues*, which the wisdom traditions identify as basically three: humility, charity, and veracity. Humility is not self-abasement. It is the capacity to regard oneself in the company of others as one, but not more than one. Charity shifts that shoe to the other foot; it is to regard one's neighbor as likewise one, as fully one as oneself. As for veracity, it extends beyond the minimum of truth-telling to sublime objectivity, the capacity to see things exactly as they are. To conform one's life to the way things are is to live authentically.

The Asian religions extol these same three virtues, while emphasizing the obstacles that must be overcome in acquiring them. The Buddha identified these obstacles as greed, hatred, and delusion, and called them the "three poisons." To the degree that they are eliminated, selflessness (humility), compassion (charity), and seeing things in their Suchness (veracity) replace them. Though the word virtue now carries a heavy moralistic ring, the wisdom traditions emphasize the root meaning of the word, which inclines toward power; philosophical Taoism has remained particularly alert to this original meaning. We catch echoes of the power component of "virtue" when people speak, as they still occasionally do, of "the virtue of a drug."

When we turn to *vision*, the wisdom traditions' rendering of the ultimate character of things, three points must here suffice.

The religions begin by assuring us that if we could see the full picture we would find it more integrated than we normally suppose. Life gives us no view of the whole. We see only snatches here and there, and self-interest skews our perspective grotesquely. Things that are close to us assume exaggerated importance, while the rest we view with cold dispassion. It is as if life were a great tapestry, which we face from its wrong side. This gives it the appearance of a maze of knots and threads, which for the most part appear chaotic.

From a purely human standpoint the wisdom traditions are the species' most prolonged and serious attempts to infer from the maze on this side of the tapestry the pattern which, on its right side, gives meaning to the whole. As the beauty and harmony of the design derive from the way its parts are related, the design confers on those parts a significance that we, seeing only scraps of the design, do not normally perceive. We could almost say that this belonging to the whole, in something of the way the parts of a painting suggest, is what religion (*religio*, rebinding) is all about; the theme of at-one-ment laces its every expression. Buddhists bring their palms together to symbolize the overcoming of duality, and Advaitic Vedantins deny duality altogether.

The second claim the wisdom traditions make about reality is implied by the first. If things are pervaded by a grand design, they are not only more integrated than they seem; they are also better than they seem. Having used art (via a tapestry) to symbolize the world's unity, we shall invoke astrophysics to allegorize this second point, reality's worth; for if the upshot of astronomy is its verdict that the universe is *bigger* than human senses disclose, the conclusion of the wisdom traditions is that it is *better* than our sensibilities discern. And better to comparable degree, which means that we are talking about the value equivalent of lightyears here. *T'ien* and the *Tao, Brahman* and *nirvana,* God and Allah all carry the signature of *ens perfectissium*—perfect being. This causes the wisdom traditions to flame with an ontological exuberance that is nowhere else to be found. This exuberance is reflected in their estimates of the human self, for in the way that the world's unity implies that selves belong to the world, its worth implies that they share in the world's exalted stature. The sheer immensity of the human self as envisioned by the world's religions is awesome. Atman and the Buddha-nature come immediately to mind, and we remember the rabbis' angels who precede human beings crying, "Make way for the image of God." Saint

Paul reports that "beholding the glory of the Lord [changes us] from one degree of glory to another" (2 Corinthians 3:18).

Beyond the unity of things and their inestimable worth is the wisdom traditions' third report. Reality is steeped in ineluctable mystery; we are born in mystery, we live in mystery, and we die in mystery. Here again we must rescue our world from time's debasement, for "mystery" has come to be associated with murder mysteries, which because they are solvable are not mysteries at all. A mystery is that special kind of problem which for the human mind *has* no solution; the more we understand it, the more we become aware of additional factors relating to it that we do not understand. In mysteries what we know, and our realization of what we do not know, proceed together; the larger the island of knowledge, the longer the shoreline of wonder. It is like the quantum world, where the more we understand its formalism, the stranger that world becomes.

Things are more integrated than they seem, they are better than they seem, and they are more mysterious than they seem; something like this emerges as the highest common denominator of the wisdom traditions' reports. When we add to this the baseline they establish for ethical behavior and their account of the human virtues, one wonders if a wiser platform for life has been conceived. At the center of the religious life is a particular kind of joy, the prospect of a happy ending that blossoms from necessarily painful beginnings, the promise of human difficulties embraced and overcome. We have only hints of this joy in our daily life. When it arrives we do not know whether our happiness is the rarest or the commonest thing on earth; for in all earthly things we find it, give it, and receive it, but cannot hold onto it. When those intimations are ours it seems in no way strange to be so happy, but in retrospect we wonder how such gold of Eden could have been ours. The human opportunity, the religions tell us, is to transform our flashes of insight into abiding light.

The world at large, however, particularly the modern world, is not persuaded by this view of things; it cannot rise to the daringness of the claim. So what do we do? This is our final question. Whether religion is, for us, a good word or bad; whether (if on balance it is a good word) we side with a single religious tradition or to some degree open our arms to all: How do we comport ourselves in a pluralistic world that is riven by ideologies, some sacred, some profane?

We listen.

Listening

If one of the wisdom traditions claims us, we begin by listening to it. Not uncritically, for new occasions teach new duties and everything finite is flawed in some respects. Still, we listen to it expectantly, knowing that it houses more truth than can be encompassed in a single lifetime.

But we also listen to the faith of others, including the secularists. We listen first because, as this book opened by noting, our times require it. The community today can be no single tradition; it is the planet. Daily the world grows smaller, leaving understanding the only place where peace can a find a home. We are not prepared for the annihilation of distance that science has effected. Who today stands ready to accept the solemn equality of peoples? Who does not have to fight an unconscious tendency to equate foreign with inferior? Some of us have survived this bloodiest of centuries; but if its ordeals are to be birth pangs rather than death throes, the century's scientific advances must be matched by comparable advances in human relations. Those who listen work for peace, a peace built not on ecclesiastical or political hegemonies but on understanding and mutual concern. For understanding, at least in realms as inherently noble as the great faiths of humankind, brings respect; and respect prepares the way for a higher power, love—the only power that can quench the flames of fear, suspicion, and prejudice, and provide the means by which the people of this small but precious Earth can become one to one another.

Understanding, then, can lead to love. But the reverse is also true. Love brings understanding; the two are reciprocal. So we must listen to understand, but we must also listen to put into play the compassion that the wisdom traditions all enjoin, for it is impossible to love another without hearing that other. If we are to be true to these religions, we must attend to others as deeply and as alertly as we hope that they will attend to us; Thomas Merton made this point by saying that God speaks to us in three places: in scripture, in our deepest selves, and in the voice of the stranger. We must have the graciousness to receive as well as to give, for there is no greater way to depersonalize another than to speak without also listening.

Said Jesus, blessed be his name, "Do unto others as you would they should do unto you." Said Buddha, blessed be his name as well,

"He who would, may reach the utmost height—but he must be eager to learn." If we do not quote the other religions on these points, it is because their words would be redundant.

Notes

1. Traditionally, philosophy and religion worked hand in hand; but because modernity has separated them we should note that Schumacher includes philosophy up to Descartes in the wisdom traditions. See his *A Guide for the Perplexed* (New York: Harper & Row, 1976), and my "Western Philosophy as a Great Religion" in Alan Olson and Leroy Rouner, *Transcendence and the Sacred* (University of Notre Dame Press, 1981).

Index

393